The foreign policies of
European Union Member States

MANCHESTER
UNIVERSITY PRESS

The foreign policies of European Union Member States

**edited by Ian Manners
and Richard G. Whitman**

Manchester University Press

Manchester and New York

distributed exclusively in the USA by Palgrave

Published by Manchester University Press
Oxford Road, Manchester M13 9NR, UK
and Room 400, 175 Fifth Avenue, New York, NY 10010, USA
http://www.manchesteruniversitypress.co.uk

Distributed exclusively in the USA by
Palgrave, 175 Fifth Avenue, New York,
NY 10010, USA

Distributed exclusively in Canada by
UBC Press, University of British Columbia, 2029 West Mall,
Vancouver, BC, Canada V6T 1Z2

British Library Cataloguing-in-Publication Data
A catalogue record for this book is available from the British Library

Library of Congress Cataloging-in-Publication Data applied for

ISBN 0 7190 5778 7 *hardback*
      0 7190 5779 5 *paperback*

First published 2000

07 06 05 04 03 02 01 00   10 9 8 7 6 5 4 3 2 1

Typeset in Sabon with Stone Sans
by Action Publishing Technology Limited, Gloucester
Printed in Great Britain
by Biddles Ltd, Guildford and King's Lynn

Contents

Contributors

Lisbeth Aggestam, Stockholm University

Margaret Blunden, University of Westminster

Rik Coolsaet, Gent University

Anthony Forster, University of Nottingham

Dimitrios Kavakas, The American University of Thessaloniki

Paul Kennedy, University of Loughborough

José Magone, University of Hull

Ian Manners, University of Kent at Canterbury

Lee Miles, University of Hull

Antonio Missiroli, WEU Institute for Security Studies

David Phinnemore, The Queen's University of Belfast

Ben Soetendorp, Rijks Universiteit Leiden

Ben Tonra, University College Dublin

Richard Whitman, University of Westminster

Acknowledgements

Despite any appearance to the contrary, this book is not just a collected volume of works on foreign policy. Nor is it the result of the editors' work alone. Rather, the book represents the end-product of an eighteen-month process that enabled the editors, the contributors, and a large number of other participants to engage in a dialogue on the distinctive nature of foreign policy analysis of EU Member States. This process created an open intellectual space where discussion, feedback and rethinking contributed hugely to the overall output.

All of the participants in this project are grateful for the opportunity to present their work at the University of Kent at Canterbury; the Centre for the Study of Democracy (CSD) at the University of Westminster; the Third Pan-European IR Conference and Joint meeting of the ECPR with the ISA in Vienna; and the University Association for Contemporary European Studies (UACES) Research Conference at the University of Sheffield.

The contributors acknowledge the helpful comments made by the participants in the research seminar programme of the Department of Politics and International Relations at the University of Kent at Canterbury: Phil Deans, Dan Heister, Keith Webb, Anne Stevens, Mervyn Frost, Athina Markantoni, and A.J.R. Groom. Suggestions by Ben Soetendorp, Lee Miles, and other participants in the UACES/CSD sponsored research workshop held at the University of Westminster in April 1998 (David Allen, Anthony Forster, Margaret Blunden, Lisbeth Aggestam, Paul Kennedy, Dimitrios Kavakas, David Phinnemore and Ben Tonra), were gratefully received, as were those provided by participants at the Joint ECPR-ISA Conference held in Vienna during September 1998, especially the input of Geoffrey Edwards, Alice Landau, Adrian Hyde-Price, Hanna Ojanen, Michael Van Cutsome, and Henrik Larsen. Thanks also go to those who participated in the final session at the UACES Research Conference at the University of Sheffield in September 1999, in particular Mike Smith, who made extremely useful comments, and Maria Strömvik.

Finally, many thanks go to all at Manchester University Press: the two anonymous reviewers for their encouragement and constructive criticism, and, in particular, former Commissioning Editor Nicola Viinikka.

Abbreviations

ACEUA	Advisory Committee on EU Affairs
APEC	Asia Pacific Economic Cooperation
ASEAN	Association of South East Asian Nations
BSCH	Banco Santander Central Hispano
CAP	Common Agricultural Policy
CCOO	Comisiones Obreras
CDS	Christian Democratic Party
CDU/CSU	Christian Democratic Union/Christian Social Union
CEE	Central and Eastern European
CEI	Central European Initiative
CEOE	Confederación Española de Organizaciones Empresariales
CFA	Communauté Financière Africane
CFSP	Common Foreign and Security Policy
CIAC	Comissao Interministerial de Assuntos Comunitarios
CiU	Convergència i Unió/Convergence and Union Party
CJTFs	Combined Joint Task Forces
COREPER	Committee of Permanent Representatives (to the EU)
COREU/CORTESY	European Correspondents Cipher Network
CPLP	Comunidade de Paises de Lingua Portuguesa
CSCE	Conference on Security and Cooperation in Europe
CSCM	Conference on Security and Cooperation in the Mediterranean
DGCE	Direccao-Geral de Assuntos Comunitarios

DREE   Direction des Relations Économiques Éxterieures

EC   European Community
ECB   European Central Bank
ECSC   European Coal and Steel Community
ECU   European Currency Unit
EEA   European Economic Area
EFTA   European Free Trade Association
EIB   European Investment Bank
EMU   Economic and Monetary Union
EPC   European Political Cooperation
ERM   Exchange Rate Mechanism
ESDI   European Security and Defence Identity
EU   European Union

FCMA   Treaty of Friendship, Cooperation and Mutual
                              Assistance
FCO   Foreign and Commonwealth Office
FDP   Federal Democratic Party
FP   Foreign Policy
FPA   Foreign Policy Analysis
FPÖ   Austrian Freedom Party

GATT   General Agreement on Tariffs and Trade
G7   Group of Seven

IGC   Intergovernmental Conference
ILO   International Labour Organisation
IMF   International Monetary Fund
INA   Instituto Nacional de Administracco
IU   Izquierda Unida/United Left Party

MEFTA   Mediterranean Free Trade Area
MERCOSUR   Common Market of the Southern Cone (Argentina,
                              Brazil, Paraguay, Uruguay)
MFA   Ministry of Foreign Affairs
MFA   Movimento das Forces Armadas
MNCs   Multi-National Corporations
MNE   Ministerio dos Negocios Estrangeiros

NACC   North Atlantic Cooperation Council
NATO   North Atlantic Treaty Organisation
NGO   Non-Governmental Organisation
Nordic   Nordic Union

OEEC	Organisation of European Economic Cooperation
OSCE	Organisation for Security and Cooperation in Europe
ÖVP	Austrian Peoples Party
PANA	Peace and Neutrality Alliance
PCP	Partido Comunista Portugues
PfP	Partnership for Peace
POCO	Political Committee of the European Union
PP	Partido Popular/Socialists Popular Party
PS	Partido Socialista
PSD	Partido Socialdemocrata
PSOE	Partido Socialista Obrero Español
SADC	South African Development Community
SFOR	Stabilisation Force
SGAE	Secretariado-Geral de Assuntos Europens
SPÖ	Austrian Social Democrats
SPR	Permanent Representation in Brussels
SSEU	Secretariat of State for Foreign Policy and the EU
TEU	Treaty on European Union
UCD	Unión de Centro Democrático/Democratic Centre Union
UGT	General de Trabajadores
UKREP	United Kingdom Permanent Representation
UN	United Nations
WEU	Western European Union
WTO	World Trade Organisation

1

Introduction

Ian Manners and Richard Whitman

Foreign Policy Analysis is overwhelmingly an American subject, despite the presence of a robust and healthy European research community.[1]

This book attempts to construct and apply a framework for the examination of the foreign policies of individual European Union (EU) Member States in order to gauge whether comparative analysis is possible and to see what insights it might provide. As a part of this exercise the crucial question which will be asked, and supported by empirical study, is whether it is valid to assert that there is a need for a distinctive Foreign Policy Analysis (FPA) approach to the study of EU states. As Walter Carlsnaes and Steve Smith have suggested (above) the application of FPA insights from outside of Europe to the Member States of the EU is an undertaking which raises questions about the value of a broad-based FPA and the role of European approaches. Thus the analysis of EU Member States' foreign policies involves tackling both theoretical questions of a FPA itself, and empirical questions of case study comparison in the European arena.

This chapter will first question the notion of 'foreign policy', next it will discuss the particular nature of FPA needed for EU states, then briefly consider the state of the art of comparative FPA, before finally proposing a framework for analysis which can be applied to case studies of EU Member States – a distinctive foreign policy analysis. The analysis contained within this chapter raises a series of questions about the possibilities for creating a FPA of EU states. The first question concerns an understanding of the European condition as currently experienced by EU citizens, the states they live in, and the scholars who study them. Clearly this is an important issue and one which will be discussed in greater detail when the justification for this work is provided in the 'distinctive foreign policy analysis' section below. The second question is just one function of this European condition and asks what the impact of the evolving

European political/economic/societal environment is on the foreign policies of EU states. This question can only be fairly answered by considering
the wealth of detail provided by empirical case studies. The third question
continues on this path by asking to what degree foreign policy formulation is being Europeanised as part of the more recent developments in the
European condition. As with the preceding question, an answer can only
really be provided by reference to empirical detail across a range of case
studies. The final question concerns the FPA of EU states and whether
there are similar forces at work in the variety of Member States under
analysis which have a common impact upon their foreign policies. It
seems fair to suggest that the changing nature of the European condition
will, and does, have a differential impact on states but there may be
common features, for example, on larger states, smaller states, or perhaps
neutral states.

What is foreign policy?

Definitions of foreign policy vary from the very narrow 'relations between
states',[2] through the broader 'governmental activity'[3] to the very broad
notion of 'external relations'.[4] Whilst this variety of definitions is interesting, the choice of definition is crucial in circumscribing the field of
investigation. Look, for example at Brian White's definition of 'foreign
policy [as being] that area of governmental activity which is concerned with
relationships between the state and other actors, particularly other states,
in the international system'.[5] This approach would naturally tend to privilege relations with other states and would tend to ignore non-state actors,
issues or even regions. This study is particularly aware of this danger but, in
the interests of brevity, will attempt to find a compromise definition.

What is important here is that the study adopts a narrow enough definition of foreign policy so that the study remains manageable. This is
achieved by keeping the focus on the foreign policy of governments, especially the activities of foreign ministers together and the offices of the
President (as in the case of France). However, the study must also ensure
that the definition of foreign policy is broad enough to be valuable and
does not exclude the most interesting elements of foreign policy activity.

Thus, a distillation of these ideas brings us to the observation that, for
the purpose of this study, foreign policy shall be defined as the 'attempts
by governments to influence or manage events outside the state's boundaries'. This definition draws largely on Steve Smith and Michael Smith
and represents a balance between external relations (between different
societies) and foreign relations (between different governments).[6] It seeks
to move the focus away from 'state' approaches (which we feel are inappropriate in the European case) to 'government' approaches (which we see
as more revealing). Clearly even this approach appears to indicate an

assumption that the government is an important actor capable of autonomous action. The basis and realities of this assumption will be discussed at greater detail in the conclusion.

European foreign policy analysis literature

Comparative foreign policy is the field of FPA that has been most subject to criticism and self-criticism.[7]

It seems clear that the existing literature has under-explored the distinctiveness of the foreign policies of European states who are members of the EU and the issues that this membership raises. Despite the observation by Margot Light (above) that the field of comparative foreign policy has been subject to critical re-evaluation, this does not seem to have extended to the area of European foreign policy analysis. The existing literature falls within two large and two small categories. The largest is the broad-based FPA literature which is primarily US written, the most recent comprehensive survey of which is by Laura Neack, Jeanne Hey, and Patrick Haney.[8] This literature has rarely sought to address the distinctive nature of the foreign policies of EU Member States. The second largest category consists of case studies concerning the impact of membership on individual EU states, for example the 'EC Membership Evaluated' series published by Pinter publishers. Although this literature is interesting, by its nature, it has rarely sought to address the issue from a directly comparative viewpoint across a series of studies. One early attempt to do so in a comparative analysis is that by William Wallace and William Paterson,[9] which poses many of the questions which we are returning to some twenty years later. The last two categories are those that look at the topic of European foreign policy[10] and states in European foreign policy.[11] These two texts have approached the subject by asking very different sets of questions about European FPA. Walter Carlsnaes and Steve Smith have as their primary theoretical concern the interparadigm and agency–structure debates. Indeed, they do not seem overly concerned with explaining the foreign policies of European states at all, focusing on issues in international relations theory rather than focusing directly upon the practice and interpretation of EU Member States' foreign policies. Christopher Hill takes completely the opposite stance by focusing almost entirely on the detail of EU states' behaviour within the Common Foreign and Security Policy (CFSP) without being overly concerned by introducing a comparative element. It is interesting to note how little Hill's project has moved since it was first written in 1983 with his list of research questions remaining remarkably unchanged.[12] An area which both of these latter two texts under-explore is the question of 'what is distinctive about the foreign policy of EU states?'

Building upon the admirable output in the English language by a small group of European foreign policy specialists (David Allen, Walter Carlsnaes, Christopher Hill, Brian Hocking, Michael Smith, Steve Smith, Ben Soetendorp, William Wallace, and Brian White amongst others), it does appear that European FPA is starting to come of age. There are several reasons why this coming of age appears to be happening in the early twenty-first century. The end of the Cold War seems increasingly to be leading to a divergence of practices between Europe and North America in terms of the development of foreign policies, and in terms of foreign policy analysis undertaken by scholars. It is increasingly questionable to what degree European scholars pay attention to the work of US scholars, and vice versa (although this may simply be a function of the proliferation of output on both sides of the Atlantic). In parallel to this divergence is the development of a critical mass of existing and new European scholars who are writing in the field of FPA in a European context. The final reason for the coming of age of European FPA is that the European condition increasingly requires scholars to adjust their models in a *sui generis* direction. These models need to take account of the triple developments of a post-Cold War Europe, a complex interdependent Europe, and an increasingly integrated Europe. This leads to the observation that European FPA seems to be becoming more endogenous, examples of which include Christopher Hill, Walter Carlsnaes and Steve Smith, and Stelios Stavridis and Christopher Hill. [13] It is the intention of this chapter to attempt to further extend this trend by building a distinctive European FPA.

A distinctive foreign policy analysis

Rare is the European foreign policy specialist who has not started [their] career by looking at a US theory.[14]

Having raised so many crucial questions surrounding the study of EU Member States' foreign policies, it is only right that the approach adopted in this chapter as part of developing a common analytical framework is justified. There are indeed two sets of justifications to be made regarding the distinctiveness of European foreign policy analysis and its application to EU Member States. These two justifications concern the necessity for a distinctive FPA, and what common framework can be supported. As Walter Carlsnaes and Steve Smith have pointed out (above) European FPA is almost inevitably situated within a theoretical framework based upon, or least informed by, US theories. Thus the first justification for a distinctive FPA is the need to escape the frameworks, or boundaries, constructed within US FP circles and move towards a more appropriate approach primarily informed by more recent European thinking. The second justification for a distinctive FPA is the attempt to construct an analytical framework which is appropriate for the European (or at least EU) condition. As William Wallace observed in the late 1970s: 'There are a number of immediate parallels between the context and conduct of American foreign policy and that of the major states of Western Europe. But the differences are as striking as the similarities.'[15] Thus it would appear clear that as these differences have become more exaggerated in post-Cold War Europe, so scholars must be prepared to construct original analytical frameworks to examine the context and conduct of European FPA.

As part of constructing a framework it is necessary to first escape the hegemonic US discourses which have tended to dominate the study of FPA. As William Paterson, William Wallace, David Allen, Steve Smith, Walter Carlsnaes, Ole Wæver, Joe Hagan, Leon Lindburg, Janne Haaland Matlary, Brian White, Helen Wallace and Hartmut Mayer have all drawn our attention to over the past two decades, there is a considerable amount of concern amongst scholars working on the relationships between the EU and the foreign policies of its Member States that the 'actor-centred rationality' dominant in American discourses on the subject in the search for 'theoretical generalisations of global reach' are increasingly inappropriate for application to the specific conditions under examination here.[16]

Existing explanations for foreign policy

Most surveys of explanations of foreign policy understate elements in the existing FPA literature, largely because of the huge wealth of existing works in the field. Undoubtedly this chapter will follow in this trend, which can largely be overcome by reading the best short summary, in its time, by Steve Smith.[17] This summary admirably illustrates the sheer range of existing explanations for foreign policy, and importantly introduces the idea of middle range theories. In attempting to generalise more for the benefit of brevity than Smith does, it may be possible to suggest that existing explanations appear to fall into three very broad categories of foreign policy analysis, which are considered here in reference to their applicability to the analysis of EU Member States' foreign policies. It is not the intention here to discuss any of these existing explanations in any great detail, but simply to acknowledge their existence and consider their value for this study. The first category is what can very broadly be called the 'rational actor' model of FPA and is generally associated with traditional analyses based on 'state-centric realism'. The focus here is on the state as an egoistic rational actor pursuing national interests.

The second category is broadly labelled the 'decision-making' model of FPA as suggested by Richard Snyder et al. and pursued by Graham Allison.[18] This second category can be further distinguished between the

'organisational process' model and the 'bureaucratic politics' model. Both
the rational actor and the decision-making models of FPA have tended to
be mutually reinforcing and predominantly suitable for application in
only one case – the US. The more interesting work to emanate from the
latter model of FPA has been in field of sub-national activity, in particular in the area of local (i.e. non-central government) foreign policy (Brian
Hocking and Eric Phillipart).[19] The focus of this second group is still
largely on the state, but represents attempts to open the black box and
look inside.

The third category is really not a category at all, but more of a grouping of more recent works attempting to move beyond the concepts of
'actorness' and 'process' in order to more fully appreciate the less tangible aspects of FPA in the form of 'societal' factors. These societal factors
have included ideology,[20] national role conceptions,[21] ethical considerations, and culture,[22] amongst others. The focus of this third category is to
move away from the state as 'agent' in order to return to the broader
questions of the roles of institutions, public opinion, and norms, amongst
others, in the analysis of foreign policy.

In parallel to these three very broad categories of FPA sit the few
attempts to explain the foreign policies of European states in any form of
comparative framework. In addition to considering the traditional areas
of FPA mentioned above (and including the largely discredited psychology
model) Christopher Hill[23] emphasised the role of domestic society and the
external environment as being important to foreign policy making in
Western European states. Five years later Hill[24] focused on a range of
cross-cutting factors as being important determinants of FP making in the
European sphere: 'extra-European distractions', 'domestic factors', the
European Community, and the 'security dilemma'. Frank Pfetsch
narrowed these explanations down to internal factors (i.e. domestic
factors) and external factors (i.e. international factors) in an attempt to
compare the foreign policies of European Community (EC) members.[25]

A common analytical framework

Any attempt to construct a common framework for the comparison of EU
Member States' foreign policies runs into a crucial criticism posed accu-
rately by A. J. R. Groom: 'since they are so different can you sensibly do
this?'[26] This chapter has sought to justify, and make the argument, that a
distinctive FPA is not only sensible but is a prerequisite for any appropriate analysis.

The common framework will initially look at the foreign policies of the
EU Member States by considering the policy variables suggested below
whilst looking at a range of interesting issues of foreign policy behaviour.
The framework for analysis consists of a series of six questions divided

into three sections. The sections attempt to delineate three different forces shaping the foreign policies of EU Member States. These three forces are foreign policy change, foreign policy process, and foreign policy actions. It is intended that this common framework can act as a starting point for consideration in the writing of the chapters looking at the individual EU Member States.

Section one: foreign policy change – adaptation and socialisation

The two questions in this first section focus on the role of dynamic change as a factor in the foreign policies of the EU Member States.

Adaptation through membership

This question considers the way in which EU Member States adapt their foreign policy through membership of the EU, as well as towards the EU itself, and towards the other Member States of the Union. Although the process of adaptation is more sudden for new Member States, even founding Member States have to change their policy towards previously external states (i.e. previously third party states) as they join. The second element of this variable concerns the adaptation of foreign policy towards third states in order to bring it into line with existing EU policies. Kenneth Hanf and Ben Soetendorp have emphasised the role of state adaptation to EU membership by looking at governmental, political, and strategic adaptation.[27] Nikolaj Petersen has also suggested this approach by looking at the case of Denmark and its national strategy as an EU member.[28]

These approaches lead us to ask what impact the changing external environment has had on the Member State's foreign policy. More specifically, a question that is particularly relevant for the more recent members is, what has been the impact of membership? Similarly, the changes introduced in the Maastricht and Amsterdam treaties cause us to ask, what has been the impact of changes to the treaty base of the EU? Finally, in the context of EU membership, what has been the impact of the end of the Cold War?

Socialisation of foreign policy makers

note must also be made of the elite socialization which is clearly event . . . [as] this socialization has practical effects . . . where there is ever any new foreign policy initiative in the making the first reflex is European.[29]

This question looks at the role of socialisation and social interaction in shaping the practices, perceptions and interests of policy makers. As Ben Tonra has previously identified (above), the practice of elite socialisation has practical effects in foreign policy making. The starting point for the contemporary discussion of the theorising surrounding social interaction is

often found in the work of Alexander Wendt who argues that 'construc-
tivists are interested in how knowledgeable practices constitute subjects,
which is not far from the strong liberal interest in how institutions transform interests'.[30] Interestingly, Wendt has also argued that European
cooperation falls into this sphere of explanation for foreign policy makers:

> A strong liberal or constructivist analysis of this problem [explaining the
> persistence of European institutions] would suggest that four decades of
> cooperation may have transformed a positive interdependence or outcomes
> into a collective 'European identity' in terms of which states increasingly
> define their 'self'-interests.[31]

These approaches lead us to ask what impact the changing internal
environment has had on the Member State's foreign policy. More specifically, the question is whether the sharing of information and common
practices leads to socialisation or *engrenage* and thus habits of working
together transform the common perceptions of policy makers. Taken one
step further, it could be asked whether a redefinition of self- or national-
interest is taking place, through which constructivist practices transform
identities. Finally, it has been argued that an extension of these practices,
through a more European orientation of policy-making groups, might
lead to an actual 'Europeanisation' of foreign policy as a logical step.
Obviously all three of these arguments are looking at a very similar
process whereby habits become practices which shape the participants
and may lead to a re-orientation of their beliefs and behaviour.

Section two: foreign policy process – domestic and bureaucratic

The two questions in this second section focus on the role of the policy
process as a factor in the foreign policies of the EU Member States.

Domestic factors in the policy process

This question looks at the important inter-relationship between the
domestic and the foreign arenas – an aspect which is even more critical in
the European context. As Charles Pentland, Carole Webb, Helen Wallace,
Christopher Hill and Simon Bulmer have been arguing since the 1970s,
'the foreign and domestic policy processes'[32] are part of the same 'political game'[33] where 'foreign policy and domestic politics [are] of vital
importance to each other'.[34] Slowly, foreign policy making among
Member States is becoming part of the EU 'multilevel political system'[35]
where its primacy amongst the hierarchy of policy making is increasingly
challenged. The idea of this 'two-level game' has been recently addressed
by American scholars, but the 'political game' between the 'two tiers' of
domestic politics and international politics has always been central to the
analysis of Member States' foreign policy making.[36]

The two-level game and its application in a European context has been gathering momentum since 1987 when Robert Putnam and Nicholas Bayne first posited its applicability to the G7.[37] Currently, the importance of the domestic–foreign relationship is being argued in several works by Peter Evans, Robert Putnam and Harold Jacobson, Thomas Risse, and Helen Milner.[38] Robert Putnam's metaphor of the two-level game is useful here in explaining how both international and domestic arenas are important in explaining foreign policy of an EU state. But clearly this is a two-way street as domestic change, such as a change of government, can have an international impact, but also EU events, such as CFSP, can have a domestic impact.

These approaches lead us to ask what impact domestic political forces have had in determining the Member State's foreign policies. More specifically, what impact has the constitutional relationship between domestic political forces had on foreign policy? Most importantly, this leads us to ask, what impact has the two-level game between the domestic and the international sphere had on foreign policy? The impact of this game will undoubtedly be different for multilevel governments as predominantly found in federal states, and so what role does this separation of government play? Finally, the impact of non-state actors at a domestic level (such as large companies, trade unions, and pressure groups, for example) cannot be ignored.

Bureaucratic politics in the policy process

Most, if not all, of those working on foreign policy analysis consider bureaucratic issues to be important factors in the determining of foreign policy. These analysts and commentators lead us to question what impact bureaucratic factors have had in determining Member States' foreign policies. More specifically, the role which the constitutional design of the bureaucratic process has had on the Member States' foreign policy. This question leads us to inquire what impact the decision-making process itself has had on the outcomes. Clearly the way in which foreign policies are initiated, sanctioned and implemented are all important here. Finally, the interrelationship between civil servants and their administrative departments or ministries is a question which must be raised, especially if this leads to rivalry or conflict which significantly effect the foreign policy process.

Section three: foreign policy action – with or without the EU?

The two questions in this final section focus on the type of action in relation to the EU as a factor in the foreign policies of the EU Member States.

With the EU: constriction or opportunity?

This question looks at the way in which participation in the CFSP of the EU and the external relations of the EC alters the foreign policy of Member States. The question that will be asked is whether this participation provides a constriction on foreign policy choice or an opportunity for foreign policy action. What is important to consider in this question is that whereas the CFSP appears to have actually achieved very little, indicating that Member States' foreign policy must be somewhat at odds with each other, external relations seems to have been somewhat more successful. An important question to consider here is how individual foreign policies have led to the reluctance to reach agreement on issues to be handled under the CFSP, and whether the submersion of national trade relations within the EC's external relations have met the same reluctance.

Hill, Wallace and Allen have all been concerned with the question of participation in the CFSP and its impact on Member States' foreign policies. These analysts have gradually moved their position from one of arguing that national interests represent insuperable obstacles to common foreign policy,[39] towards suggesting that the CFSP might actually represent the 'European rescue of national foreign policy'.[40] However, these analyses have been more reluctant to consider whether Member States' foreign policies are affected by participation within the EC's pillar I structures.

These points lead us to question what impact the EU's policy processes have had in determining the Member States' foreign policies. More specifically, whether constrictions caused by both the CFSP and the external relations of the EC have significantly altered the Member States' foreign policies. In contrast, it is also important to ask whether the opportunities provided by both the CFSP and the external relations of the EC are being used by the Member States to advance their own foreign policies.

The third question here regards the consideration of possible 'tiers of exclusivity' representing levels of hierarchy in the EU's policy processes and the impact these have on foreign policy. It can be argued that there are clear 'tiers of exclusivity' within the Union as it exists today. This is largely in terms of influence between the large and small states within the Union in terms of foreign policy clout. However, the integration process also creates new 'tiers of exclusivity' within the foreign policy field, with some members having deeper and more influential roles in the CFSP and external relations processes than others as a result of attitudes towards the integration process in general. A good example would be Sweden and Finland's observer Western European Union (WEU) status and the difficulties that CFSP cooperation creates for Denmark. This leads to the question of whether there is evidence of 'tiers of exclusivity' in the EU policy process and what impact have they have had on the Member States' foreign policies.

Without the EU: special relations and special interests

This final question looks at EU Member States' foreign policies which are 'ring-fenced' by the states concerned as being special relationships or issues beyond the call of the EU. These ring-fenced relationships are very important because they do in fact alter the behaviour of Member States towards one another and towards external states. The examples of Britain and the US, France and Algeria, and Sweden and Norway spring to mind under this heading.

The first part of this question concerns the notion of special relationships, which is fairly well accepted in FPA. What is interesting for the FPA of EU states is that these special relationships may be both internal and external to the EU. Frank Pfetsch focused primarily on 'extra-European engagements' having a colonial/post-colonial context to them.[41] Three of the most special relationships for the EU are the Franco-German relationship, the Benelux relationship, and the Anglo-American relationship (although most Americans remain unaware of their side of the bargain). Writing on this last relationship, Alex Danchev admits 'the very idea of "specialness" . . . remains radically under-thought and under-theorised'.[42] But he does observe that 'as in life, so in international relations: expectations are crucial' in a special relationship if it is to survive.

The second part of the question asks whether there are also 'special issues' which are ring-fenced by the Member States because of national sensitivities. These might include issues such as behaviour in certain international organisations (France and Britain in the United Nations (UN) for example); they might involve issues such as defence questions (for neutral states) or human rights issues. What is important to consider here is that these are special issues for those EU Member States who seek to exclude them from Union or Community processes as part of their foreign policy actions.

It should be noted that these relationships and issues might have a negative as well as a positive context to them. German relations with Turkey, Greek relations with FYROM/Macedonia, Finnish relations with Russia, and the issues of Gibraltar or Northern Ireland all spring to mind as examples here.

These observations lead us to ask, first, which special relations and special issues Member States seek to 'ring-fence' in order to keep them out of the EU's policy processes. More specifically, we are interested in special relations which are inside or outside the EU and which lead us to question what effect such a *domain privé* has on the Member States' foreign policies? Secondly, the role of special issues, whether inside or outside the EU, and the impact which these have on Member States' foreign policies must be questioned.

These six policy variables are all relevant, and should contribute to the backbone of comparative studies. However, it is important that the individual EU Member State analyses should not be wholly constrained by these variables. Indeed, it is quite clear that there will be many unique factors which do not fall easily into these variables, and may thus throw light upon some of the problems of such a comparative analysis.

Conclusion: what are we looking at?

the unilateral pursuit of all but the most limited objectives would not seem to be an option that the Member States of the Union are any longer prepared to consider.[43]

Given the analytical questions for consideration just described, it is necessary to spell out what this study is attempting to look at. As Allen has suggested above, are we looking at the foreign policies of EU Member States who conduct all 'but the most limited objectives' within an EU context? To this end we are very interested in gauging whether 'traditional' explanations, in a 'slightly amended' form, are still applicable to the FPA of EU Member States, or whether these foreign policies have been 'transformed' by the globalised, post-Cold War, post-EU accession 'European condition'. By 'traditional FPA', we are asking if we are witnessing traditional (i.e. state-centric) FPA where foreign policy remains largely the realm of the Member State. In this traditional approach the Member States remain the 'dominant actors', with a 'sharp distinction between domestic and international politics', and with the focus of foreign policy activity primarily on the 'struggle for power and peace'.[44] On the other hand, by 'transformational FPA', we are asking if we are witnessing transformational (i.e. pluralistic) FPA where foreign policy is significantly altered through membership. In this transformation approach the Member States are not the only 'significant actors', where there is a 'blurred' distinction between 'domestic and international politics', and with the focus of foreign policy activity increasingly displaced by a 'concern for economic and social matters'.[45]

In sum, this chapter briefly suggests a common framework to analyse the foreign policies of Member States which it argues is distinctive because of its appropriateness for the unique condition of membership of the EU. It asks whether we are witnessing traditional foreign policies being pursued by the states under analysis, albeit in a 'slightly amended' form, or whether in fact we are witnessing the transformation of foreign policies into a Europeanised form which demand a distinctive European FPA. Thus, this study seeks to explore whether the approach of traditionalist FPA, still largely pursued by 'the American, or neo-positivistic, approach',[46] is appropriate for the analysis of the foreign policies of EU Member States. In lieu of an answer to this question, we suggest that what is needed is a distinctive form of European FPA which is appropriate for the transformational foreign polices of EU Member States, characterised by the impact of membership, which focuses on a number of regional factors as a means of explanation.

The aim of this chapter is to provoke thinking about the comparative analysis of the EU's Member States' foreign policies. It seeks to examine the extent to which the Member States retain foreign and security policies which are separable, but not separate from, the external relations and the CFSP of the EU. The intention is *not* to examine the CFSP or external relations themselves, but rather to examine the scope of Member States' foreign policies both conducted within the arena of the EU but also, importantly, what they retain as a *domain privé*.

This chapter has argued that there are grounds for a distinctive approach to the comparative study of the foreign policy of EU states. It further suggests that the foreign polices analysis of EU states is possible within a comparative framework which considers the adaptation of their foreign policy to membership; the process of socialisation of foreign policy makers; the relationship between domestic conditions and FP (for example, a change of government); the role of bureaucratic factors in shaping FP; their participation in EC external relations and EU CFSP, including the possibility of 'tiers of exclusivity' between different Member States; and the role of 'special relationships' and 'special issues' between Member States and external actors/issues.

Notes

1 W. Carlsnaes and S. Smith (eds), *European Foreign Policy* (London, Sage, 1994), p. 11.

2 P. Calvert, *The Foreign Policies of New States* (London, Wheatsheaf, 1986), p. 1.

3 S. Smith and M. Smith, 'The analytical background: approaches to the study of British foreign policy' in S. Smith, M. Smith, and B. White (eds), *British Foreign Policy: Tradition, Change and Transformation* (London, Unwin Hyman, 1988), p. 15.

4 M. Clarke, 'Policy processes in a changing world' in *British External Policy-Making in the 1990s* (London, Macmillan for RIIA, 1992), p. 72.

5 In, M. Clarke and B. White (eds), *Understanding Foreign Policy: The Foreign Policy Systems Approach* (Aldershot, Edward Elgar, 1989), p. 1.

6 Smith and Smith, 'The analytical background', p. 15.

7 M. Light, 'Foreign policy analysis' in A. J. R. Groom and M. Light (eds), *Contemporary International Relations: A Guide to Theory* (London, Pinter, 1994), p. 100.

8 L. Neack, J. Hey and P. Haney (eds), *Foreign Policy Analysis: Continuity and Change in its Second Generation* (Englewood Cliffs, NJ, Prentice Hall, 1995).

9 W. Wallace and W. Paterson (eds), *Foreign Policy Making in Western Europe* (Farnborough, Saxon House, 1978).

10 See for example, Carlsnaes and Smith, *European Foreign Policy*, p. 11.

11 See for example, C. Hill (ed.), *The Actors in Europe's Foreign Policy* (London, Routledge, 1996).

12 Compare C. Hill (ed.), *National Foreign Policies and European Political Cooperation* (London, George Allen and Unwin, 1983), p. xi. with Hill (ed.), *The Actors*, p. xi.

13 Hill (ed.), *The Actors*; Carlsnaes and Smith, *European Foreign Policy*; S. Stavridis, and C. Hill (eds), *Domestic Sources of Foreign Policy: Western European Reactions to the Falklands Conflict* (Oxford, Berg, 1996).

14 Carlsnaes and Smith, *European Foreign Policy*, p. 11.

15 Wallace and Paterson (eds), *Foreign Policy*, p. 51.

16 W. Paterson, 'Forward' in Wallace and Paterson (eds), *Foreign Policy*, p. 1; W. Wallace, 'Old states and new circumstances' in Wallace and Paterson (eds), *Foreign Policy*, p. 51; D. Allen, 'Foreign policy at the European level' in Wallace and Paterson (eds), *Foreign Policy*, p. 135; S. Smith, 'Theories of foreign policy: a historical overview', *Review of International Studies*, 12 (1986), p. 26; S. Smith, 'Foreign policy theory and the new Europe' in Carlsnaes and Smith, *European Foreign Policy*, p. 11; W. Carlsnaes, 'In lieu of a conclusion' in Carlsnaes and Smith, *European Foreign Policy*, p. 286; J. Hagan, 'The politics of foreign policy in non-US settings' in *Political Opposition and Foreign Policy in Comparative Perspective* (London, Lynne Rienner, 1993), p. 24; L. Lindburg, 'Comment on Moravcsik' in S. Bulmer and A. Scott (eds), *Economic and Political Integration in Europe* (Oxford, Blackwell, 1994), p. 84; O. Wæver, 'Resisting the temptation of post foreign policy analysis' in Carlsnaes and Smith, *European Foreign Policy*, pp. 249–250; J. Haaland Matlary, 'Epilogue: new bottles for new wine' in K. E. Jørgensen (ed.), *Reflective Approaches to European Governance* (Basingstoke, Macmillan, 1997), pp. 201–205; B. White, 'The European challenge to foreign policy analysis' in *European Journal of International Relations*, 5:1 (1999), p. 59; W. Wallace, 'Review of W. Sandholtz and A. Stone Sweet (eds), *European Integration and Supranational Governance* (Oxford, Oxford University Press, 1998)' in *International Affairs*, 75 (1999), pp. 424–425; H. Mayer, 'Review of A. Moravcsik, *The Choice for Europe* (London, UCL Press, 1999)', in *International Affairs*, 75 (1999), pp. 684–685; H. Wallace, 'Review section: the choice for Europe – piecing the integration jigsaw together', *Journal of European Public Policy*, 6:1 (1999), p. 158.

17 Smith, 'Theories of foreign policy', pp. 13–29.

18 R. Snyder, H. Bruck and B. Sapin (eds), *Foreign Policy Decision-Making: an Approach to the Study of International Politics* (New York, Free Press of Glencoe, 1962); G. Allison, *Essence of Decision: Explaining the Cuban Missile Crisis* (Boston, Little, Brown, 1971).

19 B. Hocking, *Localizing Foreign Policy* (New York, St. Martin's Press, 1993); B. Hocking (ed.), *Foreign Relations and Federal States* (London, Leicester University Press, 1993); E. Philippart, 'Le comité des régions confronté à la 'paradiplomatie' des régions de l'Union européenne', in J. Bourrinet (ed.), *Le Comité des Régions de l'Union Européenne* (Paris, Editions Economica, 1997), pp. 147–180.

20 W. Carlsnaes, *Ideology and Foreign Policy: Problems of Comparative Conceptualisation* (Oxford, Blackwell, 1986).

21 P. Le Prestre (ed.), *Role Quests in the Post-Cold War Era: Foreign Policies in Transition* (Montreal, McGill-Queen's University Press, 1997); S. Walker (ed.), *Role Theory and Foreign Policy Analysis* (Durham, NC, Duke University Press, 1987).

22 V. Hudson and C. Vore, 'Foreign policy analysis yesterday, today, and tomorrow', *Mershon International Studies Review*, 39 (1995), pp. 209–238.

23 C. Hill, 'A theoretical introduction' in Wallace and Paterson (eds), *Foreign Policy*, pp. 7–30.

24 C. Hill (ed.), *National Foreign Policies*.

25 F. Pfesch, 'Tensions in sovereignty: foreign policies of EC members compared' in Carlsnaes and Smith, *European Foreign Policy*.

26 A. J. R. Groom's comments on an earlier draft of this chapter, Canterbury, March 1998.

27 K. Hanf, and B. Soetendorp, *Adapting to European Integration: Small States and the European Union* (London, Longman, 1998), pp. 8–12.

28 N. Petersen, 'National strategies in the integration dilemma: an adaptation approach', *Journal of Common Market Studies*, 36:1 (1998), pp. 33–54.

29 B. Tonra, 'The impact of political cooperation' in Jørgensen (ed.), *Reflective Approaches*, pp. 186–187.

30 A. Wendt, 'Anarchy is what states make of it: the social construction of power politics', *International Organization*, 46:2 (Spring 1992), p. 394.

31 Wendt, 'Anarchy', p. 417.

32 C. Webb, 'Introduction: variations on a theoretical theme' in H. Wallace, W. Wallace and C. Webb (eds) *Policy-Making in the European Communities* (Chichester, John Wiley, 1977), p. 27.

33 C. Pentland, *International Theory and European Integration* (London, Faber, 1973), p. 221 in Webb, 'Introduction', p. 26.

34 Hill, 'Theoretical introduction', p. 22.

35 C. Webb, 'Theoretical perspectives and problems' in H. Wallace, W. Wallace and C. Webb (eds), *Policy-Making in the European Community* 2nd edn (Chichester, John Wiley, 1983), p. 38.

36 S. Bulmer, 'Domestic politics and European community policy-making', *Journal of Common Market Studies*, 21:4 (June 1983), pp. 349–363.

37 R. Putnam and N. Bayne, *Hanging Together: Cooperation and Conflict in the Seven-Power Summits* rev. edn (London, Sage, 1987).

38 P. Evans, R. Putnam, and H. Jacobson (eds), *Double-Edged Diplomacy: International Bargaining and Domestic Politics* (Berkeley, University of California Press, 1993); T. Risse-Kappen (ed.), *Cooperation among Democracies: the European Influence on US Foreign Policy* (Princeton, Princeton U. P., 1995); and H. Milner, *Interests, Institutions and Information: Domestic Politics and International Relations* (Princeton, Princeton U. P., 1997).

39 Hill (ed.), *National Foreign Policies*.

40 D. Allen, 'Conclusions: the European rescue of national foreign policy' in Hill (ed.), *The Actors*.

41 F. Pfesch, 'Tensions in sovereignty: foreign policies of EC members compared' in Carlsnaes and Smith (eds), *European Foreign Policy*.

42 A. Danchev, 'On specialness', *International Affairs*, 72:4 (1996), pp. 737–750.

43   D. Allen, 'Conclusions', p. 297.
44   Smith and Smith, 'The analytical background', p. 12.
45   Smith and Smith, 'The analytical background', p. 13.
46   Carlsnaes, 'In lieu of a conclusion', p. 286.

I

Primus inter pares?

2

France

Margaret Blunden

The foreign policy environment

The idea of Europe as a political as well as an economic force has been largely inspired by French vision, pursued since the 1960s by means of a special relationship with Germany. *L'Europe puissance,* Europe as a political actor, is strategically essential to meet the aspirations of presidents from de Gaulle to Chirac that France should retain grandeur and influence beyond what its economic weight might suggest, should be a member of all the best clubs, should always have a seat at the top table. In the 1980s and 1990s, when the diplomatic environment became multilateral rather than bilateral, France strove to remain a world power and to make its distinctive voice heard in all the places that matter – the Security Council, the G8 (which represents the G7 major industrialised nations), the Council of Ministers. More than this, it seeks to promote those multilateral organisations within which French ascendance is greatest, notably the Council of Ministers, and to resist any increase in the power of those, notably the G8, which are dominated by the Americans. It is similarly seen as of great strategic importance that French nationals should hold the key executive posts both within European organisations (European Commission, European Investment Bank (EIB), Organisation for European Cooperation and Development (OECD), Council of Europe) and within multilateral ones, such as the Directorate of the International Monetary Fund (IMF).

France has sought to project a strong European political voice, to complement and amplify its national voice, in an increasingly unfavourable international environment. As Hubert Vedrine, Minister of Foreign Affairs in the present government and for fourteen years Diplomatic Counsellor to President Mitterrand, reminded his audience in a recent interview in *Politique Internationale,* it is too often forgotten that the elements of status, power and prestige which the French inherited from their history, ancient or modern, have been trivialised or relativised since 1989.[1] France's unique position and freedom of diplomatic manouevre were weakened by the sudden ending of the Cold War, the break-up of the Soviet Union, and the reunification and normalisation of Germany. When the Cold War came to an end, France's territorial strategic depth behind the Central Front, and the element of uncertainty offered by the *force de frappe,* lost much of their value. Within the European Union (EU) itself, successive enlargements, actual and prospective, have meant that those Member States committed to Europe as an economic space have gained ground over those, like France, which have urged that a stronger political architecture should precede enlargement.

But it is what Nicole Gnesotto calls the fantastic rebound of the North Atlantic Treaty Organisation (NATO), the expansion of its role as the only western organisation capable of military intervention in Former Yugoslavia, and its extension into Eastern and Central Europe, ahead of that of the EU, which has really threatened to marginalise France.[2] In the early 1990s French leaders resigned themselves to accept that NATO and the Partnership for Peace should fulfil the task of collective security in Eurasia at the expense of the Organisation for Security and Cooperation (OSCE) in Europe, and the United Nations (UN). France lost the argument that it was the natural function of the OSCE, not that of NATO, to provide the framework of cooperation with the Eastern countries of the former Soviet Union and Warsaw Pact, now no longer a military threat. The expanded role of the American-dominated NATO within post-Cold War Europe has been a serious setback to French influence and interests. But in 1994 hopes were raised in Paris that the American administration might agree to greater devolution of NATO's European operations. NATO took the decision to put its means at the disposal of the Europeans for actions which they could undertake within the framework of the EU's Common Foreign and Security Policy (CFSP), a development which facilitated French participation in combined operations in Bosnia under NATO command. After Jacques Chirac became President in 1995, French leaders came to accept that a European defence entity could only in practice be constructed within the Atlantic Alliance. France made a fundamental readjustment of its policies towards NATO in that year, normalising its relations with the military structures, and in 1996 Chirac initiated military reforms, including professionalisation of the army, which aimed *inter alia* to make possible an effective French contribution to future NATO peace-enforcing and peace-keeping operations. Chirac and his then Prime Minister Alain Juppé even allowed themselves to dream of France assuming European leadership within a reformed Alliance structure.[3] However, they failed to secure that reform of NATO, giving greater autonomy to the Europeans, without which, French logic suggests, a genuine implementation of the European CFSP declared in the Maastricht Treaty could not be implemented. Neither the Juppé

Government nor that of his successor Lionel Jospin have been able to negotiate a return to the NATO Central Military Command on terms which would build a genuine European pillar within it, as symbolised initially by the nomination of a European to head the NATO Southern Command (excluding the US Sixth Fleet). Chirac and Jospin pursued this strategy, which was intended to reinforce the political effectiveness of the EU, giving it some military credibility through its access to NATO's technical assets, in spite of the fact that there were no strong political pressures for it within France itself.[4] But the United States appears to have believed that the weakness of the French position, in political and defence terms, would force her to accept an unconditional return to NATO.[5]

French analysts find it to hard to explain why France's European partners have not given more determined support for reforms of NATO in order to promote European authority within the alliance.[6] As Jacques Attali, reflecting on his experience as a Frenchman in European politics, ruefully remarked, why was it that he always appeared to be the only one resisting the American stranglehold on European autonomy?[7] In what French leaders believe is their own more profound analysis of the interests both of France and of Europe, it seems self-evident that the emergence of a more united EU at the political level must translate into a new sharing of tasks and responsibilities within the NATO alliance. Of this there is as yet no real sign and perhaps not much understanding. In the meantime, France made the largest contribution, after the United States and before the United Kingdom, to NATO's controversial air campaign against Yugoslavia, its forces based in Macedonia operating under the American Admiral heading NATO's Southern European Command, the very post which France had sought to Europeanise. In this, the most serious military conflict in Europe since 1945, France was disadvantaged by her only partial integration into NATO. François Heisbourg described as the worst of situations that in which French servicemen risked their lives fulfilling NATO commands while their government did not participate, at the military level, in the elaboration of these orders. He argued that, paradoxical as it might seem, France must become fully integrated into NATO if it were truly to play the leading role in the Europeanisation of defence.[8]

None of the developments of the 1990s – commercial, military, technological, cultural or linguistic – have been spontaneously favourable to France. Its threatened decline is social, cultural, linguistic and psychological, as well as political – it strikes at the heart of the distinctive French identity and mission. 'La France qui soit elle-même' is at risk of being overwhelmed by more powerful people and cultures. Globalisation threatens to dissolve all that is distinctively French in what Vedrine has called 'an Anglophone, Americo-Asiatic miasma'.[9] In this alien world, French people would have no choice but to watch bad American television programmes on Japanese television sets. French leaders have worked to create a strong Europe, and constantly uphold the value of fruitful cultural diversity worldwide, as a means of protecting a French culture now in global retreat in the face of savage globalisation. The French political class are the epitome of concern for what Ole Wæver *et al* call 'societal security', in which 'survival for a society is a question of identity, because this is the way a society talks about existential threats: if this happens, we will no longer be able to live as us'.[10] The processes of *mondialisation* – uncontrolled liberalisation of trade and finance, worldwide communications, the dominance of English in business and the media – are equated with Americanisation, and threaten the distinctive French values, culture and world mission which it is the goal of foreign policy both to protect and to project. France, like the United States, is a mission country. Elie Cohen has pointed out that official discourse on the rank of France, on its status, on the defence and promotion of the French language, on its cultural exceptionalism, is quite incomprehensible unless one takes into account the fact that, like the United States, France wants to be the carrier of a universal message.[11] As the writer Pascal Bruckner sardonically puts it, for two centuries France, as a messianic nation which wants to be the teacher of the human race, exists in a competitive relationship with the United States, and tries, like the United States, to establish a model of civilisation valid for the entire planet.[12] France's foreign policy is on the defensive, operating in a domestic environment where the public mood oscillates between arrogance and self contempt, and in an international environment where it is the American mission and ideology, not the French, which are in the ascendant.

In these adverse circumstances, the conviction that the construction of political Europe is *the* effective multiplier of French power, that the EU is the only international organisation capable of counterbalancing, of redeeming and of humanising rampant globalisation, is held with extraordinary consistency across the ruling elites of the major parties, once in office.[13] Europe is to France what the United States is to Britain, the optimum multiplier of national power.[14] Hubert Vedrine articulates the view, widely shared among successive ministers, that the political construction of the Union as an extendor or amplifier of French power, does not oblige France to abandon sovereignty, since in most cases this sovereignty is already formal or illusory, and the exercise in common of sovereignty permits on the contrary the recovery of a little of what has been lost.[15] In general terms, Europe is about adding, not subtracting. In specific terms, it is about asserting independence from the United States.

Alain Juppé, successively Minister of Foreign Affairs and Prime Minister from the right-wing RPR party, shares a similar mindset with Vedrine from the socialist left. If France wants to strengthen its own security, and secure recognition for the value of its principles of world organisation, then it is through Europe that it must work. France must develop a certain idea of Europe which contains and extends a certain idea of France.[16] Indeed, within the evolving regional complexes of Asia and Latin America, where France has to make the biggest effort to modernise what Juppé calls an outdated image close to caricature, its national effort cannot be separated from the political affirmation of Europe. The EU, with its pacific reputation and freedom from the taint of imperialism, is a particularly useful vehicle for a country like France, whose record of colonialism and violently resisted de-colonisation is still remembered in the developing world. Presidents and their ministers have struggled to preserve France's traditional national advantages and freedom of movement, while at the same time benefiting from the supplementary influence, the value added, derived from *l'Europe puissance,* and the idea captured in the slogan, 'a strong France in a strong Europe'.

French leaders are then always involved in a two-level game, national and European. As Vedrine explains, a great country plays permanently on two levels: multilateral coordination when it is to its advantage, and the unilateral and sovereign *démarche* which it never renounces.[17] For Juppé, French national foreign policy and European multilateral policies are complementary, not conflicting, providing always that the EU concentrates its international attention in those areas where it can indisputably bring added value to what national policies may achieve, as the principle of subsidiarity would suggest. (Neither all of Vedrine's party, nor all of Juppé's, agree on what these areas actually are.) But Heads of State and ministers across the parties have identified Europe's distinctive value as an international actor in the fact that, having no association with external conquest and constituting in itself a model of the peaceful reconciliation of former enemies, it is able, under French prompting, to be a major player on the world stage in a way which France alone cannot do. The EU embodies the reconciliation of transnational order with the preservation of national identities, understood by the more far-sighted French leaders as a central issue for the management of international affairs in the twenty-first century. Both France, for historical and cultural reasons, and the EU, as an entity which is *sui generis* in the international system, have a special contribution to make to those issues – harmonising the interests of the whole with the parts, managing variety at different levels of the international system, and preserving heterogeneity within a collectively regulated international order – which will dominate the agenda of the future. Europe, like France, is exceptional. France is playing a two-level game in which French exceptionalism is complemented by European exceptionalism.

French leaders, as the prime movers of European political coordination, have never under-estimated the difficulties, internal and external, of putting in place this unique extender of French power. The Maastricht Treaty as a key stage in the construction of a federal Europe was, for

President Mitterrand as for his then Foreign Minister Roland Dumas, part of an ambitious design to make Europe *la première puissance au monde*. Both the President and the government of the time were alive to the complexities of formulating a common foreign policy between those countries which had never had a foreign policy and were nervous about having one, and others, among them France, which had for centuries conducted national, imperialist, global and antagonistic foreign policies and whose leaders still see it as one of the six countries of world influence, just behind the United States.[18]

Belief in the complementarity of a strong France and a strong Europe is then the norm among those in power. Politicians such as President Chirac, whose Gaullist commitment to *l'Europe des Patries* brought him closer to British ideas, are largely assimilated into the dominant view once in office. The complementarity of French and European interests is not, however, accepted across the entire political spectrum. There is agreement that France is threatened with submergence in the American way of life and liberal capitalist Atlanticism, but no agreement about the best means of combating it. *Euroallergie*, which afflicts members of the respectable right as well as Gaullists of the left, finds expression in disbelief that France's international status and Europe as an international actor can ever be compatible. In practice, it is argued, the growth of one has reduced the standing of the other, and this must inevitably be the case. The stress on France's own national role, and on the importance of bilateral rather than multilateral diplomacy, comes naturally to older members of the cadre of ambassadors of France. Giles Perol, Ambassadeur de France, former collaborator of Général de Gaulle and a prominent opponent of the Maastricht Treaty, blamed the decline in France's status and prestige during the previous thirty years, which he had experienced directly as France's ambassador in Japan, on the steady assertion of the EU as an international actor worldwide.[19] The claim of EU presidents from small countries such as Belgium or Denmark to speak in the name of France diminished France's own rank in the world. The obligation on France, as on the UK, to represent in some sense the EU within the United Nations Security Council, weakened her status and independence relative to that of the United States, Russia and China.

The dominant leaders from right, left and centre who see a strong Europe as the necessary complement to a strong France do not underestimate the scale of the challenge. Alain Juppé himself recognised in 1995 that it would become progressively more difficult for the EU to have the capacity to decide and to act. There was a real danger of returning to a concert of nations, which would satisfy all those, inside and outside the Union, who feared a genuine affirmation of European identity.[20] Only the Franco-German coupling could provide the dynamism and cohesion necessary for Europe to move forward. That coupling has however never been as strong since 1995 as it was during the Mitterrand/Kohl period. President Chirac has nothing like Mitterrand's intellectual and emotional commitment to *l'Europe puissance* and voted yes without enthusiasm in the Maastricht Treaty referendum. The special relationship with Germany threatened to unravel when he came to power in 1995 and his initial attempt to get closer to the British unfortunately coincided with the unilateral cancellation, for budgetary reasons, of large joint Franco-German armaments projects. The dissonances between France and Germany at the time of the 1996 EU Intergovernmental Conference cast doubt on the enduring harmony of the Franco-German relationship and the chances of building Europe as a political entity. This impacted on the weak outcome of the Treaty of Amsterdam, and subsequently slowed down for some eighteen months the European political and security engine.

Some of the dynamic for the integration of European security has since been revived at a practical level by the growing imperative of armaments collaboration. The escalating pace and cost of armaments development, and the challenge posed by the scale of mergers in the United States defence industry to the survival of an independent French prime contractor capability, have compelled governments to accept that a much larger fusion of French, German and British defence industries is inevitable. This will necessarily erode France's sovereign defence industrial base. Joint armaments projects with European partners currently make up more than a third of all projects, and the Jospin government's continuing concern for constructing a 'Europe de la sécurité' has led it to privilege agreements with its major partners during a time of declining budgets and cost cutting.[21] Such is the pace of technological advance, that the concern now is that not only France, but Europe too, may lose its independent defence industrial capability. French leaders are clear on this point – no European defence industrial base, no national defence policies and no Common Foreign and Security Policy (CFSP) either. Increasing armaments collaboration between France and Britain, in the context of Chirac's policy of closer relations with Britain, smoothed the way for the joint Franco-British initiative to spearhead a new defence policy for the EU as announced in the St Malo declaration of December 1998. British and French leaders committed themselves to providing the Union with appropriate structures and a capacity for analysis of situations, sources of intelligence and a capability for relevant strategic planning.

Government strategy for preserving France's distinctive identity, while simultaneously promoting the EU as an international actor to protect that identity, is a subtle and complex one, not easily communicated to the public at large. Nicole Gnesotto may argue, from the perspective of the Parisian intellectual elite, that France has become so closely identified with the European project that any reverse, indeed any slowing down, in the affirmation of Europe immediately takes the form of a French crisis of identity. In her view, it is Europe which is today the incarnation of France and of her international role, in sharp contrast with de Gaulle's time.[22] Indeed, President Mitterrand famously told the French that in serving Europe they were serving France. But public opinion polls continue to show that attachment to Europe is weaker than other territorial affiliations, to the nation, the region, the department and the commune.[23] Indeed, even for the political class, Europe is a means to French influence, it has not been entirely assimilated in that end: France must never surrender its independent role, and the status as one of the great historic powers and permanent member of the Security Council which qualifies France to pronounce on questions of world importance.[24]

Foreign policy change – socialisation of foreign policy makers

During the fourteen years of the Mitterrand Presidency, when cementing the relationship with Germany for European ends was the central plank of foreign policy, the working relationship between staff of the Élysée and the Chancellory, between those of the foreign and other ministries, and between the service chiefs, was transformed. At the heart of the conjunction between the countries was the relationship, at once professional and personal, between Chancellor Kohl and President Mitterrand. There was, as Hubert Vedrine, then diplomatic counsellor to Mitterrand, has remarked, nothing like it anywhere else in the world. In addition to the two formal Franco-German summits as specified in the 1963 Treaty, there were regular, informal meetings, in domestic and private locations as well as public ones, the close coordination during meetings of the European Council, among them, the regular breakfasting together on the second day. During the Mitterrand years, the Franco-German relationship before and during the European Council meeting was the key to French influence. The assistants and advisers to the President and the Chancellor – many of them like Vedrine still at the heart of foreign policy making – became friends as well as colleagues:

> 'Chacun est accompagné par un tout petit nombre de collaborateurs, toujours les mêmes, devenus des amis'.[25]

The friendly relationships and almost daily contact over the Mitterrand years, across the ministries of Foreign Affairs, Defence, European Affairs, Finance, Matignon and Elysee, developed habits of working together, and fostered mutual respect and a shared understanding of each other's approach, margin of manouevre and available options. The interaction was particularly instructive for the French, since their elites knew Germany less well than their German counterparts knew France.[26] The habits and understanding formed at that time have retained some continuity across administrations and presidencies. The connections between ministers, assistants and advisers in either country, many of them still in politics, have mitigated to some extent the degradation in the Franco-German relationship since the end of Mitterrand's term of office. President Chirac has never established the same kind of personal rapport with either German Chancellor as his predecessor enjoyed with Chancellor Kohl. When he first became president, some persuasion had to be brought to bear on Chirac, who had been critical of the Mitterrand project, to acknowledge the special bond with Germany by an early symbolic action. Subsequent hopes of a good rapport between the Socialist Government of Lionel Jospin and the German Social Democrats of the Schröder government have been disappointed. French socialists warmly welcomed the defeat of Helmut Kohl, which it was hoped would open the way for a new entente with the Social Democrats, and were enamoured with the new Minister of Finance, Oscar Lafontaine. After Lafontaine's sudden resignation in March 1999, the French found themselves with few friends in the Schröder government. The deterioration in the Franco-German relationship was made painfully clear when Chancellor Schröder, as President of the Council of Ministers, made no attempt to reach a prior agreement with the French on the substance of Agenda 2000, something which would have been inconceivable during the Mitterrand–Kohl years.

The relative isolation of the French military and defence communities dating from French withdrawal from the NATO central command structure in 1966 began to break down in the late 1980s. The creation in 1987 of the Council of Franco-German Defence and Security and the Franco-German brigade and, following German unification, the construction of Eurocorps, has made it necessary for the French and German military and defence specialists to work together in a way which favours the convergence of policies and doctrines.[27] The extension of the Eurocorps in 1995 as a multinational formation of five countries, and the creation that same year of Eurofor, a combined land force of France, Italy, Spain and Portugal, and Euromarfor, a combined maritime force of the same countries, has created a broader *ésprit de corps*, even though the forces have not, as hoped, been translated into the active collective management of crises. The special bond which comes from active service has been forged more with the British. The collaborative operations between the French and British forces in Bosnia and in Yugoslavia had a big impact in building mutual respect across the services involved, and played their part in supporting those better relations with Britain which distinguish Chirac's presidency from that of Mitterrand.

Habits of working together are then highly differentiated between France and its various European partners: closest by a considerable margin with Germany, followed by the other larger western European powers, and much less so with the smaller countries to the east. The attempt to coordinate foreign policy within the EC culminating in the CFSP meant that French leaders had to make an effort to familiarise themselves with smaller, hitherto little known European countries to the East. A certain amount of reorientation was necessary for the Parisian foreign policy establishment, hitherto better connected and more at home in the developing world, especially Africa, than in the Baltic. Hubert Vedrine's account of the progression of President Mitterrand and his entourage round the more obscure capitals of European Member States reads like *Venture to the Interior*. Personal relationships with the leaders of the smaller Member States of Eastern and Central Europe remain less close than those with major Western European partners, or with key collaborators in the francophone world.

Domestic factors in the foreign policy process: constitutional and bureaucratic factors

Within the constitution and practices of the Fifth Republic, as Vedrine describes them, everything or almost everything is ordered around the President, everything emanates from him or returns to him, nothing can be done without his delegation, nothing is legitimate and lasting without him.[28] The unusually long seven-year presidential term of office has been retained, in spite of periodic assaults, since the major parties tacitly accept that to reduce it would weaken presidential power, a cornerstone of the constitution of the Fifth Republic.[29] The hierarchical form of authority which the President continues to exercise within the state apparatus is, as Vedrine observes, increasingly divergent from the general evolution of society in France, *individualiste, protestataire et libertaire-consommatrice*.[30] The Presidential grip is tightest where the President himself has a coherent foreign policy vision and commitment, and in those areas where French vital interests are perceived to be at stake, and on which attention is concentrated. It does not exclude the influence of bureaucratic politics or industrial pressure in more peripheral areas.

Foreign policy is defined and conducted in almost permanent symbiosis between the Élysée and the Quai d'Orsay. It is not accurate to see the Presidency, the Prime Minister's Office, the Quai d'Orsay, the Ministry of Defence, the Ministry of Finance, as separate entities, engaging in regular but formal contact. In practice, the leaders of these institutions – ministers, secretaries general, *directeurs de cabinet*, counsellors, in all twenty or thirty people – are in uninterrupted contact between themselves, twenty-four hours a day, fifty-two weeks a year, by means of telephones, inter-ministerial telephones, protected communications networks, mobile phones, car phones, faxes, meetings, breakfasts, lunches and dinners. Wherever they are in the world, in the air or on land, they are all informed of the same events, often some minutes before these are made public. The members of the groups acquire a distinctive common culture, which goes far to explain the exceptional and much noted continuity of French foreign policy. Elites in France are densely interlinked, with no sharp divide between civil servants and politicians, and circulate between ministerial office, the civil service, mayoralties of major towns, the top policy institutes, the President's advisory posts, and indeed leadership of major companies. The brilliant products of the École Nationale d'Administration continue to colonise the highest posts across the public sector. However, parliamentarians, both national and European, are not necessarily part of the political elite and there has commonly been less coordination between French governments and French members of the European Parliament than is the case in Germany.

Hubert Vedrine, during his fourteen years at the Élysée as Diplomatic Counsellor to President Mitterrand, worked closely with all the ministries of those years, both right and left. As Foreign Secretary in Lionel Jospin's government, he enjoys a good relationship with President Chirac, the fruit of many years of working in the same milieu, a kind of experience which it would be rare to find across the party divide in Britain. The habits of collaboration foster a shared view of the world, which spans political parties, and makes possible a consistency across governments and presidencies, extending to the leaders of the major French companies. President Mitterrand, following German precedent, associated the business community more closely with foreign policy by inviting prominent business leaders to form part of his entourage on official visits abroad.

There are of course some differences of emphasis and some tensions within this broad consensus, both institutional and party political, the latter particularly during periods of cohabitation. It is believed that the Quai d'Orsay has definitely shown itself closer to the 'sovereignty' position of the British than to the federalist position of the Germans on the institutional and decision-making modalities of the CFSP and the third pillar, and consequently, on the very structure of the future Union.[31] The Presidential domination of foreign policy claimed by President Mitterrand did not go unchallenged. In 1986 the incoming Prime Minister Jacques Chirac wanted to implement his election pledge that France would participate in the American Strategic Defence Initiative research programme. Mitterrand insisted that this would never happen as long as he was President, and his threat to call a referendum if Chirac persisted won the day.[32] During the second Mitterrand cohabitation of 1993 to 1995 Eduard Balladur and Jacques Chirac tried to establish that Article 20 of the constitution allowed the government, rather than the President, to determine and conduct the foreign policies of France. The outcome of this public power struggle was a compromise, an agreement that foreign policy was a shared domain. In practice, the quartet of Mitterrand–

Balladur–Juppé–Leotard, Head of State, Prime Minister, Foreign Minister, Defence Minister, managed to conduct foreign policy in a relatively coherent fashion, except in respect of Algeria where it was mainly disagreements between ministers, not between the ministers and the President, which were at issue. But in Vedrine's view, the formulation of a common foreign policy position within each government is always a process of alchemy. Even outside periods of cohabitation, the President, the Prime Minister and the Minister of Foreign Affairs do not automatically react in the same way from the start. There is a permanent process of mutual adjustment between the personalities and the interests, arbitrated at the last count by the Prime Minister, and by the Head of State. Cohabitation is from this point of view only a particular case of a more general process. Since 1997 President Chirac and the government of Lionel Jospin have succeeded in developing common positions without real difficulties and went out of their way to demonstrate their perfect coordination when the NATO air bombardments of Yugoslavia began.[33]

There are, of course, inter-ministerial tensions and the unusual political prominence of the Head of State complicates the lives of ministers and may overshadow their role, relative to that of their co-equals from other European states. Ministers of Foreign Affairs work closely with Ministers of European Affairs but, considering themselves the true head of foreign policy within the government, do not want the Ministers of European Affairs to have too close or direct relations with the President and his close advisers, or direct communications with the press without advance coordination with the Quai d'Orsay.[34] At European Councils the large French delegation including advisers consists of some thirty people. It is led, typically, by the Head of State, with the second seat held by the Minister of Foreign Affairs. The Minister of European Affairs is reduced to hanging about in one of the delegation offices, hoping that the Minister of Foreign Affairs will vacate a seat for a moment, or that the President will ask the European Minister to come in whilst taking a break.[35]

In France as elsewhere inter-ministerial rivalries and structural factors impact on the policy-making process, despite the strong consensus among foreign policy elites and the powerful role of the President. This is particularly the case in those areas of the world, such as Asia, where big policy issues affecting core French interests are not generally perceived to be at stake and which attract little concentrated attention in normal times. Asia is dealt with by both the regional and the functional administrations within the principal ministries – Foreign Affairs and the Economy and Finance Section of the Direction des Relations Économiques Extérieures (DREE), but it does not loom large in the ministerial offices which help to structure policy.[36] Within the Quai d'Orsay, Asia is often handled with Latin America, the area of the world where France's interests and influence are at their weakest. Long standing rivalry between the Ministry of

Foreign Affairs and the DREE has been only partly mitigated by Alain Juppé's attempts, as Prime Minister, to bring them together. French ambassadors in the Asia region are said to be torn between their position as political representatives and their expanding role in promoting high-level commercial interests. The lack of diplomatic preparation in the Asia-Pacific region before the relaunching of the French nuclear tests in 1995 was one manifestation of this lack of coherence, both in Paris and in the field.

Swings in policy towards rival or competing countries in the area, India and Pakistan, China, Taiwan and South Korea, with France inclining now to one side, now to the other, derive from perceived short-term opportunities in the arms sales market. The shifts in French policy towards India and Pakistan are a case in point. In East Asia, the 'all-China policy' of the 1970s was followed in the early 1980s by an 'all Vietnam policy': the scientific and cultural programme with Vietnam was the only one to escape the budget cuts then in force. After their return to power in 1988 the Socialists turned their attention from China towards South Korea, towards the Association of South East Asian Nations (ASEAN), and towards Taiwan, where arms sales between 1991 and 1993 alone equalled five years of arms exports to China, and are said to have helped to stabilise the franc during the financial turbulence of autumn 1993.[37]

Godement argues that two competing industrial influences have contended to drive French foreign policy in the region. The energy, telecommunications, automobile and wheat industries have inclined towards China, and the Franco-Chinese declaration of 1993, to the detriment of Taiwan, and have formed the high point of this orientation in foreign policy. The high technology industries, electronics, space and armaments, on the other hand, have seen their main opportunities in the markets of the maritime states of Taiwan, Korea and ASEAN. The launching of the French initiative towards Asia in 1994, a classic instance of commercial diplomacy, reflected this orientation and interest. It should be stressed however that competing industrial pressures, and indeed the influence of bureaucratic politics, prevail only when no overriding French interests are held to be at stake. Strong protests from French industrial interests in the Asia–Pacific region were no more effective than protests from within European partner countries in deterring President Chirac and the Juppé government from seeing the French nuclear weapons tests through to the end.

If there is an exception to the general rule that bureaucratic politics and inter-ministerial tensions only impact on peripheral areas of foreign policy, that exception has been Algeria. The existence of a large population of Algerian descent within France, and fears of the impact of the Algerian crisis within the hexagon, has brought French policy in this area within the ambit of the Minister for the Interior as well as of the Quai

d'Orsay. During the cohabitation period of 1993–95, the strong personality and convictions of Charles Pasqua as Minister for the Interior made
his Ministry as powerful an influence over Algerian policy as the Foreign
Ministry of Alain Juppé, at a time when Mitterrand's grip was weakened
by failing health, the approaching end of his period of office, and his
preoccupation with the Bosnian crisis. After the annulment of the
Algerian elections in 1991 which was won by the Islamist Front Islamique
de Salut, an annulment received in Paris with a sigh of relief, ministers
were preoccupied with sheltering France from the repercussions of the
ensuing conflict.[38] The possibility that hundreds of deaths in Algeria
might drive boat people across the Mediterranean to Provence, impacting
on municipal, parliamentary and presidential elections, was a nightmare
for electoral strategists. Pasqua saw himself in part as Minister for
Algerian Affairs, in the name of an extended notion of security, not a new
phenomenon during the Fifth Republic. His stance had a big impact on
what was defined as much domestic as foreign policy. He often articulated
loud and clear a policy line which appeared to contradict that of ministerial colleagues. He regularly expressed extreme scepticism towards all idea
of dialogue with Islamists, even when the activities of some of his
colleagues might suggest otherwise. In times of tension, he appeared the
strongest supporter of the Algerian government. The strong line which he
pursued within his own domain – denial of Islamist leaders in exile a voice
or a power base within France, destabilisation of the potential Islamist
networks, a dramatic reduction in the issuing of visas, regular expulsion
of Algerian refugees, and a high level of cooperation between the French
and Algerian police and security forces – were simultaneously foreign and
domestic policy in action. After the hijacking of the Air France Airbus in
Algeria at Christmas 1994, the French government tried to harden its
position towards the Algerian government, but was somewhat restrained
by the desire not to inflame existing inter-ministerial disagreements.[39]

However, such ministerial disarray has not normally exposed French
governments to the parliamentary censure likely to follow in other
Western European states. The French parliament has a distinctively
limited role in foreign policy. Although the President receives parliamentary spokespersons, these are protocol contacts, and the Assemblée
Nationale and the Senate vote on treaties or international conventions,
they nevertheless tend to be wrong-footed in terms of foreign policy decision making, which depends on adequate information at the appropriate
time, speed of reaction and unity in execution. What is more, parliamentary influence had been systematically limited, partly by the constitution
of 1958 and partly by the institutional practice of the intervening years.
Neither Mitterrand nor Chirac have shown any inclination to change this.
Parliament was not asked to vote on French participation in the NATO
bombing campaign in Yugoslavia, and was only informed after the event,

in spite of the fact that Article 35 of the Constitution says that the declaration of war is authorised by parliament. During the Mitterrand period
French leaders took it for granted that the crucially important project of
Europe could easily be imperilled if populist, nationalist or demagogic
pressures on public opinion were allowed free rein to influence policy.
There were always unscrupulous politicians willing to exploit nationalist
fears or ancient hatreds, particularly in relation to Germany. The public
at large was fearful of being dominated by Germany, by the outside
world, by the blind laws of the market, of losing sovereignty, its soul, its
autonomy, its way of life, and these fears could all too easily be translated
into opposition to the government. So, in addition to what Vedrine calls
the natural tendency of governments to keep as free as possible a hand
over policy, there was a settled assumption that governments should not
imperil the negotiations and discussions in hand, whether relating to
Germany or to Europe, by imprudent consultation which might revive the
nationalisms which had been at the root of two world wars. At best, it
occurred to French leaders from time to time that it might be expedient to
keep parliament informed, a strategy which almost came adrift when it
became politically impossible to avoid a referendum on the Maastricht
Treaty.

The patrician view of policy making which Vedrine epitomises, and
expresses with a frankness which would be startling anywhere other than
in France, is based on a disdainful estimate of popular capacities and prejudices. 'What force other than nationalism or expansionism, or on the
other hand, withdrawal into isolationism, has ever come spontaneously
from the people in terms of defining their relations with other peoples?'[40]
French leaders have taken it for granted that the building of Europe could
never be a popular or democratic process. It could, says Vedrine:

> 'only have been accomplished by enlightened despots convinced of the justice
> of their cause in going beyond the European curse and equally convinced of
> the incapacity of people intoxicated with nationalism for two centuries to
> approve, or even to conceive of, their grand design if exposed to it in its full
> amplitude too soon'.[41]

The extent to which the French constitution, practices and attitudes
allowed Mitterrand's governments to ignore nationalistic pressures from
press or public, goes a long way towards explaining their success in
coupling with Germany and promoting l'Europe puissance. The contrast
with Britain, where parliament has a much greater influence over
European policy, and where governments take very seriously in electoral
terms the influence of the popular press and the media, particularly the
anti-European, Murdoch-dominated media, is instructive.

This is not to say that the intense interest of the media in selected
foreign policy issues such as the Bosnian crisis has no effect on policy. Of

all the non-state actors with an interest in foreign policy, the media, and particularly television, have become the most prominent. The prejudices and passions of public opinion are easily aroused by the all pervasive influence of the media, particularly television, which has created a newly mediatised public, liable to make snap judgements on the issue of the day and susceptible to highly emotional responses to simplified images of complex situations. Media personalities, in France, as elsewhere, have more to gain from attacking than from supporting government policies. From Vedrine's former perspective in the Élysée Palace, the growing symptoms of mediatised societies were their futility, their credulity and the difficulty in distinguishing what was real from what was unreal. It is the case that, during the Bosnian crisis in particular, French television largely projected ignorant and oversimplified representations of the complicated issues involved. All countries have their mediatised public opinion, but within France there is a special role and status attached to media intellectuals such as Bernard-Henri Lévy. Vedrine argues persuasively that after 1992 the French media intellectuals' taking up of the 'Bosnians' (the Bosnian Moslems) smacked more of arousing the emotions of the public in favour of summary solutions which could only lead to an impasse, than of the courage and lucidity needed to formulate serious ways forward to a genuine political solution of the conflict. The strong constitutional position of the President, insisted on by de Gaulle, enables presidents with sufficiently robust personalities to resist the onslaught of media attacks on foreign policy issues, that is, it is less necessary than elsewhere, where foreign policy is more democratised, to play a two-level game domestically and nationally. However, in the Bosnian case the execution of foreign policy, and particularly the inestimable benefits of ambiguity in diplomatic discourse, were compromised by the media campaign. Mitterrand's cold fury at sustained, mischievous and personalised attacks led him to repeat, much more explicitly than would otherwise have been the case, that he had no intention of adding another war to the one already in progress. This sent an unfortunate signal to the Bosnian Serb leaders and may have encouraged them to persist in their actions.[42]

Many of the themes of this chapter – the unaccountability of French foreign policy makers and their capacity to withstand, at least in the short run, concerted press and public campaigns, the influence of bureaucratic politics, the continuing aspirations to be a world power, and the habit of playing the European card in a two-level game when it suits them – are best illustrated by reference to Africa. France's position vis-à-vis her European partners is at its most distinctive in Africa, where France alone of the former European colonial powers has retained a leadership role. Many different actors have been involved in African policy, including the ministries of Foreign Affairs and Cooperation, Defence and Finance, the

Caisse Française de Développement, and the 'African cell' at the Élysée, which has on occasion overruled government departments. There is no parliamentary debate on the basis of financial cooperation with African countries, despite the large sums involved. Bureaucratic complexities muddle political priorities, give scope for secret deals, and open the way for manipulation by African Heads of States themselves. There are said to be powerful organised networks surrounding politicians and the directors of big companies, which confuse public and private interests and corrupt the policy-making process.[43] Thanks to its relations with francophone Africa, France disposes at the international level a group of about thirty countries which systematically place themselves at its side in the international organisations. Francophone countries gave France more consistent support during the international furore following the resumption of nuclear tests in 1995 than did its European partners. France has always wanted to keep francophone Africa as part of a *domain privé*. The regular Franco-African summits with Heads of State of France and Africa, France's role in the *Communauté Financière Africaine* (CFA) area, despite the devaluation of 1994, all bear witness to France's special position. France comes closer to being a world power in Africa than anywhere else, and as such deals more with the United Nations, and head to head with the United States, than with the other states of the EU. The support of its African partners allows France to play a role which exceeds its normal limitations as a medium power.[44] As far as Africa is concerned, the EU in only one of the multilateral fora within which France acts as intercessor for African interests. While preserving and indeed extending French national influence in Africa during the 1990s beyond the francophone area, France has buttressed that position by acting as intercessor for Africa with its European partners, since European financial aid and investment are a valuable reinforcement of French influence. But during the Mitterrand period France also regularly interceded, almost alone among the industrialised countries, for greater international aid to African development in all the centres of power, the Group of Seven (G7), the International Monetary Fund (IMF), the World Bank, as well as the EU.

France's standing in Africa is, however, widely seen as on the wane. A series of controversial interventions during the 1990s have aroused mounting criticism, in France and in Africa, of both the means and the ends of French policy in Africa. Critics of French intervention in Rwanda in 1994, including leaders of prominent French humanitarian organisations, accused France with some reason of knowingly supporting the French-speaking Hutu regime in its genocidal attacks on the English-speaking Tutsis, and went on to attack the whole of French policy in Africa, seen as in pursuit of aggressive expansion beyond the francophone zone itself. Mounting outrage at Opération Turquoise did not succeed in deflecting French policy in Rwanda at the time, nor indeed did it inhibit a subsequent French government from supporting the tyrannical General Mobuto of Zaire to the very end in 1997. The crises in Zaire and in the Central African Republic demonstrated that the presence of large French forces in a country did not necessarily guarantee political stability. Exposure of the involvement of the African cell at the Élysée in the recruitment of Serbian mercenaries, former war criminals, was particularly damaging to the Juppé government. Lionel Jospin's concern to distance himself from some of the more dubious aspects of his predecessors' African policies, and the diminishing economic importance of Africa for France, have encouraged plans for reform, including changes to the responsibilities of ministries aimed at integrating development with foreign policy, a planned reduction in the numbers of French troops stationed in Africa, and a review of all defence agreements to cancel articles which provide for French intervention in the event of internal conflict. (France had in 1998 defence treaties with eight African countries and military cooperation agreements with twenty-six others.)[45]

In these delicate circumstances, when France's national *modus operandi* has run into opposition, one may expect her to play the European card. The EU is a particularly helpful mechanism for countering American competition, and multilateral aid supplied by EU members as a whole is widely credited by African leaders to French advocacy. Efforts will probably be made to get other Europeans, particularly the British, to define common criteria for Africa, as long as these reinforce, rather than undermine, France's special position. But as Hubert Vedrine emphasised in his 1998 interview with *Politique Internationale*, the French government has no intention of disengagement in Africa. On the contrary. France aims to hold dialogue with the whole of the African continent, anglophone and francophone, and will, he claims, be all the more useful to its European partners if it is able to do so. Africa remains central to France's status as a world power.

Foreign policy action – with or without the EU?

Aspirations to harmonise European foreign policies have on occasion constricted France's own policies, notably towards Former Yugoslavia, and have more often provided an opportunity to reinforce her own national interest. Considerations of European solidarity affected French foreign policy well before the advent of the CFSP. President Mitterrand supported Britain during the Falklands War, on the grounds that European solidarity weighed more heavily than France's traditional Third World sympathies and straddling of the North–South divide. French policy was actively influenced by European considerations when a crisis erupted in the Gulf in 1990, at the very time when Mitterrand was doing everything possible to secure, through intergovernmental conferences, a treaty putting in place the CFSP. The problem of French policy towards Iraq was thus posed as 'Être dans le Golfe ou perdre notre leadership en Europe'. The choice was clear and everything flowed from it.[46] The same considerations did not apply in 1998/99 when American and British military action in Iraq had nothing like the support elsewhere in Europe, or indeed in the Arab world, which it had earlier enjoyed. The French government, keen to be well placed for a return to Iraq when normalisation does eventually occur, had much to lose and nothing to gain by supporting the Anglo-Saxons on this occasion.

But the most significant constraint, not so much of solidarity with Europe as of solidarity with Germany, was on France's Yugoslav policy in the early stages of the crisis, which coincided with the putting in place of the Maastricht Treaty. Mitterrand's first reaction to the onset of the Yugoslav crisis was a reluctance to see the country break up. He believed that stability was rarely served by the dismemberment of states. The President took the view that the dismantlement of empires benefited only the United States and Germany, not Europe, and it was more important for him to preserve the promises of Maastricht than to stand by French convictions on the Yugoslav affair. On the specific question of the recognition of Croatia and Slovenia, he initially adhered to the position, long sanctified by diplomatic practice, that recognition was an acknowledgement that a government already controlled its territory. The independence of Croatia should not be conceded before its frontiers were accepted by all its neighbours. The same applied to Slovenia. Mitterrand and his Foreign Minister Roland Dumas succeeded in restraining Germany, where public pressures for the recognition of Croatia were almost irresistible, for some six months. Unilateral German recognition of Slovenia at the end of 1991 was a grave reverse for France. What was to be done? Refusal of recognition on France's part would make public the divisions among Europeans at this peculiarly delicate stage in the Maastricht process. In the event, Mitterrand and Dumas reluctantly resigned themselves to recognising Slovenia and Croatia, for reasons of 'discipline européenne' and concern for the future rather than solidarity.[47] France recognised the two new Yugoslav republics in order to restore, after the event, the formal unity of the Community. Nothing could be allowed to call into question the Franco-German relationship – not commercial or industrial rivalries, nor the radical divergence in their response to Slovene and Croat demands for diplomatic recognition.[48] When the then EC Twelve recognised Slovenia and Croatia on 15 January 1992, the French government wanted to believe that this was the first step towards a CFSP. Similarly in the case of Bosnia, Vedrine says that everyone knew that the new state was not viable, but France was on a diplomatic toboggan and felt impelled to recognise Bosnia-Herzegovina, along with its eleven European partners.[49] Tragically, responsibility towards Europe led to irresponsibility towards Yugoslavia, in conscious violation of the hard learnt lessons of diplomatic history and practice. Yugoslavia paid a terrible price for the preservation of the Franco-German alliance at the heart of Europe, and the susceptibility of the German government to the kind of hysterical public opinion which it is the strength of the French political system to be able to resist.

In the last resort the French government was willing to allow solidarity with European partners to constrain its own policy in Yugoslavia, only because no vital French interests were perceived to be at stake. Where French governments identify special interests or have special relationships outside the EU, then general aspirations to harmonise European foreign policy is not allowed to restrict their own independence of action. Yugoslavia is much less important to France, economically, culturally and in terms of domestic politics, than North Africa, where French governments have been more assertive both in shaping EU policies, and in maintaining their national bilateral strength. The three main countries of the Maghreb, Morocco, Algeria and Tunisia, France's neighbours to the south, are as important to it, in geopolitical and security terms, as those of eastern Europe are to the Germans and other Europeans. The French stake for France in the stability of this area is considerable, not only in terms of illicit immigration, but because the Maghreb is the fulcrum between the rest of the Arab world and Europe.[50]

In Algeria, where a special relationship and special interests are particularly strong, national rather than European policies has been pursued most conspicuously. In spite of conflicting and sometimes passionate differences of opinion within the French political classes, French policy has as we have seen been consistently to support the Algerian government in its armed struggle with the Islamist opposition groups, since the overthrow of the elections in January 1991. This support, political, economic and security, running across Socialist and Gaullist governments and the presidencies of both Mitterrand and Chirac, has taken the form of large French loans, of decisive intercession on Algeria's behalf for the 1994 agreement between Algeria and the IMF, of consistent political and diplomatic support for the Algerian government, and close cooperation between the security forces of the two countries. French governments have taken a strong bilateral line on Algeria, although some policy insiders, notably Thierry de Montbrial, have argued the need for a greater involvement of the EU.[51] First of all, there is the underlying assumption that French, rather than European, interests are at stake in Algeria, which France has struggled to retain as a *domain privé*. When the troubles started, France enjoyed particularly close political relations with the Algerian government of President Chadli, French economic interests in

Algeria were greater than any of its European partners and French linguistic and cultural influence, a particular target of the Islamist opposition, was strong in this bastion of the francophone area. The large population of Algerian origin within France itself was, as we have seen, a critical consideration: the coming to power of an Islamist government in Algiers would not only signal the end of French political, economic and cultural influence in Algeria, it might well, it was feared, unsettle the Algerian population within France itself. The influence on the Parisian press and public opinion of the brilliant Algerian francophone intelligentsia, including fashionable feminist groups, served to rally support for the *éradicateurs* within Algeria and to focus blame for all atrocities on the Islamists. For all these reasons, France has followed a strong bilateral line, seeking to preserve French political, economic and linguistic interests, and to retain Algeria as a major interlocutor for France in the Maghreb and the whole Mediterranean region.[52] The present French government continues to support the Algerian regime, in spite of considerable disquiet on the left, encouraged by what Vedrine maintains are hopeful signs of progress by the government towards democracy and the rule of law.[53] French support for European initiatives in this area, including the exploratory visit of the troika in 1996, has been muted.

In the Mediterranean and the Middle East region more broadly, however, French governments have identified an opportunity to use a multilateral, European approach to promote French interests. French involvement in the Gulf War of 1991 had as its principal effect accelerating the Europeanisation of its foreign policy in the Arab world.[54] France espoused European initiatives in the Mediterranean to counterbalance the slippage of the European centre of gravity towards the north-east as a result of the enlargement process, to find some small financial counterbalance to the financial expenditure of the EU in Eastern Europe and to mount more effective competition to the dominant American position in the region.[55] This has not of course excluded the simultaneous and complementary invocation of privileged bilateral links with a number of countries in the Mediterranean area, in the hope of seeing itself preferred to its European partners in the markets of the region. In the Middle East, France, once a great historic power in the Lebanon and elsewhere, is now seen as a middle ranking power with little influence, whereas the EU is taken very seriously, both as a model of regional integration and a global actor. The EU does therefore offer effective leverage, an unparalleled vehicle for reasserting French influence in the region. The high levels of EU aid to the Palestinian state has amplified in classic fashion the not insignificant French bilateral financial protocols. As Kodmani-Darwish puts it, French policy of financial and diplomatic support of the Palestinians has become European policy, thus putting European means in the service of a French vision of the Arab–Israeli conflict and its solution.[56]

The Euro-Mediterranean Partnership Initiative, launched by the Barcelona conference of 1995, shaped by French strategic perspectives, policies and interests, and hailed as a success for the southern countries of the EU as a whole, is a prime example of adroitly exploiting the opportunity to work at the European level in a broad area extending beyond French special interests and relationships. France, more than any other country, has an interest in seeing this partnership succeed, as a means of maintaining her rank and influence, of balancing German dominance in Eastern and Central Europe, and of re-establishing the link between the Maghreb and the Mashreq at the expense of the United States, in the classic tradition of de Gaulle. It is a prime example of how close French bilateral accords, political and financial, can be amplified by European multilateral accords, political and especially financial. This is a textbook case of how European policies were intended to work, as an enlargement of French bilateral influence and policies. Pierre Moscovici, Minister of European Affairs in the Jospin government, explained to the journal *Euromag* in February 1998 that although the European initiative in the Mediterranean took place in a multilateral framework, it did not exclude, quite the contrary, bilateral initiatives between Member States and south Mediterranean countries. The French, at the national level, increased their instruments of financial aid and maintained at a high level their cultural, scientific and cultural cooperation of which the total comprised, for the whole of North Africa and the Middle East, one thousand million francs.[57] Kodmani-Darwish estimates that France has gained in effectiveness much more than it has lost by acting within the European framework, which offers the opportunity to exercise uncontested leadership, to maintain her existing advantages in those countries linked by her historic Arab policy, and to extend relationships with new countries of the region previously outside her range. For the first time, France is able to adopt a regional approach by which it can defend its markets in the monarchies of the Gulf, aid Lebanon in its reconstruction, maintain itself in readiness for a return to Iraq when the opportunity presents itself, and simultaneously, develop its relationship with Israel and Turkey.[58]

The EU has similarly provided the opportunity to amplify French influence in Asia. French commercial interests in Asia, particularly the high technology ones, find themselves competing with the Americans on an unequal playing field, without the political assets which the Americans enjoy in the Asia–Pacific region. In this situation, it is very much in French interests to promote European region to region connections, at a time when Asia Pacific Economic Cooperation (APEC) seems designed to exclude the Europeans. The EU has however established good links since its creation with the ASEAN regional forum, although France has considered it necessary to reinforce these European links with French national links. Despite concerns about the weakness of European structures and the changing Presidency every six months, the firmness of EU representations on Chinese entry to the World Trade Organisation, the flexibility displayed in reaching a pragmatic trade agreement with Japan, and progress in opening up the South Korean markets, are taken as indications that Europe has now achieved the kind of critical mass necessary for success in the big commercial negotiations.[59] But, it is argued, Europe still needs to assert a political as well as a commercial influence in the area, if it is not to succumb to overwhelming American dominance. Working within European structures is particularly convenient for France since it allows it to bury its reputation for protectionism while promoting its own interests.[60] France is playing a classic two-level game in Asia. Its national influence remains in place thanks to its historical experience and the 'soft power' of its cultural inheritance, its territorial presence in the South Pacific, and its role within the UN and its work for world order. The European region-to-region initiatives serve to combat the dominance of Asia–Pacific regional organisations oriented towards the commercial needs of the United States, and can be presented as diversifying the options available for Asian countries themselves.

Conclusion

French leaders have a widely shared, well thought out and sophisticated view of the relationship between French foreign policy and a European CFSP. French governments have promoted the EU's international activity as a vehicle for those initiatives which France alone cannot accomplish, and which are intended to supplement French efforts at a national level. The European presence is particularly useful in those areas of the world where French influence is weak and American hegemony is strong, where memories of France's colonial past still linger, and where the scale of economic aid and investment required is beyond the scope of French bilateral capabilities. French governments have sought to keep their *domain privé* those areas, particularly francophone Africa, where France managed to retain much of her historic national influence, and which are vital if it is to continue to lay claim to the status of a world power. In these areas, French leaders have neither wanted nor needed the EU to assert an international presence

French foreign policy is on the defensive in a global environment which weakens French prestige and authority and reduces her freedom of manoeuvre. The United States, its culture, its language, its economic interests and its political clout, are on the ascendant even within the traditional French spheres of influence. While French governments may be expected to fight to retain national freedom of action and historic political assets at all costs, we are likely, in this adverse situation, to see a shift in the balance of the two-level game, with the European region-to-region card increasingly deployed to counter that globalisation which, in French eyes, is inseparable from Americanisation.

Notes

1 H. Vedrine, 'Entretien avec la revue' *Politique Internationale*, La Documentation Française, Textes et Documents, Ministère des Affaires Étrangères, Paris, February (1998), p. 150.
2 N. Gnesotto, *La Puissance et l'Europe* (Presses de La Fondation Nationale des Sciences Politiques, Paris, 1998), p. 66.
3 A. Sauder, 'Les changements de la politique de defense française et de la coopération franco-allemande', *Politique Étrangère*, 3 (1996), p. 588.
4 G. Andréani, 'La France et l'OTAN après la guerre froide', *Politique Étrangère*, 1 (1998), p. 90.
5 Gnesotto, *La Puissance*, pp. 58–59.
6 Andréani, 'La France et l'OTAN', p. 78.
7 H. Vedrine, *Les Mondes de François Mitterrand* (Fayard, Paris, 1996), p. 240.
8 F. Heisbourg, 'Kosova: trois leçons pour la France', *Le Monde*, 15 April 1999, p. 17.
9 Vedrine, *Les Mondes,* p. 747.
10 O. Wæver, B. Buzan, M. Kelstrup and P. Lemaitre, *Identity, Migration and the New Security Agenda in Europe* (Centre for Peace and Conflict Resolution, Copenhagen, Pinter Publishers, London, 1993), pp. 25–26.
11 E. Cohen, *La Tentation Hexagonale; la Souveraineté à l'Épreuve de la Mondialisation* (Fayard, Paris, 1996), p. 23.
12 P. Bruckner, 'La France, victime universelle?', *Le Monde*, 2 April 1998, p. 2.
13 Vedrine, *Les Mondes*, p. 58.
14 Gnesotto, *La Puissance*, p. 93.
15 Vedrine, *Les Mondes*, p. 293.
16 Alain Juppé, 'Quel horizon pour la politique étrangère de la France?', *Politique Étrangère*, 1 (1995), p. 258.
17 Vedrine, *Les Mondes*, p. 248.
18 Vedrine, *Les Mondes*, p. 476.
19 G. Perol, *La Grandeur de la France* (Albin Michel, Paris, 1992), pp. 136–137.
20 Juppé, 'Quel horizon', p. 247.
21 J. Isnard, 'La revision des programmes de défense, un casse-tête', *Le Monde*, 18 March 1998.
22 Gnesotto, *La Puissance*, p. 109.
23 C. Dargent, 'Si proche, si lointaine', *Le Monde*, 14/15 February 1999.
24 J. Andréani, 'Les rélations franco-americaines', *Politique Étrangère*, 4 (1995), p. 891.
25 Vedrine, *Les Mondes*, p. 575.
26 Vedrine, *Les Mondes*, p. 426.
27 Sauder, *Les Mondes*, p. 584.
28 Vedrine, *Les Mondes*, p. 43.
29 A. Juppé, *La Tentation de Venise* (Grasset, Paris, 1993), p. 112.
30 Vedrine, *Les Mondes*, p. 42.

31 L. Cohen-Tanugi, 'La politique éuropéenne de la France à l'heure des choix', *Politique Étrangère,* 4 (1995), p. 858.
32 Vedrine, *Les Mondes,* p. 367.
33 Vedrine, 'Entretien avec la revue'.
34 Vedrine, *Les Mondes,* p. 48.
35 Vedrine, *Les Mondes,* p. 281
36 F. Godement, 'Une politique Française pour l'Asie-Pacifique?', *Politique Étrangère,* 4 (1995), p. 959.
37 Godement, 'Une politique Française', p. 965.
38 A. Chenal, 'La France rattrapée par le drame Algerien', *Politique Étrangère,* 2 (1995), p. 418.
39 Chenal, 'La France', p. 424.
40 Vedrine, *Les Mondes,* p. 299.
41 Vedrine, *Les Mondes,* p. 555.
42 Vedrine, *Les Mondes,* p. 638.
43 R. Marchal, 'France and Africa: the emergence of essential reforms?', *International Affairs,* 74:2 (April 1998), pp. 357 and 361.
44 R. Marchal, Roland, 'La France en quête d'une politique Africaine?' *Politique Étrangère* (1995), p. 904.
45 Marchal, 'France and Africa', pp. 363–364.
46 Vedrine, *Les Mondes,* p. 527.
47 Vedrine, *Les Mondes,* p. 620.
48 Vedrine, *Les Mondes,* p. 578.
49 Vedrine, *Les Mondes,* p. 623.
50 Vedrine, 'Entretien avec la revue', p. 154.
51 T. de Montbrial, *Mémoire de Temps Present* (Flammarion, Paris, 1996), p. 95.
52 P-M. De la Gorce, 'La France et le Maghreb', *Politique Étrangère,* 4 (1995), p. 927.
53 Vedrine, 'Entretien avec la revue', p. 155.
54 B. Kodmani-Darwish, 'La France et le Moyen-Orient: entre nostalgie et réalisme', *Politique Étrangère,* 4 (1995), p. 942.
55 P. Moscovici, Pierre, 'Avant-propos du ministre délégué chargé des affaires européennes pour la revue euromag', *La Documentation Française, Textes et Documents,* (Ministère des Affaires Étrangères, Paris, February 1998), p. 188.
56 Kodmani-Darwish, 'La France et le Moyen-Orient', p. 949.
57 Moscovici, 'Avant-propos', p. 189.
58 Kodmani-Darwish, 'La France et le Moyen-Orient', p. 951.
59 Godement, 'Une politique Française', p. 969.
60 Godement, 'Une politique Française', p. 970.

3

Britain

Anthony Forster

Introduction

The importance of the Europeanisation of British foreign policy is a consequence of the significance of European union to the governance of Britain. A wide range of policy issues previously considered solely of British domestic concern has withered to a small number. British agricultural, economic and commercial policy were the first and most directly affected by Britain's membership of the European Union (EU), but increasingly membership of the EU directly or indirectly impacts upon most, if not all government departments. Moreover, the involvement of domestic ministries in the EU's common policies is challenging the dominance of the Foreign and Commonwealth Office (FCO) in managing Britain's external relations and events 'outside the state's boundaries' and can no longer be considered solely by a focus on the FCO.[1] Analysis of the impact of the EU leads to the overwhelming conclusion that it is no longer possible to make a clear distinction between European foreign and domestic policy, since functionally – and increasingly given the importance of European issue in the United Kingdom – politically, both are intrinsically interlinked with each other.

In the last twenty-seven years, membership of the EU has also had far-reaching consequences for the way in which policy is made. Not only are diplomats spending greater amounts of time in Brussels, but officials in other ministries now also have daily contact with their opposite numbers in other Member States. Ministers too are drawn into this permanent negotiating forum. Bilateral and multilateral summits have increasingly become part of the routine diplomacy, both in the EU with its scheduled twice-yearly European Councils, and in other international organisations such as the North Atlantic Treaty Organisation (NATO) and the Group of Seven (G7) summits. Pressure group activity has dramatically increased, both in terms of think-tank contributions to various aspects of British foreign policy, and through the broadening of lobby groups beyond purely economic interests. Likewise, transnational groups now exist on almost all issues and lobby governments simultaneously across national frontiers that reinforce the importance of the EU both as a policy and an arena.

This chapter argues that the UK operates in a system in which it has allowed ambitious declaratory commitments to a Common Foreign and Security Policy (CFSP) to develop which are not supported by procedural mechanisms to achieve these goals. However dysfunctional this might be, there is no appetite in London for a step change away from intergovernmentalism towards supranational decision making. In terms of policy, this chapter suggests that membership of the EU has steadily and quietly transformed not just the process of making British foreign policy, but also in certain key areas the options for achieving national goals. However, while Europeanisation in some Member States has led to a 'European rescue of national foreign policies', this thesis is of more limited relevance to Britain.[2] British governments retain an important (though decreasing) national capacity to act and a willingness to use the opportunities of a CFSP to supplement this wherever possible. British policy makers use the European arena instrumentally and are not committed to its development as part of the integration project. However, while there is a recognition that EU membership necessitates restraints on national autonomy, except in a few limited areas, these remain relatively weak.

Foreign policy change – adaptation and socialisation

Adaptation through membership

The economic and political impact of EU membership on Britain is an important one. In many core EU areas including the budgetary arrangements, the Common Agricultural Policy (CAP), or the social dimension, the British government has felt compelled to challenge the legitimacy and efficacy of the policies being pursued.[3] Even when policies have converged with British preferences such as trade liberalisation or monetarist policy the government '... has missed out on feeling a sense of achievement on the EC/EU issues that had apparently been important for them'.[4] However, one exception to this tendency throughout most of the UK's twenty-seven year membership of the EU, is in the area of foreign policy coordination, where joint action has taken the guise, first of European Political Cooperation, and subsequently the CFSP.[5]

Within important parameters, the UK has been supportive of greater foreign policy cooperation along intergovernmental lines. There is, however, a significant distinction to be made between informal cooperation and formal treaty enhancements of EU foreign policy cooperation.[6] A consistent British predisposition has been to support 'quiet' informal developments, with a preference for practical developments rather than

treaty amendments. In part this is so because routine foreign policy cooperation takes place away from the glare of parliamentary scrutiny, it
reinforces executive dominance over the direction of policy and allows the
government to hide from potentially awkward and increasingly volatile
domestic forces.[7]

By contrast treaty amendments focus attention on what government
policy is, how far integration has taken place and what concessions the
government is willing to make. Unsurprisingly then, treaty changes have
therefore presented greater domestic and EU-level difficulties for British
governments who find the process difficult to manage. This is perhaps
unsurprising on such a core sovereignty issue as foreign policy, which
raises important matters concerning the role of the nation-state, and for
some is a key indicator of the transformation of the EU into a European
federation.[8] Britain has therefore been a reluctant, though full, participant
in treaty negotiations while routinely giving the impression that it would
have been happier if this form of negotiations evaporated.[9] Given the
fundamental differences between leading Member States of the EU, treaty
amendments also routinely use rhetorical declarations as a substitute for
substantive agreement, which also challenges the pragmatic self-image of
British policy-makers, with an instinctive dislike of substituting symbolic
declarations for detailed policy commitments.[10] The domestic resonance
of this is to raise both fears and expectations among the political elite
concerning the limits and possibilities of the EU's foreign and security
policy.

Despite these reservations, at one level the three treaties of the Single
European Act, the Maastricht Treaty on the EU and the Amsterdam
Treaty, have broadly matched British policy preferences. In terms of the
institutional structure of the Union, London has won some important
successes in securing a distinctive alternative to the 'Community method'
through pillarisation which separates foreign and security policy (and to
a lesser extent justice and home affairs issues) from other *communautaire*
policy sectors.[11] In this way, British governments have attempted to secure
the primacy of the Council of Ministers, and in doing so have tried to use
European-level foreign policy cooperation as a means to strengthen
national policy rather than a means of deepening integration.[12]

Socialisation of foreign policy makers

One paradox of British involvement in the development of foreign policy
cooperation is that while generally successful in shaping the symbolism of
foreign policy cooperation, contrary to the British self-image, the government has routinely sacrificed its preferences on procedures in order to
secure an acceptable intergovernmental structure. Put another way, for
most of the period of Britain's membership of the EU, the volatility of
domestic support, the sensitivity to the issues involved, and the difficulty

of managing the European issue within the governing party and Parliament, has made presentation crucial in deepening integration in this policy sector.

The symbolism of British involvement in foreign and security policy cooperation has become as important as the substance. In the case of European foreign policy cooperation, the imagery of intergovernmentalism, first through the development of European Political Cooperation (EPC) outside the Community structure and then pillarisation of CFSP, has been used to deliberately obscure important concessions on substance, including the incremental introduction of majority voting, the merger of the EPC and Council Secretariat and the developing linkage between the *communautaire* and intergovernmental pillars, both functionally and through the budget.[13] As a result of this 'ratchet effect' British governments have been drawn into integration in foreign policy without ever admitting to a domestic audience how far integration in this policy sector has proceeded. It has also led to a dysfunctional policy. British officials have supported pragmatic informal strengthening of foreign policy cooperation and London has been at the forefront of advocating improvements to the machinery of CFSP, especially planning and analysis, and yet has been reluctant to acknowledge the contribution this makes to the momentum for formal treaty change.[14]

In shaping British foreign policy, the impact of the end of the Cold War has been slow to have an effect despite the fact that in this and other respects, the context in which British foreign policy is conducted has changed dramatically over the last decade. Externally, the fundamental structure of international society has been transformed by the dramatic increase in the number of states to nearly 200, the disappearance of the Soviet Union and the growing importance of international rules, norms and procedures in legitimating foreign policy actions.[15] The context in which policy is conducted has been further transformed by the growing importance of multilateral organisations such as the United Nations (UN), North Atlantic Treaty Organisation, Western European Union (WEU), Organisation for Security and Cooperation in Europe (OSCE) and the EU itself.[16]

Yet despite these changes, the volatility of the European issue has been sufficiently destabilising to dampen down debate and to discourage explicit rethinking of the fundamental assumptions of British foreign and security policy.[17] Indeed the most remarkable aspect of the British foreign policy debate is how little it appears to have been affected by the transformation of international order. The debate on Britain's place in the world has therefore continued along familiar lines. There remains an assumption that the United States, rather than EU Member States, is Britain's preferred partner. In security matters there is continued commitment to retaining a privileged role within NATO and a dominant role for that organisation in European security. Continuity rather than change and denial rather than adaptation appear to have been the predominant British response to changes since the end of the Cold War. Thus, reshaping British foreign policy has been perceived through a very strong domestic politics filter throughout the political elite.[18]

It is characteristic of the British foreign policy elite who cherish a 'pragmatic' self-image, that in the last decade the absence of any dramatic reappraisal has been accompanied by incremental adaptation, good administration and effective use of restricted resources.[19] This has led to active engagement of the FCO and British ministers in CFSP. But at the same time, rather limited success in developing a coherent EU foreign and security policy has been accompanied by a growing dominance of NATO and to a lesser degree a renaissance for WEU. The development of the North Atlantic Cooperation Council (NACC) and Partnership for Peace (PfP) have offered an institutional framework through which to colonise areas of cooperation with partner states on the borders of the EU, where one might have expected the EU through its CFSP to take the lead, especially Russia and the Ukraine. Likewise, NATO through Combined Joint Task Forces (CJTFs) has been the lead organisation in European and global crises like those in Bosnia, Kosovo and Iraq. This has not been an unwelcome development and the FCO and the Ministry of Defence (MoD) have been relatively satisfied both with the central role of NATO and the important role Britain plays within its military and political structures. This role has recently been reinforced with the appointment of the Defence Minister George Robertson as the new Secretary-General of NATO, much to the pleasure of the British government. These developments have also allowed successive British governments to pick and choose between organisations, a process which strengthens the role of governments in foreign policy decision making.

Foreign policy process – domestic and bureaucratic

Bureaucratic factors in the foreign policy process
As with many Member States, the impact of domestic factors has been crucial in shaping Britain's foreign policy. In part, the constitutional arrangements are an influential constraint. Since joining the European Community, the government has insisted on a tightly organised and highly centralised policy-making process. While the Scottish Office has an industry section to coordinate EU issues within each department, London retains the lead role and ensures that the government speaks with one voice in Brussels concerning the British national interest.[20] The recent creation of devolved assemblies in Scotland and Wales will not change this pattern, since a new structure of joint ministerial committees will decide the UK line in advance of key negotiations; in addition, there will be no

question of splitting the UK's block vote between regions.[21] This centralised system removes the need for vertical sub-national coordination, with efforts tightly focused on horizontal coordination between ministries in London. Combined with cabinet government and collective responsibility, ministers and the Permanent Representative work to a tight brief from London, and in contrast to colleagues from other Member States, British ministers have less autonomy and less flexibility to bargain within the Council of Ministers in situations where coalition building and fluidity are the dominant characteristic of negotiations.[22]

From the outset the Cabinet Office, rather than the FCO, was identified as the lead institution in coordinating government policy and it has retained its dominant position ever since. In part this is so because of fears that Whitehall departments might consider the FCO to be too willing to advance diplomatic and political solutions at the expense of other legitimate interests and that the Cabinet Office could therefore better present a consensus view.[23] This arrangement had the further advantage that it allowed the FCO to argue for a particular departmental view on EC issues. As a former head of the European Secretariat noted, '. . . it could not do this and at the same time hold the ring in Whitehall'.[24] In part the role of the Cabinet Office also reflected the fact that most early Community business addressed issues on which the FCO had little direct experience and a non-departmental view was best.[25]

In the past it was a widely held view that EU membership would give FCO diplomats 'a new place in the sun'.[26] Today the picture is far more complicated. Since the Single European Act Britain's EU relations have been characterised by domestication of EU policy through the direct engagement of domestic ministries, the growing influence of the Treasury in policy making with financial implications, and the fact that the Euro casts a long shadow over most policy making. To this can be added the growing frequency of emergency European Councils, called to address specific internal and external crises, which directly engage the Prime Minister in foreign policy making.[27]

This leaves the FCO with formal responsibility for communicating instructions to Britain's Permanent Representation in Brussels, though even here established practice is that individual departments contact the Commission and United Kingdom Permanent Representation (UKREP), bypassing the Cabinet Office and the FCO.[28] Both in theory and practice, the FCO also monitors European policy developments and provides advice to domestic ministries when necessary. Reflecting this wider role, the FCO therefore has departments divided between issues which have an internal and external impact on the EU, the former providing assistance to departments which have only recently established EU coordinating units and are dependent on FCO advice, and the latter concerned with external relations.[29]

However, the FCO continues to play three important roles. First, departments provide advice on bilateral relations with Member States and those outside the EU, through departments covering Central and Eastern Europe, Eastern, Eastern Adriatic and Southern Europe and Western Europe. Secondly, the FCO prepares the Foreign Secretary for General Affairs Councils and the rotating Presidency of the Council of Ministers (for which special arrangements are put in place).[30] Thirdly, the FCO has a particular role concerning CFSP with little involvement from other Whitehall departments which has given the FCO its own *domain privé*.[31] The organisation of the FCO reflects this, with a European Correspondent covering economic and political issues who is also head of the CFSP department. The Political Director is the senior European policy advisor to the Foreign Secretary and Prime Minister, with overall responsibility for CFSP and the European Correspondent. The CFSP department has six desk officers, divided into two sections covering institutional and operational matters.[32] The former deals with European defence, institutional developments including the implementation of the Amsterdam Treaty and institutional issues (and works closely with the International Security Department), while the latter covers preparations for the General Affairs Council, Political Committees and the twenty-eight working groups which cover all aspects of foreign policy.

These officials provide advice to the Political Director with little involvement beyond a watching brief from the Cabinet Office or other departments with the exception of coordination with the Security Policy Department of the Ministry of Defence.[33] Depending on the issue under discussion, this advice is further supplemented by that from the UK Permanent Representative at NATO and the WEU Ambassador. The result is a very informal but highly effective system of coordination between ministries and officials, which generates a shared perception of the problems and a unity of purpose concerning objectives, and which is capable of rapid decision making.[34]

The system of coordination ensures that on routine matters whenever the UK needs a policy on a foreign policy issue it has one, and that the policy is advanced consistently by ministers and officials in the various fora of the Union. The speed with which officials operate also ensures the British are one of the first to set out a position. This procedure has delivered important negotiating benefits: it ensures that the British speak with authority and establishes a posture which other Member States must accommodate if an EU policy is to be acceptable to London. The downside is that there is little flexibility once a British position is established, but in a sub-system in which the lowest common denominator bargaining often prevails and where key decisions rest with the Foreign Secretary and Prime Minister, this is less of a disadvantage than in other aspects of EU decision making. Moreover, since a growing feature of CFSP is the need to negotiate simultaneously in the EU, NATO, WEU, and increasingly the UN, the British system has proved an important bureaucratic advantage in the pursuit of British policies.[35]

Few quibble with the efficiency of British foreign policy making, but the institutional interest of the FCO in the European arena has led some to argue that the FCO has become 'pro-European', always willing to compromise and subordinate specific policy preferences to the general interest. However, as Buller and Smith note, the role of the FCO is to act as a messenger, identifying the bounds of negotiability and the possibilities of success, so there is sometimes a tendency to misinterpret this for pro-Europeanism.[36]

In terms of CFSP, there is certainly a greater degree of flexibility among FCO ministers and officials concerning the notion of sovereignty, and most take a pragmatic view accepting (even if not liking) the fact that the EU can offer a useful arena as a means to pursue British interests in a hard-headed and unsentimental way.[37] Most officials share no particular European idealism and have a realist(ic) view of cooperation, which in their view is best based on convergence of national interests and an awareness of the limits of institutional and procedural tinkering.[38] However, widespread distrust of the FCO amongst the political class in the first two decades of EU membership led into the decision not to establish a Ministry for European Affairs, the momentum behind the decision to create the European Secretariat and for a period of eight years between 1984 and 1992 led to the appointment of a Foreign Policy Advisor in order to avoid reliance on FCO advice alone.[39] The new Labour government has proved itself more relaxed about the criticism of socialisation, but has been at the forefront of attempts to open up the policy-making process, and measures have included formalising contacts with academics in the field and creating the Foreign Policy Centre in an attempt to provide fresh thinking an alternative source of ideas and to make the policy-making process more transparent.[40]

At the political level coordination can also be extensive depending on the sensitivity and perceived importance of the issues in question. The lead Cabinet Committee responsible for EU matters is EDOP (UK ministerial sub-committee on European questions), which is chaired by the Foreign Secretary and has a remit to cover issues related to the UK's membership of the EU and reports to OPD (Committee on Defence and Overseas Policy). OPD is chaired by the Prime Minister and has a broader remit to review Britain's defence and overseas policy.[41] Most foreign and security policy decisions never reach Cabinet for discussion and are decided bilaterally between the Prime Minister, the Foreign Secretary and other relevant ministers or even lower down the bureaucracy.[42] In comparison with other Member States, the large measure of cohesion across the political elite concerning British foreign policy objectives, leaves the government relatively free to decide the best means of securing its objectives. The important exception is when a foreign policy issue is embroiled in questions concerning European integration when Parliamentary and party management issues take on greater significance in constraining policy.

Domestic factors in the foreign policy process

While incremental adaptation has been a feature of the administrative response to EU membership, Parliamentary scrutiny and oversight has been less radical and is generally considered to be rather ineffective in holding the government to account.[43] While both chambers have permanent committees dealing with European issues and foreign policy, Parliament has a limited input into the policy-making process, designed more to scrutinise how policy had worked and to provide a forum for expert opinion, than as an alternative source for forward planning. Recent procedural changes have resolved the issue of how to deal with the CFSP, caught as it is between the European and Foreign Policy Committees. Since 1998 the government requires policy documents to be deposited in the Select Committee on European Legislation and European Community Committees within ten working days of receipt of EU documents (with a 'fast track' procedure for emergencies) and prior to any ministerial decision.[44] These documents are accompanied by an explanatory memorandum setting out the government's position and addressing the implications for British policy. Since all select committees are dominated by the ruling party, a bias exists towards adopting positions that avoid directly confronting government policy and towards accepting the prevailing orthodoxies. Moreover, the European Committees of both Houses are already overworked, and relatively ineffective in coping with the existing flow of information, giving the government significant leeway in shaping current policy.[45]

Despite this weak structure, the volatility of the European issue on the backbenches ensures that the British government must remain constantly vigilant. When policies get caught up in the European issue, the government is forced to tread warily and on occasions decisions in Brussels are decisively shaped by what is acceptable in London. Excellent administrative coordination and recognition of the skills of diplomats as a valued resource are sometimes undermined by the prevailing political volatility in London. Policy, especially during the Conservative period in office between 1990 and 1997, was frequently driven by domestic political constellations – what might be acceptable to the ruling political party – though with a large majority and greater cohesion on the European issue than any previous administration, the current Labour government has been less constrained by parliamentary arithmetic.[46]

One striking aspect of British policy making is the role of non-state actors in British foreign policy making. First, almost all lobby groups previously concerned with domestic policy now have a European dimension to their activities. Menon and Wright note the close relationship between British officials and private interests and the effectiveness with which British officials across the board work with interest groups.[47] This characteristic is also prevalent in foreign policy making where consultation and dialogue routinely takes place with 'flag-ship' non-governmental organisations (NGOs) who have a close working relationship with the FCO and MoD. On human rights issues, Amnesty International has played an influential role and currently has a secondee in the Human Rights Policy Department; Greenpeace has close links with the Department for International Development and Saferworld has produced highly respected and influential reports on non-proliferation and security policy.[48] While Europeanisation has spurred on NGOs to operate at the transnational level, many UK NGOs find it easier to operate in London where there is considered to be a more open policy-making style than in France or Germany where access is more limited.

Foreign policy actions: opportunities

In terms of policy content, Britain has been centrally engaged in the process of EPC, and since 1993 CFSP, and the growing coherence of the EU's CFSP has provided London with a number of important opportunities for foreign policy action. First, EU-level action has made it possible for the UK to pursue policies increasingly beyond the UK acting on a unilateral basis. The Middle East peace process and the events in North Africa are examples of this, where British diplomats have worked alongside EU partners to form a common front offering influence unavailable to Britain alone. On trade and commercial issues too, a united EU position brings added value in negotiations with the United States and Japan.

Secondly, over the last twenty-seven years, the British government has used EU structures to multilateralise British policy and to provide leadership to EU Member States on issues which the government felt were important. Indeed the aspiration to provide foreign policy leadership is an enduring feature of British engagement in the CFSP. This was the case for counter-terrorism measures in the late 1980s and more recently, in June 1998, the British government used the opportunities provided by CFSP to secure a politically (though not legally) binding EU code of conduct on arms sales. The latter is a *locus classicus*, since the UK had unilaterally set in place a restrictive national policy on export licences and EU-level action established criteria, transparency and a consultation mechanism, to prevent British firms from being undercut by competitors in other Member States.[49] The British government has also used the EU as a multiplier to deliver financial benefit in the pursuit of national policy. During the Kosovo crisis the government allocated 'seed corn' funding of £10 million to support countries in the southern Balkans which attracted a further £250 million from the Community budget. It also provided £1.5 million for monitoring the Indonesian elections planned for June 1999, securing a further £7 million for the project. In both cases the effectiveness of British lobbying and the clever linkage of traditional foreign policy to first pillar external aid funding has operated as a classic financial multiplier at a time when the FCO budget is facing cutbacks.[50]

The government has also used the obligation of forming a common EU-wide policy to protect itself from unpalatable decisions. For example, Christopher Hill points to a British reluctance to follow American policy in Central America in the mid-1980s and Percy Craddock remarks that, concerning policy towards South Africa in 1986, the British government consciously opted for lighter EC measures rather than Commonwealth sanctions.[51] More recently, in 1996 a progressive EU common position on Cuba has provided shelter from rather aggressive US policies. Likewise the Berlin Declaration on the Middle East Peace Process was built around a British position, but without exposing it to a focused reaction from Israel or Arab governments. Unlike many other policy sectors in the EU, on a vast majority of occasions the British government has been able to use membership of the EU to reinforce its substantive interests and foreign policy.

Foreign policy actions: constraints

The opportunities which EU membership has provided for the British government have been accompanied by important constraints. The most significant of these relate to the competences of the Commission which have constrained the UK insofar as policies it previously pursued on a unilateral basis now require EU-level agreement. This has been particularly noticeable concerning trade and economic issues such as the General Agreement on Tariffs and Trade (GATT), the Lomé Convention and various international and EU-wide trade negotiations. In these areas the Commission, through its responsibility for the common commercial policy, has an indisputable lead role and the UK is bound by the legal requirement of collective action.

CFSP has also constrained the UK in a softer sense, generating pressures for the government to 'trim' its unilateral position, either to secure EU-level backing for a preferred policy or for the sake of maintaining an existing common position. However, in the case of much of the substance of CFSP, ultimately if the British government does not secure most of its objectives, it rarely feels obliged to support or follow a particular policy.

Notwithstanding the flexibility built in to EU common positions, joint actions and common strategies, the British government has on occasions been unwilling to stand out against a policy to which it is opposed, either for the sake of EU unity, or because the diplomatic price of defection was too high. Perhaps the most publicised case concerned the EU's recognition of Slovenia and Croatia in January 1992, when Douglas Hurd was willing to sacrifice the Carrington Plan and chose to side with the EU rather than the United States for the sake of a common front with Germany.[52] However, only on a handful of issues in the last six years has the UK felt national interest was significantly divergent from Member States and was therefore unable to support an EU decision. The most recent examples concern the possibility of EU/WEU deployment of military forces to Albania in 1997, to which the British government was vehemently opposed, leaving an *ad hoc* intervention force to be deployed under the auspices of UN and OSCE. In March 1998 the British government came under sustained pressure to allow the Burmese Foreign Minister to attend the EU–ASEAN ministerial meeting, though in this instance the British government found support from three other Member States to oppose this.

However, despite the near universal acceptance of the value of coordinating policy at the EU level, the emergence of a strong 'first reflex' of consulting European partners and socialisation within EU networks has not yet led to complete, or even widespread, dependence on CFSP. The UK has routinely been willing and able to break free from EU level commitments. Successive British governments have proved themselves willing to act alone or in partnership with other countries when they deem it necessary. The most striking example is the bombing of Iraq in 1999, when the British government pursued a bilateral policy with Washington, rather than negotiating alternative policy options with its EU partners which it considered unlikely to succeed from the outset.

The UK, alongside France, is the most embedded in foreign policy networks outside the framework of CFSP both in terms of exclusivity and in terms of the special relationship with the United States.[53] Malcolm Rifkind argued that Britain was a member of 120 intergovernmental organisations, which gave Britain the authority to influence international society and exercise authority.[54] Most obviously it is a member of the UN Security Council with all the rights and obligations which follow from this.[55] Both Britain and France have been insistent that while they accept the obligation to consult, they are unwilling to be bound by their partners in the Security Council. The legitimacy of the global interests of Britain has also led to tacit acceptance by EU partners of Britain's special role in contact groups, comprising EU and non-EU Member States with special interests on issues as wide ranging as Namibia to Kosovo. Britain has also had a leading role in providing EU special emissaries, most notably Lords Carrington and Owen and on a bilateral level, Sir David Hannay addressing the issue of Cyprus.

If, in the past, the Commonwealth was an important tier of exclusivity, it is becoming increasingly less important as an arena for the pursuit of British interests. Special interests in the remaining thirteen Overseas Territories as well as Northern Ireland and Gibraltar remain *domaines privé* to the British government.[56] However, Gibraltar continues to sour bilateral relations with Spain, with consequences for the broader relationship inside the EU in both the first and third pillars, with the current Spanish government unwilling to countenance partial British membership of the Schengen Agreement until a settlement is reached on the future status of Gibraltar.

One paradoxical aspect of the importance of the EU in shaping British foreign policy has been to strengthen the bilateral relationship between Britain and France. Experience of the CFSP over the last six years (and the EPC before that) has increasingly led to the view in London that leading the EU on a unilateral basis has not been altogether successful. There is a widespread feeling in London that bilateral partnership is the most useful vehicle to provide policy leadership. The corollary is that when important differences exist between Britain and France the Union's foreign policy is ineffective. The Franco-British St Malo Declaration of December 1998 provides the basis for closer cooperation across a wide range of defence and foreign policy issues, not only at ministerial level in areas of mutual interest such as Africa, but also at official level where the 'default setting' is to coordinate with counterparts in the *Quai* prior to any foreign policy meetings in the Union.[57] More recently, it has also led to a relaxation of traditional British positions on the NATO, EU–WEU relationship and opened up the possibility of Europeanising NATO structures and on the basis of intergovernmental procedures, permitting the Union to take over some of the security functions of the WEU.[58]

Notwithstanding intra-European relationships, that of Britain and the United States remains a long-standing and core feature of Britain's foreign policy partnerships. The reflex of coordination with Washington remains powerful, though as a number of commentators have pointed out, the EPC and the development of the CFSP have directly challenged the restricted nature of this relationship.[59] The answer from British policy makers is to pick and choose whom to consult first, depending on the issue in hand, whether defence, foreign or economic policy, and an assessment of which channel might be most effective in achieving British policy goals. The special relationship retains a leading position on matters of defence (and to some extent security), not least because of the permanent structures in NATO, the close proximity of British and American views on many issues and the important intelligence-sharing arrangements.[60] In economic, and increasingly foreign policy, the preference for Anglo-American coordination prior to consultation with EU partners is diminishing, though British officials retain their self-image of being in a privileged position in trying to explain EU policy to their American counterparts.[61]

The balance of opportunities and constraints therefore depends as much on the type of policy, whether declaratory or substantive, as its sectoral specificity. Moreover, British membership of the CFSP cannot be seen in zero sum terms. Participation in the process has allowed the government to initiate important proposals and influence decision making in the Council of Ministers, through voting and adopting the lowest common position and finally through derogations, opt-outs and evoking British national interest to step aside from decisions, as well as more informally honouring policy in the breach.

Conclusion: playing the European game?

Despite the changes in international order since the end of the Cold War and the new arena which the EU represents for the pursuit of British foreign policy, there remains a strong sense of continuity in the objectives of British policy and norms and values held by officials. There is little evidence to suggest that membership of the EU has led to the widespread transformation of British national objectives as some scholars have predicted.[62] Twenty-seven years of European foreign policy collaboration does not appear to have led to a new and wholly different European identity for British foreign policy. Through tight policy coordination and excellent administrative control, policy makers have used the opportunities of the EU as a new arena for the pursuit of national objectives. The choice of which institution through which to pursue foreign policy objectives is based on a robust cost/benefit analysis of the competing advantages and disadvantages of different institutions and the extent of their legal competences. With the important exception of the economic and external competences of the first pillar of the Union, membership of the EU appears to have left the majority of British objectives remarkably unchanged, though membership has significantly affected the options (and in some cases compensated the loss of influence in the world) in the pursuit of that policy.

For Britain, there are a number of remarkable features of the EU framework which highlight British engagement from other international obligations. The first is a breakdown of the domestic and foreign (and increasingly the political–economic) distinction. On this point, the fact that the EU has direct competence for many economic, agricultural and commercial issues marks out the EU as *sui generis*. It is these policy areas which most directly constrain autonomous British action through the legal competences of the European Commission to manage the Union's common commercial policy. But this is not a zero-sum game and membership also offers important opportunities in the pursuit of British interests, through effective linkage, access to financial resources and a wide range of economic instruments and a 'multiplier effect' of securing EU support. A further aspect of the unique aspect of EU membership is the way in which the range of policy competences encourages issue linkage across traditional foreign policy to other issues that are not functionally, though politically, connected.

A second characteristic is the link between foreign policy cooperation in the Union and the broader European integration project. Though the British government does not use the development of foreign and security policy cooperation to advance the development of the EU, it has been quiescent in this. In part the awkward domestic circumstances which prevailed during the Thatcher and Major years led Conservative governments to invest in the imagery of intergovernmentalism at the expense of endorsing procedural developments which are steadily drawing the CFSP into the core functions of the Union and leading to creeping *communitarisation*. At the same time Britain has been at the forefront of informal improvements to the machinery of European foreign policy-making – through the St Malo Declaration and more recently Robin Cook's proposal for a foreign policy committee made up of deputy political directors permanently based in Brussels – which have added to the momentum for formal treaty changes. How long this contradiction can be sustained before the CFSP significantly constrains British foreign policy and directly raises issues concerning sovereignty, the role of the nation state, and European federation will depend on the domestic political constellation. Britain is therefore still wrestling with the contradictions of trying to use EU membership to manage and adapt to changes in the international system, while reluctant to acknowledge the consequences for the integration project.

Notes

1 M. J. Smith, *The Core Executive in Britain* (London, Macmillan, 1999), p. 234.
2 The relevance of Alan Milward's rescue thesis is noted by David Allen, 'Conclusions: the European rescue of national foreign policy' in C. Hill (ed.), *The Actors in Europe's Foreign Policy* (London, Routledge, 1996), p. 290.
3 H. Wallace, 'Britain out on a limb', *Political Quarterly*, 166:1 (1995), p. 49.
4 For a different interpretation see Anand Menon and Vincent Wright, 'The paradoxes of failure: British policy making in comparative perspective', *Public Policy and Administration*, 13:4 (Winter 1998), pp. 46–66.
5 For an overview of the development of the EU's CFSP see A. Forster and W. Wallace, 'Common foreign and security policy', in H. Wallace and W. Wallace (eds), *Policy Making in the European Union* (Oxford, Oxford University Press, 1997).

6   W. Wallace, 'What price interdependence? sovereignty and interdependence in British politics', *International Affairs*, 62:3 (1986), p. 367.

7   A. Butt Philip, 'Westminster versus Brussels', in Jolyon Howarth and John Maclean (eds), *Europeans on Europe*, (London, Macmillan, 1992), p. 188.

8   See N. Gnesotto, 'Défense européenne: pourqoui pas les Douze?', *Politique Étrangère*, 55:4 (1990), pp. 881–883.

9   A. Deighton, 'On the cusp? Britain, Maastricht and european security', paper presented to the European University Institute, Florence, May 1996, p. 3.

10 Many maximalist states have routinely placed greater value on establishing a political commitment to a policy objective, than on the presence or absence of particular procedural methods to achieve it. See for example Jacques Delors' comments that ambitious objectives in the TEU were not matched by the procedural requirements to achieve them. Speech to the EP reproduced in Bulletin to the European communities, supplement 1/92, Luxembourg 1992. W. Wallace, 'British foreign policy after the cold war', *International Affairs*, 68:2 (July 1992), p. 442.

11 For a discussion of the British position concerning the Single European Act see P. Budden, *The Making of the Single European Act: the United Kingdom and the European Community 1979–1986* (Oxford, D Phil thesis unpublished, 1994). For the TEU see A. Forster, *Britain and the Maastricht Negotiations* (Basingstoke, St. Antony's/Macmillan Press, 1999).

12 In this respect, until April 1990, the French government were a reliable British partner, but the Mitterrand-Kohl initiative to use the transformation of EPC into CFSP as a defining feature of political union called this into question. For the Mitterrand and Kohl proposal see *Agence Europe* 5238, April 20 1990.

13 For a further discussion of this point see G. Howe, 'Britain and the European community: a twenty year balance sheet', *Occasional Paper* (Cambridge, Tory Reform Group/Elitian, January 1994); see also W. Sweeney 'Falsehood that Maastricht Pillars can be kept separate', in I. Duncan Smith, B. Jenkin, B. Legg and W. Sweeney, 'Game, set and match?', *Conservative Way Forward, Occasional Paper No.2* (1993), pp. 49–55.

14 For the most recent proposal see D. Buchan, 'Cook to propose EU foreign policy committee' *Financial Times*, 13 March 1999.

15 L. Martin and J. Garnett, *British Foreign Policy: Challenges and Choices for the Twenty-First Century* (London, RIIA/Cassell, 1997), p. 26.

16 The UK now belongs to over 120 international organisations.

17 The previous government tried to facilitate a debate through a RIIA/British Government conference on British foreign policy in March 1995 but with very limited success.

18 David Allen notes that the 1992 Structural Review, 1995 Fundamental Expenditure Review and 1996 Senior Management Review contrast with previous reports, all being conducted in-house. The other major review, the 1994 White Paper on the Civil Service recognised the distinct nature of the Diplomatic Service. See D. Allen, 'The United Kingdom: adapting to the European Union within a transformed world', in D. Spence and B. Hocking (eds), *European Union Member State Foreign Ministries: Change and Adaptation* (Basingstoke, Macmillan, forthcoming 2000), p. 4 and p. 18. For a further discussion of this see W. Wallace and A. Forster, 'British approaches

to rethinking European order since 1989' in R. Niblett and W. Wallace (eds), *Rethinking European Order: West European Responses, 1989–1997*, unpublished manuscript.

19 David Allen notes that the UK spends half as much on overseas diplomacy as France and one third of German expenditure. D. Allen, 'The United Kingdom' in D. Spence and B. Hocking (eds), *European Union Member State Foreign Ministries* (Basingstoke, Macmillan, forthcoming 2000), p. 23. For an analysis of pragmatism in British decision-making see J. Bayliss, *British Defence Policy* (London, Macmillan, 1989), pp. 5–12, and M. Clarke, 'The policy-making process', in M. Smith and S. Smith, B. White, *British Foreign Policy* (London, Unwin Hyman, 1988), p. 76.

20 S. Bulmer and M. Birch, 'Organising for Europe: Whitehall, the British state and the European Union', *Public Administration*, forthcoming; and A. Menon and Wright, 'The paradoxes of failure', *Public Policy and Administration*, 13:4, p. 47.

21 However, assembly politicians may join the Cabinet ministers in Council of Ministers meetings see V. Elliott, 'Cook forestalls 'meddling' by new assemblies', *The Times*, 15 March 1999. See also Joyce Quin, 'Devolution and foreign affairs', speech to the Northern Ireland Assembly, 26 February 1999, http://www.fco.gov.uk/news/speechtext.asp?2063.

22 H. Wallace, 'Negotiations and coalition formation in the European Community', *Government and Opposition*, 20:4 (1985), p. 456. J. Buller and M. J. Smith, 'Civil service attitudes towards the European Union', in D. Baker and D. Seawright (eds), *Britain For and Against Europe* (Oxford, Clarendon Press, 1998), p. 169.

23 A. Blair, 'The 1990–91 Intergovernmental Conference', *Diplomacy and Statecraft*, 9:2 (1998), p. 163; B. Bender, 'Co-ordination of European Union policy in Whitehall,' paper presented at St. Antony's College, Oxford, 5 February 1996, p.5; see also D. Spence, 'The Co-ordination of European Union policy by member states' in Martin Westlake (ed.), *The Council of the European Union* (London, Cartermill), p. 365.

24 B. Bender, 'Governmental process: Whitehall, central government and 1992', *Public Policy and Public Administration*, 56 (1991), p. 18.

25 Central Policy Review Staff, *Review of Overseas Representation* (London, HMSO, 1977).

26 P. Hennessy, *Whitehall* (London, Fontana, 1988), p. 404.

27 The EUROPES system requires compensatory budget cuts for extra EU spending which Menon and Wright argue often encourages spending ministries to side with the Treasury in negotiations. A. Menon and Wright, 'The paradoxes of failure', *Public Policy and Administration*, 13:4, p. 49.

28 J. Buller and M. J. Smith, 'Civil service attitudes', in D. Baker and D. Seawright (eds), *Britain For and Against Europe* (Oxford, Clarendon Press, 1998), p. 172.

29 The EU internal and external departments report to the FCO Economic Director.

30 For a discussion of the recent Presidency see P. Ludlow, 'The 1998 UK presidency: a view from Brussels', *Journal of Common Market Studies*, 36:4 (December 1998), pp. 573–583.

31 During the Maastricht negotiations one Department of Employment official remarked ruefully that unlike the FCO and the development of a CFSP his department had nothing to gain and everything to fear from a social policy agreement at Maastricht. A. Forster, *Britain and the Maastricht Negotiations* (Basingstoke, St. Antony's/Macmillan Press, 1999), p. 168.

32 In addition there are three support staff and a research officer and this is therefore one of the smallest departments in the FCO.

33 The Head of the Security Department reports directly to the Policy Department Assistant Under Secretary in the MoD.

34 A. Forster, *Britain and the Maastricht Negotiations* (Basingstoke, St. Antony's/Macmillan Press, 1999), p. 168.

35 This is especially true of IGC negotiations which share this triple personality. German officials in the Auswärtiges Amt have pointed to the fragmented nature of their own foreign and security policy policy-making, which places them at a disadvantage relative to their colleagues in London.

36 J. Buller and M. J. Smith, 'Civil service attitudes', in D. Baker and D. Seawright (eds), *Britain For and Against Europe* (Oxford, Clarendon Press, 1998), p. 176. See also J. W. Young and A. Sloman, 'No Minister' London, BBC, 1981; T. Benn, *Arguments for Socialism* (London, 1979); D. Owen, *Time to Declare* (London, 1991); M. Thatcher, *The Downing Street Years* (London, Harper Collins, 1993).

37 See for example G. Howe, 'Sovereignty and independence: Britain's place in the world', *International Affairs*, 66 (1990), pp. 675–695. P. Craddock, *In Pursuit of British Interests* (London, John Murray, 1997), p. 209.

38 This view has been articulated most clearly by Douglas Hurd a former Foreign Secretary and diplomat.

39 J. Buller and M. J. Smith, 'Civil service attitudes', in D. Baker and D. Seawright (eds), *Britain For and Against Europe* (Oxford, Clarendon Press, 1998), p. 169. P. Craddock, *In Pursuit of British Interests*, (London, John Murray, 1997), p. 10.

40 The Foreign Policy Centre was created in 1998 with the Patron Tony Blair and the President Robin Cook. See Stephen Castle, 'Cook opens rival to Foreign Office', *Independent on Sunday*, 1 March 1998. The FCO has also opened itself up to the academic community running a focus group of half a dozen academics which meets with the Political Director four times a year and a larger grouping of academics, journalists and policy specialists which meets with the Foreign Secretary less frequently.

41 OPD has six members, the Prime Minister, Foreign Secretary, Chancellor, President of the Board of Trade and Secretary of State for Defence and the Attorney General.

42 As a corollary, at the European level, most decisions are taken in the Political Committee with the Foreign Secretary directly involved in the agenda of the General Affairs Council.

43 P. Norton, 'The United Kingdom: political conflict, parliamentary scrutiny', in *National Parliaments and the European Union* (London, Frank Cass, 1996).

44 The Foreign Affairs Committee has also indicated it wishes to see all relevant documentation.

45 P. Norton, 'The United Kingdom', in *National Parliaments and the European Union* (London, Frank Cass, 1996), p. 96.

46 See for example the negotiations of the Maastricht Treaty, A. Forster *Britain and the Maastricht Negotiations*, (Basingstoke, St. Antony's/Macmillan Press, 1999). Menon and Wright make a similar point in relation to broader UK–EU policy-making. A. Menon and Wright, 'The paradoxes of failure', *Public Policy and Administration*, 13:4, p. 61 and p. 53.

47 A. Parker, 'Cook sees more Foreign Office-industry ties', *Financial Times*, 3 November 1998; A. Menon and Wright, 'The paradoxes of failure', *Public Policy and Administration*, 13:4, p. 55.

48 This a two-way street with over 100 diplomats who have used the opportunity of Special Unpaid Leave (SUPL) to take career breaks, some taking up temporary positions in NGOs.

49 It has however also necessitated a trimming of the government's position to secure backing from its partners.

50 For the financial year 1999–2000, the EU's CFSP budget is £30 million. Reportedly most of this had been spent by the end of April 1999.

51 C. Hill, 'United Kingdom: sharpening contradictions', in C. Hill, *The Actors in Europe's Foreign Policy* (London, Routledge, 1996), p. 75; P. Craddock, *In Pursuit of British Interests* (London, John Murray, 1997), p. 151.

52 P. Craddock, *In Pursuit of British Interests* (London, John Murray, 1997), p. 191.

53 Christopher Hill notes that in John Major's address to a RIIA/British Government conference on British foreign policy in March 1995, Major did not once mention the CFSP, preferring to emphasise Britain's global orientation. See C. Hill, 'United Kingdom', in *The Actors in Europe's Foreign Policy* (London, Routledge, 1995), p. 89, footnote 28.

54 This point is made by L. Martin and J. Garnet, *British Foreign Policy* (London, RIIA/ Pinter, 1997), p. 46.

55 Membership of the Security Council, alongside the possession of nuclear weapons, are also part of a wider set of great power symbols of Britain's world role. J. Young, *Britain and European Unity: 1945–1992* (London, Macmillan, 1993), pp. 171–172.

56 However the British government has been effective in securing special funding for the province in the EU budget settlement of March 1999.

57 The full declaration is available at the British Embassy in France web site, 'déclaration franco-britannique sur la défense européenne', Saint-Malo, 4 décembre 1998 http://www.amb-grandebretagne.fr/decl/decl.html. For press comment on the initiative see R. Graham and A. Peel, 'Britain and France to press for EU defence pact', *Financial Times*, 5/6 December 1998. On Franco-British cooperation on Africa see Quentin Peel, 'White man's burden sharing', *Financial Times*, 11 March 1999.

58 G. Robertson, 'NATO alliance and military capabilities for European security', speech delivered at the Royal United Services Institute, 10 March 1999.

59 C. Hill, 'The United Kingdom', in *The Actors in Europe's Foreign Policy* (London, Routledge, 1996), p. 84.

60 There is some concern in London that an exclusively European intelligence capacity might weaken US links in this area, since Washington might be

reluctant to share information with Member States who might be considered 'indiscreet'. Indeed an unwillingness in London to consider closer EU intelligence cooperation stems from a poor experience of sharing information between EU partners during the bombing of Former Yugoslavia which was reportedly passed on to Belgrade within hours.

61 See for example Tony Blair, 'The doctrine of the international community', speech to the Economic Club of Chicago, 22 April 1999, http://www.fco.gov.uk/news/speechtext.asp?2316.

62 A.Wendt, 'Collective identity formation and the international state', *American Political Science Review*, 88:2 (1994), pp. 384–396.

4

Germany

Lisbeth Aggestam

Introduction

The idea of a 'European Germany,' first formulated by Thomas Mann, has constituted a powerful normative idea for the formulation of German foreign policy after the Second World War.[1] The notion of a European foreign policy thus has positive connotations in Germany, replacing the discredited conception of national interest as the guiding principle in foreign policy.

The Adenauer legacy of *Westbindung*, emphasising multilateralism and European integration, formed the central axioms of the West German 'transformationalist' foreign policy. In order to break with Germany's history of militarism and authoritarianism, the post-war political leader-ship strove to enmesh Germany in Western institutional structures, of which North Atlantic Treaty Organisation (NATO) and the European Union (EU) provided the primary anchors.[2]

German membership in these two organisations constitutes the two pathways through which German conceptions of security have been, and still are, pursued today. NATO has primarily accommodated German interests in the hard core of security policy, that is, collective defence. The broader notion of security in terms of *Friedenspolitik* (peace policy) has, however, been channelled through membership of the EU, reflecting the liberal idea that economic and social interdependencies arising from the integration process in themselves lead to peaceful relations between states.

The chief trait of German post-war foreign policy has therefore been that of a civilian power.[3] Both the European Community (EC) and Germany were described as 'economic giants but political dwarfs' during much of the Cold War. However, the end of bipolarity has challenged the civilian conception of both the EC and Germany. In 1990, the Eastern and Western parts of Germany were unified, restoring formal sovereignty in foreign and security policy. Shortly afterwards, the EC Member States decided to establish European Union and deepen integration within a

Common Foreign and Security Policy (CFSP) which eventually could lead to a common defence policy.

Since the end of the Cold War, the 'logic of the nation-state' has permeated the 'logic of European integration' in Germany. This has been accompanied by intensive debates both among practitioners and academics about the meaning of 'normality' in German foreign policy.[4] The aim of this chapter is to explore the two developments of 'normalisation' and 'Europeanisation' of German foreign policy in the 1990s with particular reference to the CFSP.

The basic argument of this chapter is that German foreign policy is exerting a remarkable continuity despite fundamental changes in its environment. The overall diplomatic strategy of multilateral institutionalism still characterises the main thrust of German foreign policy. However, one must distinguish between the *normative* and *instrumental* dimensions of German foreign policy. As a normative idea, the CFSP is of central importance in German thinking of the EU as a political union. Yet, from an instrumental point of view, the CFSP framework is only one, and not necessarily considered the most important, forum in which to exercise German foreign policy interests.

This chapter is structured in six parts. The first part considers how notions of German identity and German foreign policy have evolved through integration and membership of the EU. This first part discusses the ideational dimension of foreign policy in terms of a German and European identity. The second part considers the importance of socialisation as it seeks to clarify what the Europeanisation of foreign policy means in the German context. It draws attention to the reflexivist tradition in German foreign policy making and the '*Sowohl-als-auch*' (as well as) approach of considering international institutions as mutually reinforcing. The third part considers domestic factors as it examines the *Normalisierung* of German foreign policy, emphasising that this process is primarily a concern with formulating German responsibilities (*Verantwortung*) in post-Cold War Europe, rather than a return to *Realpolitik* and German unilateralism (*Sonderweg*). The fourth part considers the German debate over whether the EU represents a constriction or opportunity for its foreign policy by looking at its attempts to reform the EU's foreign policy mechanisms. This part analyses German proposals relating to the CFSP at the 1996 EU Intergovernmental Conference, arguing that German negotiations were characterised by a move from idealism to pragmatism. The fifth part considers German's special relationships that it privileges, both within the EU and without the EU. This part focuses on Germany's strategic partnerships in foreign policy, particularly with France and the United States, and discusses how these reflect on cooperation in the CFSP in particular, and visions of Europe in a broader sense. The final part draws together the different

issues and themes raised in this chapter with the concluding question –
will the *Berliner Republik* be a civilian power at the turn of the millennium?

Foreign policy change – adaptation and socialisation

Adaptation through membership: the politics of
German and European identity

Collective identities express ideas about membership within a social
group. As such, they provide a system of orientation for self-reference and
action. Culture is in this chapter interpreted as the broad context in which
individual and collective identities are linked producing shared meanings
that influence the framing of political action. The *politics of identity* refers
to a particular set of ideas about political community that policy makers
draw on in order to mobilise a sense of cohesion and solidarity to legitimate the general thrust of foreign policy.[5]

In the discourse on German foreign policy after the Second World War,
the idea of national identity and interest was largely absent from the
diplomatic vocabulary. Nonetheless, a West German identity constructed
by the political elite in Germany evolved in the post-War period along
four central dimensions. First, a German identity was defined in opposition to the Third Reich. German authoritarianism and Nazism constituted
the 'Other' against which a new conception of a German identity based
on civic political rights was formulated.[6] Secondly, a West German identity was defined as firmly belonging to 'Europe' and the 'West': a western
community of democracies.

The third component of a West German identity was tied to domestic
institutions and policies, particularly the federal constitution
(*Grundgesetz*), the national currency (*Deutsche Mark*) and the social
market economy. This combination resulted in the growth of a constitutional patriotism (*Verfassungspatriotismus*). Finally, reconciliation with
former enemies and a rejection of military power projection for other
purposes than territorial defence through NATO should constitute the
core of a West German identity. The tenacity of these four dimensions of
German identity after unification indicates the extent to which they
became institutionalised in the political culture of West Germany.[7]

Yet, German reunification and full sovereignty brought back the historical idea of a nation with full force based on the notion *Wir sind ein Volk*
('we are one people'). Furthermore, the implications of Germany's central
geographical position in the middle of Europe were once again starkly
apparent and came back to haunt policy makers with their overriding
concern for stability (*Stabilität*). Both internally and externally, questions
were raised regarding the implications for German identity and foreign
policy orientation, given its central location on the line between the

eastern part of Western Europe, on the one hand, and the western part of Eastern Europe on the other.

A long-standing theme in political speeches and slogans has been that Germany's reunification must take place hand-in-hand with European unification (*Geeintes Vaterland – Vereinigtes Europa*). It is a widely held view among German foreign policy makers that only through a deepening of European integration can Germany be assured of a durable peace in Europe. It was, therefore, particularly important that the Maastricht Treaty which followed shortly after German unification, should contain explicit reference to a European political union, including strengthened cooperation in foreign and security policy. As Helmut Kohl continually reiterated, the European integration process must both be widened and deepened in the new Europe to guarantee peace in the next century. The integration process must be made irreversible.[8]

Thus, a European identity in Germany is formulated in a language characterised by existential notions of a shared European destiny (*Schicksalsgemeinschaft*). The commitment to European integration is a powerful symbol that testifies that Germany has indeed become 'emancipated and learnt from history'.[9] As Volker Rühe, former defence minister, asserts, 'Europe was and remains a political and cultural conception. European unity is the vision of lasting pacification in freedom and prosperity.'[10] The major political parties agree that the historical legacy necessitates that Germany takes an active part in promoting European unity – being the motor that drives the construction forwards. As a consequence, the formulation of German and European interests has become blurred because legitimation is sought both on a European and national basis. In a way reminiscent of the end of the 19th century under Bismarck, Germany is again a pivotal political and economic power in the centre of Europe. The great difference between the two time periods is how German politicians in a fundamentally different way both reason and conceive of their interests.[11] As the German foreign minister, Joschka Fischer, has described the German pursuit of its interests: 'You have to first build up a stock of trust (*Vertrauenskapital*) and then present your interests at the table'.[12]

Though German identity is still framed in terms of a sense of guilt and shame about its Nazi past, a certain pride is evident in German foreign policy speeches arising from the new German identity and state (*Rechtsstaat*) which several decades of democracy has generated. The German model founded on a federal constitution enshrining the principles of subsidiarity and power-sharing is considered a desirable norm to be promoted in the EU. As the Federal President of Germany Roman Herzog mused:

> The best policy contribution Germany can make towards political union in Europe consists of federalism and the principle of subsidiarity. Let us proffer

these until the time comes when our British friends realize that federalism is the opposite of centralism, and our French friends develop a sense for the fact that the formation of a federation does not mean the disappearance of the nation state and all that it stands for in the minds of its citizens.[13]

The decentralisation of power in Germany to the federal states (*Länder*) brings them, for example, extensive competency as sub-national actors in foreign economic policy.[14] However, the overall coordination and guidelines (*Richtlinien*) of German foreign policy remains firmly in the hands of the *Bundeskanzler*.[15]

The democratic idea combined with the immense economic power of Germany have generated two self-images of German foreign policy: as a trading state (*Handelsmacht*) and as a civilian power (*Zivilmacht*). Though the two role conceptions are interlinked, they have also conflicted in the past in situations where the safeguarding of German foreign trade has been given primacy. A visible example of this was Germany's reluctance to join its partners in European Political Cooperation (EPC) in the 1980s over a tightening of economic sanctions against South Africa.[16]

Socialisation of foreign policy makers: the Europeanisation of German foreign policy

Since the end of the Second World War, the formulation of German foreign policy has been a clear rejection of a *Realpolitik* based on a narrow focus on national self-interests. Instead, Germany is known for its extensive reflexive consultation procedures in foreign policy making before a position of interests is finally formulated. This is part of the Adenauer legacy of enmeshing and anchoring German interests within multilateral institutions.

This approach reflects an underlying re-conceptualisation of the interconnection between foreign policy and state sovereignty. It involves a move away from the realist conception of the 'security dilemma' towards the idea of security community, in which the security of every member of the transnational community is perceived as the responsibility of all.[17]

Academically, these ideas were already formulated by Karl Deutsch in the 1950s. He stressed how intensive interactions between states on all levels would transform their relations, in terms of a decline of military force as an instrument in foreign policy, and give rise to an expectancy of peaceful relations. These social-communicative processes between states may, according to Deutsch, lead to the development of a growing 'we-feeling' and sense of belonging to a 'security community'.[18]

German policy makers frequently express this notion of a security community by stating how war between the states in Western Europe has become unthinkable through the process of European integration. The unification of Europe, pooling sovereignty in the fields of economics and politics, is, in itself, security policy.[19] The problem that has preoccupied German foreign policy makers since the end of the Cold War is how to extend this zone of peace and stability to the rest of Europe.

German conceptualisations of security and power differ from those of the French and British (as German foreign policy makers are keen to point out).[20] Rather than equating security with defence issues, a broader view is adopted which emphasises the non-military aspects of security.[21] Within the CFSP, Germany has traditionally emphasised 'soft power' as an instrument of foreign policy, for example, trade policy and economic and political assistance to strengthen democratic structures. Given that economic instruments are located within the first and more supranational pillar of the EU, Germany has been critical of the artificial distinction between the 'high' and 'low politics' that the pillar-construction rests on.

It is, however, important to point out that when discussing the Europeanisation of German foreign policy, the term should be understood in a broad sense and not confined simply to the socialisation mechanisms that may be found within the CFSP framework. German multilateral insti-tutionalism is, as Timothy Garton Ash points out, generally characterised by a *Sowohl-als-auch* approach, which means an avoidance in explicitly privileging a particular institution in favour of others.[22] Thus, Germany discretely pursues its interests in a multitude of European and interna-tional institutions. During the Cold War, Germany conducted its *Ostpolitik* through a number of different channels, rather than submerg-ing it within a common policy of EPC.

Nonetheless, the CFSP is an integral part of the German idea of constructing a European political union. The CFSP framework is essential to German aspirations of continuing to build trust and confidence between itself and the members of the EU. As Gerd Langguth asserts, 'German foreign policy will – and indeed must – continue to be something our partners can predict'.[23] The norms that guide the political cooperation between the EU members, such as transparency, consultation and compromise, are fundamental to the goal of maintaining stability and predictable relations in foreign policy.

Through a high density of continuous communication and adjustments (the so-called coordination reflex), a package of common European foreign policy standpoints has been built up over the last three decades. This points at certain new qualitative features of solidarity between EU members. EPC was, for example, successful in speaking with 'one voice' at the Conference on Security and Cooperation in Europe (CSCE) – an important multilateral framework for the German foreign policy goal of building common security in Europe. The Middle East is another area where the EC members succeeded in developing a common policy, despite historically disparate interests. The Venice Declaration of 1980 recognised the legitimate Palestinian right to self-determination and endorsed the PLO as a negotiating partner in a future peace process. Given the special relationship and reconciliation that Germany has developed with Israel after the Holocaust, this was a remarkable reorientation of policy not conceivable outside the EPC framework.

Yet, the CFSP remains a largely declaratory political framework and by no means constitutes an integrated common European foreign policy. The decentralised structure of the CFSP has been a continuous problem. Policies have consequently tended to be more reactive rather than proactive in relation to international developments. The continued predominance of intergovernmental procedures indicates that the members involved – including Germany – still regard their interaction in a strategic and self-interested manner.

Though Germany mostly pursues its foreign policy goals in a discrete manner by embedding its political actions in the framework of the CFSP if possible, the controversy surrounding the recognition of the former Yugoslav republics in the early 1990s indicates that European norms do not necessarily lead to intersubjective understandings between the EU members. Dissension on whether and when to recognise the independence of Slovenia and Croatia illuminated the considerable influence and political clout that the newly reunified Germany possessed once it decided on a particular course of action. Furthermore, it is important to remember that the failure of the EU to manage the Balkan crisis gave raise to the Contact Group consisting of five major powers, including Germany.

Yet, at the same time, it should not be underestimated how perceptions of German interests are largely fused with collective European interests. This signals a combination of a genuine idealistic commitment to European integration in foreign policy and a rational strategy to suffuse German power. As a German foreign policy maker asserts: 'The European interest and the German interest match, because it is in nobody's interest in Europe to make Germany deal with its neighbours in a bilateral manner, but to keep it within integrated structures.'[24] The CFSP provides a useful channel to exert an international influence without raising historical fears of Germany hegemony. The concept of power can be understood in different ways. Within a security community, it may be interpreted in terms of having a considerable influence on the norms that stipulate common interests and action.[25] Given its size, resources and pivotal position in the centre of Europe, Germany will remain highly influential even in an integrated European foreign policy.

Foreign policy process – domestic and bureaucratic

Domestic factors in the policy process: normalisation of German foreign policy

> Gone are the times when Germany could merely go along for the ride, as a passenger without any responsibilities. It is now – whether it likes it or not – a fully fledged member of the team of great democracies.[26]

The German debate on *Normalisierung* does not signal a return to realist balance-of-power thinking in German foreign policy. As Volker Rühe has clearly stated: 'Within the European Union, no country can go its own way, nor can there be any possibility of thinking in terms of spheres of influence, coalitions and counter coalitions, containment and hegemony . . . Thinking exclusively in terms of the balance of power is the thinking of the past.'[27] Nevertheless, as the term itself implies, normalisation is linked to questions of Germany as a nation-state and thus opens up a previous taboo: a discussion of German national interests in foreign policy.[28] It is important to stress that this debate has both internal and external dimensions. The internal debate is bound up with a discussion about the *Bonner vs. Berliner Republik*. This section will primarily focus on the external dimension of this debate, which has been conducted and shaped with an attentive eye to the role expectations that external actors have expressed regarding German foreign policy since unification.

According to a German diplomat involved in the CFSP, 'normalisation' focuses on four dimensions of German foreign policy:

- to be less reliant on partners and more self-confident in the formulation of German interests;
- to take on greater responsibilities internationally;
- to assure neighbours of good relations; and
- to affirm that there will be no repeat of the past.[29]

The first dimension refers to the German tradition of reflexive consultation. The end of the Cold War entailed a 'qualitative jump' in foreign policy making, which departed from the standard mechanisms of reflexive consultation with partners. German policy makers found themselves in a situation where they were under great pressure to develop their skills in analysing and reaching policy conclusions *before* entering multilateral consultations and discussions. As a German foreign policy maker remarks:

> We have to formulate a national position before we start discussing with our partners. We need to know in advance what we are actually looking for and what we are striving for. We have to define the objectives and aims of a certain policy and then discuss it. That is different from the time before 1990.[30]

This does not, however, imply that Germany will pursue unilateralist policies. The conduct of German policy regarding the recognition of the Balkan Republics has been widely seen as an aberration and failure in German foreign policy – a mistake not to be repeated again.

The second dimension of German responsibilities has been, and is still, widely debated. It is frequently expressed as a German duty (*Verpflichtung*) to become more active and shoulder the responsibility to secure peace and stability in Europe (*Friedensverantwortung*).[31] When, a few years after unification, Germany applied for permanent membership on the UN Security Council, it raised the question of whether Germany was prepared to take on the global responsibilities, including military issues, that such a position would entail. From a global perspective, German interests as a *Handelsstaat* have predominately been concerned with foreign economic policy. However, throughout the 1990s Germany has increased its participation, step-by-step, in issues and conflicts involving the use of military power (the so-called 'salami tactic').

Two conflicts, in particular, have been important to the development of German security policy since the end of the Cold War. The Gulf Conflict in 1991 was the first learning experience where the previously favoured 'cheque-book diplomacy' lost credibility in the minds of policy makers. The second conflict concerns the instability in the Balkans, which triggered German discussions of participating in the so-called out-of-area operations outside the collective defence of NATO territory. The argument that Germany is prohibited in its constitution from participating in multinational forces outside NATO was dissolved with a constitutional court ruling in 1994. The variety of instruments available to support German foreign policy now includes military resources: a standpoint supported by the main German political parties, including the Green Party, *die Grüne*, which now holds the key post of the foreign ministry in the red–green coalition government.[32]

The third and fourth dimensions are closely inter-linked in the sense that they express a clear ambition that a reunified Germany does not mean a return of history. Germany's pursuit of establishing good neighbourly relations through bilateral declarations and treaties with the countries in Eastern Europe, especially with Poland, was particularly crucial in the immediate aftermath of German unification.[33]

These policies have been further cemented by Germany becoming the chief proponent of a widening and deepening of European integration into Eastern Europe. They indicate how German foreign policy is still being formulated in the light of the experiences of the two World Wars, which devastated Europe this century. From a German perspective, Eastern enlargement of the EU (and NATO) is considered to have stabilising effects by surrounding Germany with allies and partners.[34]

Foreign policy actions – with and without the EU?

With the EU: German idealism and pragmatism

A political union between the EU Member States requires an effective CFSP – this was, in short, the starting point of Germany's approach to the negotiations at the EU's 1996 Intergovernmental Conference, which aimed to bring the CFSP closer into the Community framework. In contrast to the sensitive debate on economic and monetary union, there is a broad political consensus on European integration in foreign policy, which is based on two considerations.[35] First, foreign policy integration is a desirable strategy to harmonise and accommodate Germany's geographical position and power in the middle of Europe. Secondly, reinforcement of the CFSP restrains any potential 're-nationalisation' of foreign policy that may arise among the EU Member States after the end of the Cold War.[36]

Germany's position in the Intergovernmental Conference (IGC) was characterised both by idealism and pragmatism. An analysis of German foreign policy in the 1990s suggests that until the IGC got under way the foreign policy was characterised by idealistic overtones that stressed the existential notion of making European integration irreversible. The peak of the influence of this idealism on European integration was probably reached when the two Christian Democratic Union (CDU) politicians, Wolfgang Schäuble and Karl Lamers, presented their party manifesto in the autumn of 1994. This document outlined the idea of a semi-federal core Europe with a supranational foreign policy, which was perceived to solve the problem of both widening and deepening the EU. The proposals were bold and controversial, particularly as Schäuble and Lamers included a reference to which states they foresaw as members of this inner core within a wider Europe.[37] To their disappointment, France did not endorse the idea of a core Europe, which meant that Kohl himself did not openly come out in full support of the idea.

In the Whitebook on Germany's position at the IGC, and the coalition agreement between the CDU/Christian Social Union (CSU) and the Federal Democratic Party (FDP) in November 1994, there are no references to the idea of a core. However, a number of supranational proposals remain in the document. As a whole, the German government was critical of the pillar structure and wanted to see the CFSP as more integrated in the first supranational EC pillar, thereby achieving a better coordination and implementation between the CFSP declarations and the economic instruments to support these goals. Germany was also in favour of seeing an extension of majority voting in the CFSP and for the European Parliament to gain greater access to, and democratic control over, the CFSP. This communitarisation of the CFSP did not, however, include a future common defence policy, which was to remain strictly under the intergovernmental responsibility of the European Council.

Illustrative of the Franco-German directional leadership in the EU, Germany and France formed a common platform in the IGC negotiations. In particular, the two states jointly voiced their desire to develop the operational capability of the Western European Union (WEU) as the defence component of the EU. The German defence minister declared the need for the EU to develop a 'strategic capacity', which builds on the idea that the EU should be able to act more independently from NATO on issues involving military instruments, such as the Petersberg tasks.[38]

In a meeting in Rome in November 1998, a timetable was put forward by the German and French governments for how the WEU should be phased into the EU framework. It was proposed that the operational capabilities of the WEU should be built up step-by-step and finally, around 2010, the WEU should be amalgamated with the EU. The proposal received support from the Benelux countries, but a majority of EU members, particularly the new non-aligned members, considered the timetable too ambitious. The British government rejected it on the grounds that it would debase NATO's political role in Europe.[39]

It is interesting to analyse German ideas on the WEU as the defence component of the EU. On the one hand, the Germans seem even more eager than the French to devise a timetable for how to integrate the WEU in the organisational framework of the EU. On the other hand, they continue to emphasise the WEU as the European pillar within NATO. Germany has no wish to destabilise NATO or to alienate the US from Europe. As stated earlier, an EU common policy, particularly on security, must take into account transatlantic interests. Nonetheless, the general view that Europe must shoulder a greater responsibility for its own security, and become more of an equal partner to the US, is apparent from statements by the German government.[40]

Germany would like to see a more cohesive actor capacity of the EU in foreign and security policy, but this conception does not match the French vision of the EU as an independent world power. Instead, the German vision of the EU in security and defence is situated within the Atlantic context, in which the CFSP/WEU are useful in those crisis situations when the US does not wish to become involved. From a German perspective, the key contribution of the EU in international affairs lies in the area of 'soft security' where the EU can exert a powerful influence through its economic and commercial power.

A reflection of these differing views arose between Germany and France during the IGC negotiations, when the question of the CFSP's international representation was discussed. The German foreign minister at the time, Klaus Kinkel, was firmly opposed to the French idea of a *Madame/Monsieur PESC,* who would be able to act as a kind of European foreign minister and provide the CFSP with a distinct profile in international affairs. Instead, Kinkel proposed a general secretary, with a lower profile, working under the authority of the Council of Ministers – a post that could be combined with the equivalent position in the WEU.

As the IGC negotiations proceeded, the initial idea of the German government to develop the CFSP into a more *communautaire* direction was asserted less. The image of a 'United States of Europe' was dropped in speeches. The idea of an integrated core of countries and the extension of majority decisions were replaced by a new key concept – 'flexible integration'. This indicated a more pragmatic approach on the part of the German government to what was considered feasible to reform at a time when 'Euro-realism' increasingly reflected the mood in a number of European capitals. Significantly, some policy makers in the German *Auswärtiges Amt* even went as far as describing this new-found pragmatism in terms of a more 'British approach' to European integration, moving forwards step-by-step in the field of foreign policy.[41] As a senior German diplomat contemplated after the signing of the Amsterdam Treaty: 'In foreign policy *within* a nation where you *do* have the possibility to take majority decisions, you work nonetheless as far as possible to create consensus between different parties. If this is true *inside* the nation, how much more is it not true for decisions *between* nations?'[42]

Without the EU: strategic relationships and visions of Europe

Below the surface of German multilateralism, a number of strategic and special relationships may be discerned. These are not considered to be exclusive relationships that ring-fence German interests in terms of a *domain privé*. That would be contradictory to the strongly held belief that Germany's multilateral relations are complementary.

Nonetheless, just like most other states, Germany puts a higher premium on cultivating some particular relationships. Germany's special and sensitive relationship with Israel has already been mentioned. The relationship between Germany and Poland has been granted a high symbolic importance after the end of the Cold War, pursued in a similar vein to that of Franco-German reconciliation in the post-war period. In fact, France has been incorporated in this special relationship in the so-called Weimar Triangle. Furthermore, Germany has invested a great deal of energy in building a relationship of trust with Russia. This has been important not least because after unification Germany had to negotiate the large Russian troop withdrawals from East Germany, which was completed in 1994. In addition, a cooperative relationship with Russia is of particular importance in attempting to calm Russian fears and antagonisms towards an extension of the EU and NATO into Eastern Europe. Germany has therefore sought to embed its bilateral consultation mechanisms with Russia in partnership cooperation agreements between the EU and Russia on the one hand, and NATO and Russia on the other.

In key foreign policy speeches, German visions of a European order after the end of the Cold War are clearly stated. These are as follows:

- to construct a lasting, liberal, democratic and peaceful order throughout Europe, which importantly builds on a cooperative relationship with Russia;
- to develop the EU into a political union including security and defence; and
- to maintain and further enhance Euro-Atlantic relations, primarily through NATO.

Two relationships are of primary importance to Germany in pursuing these European visions: the Franco-German relationship and the transatlantic relationship with the United States. These two relationships will be analysed below and bring to the fore the key question how Germany interprets the construction of a European Security and Defence Identity (ESDI).

The Franco-German relationship

The idea that a stable peace in Europe must be founded on reconciliation and a close relationship between Germany and France is strongly held across the political spectrum in Germany.[43] The *rapprochement* between France and Germany was sealed with the Élysée Treaty in 1963, which initiated an institutional approach towards building a strategic relationship between the two countries. However, in contrast to their close cooperation in the economic field, a close relationship has proven difficult to build in the area of security and defence, not least because France decided to leave NATO's military command in 1966. During the Cold War, the Franco-German relationship was largely built on the fact that Germany chose to maintain a low profile in foreign and security policy, which facilitated a French dominance of the agenda.

German reunification and territorial extension eastwards therefore raised a certain anxiety in France that Germany would re-evaluate their partnership, particularly when addressing German interests in Eastern Europe.[44] It is known that Franco-German relations have become more tense and complex to handle since the end of the Cold War. Germany's foreign policy interests are clearly focused towards the stabilisation of Eastern Europe, whilst French concerns are concentrated towards the south around the Mediterranean. Furthermore, the enlargement of the EU towards Eastern Europe will place Germany at the heart of Europe, while France's geopolitical position will become more peripheral.

The Franco-German relationship is highly complicated. It is, in some respects, an enigma as to how the two states continue to differ in their world views despite a high degree of institutionalisation and interaction.

Yet, at the same time it is a deeply held belief in both states that their relationship is a key to preserving an integrated cohesive EU. From a German perspective, the necessity of a functioning Franco-German relationship is frequently asserted. As Wolfgang Schäuble, party leader of the CDU, emphasises: if France and Germany cannot agree, 'things will go wrong in Europe'.[45] To overcome these centrifugal forces in the relationship, France and Germany have attempted to address and become actively involved in each other's concerns. For example, Germany has supported France's pursuit of developing a common EU policy towards the Mediterranean.[46]

Symbolism is important in this partnership. The political leaders frequently appear together launching political initiatives to set the agenda of the EU, wishing to portray how the two countries share similar foreign policy interests. For example, the setting up of the *Eurocorps* was initiated by France and Germany, to which other EU members were later invited to participate.

France and Germany provide the 'directional leadership' of the EU when it comes to promoting new ideas and setting the pace of European integration.[47] Whilst the Germans are generally cautious about raising the notion of leadership, the deepening of the European integration process is perceived as a particular historical responsibility that Germany must take a leading role in pursuing: 'no single country can lay claim to leadership in Europe, at least not in terms of power. But in terms of ideas and of their tenacious pursuit, a number of nations can and must lead the process of European unification.'[48] Karl Lamers and Wolfgang Schäuble of the CDU launched, for example, the controversial idea of a core Europe (*Kerneuropa*) in which Germany and France, along with the Benelux countries, would constitute the 'magnetic centre' of the integration process.[49] Part of the reason why this idea was so disputed at the time was that it seemed to indicate an exclusive semi-federal core rather than the French inclusive idea of concentric circles of integration.

The key problem that France and Germany have in providing leadership in the field of integration in foreign and security policy is that they have fundamentally different conceptions of political union, which is reflected in their views about the European Security and Defence Identity (ESDI). First of all, they appear to differ in their emphasis on the extent to which the CFSP should remain an essentially intergovernmental framework. Whilst Germany is a keen advocate of majority voting and wishes a greater involvement of the European parliament, France wants the CFSP to be developed within the strictly intergovernmental European Council. Secondly, France and Germany appear to dissent on the ultimate aim of the CFSP. The French vision of a European foreign policy concerns the projection of power and independence as a global actor (*l'Europe puissance*).[50] For the Germans, the deepening of foreign policy integration is less about exerting European power and more about diffusing it, thereby preventing a renationalisation of foreign policy that could lead to national rivalry and mistrust between the EU members.

The transatlantic relationship

A strategic partnership with the United States dates back to the West German tradition of *Westbindung*. The German armed forces (the *Bundeswehr*) are deeply integrated into NATO military structures. Furthermore, the transatlantic relationship contains a strong ideational dimension in Germany of belonging to a western community of shared values. Thus, despite the end of the Cold War, the continued military presence of the United States in Europe and the perseverance of NATO are fundamental interests in German foreign policy.[51]

Despite the importance attributed to the Franco-German relationship, Germany remains a loyal ally to the United States. The fact that it was the US administration that first came out in full support of Kohl's ambitions to swiftly seek German reunification was an important landmark in their relations. For Germany, it is also essential to remain close to the only remaining superpower after the end of the Cold War.

From an American perspective, a reunified Germany is a key partner for the US in the construction of a new security order in Europe. These views have been explicitly expressed, to the consternation of France and Britain, on two occasions with different US presidents in power. In the early 1990s, George Bush attempted to encourage Germany to shoulder a European leadership role with the motto 'Partnership in Leadership'. A few years later, Bill Clinton spoke of a 'Unique Relationship' with Germany.[52]

What is interesting (if not so surprising) is that Germany declined these invitations. An acceptance would have run the risk of raising renewed misgivings about Germany as a hegemonic power in the centre of Europe and would have seriously undermined the Franco-German relationship. German foreign policy speeches regularly contain references to the importance of respecting the equality between large and small states. Germany is, therefore, of its own will a 'tamed power'.[53]

There is a tension between a European and transatlantic orientation in German foreign and security policy, noticeable within political parties and ministerial rivalries, for example, in the emphasis being put on the enlargement processes of NATO and the EU. However, the view of international institutions as mutually reinforcing means that German foreign policy makers are reluctant to recognise that multilateral engagement may generate role conflicts. Instead, Germany sees itself as playing an essentially mediating role between European and transatlantic visions of Europe.

On the one hand, Germany emphasises the need to build a strong cohesive CFSP capable of acting outside the NATO framework in those instances when the US government does not want to become involved. On the other hand, and in opposition to French long-term views, the development of EU foreign policy action and policies must be situated and constructed in consultation with the Americans. The rift that surfaced between the Europeans and the US over the Bosnian crisis in the first part of the 1990s has been seen as a low point caused by a lack of consultation.

To prevent future ruptures in transatlantic relations, Germany is a keen proponent of the idea of a Euro-Atlantic Union, which extends cooperation beyond security policy to include economics and culture. Furthermore, this thinking is connected to the process of enlargement and the evolving political role of NATO in post-Cold War Europe which, from a German perspective, must be followed by a parallel restructuring of transatlantic relations.

The attempt to reach a common ground on what an ESDI may entail in the future has to some extent been facilitated by the French *rapprochement* to NATO and the Americans' more relaxed view under the Clinton administration of a European foreign policy, that includes security and defence dimensions. However, it is a delicate balancing act for the German government to be endorsing a more cohesive European foreign policy that does not appear to undermine NATO.

Conclusion: Berliner Republik – still a civilian power?

Deutsche Außenpolitik ist und bleibt Friedenspolitik.[54]

As a newly elected Bundeskanzler, Schröder proclaimed, in the autumn of 1998, that German foreign policy is, and will remain, a 'peace policy'. Four months later, Germany was, for the first time since 1945, engaged in offensive military action against a sovereign state. Overshadowed by the Kosovo War, the Bundestag convened its first parliamentary session in Berlin on 19 April 1999, signalling the official move of government from the provincial setting of Bonn to the metropolitan city of Berlin in the north-east. As the Speaker of the Bundestag, Wolfgang Thierse, pointed out in his opening speech, there is a 'tragic historical dialectic' between German unification and the war in Kosovo. 'The return of the all-German parliament to Berlin and the warlike conflict in and around Kosovo have a common cause', he argued, 'the end of communism'. 'It presented us with the gift of German unification, but unfortunately not, as many people hoped in 1989/90, with a golden age of peace ...'.[55] In Germany, the Kosovo War presented complex moral and political dilemmas, frequently discussed with reference to German history of the Holocaust. Thus for many Germans, it was imperative that their country participated and assumed its responsibility to act at the core of the NATO coordinated action against the flagrant human right abuses in Kosovo.

The early twenty-first century is, therefore, marked by a number of symbolic and historical events. They bring to the fore the key debates about German foreign policy since unification, that is, the normalisation of German foreign policy and its status as a 'civilian power'. The debate on normalisation is somewhat confused, because it is difficult to specify what the general norms of a 'normal' state are in foreign policy. In the German context, the issue of normalisation is however interesting to study, because it blends an instrumental interest-based view of foreign policy with normative ideas of responsibility within a security community. Moral and strategic interests are for historical reasons tightly interwoven in German foreign policy.

Normalisation of German foreign policy does not imply unilateralism. The core thinking of German multilateral institutionalism remains as relevant today as it did after the Second World War. The majority view in Germany is that foreign policy must continue to be predictable, transparent and exert a strong element of continuity. The CFSP constitutes an ideal framework for these endeavours. German foreign policy makers will thus continue to attempt to enmesh German interests in the EU. Yet, as the response to the instability and wars in the Balkans has indicated throughout the 1990s, the failure of the EU to act has implications for where Germany decides to exercise its multilateral activity. Clearly, the socialisation mechanisms of the CFSP still have a limited impact on the outlook of foreign policy makers, which in part inhibits the EU to act decisively.

Despite a strong sense of continuity in German foreign policy, there are also visible changes, particularly on the view of using military force outside territorial defence, to address new instabilities and threats arising after the end of the Cold War. The description of Germany as 'an economic power but political dwarf' is no longer suitable. This change in thinking calls into question the idea of Germany as a 'civilian power'. The notion of a civilian power is notoriously vague and often poorly defined, which perhaps accounts for its attractiveness to politicians. Yet, it should be pointed out that the idea of civilian power does not necessarily equate a pacifist renunciation of the use of military force under any circumstances.

Clearly, the tragedy in Kosovo demonstrates the analytical limitations of the notion of civilian power when confronted with the dilemmas of military intervention for humanitarian purposes. However, the continued reiteration of key beliefs in German foreign policy, such as a concern for human rights; moderateness of approach; extensive consultation with partners; a clear renunciation of unilateral action; and a willingness to seek compromise, offers strong evidence to suggest that Germany will remain a civilian power in the beginning of the twenty-first century. Perhaps in contrast to the Rhineland Republic of Bonn, the Berlin Republic will be more of a 'normal' civilian power.

Notes

1 See for example, Hans-Dietrich Genscher, Speech at the UN General
   Assembly, New York, 26 September 1990; see further J. Janning, 'A German
   Europe – a European Germany? On the debate over Germany's foreign
   policy', *International Affairs* 1 (1996).
2 K. Adenauer, *Erinnerungen 1945–1953* (Stuttgart, Deutsche Verlags-Anstalt,
   1965), pp. 245–246.
3 H. Maull, 'Zivilmacht Bundesrepublik? Das neue Deutschland und die internationale Politik', *Blätter für Deutsche und Internationale Politik*, 38 (1993).
4 See for example, A. Baring, (ed.), *Germany's New Position in Europe:
   Problems and Perspectives* (Oxford, Berg, 1994); J. Habermas, *Die
   Normalität der Berliner Republik* (Frankfurt, Suhrkamp, 1995); G.
   Hellmann, 'The sirens of power and German foreign policy: who is listen-
   ing?', *German Politics*, 6:2 (1997); Janning, 'A German Europe'.
5 For a more extensive theoretical discussion see L. Aggestam, 'Role conceptions and the politics of identity in foreign policy', *ARENA Working Paper* 8
   (1999).
6 However, the right to German citizenship, and the advantages that spring
   from this privilege, remains predominantly ethnic in conception. The new
   red–green coalition government has made pledges to address this anomaly
   from the past.
7 The political structures of the former East Germany was in the main part
   supplanted by the West German political system, which later in the 1990s has
   led to a certain resentment and divide between the eastern and western parts
   of Germany in public opinion. The PDS, the reformed communist party,
   largely draws its political support from this dissatisfaction and nostalgia of
   East Germany. This divide between the eastern and western part of Germany
   seems to be reflected in public opinion on foreign policy. For example, a
   majority (53 per cent) of Germans in the East are against German participation in the NATO airstrikes in the Balkans, whilst a majority (59 per cent) of
   Germans in the western part support the action. ('Ostdeutsche gegen diesen
   Krieg', *Stern*, 15 April 1999). For an excellent overview of the variety of
   views regarding Germany as a nation-state see R. Voigt (ed.), *Der Neue
   Nationalstaat* (Baden-Baden, Nomos Verlagsgesellschaft, 1998).
8 See for example, Helmut Kohl, Regierungserklärung vor dem Deutschen
   Bundestag, Bonn, 11 November 1993.
9 As a German policy maker put it in an interview with the author (Bonn,
   November 1997).
10 V. Rühe, 'Growing responsibility', *German Comments* 42 (1996), p. 32
11 P. Katzenstein, 'United Germany in an integrating Europe', *Current History*
   March, (1997).
12 Interview in *Der Tagesspiegel*, 5 November 1998.
13 R. Herzog, 'Globalization of German foreign policy is inevitable', *German
   Comments* 39 (1995).
14 The position of *die Länder* was strengthened after Maastricht, which brought
   new extensive co-decision-making powers at the federal level.
15 See C. Clemens, 'The Chancellor as manager: Helmut Kohl, the CDU and

governance in Germany', *West European Politics* 17:4 (1994). J. Siwert-Probst, 'Die klassischen aussenpolitischen Institutionen' in W-D. Eberwein and K. Kaiser (eds), *Deutschlands neue Außenpolitik*, Band 4, DGAP (München, Oldenbourg Verlag).

16 See further, M. Holland, 'Three approaches for understanding european political co-operation', *Journal of Common Market Studies* 25:4 (1987).

17 A. Wendt, 'Anarchy is what states make of it: the social construction of power politics', *International Organization* 46 (1992), p. 400.

18 K. Deutsch et al., *Political Community in the Northern Atlantic Area* (Princeton, Princeton University Press, 1957). For more recent research on the concept of 'security community' see E. Adler and M. Barnett (eds), *Security Communities* (Cambridge, Cambridge University Press, 1998).

19 See W. Hoyer, 'Die Außen- und Sicherheitspolitische Handlungsfähigkeit der EU und die Gesamteuropäische Sicherheitsordnung'. Speech in Cologne, 22 February 1997.

20 A round of interviews (fifteen) were conducted with politicians and policy-makers at the Ministry of Foreign Affairs and the Ministry of Defence in Bonn, November 1997.

21 See further the German Whitebook on security and defence, *Weißbuch zur Sicherheit der Bundesrepublik Deutschland und zur Lage und Zukunft der Bundeswehr* (Bonn, Bundesministerium der Verteidigung, 1994).

22 T. G. Ash, 'Germany's choice' in M. Mertes, S. Muller and H. Winkler (eds), *In Search of Germany* (New Brunswick, Transaction Publishers, 1996), p. 92.

23 G. Langguth, 'Germany's role in Europe', *German Comments* 31 (1993), p. 6.

24 Interview at the Ministry of Foreign Affairs in Bonn, November 1997.

25 Adler and Barnett, *Security Communities*, p. 52.

26 Herzog, 'Globalization', p. 5.

27 V. Rühe, 'Germany's responsibility in and for Europe', The Konrad Adenauer Memorial Lecture 1994, St. Antony's College, Oxford, p. 5.

28 See for example, E. Bahr, 'Die "Normalisierung" der deutschen Außenpolitik', *Internationale Politik* 54:1 (1999); C. Hacke, 'Die nationale Interessen der Bundesrepublik Deutschland an der Schwelle zum 21. Jahrhundert', *Aussenpolitik* 2 (1998); G. Schöllgen, 'Die Berliner Republik als internationaler akteur – gibt es noch eine deutsche intressenpolitik?', *Aussenpolitik* 2 (1998).

29 Interview in Bonn, November 1997.

30 Interview in Bonn, November 1997.

31 Klaus Kinkel, 'Deutsche Außenpolitik in einer neuen Weltlage', Speech in Bonn, 24 August 1995.

32 See J. Fischer, *Risiko Deutschland: Krise und Zukunft der Deutschen Politik* (Köln, Kiepenheuer and Witsch, 1994); L. Volmer, *Die Grünen und die Außenpolitik – ein schwieriges Verhältnis* (Münster, Verlag Westfälisches Dampfboot, 1998), p. 513.

33 See A. Hyde-Price, *The International Politics of East Central Europe* (Manchester, Manchester University Press, 1996).

34 V. Rühe, *German Comments* (1996), p. 34.

35 The knowledge about the CFSP is weak among the general public. See J.

Janning and F. Algieri, 'The German debate' in *The 1996 IGC – National Debates (2)*, Discussion Paper 67, London, The Royal Institute of International Affairs, 1996, p. 73.

36 P. Schmidt, 'Security challenges and institutional responses: a German perspective' in G. Herolf (ed.), *Europe: Creating Security Through International Organizations*, Conference Papers 17, Stockholm, Utrikespolitiska institutet, 1996, p. 73.

37 Primarily France, Germany and the Benelux countries.

38 See V. Rühe, 'Strukturreform der NATO: atlantische, europäische und strategische Dimension' *Internationale Politik* 51:4 (1996). The Petersberg-tasks include humanitarian actions, crisis management, peacekeeping and peace-enforcing with military means.

39 Y. Boyer, 'France and the European project: internal and external issues' in K. Eliassen (ed.), *Foreign and Security Policy in the European Union* (London, Sage Publications, 1998), p. 104.

40 K. Kinkel, 'The new NATO: steps towards reform' *NATO Review*, May 1996.

41 Interviews at the Ministry of Foreign Affairs in Bonn, November 1997; See also A-M Le Gloannec, 'Germany and Europe's foreign and security policy: embracing the "British" vision. AICGS Research Report No 8. *Break Out, Break Down or Break In? Germany and the European Union after Amsterdam* (1997), p. 29.

42 Interview at the Ministry of Foreign Affairs in Bonn, November 1997.

43 See for example, G. Schröder, 'Regierungserklärung vor dem Deutschen Bundestag', Bonn, 10 November 1998.

44 See D. Vernet, 'The dilemma of French foreign policy' *International Affairs* 68:4 (1992).

45 Interview with W. Schäuble in Bonn, November 1997. See also, Speech by R. von Weizsäcker, 'Zur deutschen Außenpolitik', Hamburg, 2 December 1993.

46 See Rühe, 'Growing responsibility', p. 35 who speaks of the 'security in and for Europe'.

47 See T. Pedersen, *Germany, France and the Integration of Europe: A Realist Interpretation* (London, Pinter Publishers, 1998).

48 K. Lamers, *A German Agenda for the European Union* (London, Federal Trust, Konrad Adenauer Foundation, 1994), p.10.

49 For an indepth elaboration of the idea of a core Europe see C. Deubner, *Deutsche Europapolitik. Von Maastricht nach Kerneuropa?* (Baden-Baden, Nomos, 1995).

50 See for example the speech by Jacques Chirac in Paris, 29 August 1996.

51 See speech by Klaus Kinkel, 'Deutsche Sicherheitspolitik in den 90er Jahren', Hamburg, 9 November 1993.

52 For an indepth study of German–American relations see W. Hanrieder, *Deutschland, Europa, Amerika: Die Außenpolitik der Bundesrepublik Deutschland 1949–1994* (Paderborn, Schöningh, 1995).

53 P. Katzenstein (ed.), *Tamed Power: Germany in Europe* (Cornell, Cornell University Press, 1997).

54 G. Schröder, 'Regierungserklärung vor dem Deutschen Bundestag', Bonn, 10 November 1998.

55 Quoted in *Die Tageszeitung*, 20 April 1999, p. 1.

II

Commonalities and difference

5

Italy

Antonio Missiroli

Italy's European policy: a profile

Since the inception of the EC, Italy has managed to play a multiple role within the Community. First, it was a *founding member* and a major actor in the setting up of the European Coal and Steel Community (ECSC) and the Common Market. In fact, Italy was the 'ceremonial heart' – as Roy Willis puts it – of the fledgling Community between the Messina Conference (1955) and the Rome Treaties (1957).[1] In actuality, however, Italy had been quite reluctant to join both the Organisation of European Economic Cooperation (OEEC) – it was the United States that ultimately convinced it to do so – and the ECSC in the first place. Later on, the crucial factor in dispelling the fears of Italian industry vis-à-vis the Common Market was the country's overall economic and trade performance in the 1950s, which proved surprisingly successful and, therefore, reassuring.[2]

Inside the 'Club of Six' Italy also played – from the outset – the role of the *poor relative* which it actually was, in terms of gross domestic product (GDP) per capita: hence the special Protocol attached to the Rome Treaty that awarded Italy the right to take special measures against the other economies, if need be, as well as the insistence on setting up the European Social Fund and on creating the European Investment Bank.

Ever since, Italy has played the role of the *laggard*. It demanded (and usually achieved) special conditions for the introduction of VAT (two years later than its partners), a wider *ad hoc* designed fluctuation band of 6 per cent for the Lira within the newly established Exchange Rate Mechanism (ERM), and *ex post facto* financial compensation for Mediterranean products within the Common Agricultural Policy (CAP) framework. In addition, Italy, more so than any other Member State, suffers from ever increasing delays in transposing EC directives into national legislation and in allocating, and spending, the structural funds.[3]

An important corollary of this 'triple' role has been the relatively low diplomatic and political profile kept by Italy in (Western) Europe. This tendency was shown at different levels. At the 'high politics' level, Italy basically made virtue out of necessity: through NATO and EC member-ship, in fact, the country managed to regain sovereignty and international rank.[4] Since the mid-1960s, when that primary goal was by and large achieved, the same low profile served mainly a domestic purpose – i.e. to prevent a further deepening of the political divisions between the centrist majority and the left-wing opposition[5] – while anchoring the country more firmly in the Western security and economic community. Italy showed a clear preference for playing the role of *honest broker* – along-side the Benelux countries – between France and Germany, while enjoying the full benefits of American protection and thus picking up the gleanings from all three 'circles' of its foreign policy: the transatlantic partnership, the EC, and the Mediterranean basin.[6]

Against this background, since 1970, the European Political Cooperation (EPC) machinery suited Italy's foreign and European policy handsomely: it sheltered Italy's occasional detours from pro-American positions on *détente*, North Africa or the Middle East, yet its weaknesses did not at all affect Italy's 'hard' security.[7] Such detours, again, were primarily linked to widespread sentiments in Italian public opinion, supported and at times sparked by the two-and-a-half main non-state actors in the country's foreign policy making process: the Communist Party (PCI), the Catholic Church, and the national oil company ENI, each with their own 'parallel' network of interests and preferential foreign rela-tions.[8]

In the realm of defence proper, by contrast, Italy joined the United Kingdom in countering Franco-German attempts at creating a more genuinely European security framework: indeed, in the late 1980s Italy did not join the Franco-German Brigade and, in October 1991, famously signed a joint declaration with Britain to offset Franco-German initiatives. Such a convergence, however, was mainly instrumental – on both sides – and could not make up for otherwise radically different views concerning European integration.[9]

As far as European institutions are concerned, Italy's low profile was partly due to a substantial lack of interest in taking on top political responsibilities in Brussels. Just consider the Commission: a first offer to put up a candidate for the presidency was made to Italy in 1967 and turned down, thus forcing the Belgian Jean Rey to come to the fore; Franco M. Malfatti eventually took over in 1971, only to resign before mid-term in order to return to Parliament in Rome. Until 1999 no Italian leader had claimed the presidency of the Commission or used his/her tenure in Brussels to make political capital at home. Or consider, for that matter, the European Parliament: alone among the five bigger EC/EU countries, Italy has never held the chair of the Assembly, nor of either of the two main political groupings, despite her supposed Euro-federalist enthusiasm. The important role played by Altiero Spinelli in Strasbourg in the early 1980s has proved more an episode than an isolated example to be followed.[10]

Finally, at the 'low politics' level, Italy has traditionally displayed little assertiveness in the smoke-filled rooms in which horse-trading usually takes place, and little efficiency in implementing EC legislation and provisions domestically. This is true of the CAP as well as other policies. Many explanations have been put forward for such behaviour. First and foremost, poor coordination among ministries (and between them and other public institutions) as well as administrative segmentation, in both the ascending and the descending phases of EC policy making. Secondly, the central role of the Foreign Ministry in orchestrating Italy's European policy in Brussels: its rather 'generalist' approach to negotiations and its emphasis on getting deals for the sake of 'Europe' may have weakened Italy's hand on some occasions, without strengthening the overall domestic institutional coordination. Thirdly, too few incentives on spending Community funds at the local/regional level: it has long been perceived to be easier to get money directly from Rome than from Brussels.[11]

Last but not least, the slowness and unreliability of the domestic law-making process: although, with the introduction in 1989 of the so-called 'Legge Comunitaria' (a single annual law which basically consists of the delegation of legislative powers in this field to the government) and with the creation of a dedicated Department (later Ministry) for Community Affairs within the Prime Minister's office, Italy significantly improved in terms of efficiency at transposing EC directives, it did not become more effective. As a result, the number of infringement procedures against Italy soared.[12] Curiously enough, the Italian Parliament – usually considered, for better or worse, the pivot of the Italian political and legislative system – has never played a significant role in the ascending phase of European policy formulation (while its role was mainly negative in the descending phase): it was relevant only at the stage of treaty ratification.[13]

All this may be seen as the dark, or rather grey side of Italy's European policy. Italy was not alone, of course, but no other major Member State has ever gone so far in decoupling political commitment to 'Europe' and actual compliance with it. Yet, on a more positive note, Italy has always been:

- an integrationist power, often willing to pay a price in terms of strict defence of national interests in order to benefit the wider Community;
- an early and strong advocate of cohesion and structural rebalancing – the European Investment Bank stemmed from an Italian demand – as well as of the free circulation of workers inside the EC, a philosophy that has benefited also (and, recently, mainly) other Member States;

- a warm supporter of enlargement, even when it threatened its position and interests within the Community (as with Spain and Portugal in the mid-1980s); and
- a keen advocate of inner EC democracy, ready to fight against emerging or self-styled *directoires* (particularly when it felt preliminarily excluded) and in favour of ever stronger supranational institutions.

When the hypothesis of giving constitutional powers to the European Parliament was put to a (purely consultative) referendum in June 1989 on the occasion of the European elections, it was accepted by 88.1 per cent of the voters, with an 81.5 per cent turnout.[14] An important precondition for this to happen, of course, has been the growing, all-party support for European integration, which has made Italian participation in elections to the European Parliament one of the highest in the EC/EU, second only to Belgium's and Luxembourg's (where voting is, anyway, compulsory).[15]

On the whole, therefore, it is arguable that Italy's European policy has aimed at enjoying the benefits of membership – markets, modernisation, status – without paying too high a price in terms of adjustment to common rules and regulations. In terms of 'high politics', the main goal has been the re-establishment and the preservation of Italy's regional middle power rank: to this end, the EU has played a parallel role to NATO in sheltering the country and its ambitions as well as weaknesses.[16]

Italy has consistently adopted a clearly *reactive* style towards Brussels. Herein lies also its main domestic implication, notably the fact that 'Europe' has been claimed and used by elites – given the overwhelming, if somewhat superficial, popular support for integration – as a sort of external constraint in order to by-pass the country's political and administrative system and to enforce decisions and policies which would not have been agreed upon (nor accepted) otherwise.[17] On top of that, such discourse and tactics further helped Italian governments to get rebates, delays, special clauses and *ad hoc* conditions in Brussels: in particular, the Commission – especially during Delors' tenure – never had any interest in antagonising (nor in penalising) such a warmly supportive Member State. Of course, again, Italy has not been the only Member State to resort to that, but it has been the first and the most consistent larger EC/EU country to systematically and openly play the multi-level game.

After Maastricht

When the Treaty on the EU was signed, most Italian leaders did not perceive all its potential implications for the country. The negotiators claimed to have reached a good deal in that the implementation of the European and Monetary Union (EMU) was defined as an eminently political decision to be taken on the basis of each country's 'trend' towards macro-economic convergence, while the timetable was primarily meant to tie the hands of Germany rather than to force others to increase their consolidation efforts. The fact that it seemed unlikely that Italy would meet the criteria by 1997 was somewhat balanced by the Lira's recent joining of the narrower fluctuation band of the ERM, seen as a good omen for eventual macro-economic compliance.[18]

Precisely that joining, however, proved to be an act of hubris and helped trigger the big EMS crisis of September 1992: in the end, the Lira was ejected out of the ERM and strongly devalued, while interest rates started soaring, impinging upon an already huge public debt. On top of that, the financial crisis coincided with an even deeper domestic political crisis: in the wake of the *Tangentopoli* scandal, an entire political elite was wiped out almost overnight, making the country more unstable, unpredictable and inward-looking than ever. The uphill struggle to regain some credibility on financial markets, therefore, took place in a sort of political vacuum, or rather limbo, with such key measures as the wage pact of 1993 and the pension reform of 1995 enacted by governments led by 'technicians' (respectively, Ciampi and Dini, both from the Bank of Italy) resting upon fuzzy and volatile parliamentary majorities.[19]

All this, of course, strongly affected the country's international profile. The decline in Italian influence was heralded by the onset of the post-Yugoslav crisis: the Italian government of the time long supported the preservation of the Federation's unity (thus reflecting also a traditional inclination of the Foreign Ministry), while other actors – the Catholic Church, the regional administrations in the North-East – sided with the secessionist Republics. The crisis was particularly relevant because it also raised the old and still unresolved problem of the Italian minorities in Croatia and Slovenia, of the properties of Italian exiles, and of the feuds and acts of vengeance of the immediate post-war years: all this stirred controversy among political parties and made it more difficult for the country to act internationally.[20] From the outbreak of *Tangentopoli* onwards, then, Italy was *de facto* marginalised from the management of a conflict that was unfolding at its immediate borders: if Italy's initial exclusion from the so-called 'Contact Group' appeared only natural at the time, its struggle to be taken on board was ruthless (the Dini government went as far as denying the use of Italian military bases for the air operations against the Bosnian Serbs) and succeeded – similar to what happened with the G7 in the mid-1970s – only by eventually gaining the support of the United States.[21]

Yet *Tangentopoli* affected Italy's international profile also by involving, in the spiral of political scandals, an entire department of the Foreign Ministry, namely the one in charge of overseas development aid, that had enormously increased its budget since the late 1980s. Ever since, Italy's bilateral aid policy has been partly scrapped and partly delegated to multi-lateral fora, especially the World Bank and the EU itself.[22]

In the end, the joint effect of the weak Lira – whose free-floating actually unleashed an export boom, pushing some EU partners to point to Italy's alleged 'competitive devaluation' policy – and the rise in domestic taxation to tackle the growing deficit and debt, coupled with the frustration over nearby Yugoslavia, resulted in a temporary anti-Maastricht backlash in public opinion. To a certain extent, the short-lived experience of the Berlusconi government (April–December 1994) may be seen as evidence of that, combining, as it did, an element of tax revolt with the temptation to play the free-rider inside the fledgling single European market. It was also reflected in Italy's lukewarm support for the new round of enlargement, which was felt as potentially shifting the centre of gravity of the EU further North and East-Central. The main spokesman for such (mild) Euro-scepticism 'Italian-style' was the then Foreign Minister Antonio Martino, a convinced monetarist of the Chicago School and, ironically, the son of the Foreign Minister, Gaetano Martino, who convened the Messina Conference. His outspoken criticism of EMU, however, never really won the day even inside the centre-right, and was replaced first by the more pragmatic and mainstream pro-European attitude of his successor Susanna Agnelli and later (in spring 1996) by the unequivocal, almost unidimensional commitment to 'Europe' of the new centre-left majority led by Romano Prodi.[23]

Interestingly, the change of the geopolitical setting that followed the end of the Cold War in Europe – along with the overall crisis that affected Italy, with its psychological multiplier effect – triggered a cultural revival of 'geopolitical' approaches, stirring up a controversy among elites on the 'national interests' and the contours of what was called the 'sistema Italia' in Europe and the wider world. In part, this revival was also due to the weakening of domestic/national cohesion reflected in the electoral rise of the Northern League and in the breakdown of the old party system.[24] In part, however, the discussion reflected sincere worries about the future of Italy in post-Maastricht Europe. The bumpy road towards EMU, the initial exclusion from the Contact Group and from the Schengen Agreement, even the fledgling debate over a 'hard core' Europe that would not include Italy, all seemed to radically put into question the country's multiple role game in the EC/EU. Being a founding member of the Community no longer granted a position in any 'hard core' or exclusive 'club'; Italy could not claim any more to be a poor relative in terms of the GDP (actually, at Maastricht, it accepted not to be a recipient of 'cohesion' funds); and the laggard could no longer 'get away with it'.

Such widespread awareness – or rather common perception – of the critical juncture at which the country found itself helped mobilise the political and administrative resources needed to meet the new challenge(s). For almost two years (1996–98), the public discourse was dominated by the primacy and urgency of 'bringing Italy into Europe': the Prodi government focused almost exclusively on the goal of meeting the EMU criteria – which it eventually (almost) did, thus confirming the eminently reactive nature and style of Italy's European policy. After a dramatic recovery, in fact, first the Lira re-entered the ERM (November 1996), then the country met four out of five convergence criteria – the debt being out of the question – and was taken in the first wave of entrants in the single currency (May 1998).

Yet the European performance of the Prodi government went largely beyond the EMU. After some panting and bickering, due to the increasingly sophisticated technical requirements to be met, Italy was allowed also into the Schengen Agreement: partially from October 1997, fully from April 1998. In the face of the Albanian crisis of 1997, Italy took the initiative and the leadership of a peacekeeping mission to restore some form of law and order in the country (spring–summer 1997), which proved relatively successful.[25] Finally, Italian diplomacy and business are again actively present in such nearby regions as the Balkans and Central-Eastern Europe, and Italy is also now 'sponsoring' some of the candidates, especially neighbouring Slovenia and, to a much lesser extent, Catholic Lithuania. The country's overall attitude vis-à-vis the next round of enlargement(s), however, remains somewhat ambivalent. On the one hand there is widespread support – especially among the public, less so among opinion leaders – for the integration of the new democracies and the opening of new markets. On the other hand, foreign policy elites maintain that a further 'deepening' of the EU institutional set-up should precede any further 'widening' of its membership. They would also prefer to balance new openings to the East with openings to the South of Europe – although the impact and relevance of Malta and Cyprus joining the Union clearly does not match, say, Poland's or, for that matter, even Estonia's.[26]

In the event, the Prodi government collapsed in Parliament in October 1998, formally because of Rifondazione Comunista's withdrawal from the majority, but probably also owing to an apparent loss of purpose after achieving all its political goals: Italy's international and regional rank was restored, the country was fully reinserted in the European core, her political profile and reliability were significantly enhanced. The successor government, led by the Massimo D'Alema and backed by the 'Olive Tree' and some centrist splinter parties, would find it much more difficult to spell out and agree on an equally mobilising, all-encompassing *raison d'etre*.

In the end, forty years after the signing of the Treaties of Rome, of the original three 'circles' of Italian foreign policy, the European one had definitely prevailed. Rome found itself on the forefront of European opposition to American unilateral sanctions and embargoes against the 'rogue States' Cuba, Iran, and Libya, and that – similarly to other EU partners – out of commercial as well as 'cultural' considerations. Italy was also critical of the way in which NATO was enlarged to include Poland, Hungary, and the Czech Republic, and sided with those European allies (a large majority) that would have preferred a slower and, above all, wider and more comprehensive enlargement policy.[27]

This does not mean, of course, that the transatlantic link has been put into question. However, even in the field of security and defence – the primacy of NATO notwithstanding – Italy has gradually adopted a more pro-European attitude, thus partially bridging the lingering gap and the potential dichotomy between its foreign (EPC/CFSP) and its security and defence (NATO) policy. Italy has not joined the Eurocorps but, along with the five EU partners that adhere to it, strongly supported the (eventually failed) full integration of WEU into the EU at the Intergovernmental Conference that led to the Amsterdam Treaty. Furthermore, it was proactive in promoting new multinational forces: Eurofor and Euromarfor (with France, Spain and Portugal in 1995), whose headquarters are based in Florence, an Italo-Spanish amphibious unit (1998), and an Italo-Slovenian-Hungarian alpine brigade (1999) meant also to strengthen NATO's Southern command. Finally, Italy set in motion a review of its defence policy centred upon the concept of a 'new model of defence': namely, one more up to the operational challenges of the post-Cold War era. After almost a decade, the exercise has not yet generated substantive policy change. The legacy of a mainly conscript-based, cheap (in terms of absolute budget share and in percentage of GDP) but basically inefficient military machinery, though, is being put under pressure by Italy's ever-increasing involvement in multinational peacekeeping operations. The same applies to Italy's defence industry vis-à-vis the restructuring that has taken place at the international and European level over the past years. In both policy areas, Italy seems ever more inclined to give priority to the European 'circle', though not necessarily to the detriment of the 'Atlantic' one.[28]

In the Mediterranean basin, finally, the *de facto* abandonment of the project of a Conference on Security and Cooperation in the Mediterranean (CSCM) in the early 1990s was followed by a declining financial and political engagement in the area: in a way, Spain has taken over the role of champion of 'Club Med' interests inside the EC/EU, as the coming about and the implementation of the so-called Barcelona Process have clearly showed.[29]

If Italy's main focus of political concentration now lies in Europe, its interests still have a wider reach. Economically, the country has a dynamic export industry that covers the world: its trade, aid, and energy flows go far beyond the borders of 'Europe'. Trade and investment involve the Far East as well as North America. In spite of the downsizing of bilateral aid mentioned above, Italy still preserves some exclusive or preferential ties with its former African colonies and with Latin America. Its energy supply (oil and natural gas) implies some dependency on the Maghreb region, Iran, and the former Soviet Union. Finally, there still is a significant Italian 'diaspora' across the world, especially in such countries as Argentina, Venezuela, Canada and Australia (let alone the United States), which demands special attention and *ad hoc* cultural, commercial and even constitutional provisions.[30]

In the late 1990s legal and illegal immigration flows from Albania, Former Yugoslavia, Turkey (the Kurds) and North Africa put additional pressure on Italian policy makers. It is worth noting, however, that they have mostly insisted on finding 'European' rather than purely national solutions – i.e. in the framework of the Schengen Agreement and of the so-called 'third' pillar – as the cases of the Kurdish asylum seekers (January 1998) and, most dramatically, the 'Ocalan affair' (autumn 1998) have showed. Such an attitude may stem from an acute awareness of the inadequacies of Italian public structures in dealing with these problems, but it is also evidence of a genuine commitment to common policies, and has ultimately strengthened the country's European credentials.

Against this background, therefore, it is by no means surprising – contingencies of the nomination apart – that Romano Prodi was chosen as new President of the Commission by the Berlin European Council in March 1999. On top of that, a few weeks later, Carlo A. Ciampi – a former long-serving Governor of the Bank of Italy, former Prime Minister, and Prodi's Treasury Minister – was elected President of the Republic, thus emphasising also the crucial role played by *Bankitalia* (and the Treasury) as a foreign policy actor in the run-up to EMU; and it is not by chance that Lamberto Dini, deputy to Ciampi at the Bank of Italy and another former Prime Minister, has been the Foreign Minister to both Prodi and D'Alema.

Conclusions

As compared to the pre-Maastricht era, Italy's European policy has not fundamentally changed its goals, but it has significantly changed its means. The new rules and procedures of EC/EU policy making – as modified also through treaty changes that Italy has not only supported throughout the last decade, but would have preferred to be even more radical – have increasingly created a level playing field where it is no longer possible for the country to resort to the triple role of the previous decades. The fact that such change coincided with a serious domestic political crisis – a crisis that analysts have labelled as the transition from the 'First' to a still unqualified 'Second' Republic – has made its impact more dramatic and its implications more far-reaching. As a result, the stakes are higher and the efforts at adjusting to the new environment more challenging.

The implications of joining EMU for the 'political economy' of the country are quite clear already, much as this does not make them any easier to address: as a matter of fact, the EMU has soon unveiled its real nature of point of departure, rather than of arrival, of policy adaptation. In a way, however, such (predictably painful) implications represent a further step on Italy's path towards industrial, social and bureaucratic modernisation. A good case in point are the renewed efforts put in place by the Treasury – through special 'task forces' and legislative measures – to mobilise and activate local and regional administrations in both the ascending and the descending phases of the allocation of structural funds and European Investment Bank loans. Procedures and deadlines have become much stricter, and especially some Southern regions risk losing valuable financial resources (to the advantage of other less developed areas of the EU) at a time when the budgetary discipline imposed by EMU and the Stability Pact makes it much harder than in the past for the central government to step in and invest.[31]

'Staying in Europe', possibly in its core and with a higher profile, has thus become a particularly challenging task for the Italian political and administrative system. For the latter, the run-up to full membership of 'Schengen' already represented an ordeal. For the former, the need for a more coordinated, responsive and accountable system of government still clashes with the unresolved problems of the Italian political 'transition'. On the one hand, the on-going debate on electoral systems and constitutional reforms – prime ministerial or semi-presidential system, federalism or devolution – clearly points to possible ways out of the traditional lack of efficiency, effectiveness, and transparency. On the other hand, political indecisiveness and bureaucratic or intra-institutional resistance slow down the process. The overall result is that a new point of equilibrium is not in sight yet. 'Palazzo Chigi', i.e. the office of the Prime Minister (Presidente del Consiglio), has significantly increased its competencies and supervisory role. The sheer fact that the barriers between purely domestic and purely foreign/European affairs are crumbling has helped, of course, although the Department/Ministry for Community Affairs still has no role in the ascending phase of policy-making – which falls rather in the sphere of a deputy Foreign Minister in charge of 'European' affairs – and is hardly comparable even to similar instances in other EU Member States.

The Treasury, too, has remarkably increased its influence over the formulation of policies related to the EC/EU: predictably, the primacy given to EMU compliance has involved the Ministry – that now encompasses also the previous Ministry of the Budget – in almost all macro- and micro-decisions related to monetary matters and public expenditure. In addition, as already mentioned, the Bank of Italy has grown into a semi-autonomous actor, by dint of its statutory role and of its unrivalled prestige and clout: it has increasingly done so since the inception of the

ERM (after initially opposing Italy's adhesion to it) and it has played a function, also politically, that goes far beyond its formal mandate – even more so, paradoxically, after handing over its monetary competency to the European Central Bank (ECB).

Finally, as compared to the pre-Maastricht era, some Ministries have increased their autonomous bargaining power in Brussels through peer review, i.e. through the socialisation and emulation effects generated by the Council machinery. Although still reliant in many respects on the Treasury, the Ministries for Industry, Agriculture, Transport and Environment, for instance, have doubtless strengthened their intra-governmental position via 'Europe'. Hence, also, the need for a stronger 'referee' and 'initiator' role of the Presidente del Consiglio – a role that, however, is not formally allowed by the Italian Constitution.

Not so the Ministry of Defence, partly for historical reasons – a century-long history of military blunders and the legacy of fascism, that have coalesced in keeping the prestige of the military at a very low level among both public opinion and political elites – partly for political ones, such as the American hegemony inside NATO and the lack of a specifically European dimension in security and defence matters. Recurrent attempts at streamlining and reforming the armed forces, especially after the end of the Cold War, have attained very little so far. Again, it is on the fledgling security and defence component of the CFSP – in both industrial and strictly military terms – that Italy seems to rely in order to modernise and upgrade its overall capabilities.[32] At the same time, for her part, the country certainly needs to clarify better the constitutional procedures and the political chain of command and responsibilities (involving not only the government, but also the two chambers of Parliament and the Presidency of the Republic) that should preside over future military engagements of Italian military forces in peace keeping missions 'out of area' and, above all, out of the traditional NATO framework, be it under the EU/WEU cover or *ad hoc* as in Albania.[33]

At any rate, the Foreign Ministry is no longer the sole nor the main policy-making body for EU affairs. It is not by chance that the 'Farnesina', too, has long been the focus of recurrent (and mostly failed) reform attempts, and that its grip on Community matters – through the pivotal role of the Secretary-General of the Ministry and of the Department of Political Affairs – has been put into question. However, if the decline of its 'generalist' competence is a foregone conclusion, the Foreign Ministry still oversees many EU policies through the seconded career diplomats that advise other Ministries as well as through the Permanent Representation in Brussels (officers of the 'Farnesina' still make up more than half of its staff).[34]

All in all, the intra-governmental division of labour in relation to EU affairs is in a state of flux, and such complicated negotiations as those related to 'Agenda 2000' have further highlighted the existing tensions between services, departments, and Ministries. At the same time, Italy's guiding principle in the EU is to share risks and responsibilities with its partners as much as possible, in terms of both policies and political decisions. In order to achieve this goal, the country seems ready, if not yet entirely able, to tackle long overdue constitutional and structural reforms. Italy seems also willing to push for more effective decision-making procedures – institutional flexibility, enhanced/closer cooperation, 'hard cores' – not only in the Community pillar but also in the CFSP, including security and defence. This is a major change in attitude vis-à-vis the recent past, including the latest IGC that led to the Amsterdam Treaty.[35] It is arguable that Italy's eventual inclusion in both the EMU and Schengen and their present membership – much wider than initially foreseen or expected – has dispelled previous Italian fears and boosted national and bureaucratic self-confidence. It remains to be seen whether the political system will be up to such dual (internal and external) challenges.

What is clear, at any rate, is that political parties and non-state actors do not have the same influence on Italy's European and foreign policy as before. The party system, too, is in a state of flux, and it looks more *influenced by* the shape and orientation of the main EU political families than capable of *influencing* national policy in a field where there no longer is any fundamental domestic cleavage. Again, 'Europe' is seen and perceived as a set of behavioural rules to be imported in order to overcome Italian weaknesses and shortcomings.

For its part, the Catholic Church now plays a minor role in European affairs: it supports, for instance, EU membership for Slovenia, Poland and Lithuania, and is not very keen on having Turkey as a full member. In the latter case, however, other considerations (mainly strategic ones) have influenced Italy's rather open position vis-à-vis Turkish formal inclusion in the EU enlargement process. Moreover, the dissolution of the Christian Democratic Party in 1993 has deprived the Holy See of an important interlocutor – and a quasi-permanent holder of the foreign policy portfolio – in government and parliament. At the same time, the influence of the Catholic Church over Italy's foreign policy has taken new avenues, mainly through the humanitarian activism of non-governmental organisations – especially in the Balkans and in Africa – or through the international mediation and conflict resolution efforts undertaken by the Comunita' di S.Egidio in Rome, most recently in Mozambique and Guatemala (quite successfully), and also in Algeria (much less so).[36]

Notes

1 A certain inclination, if not a demand, for starting up things as a host has endured over time: the institutional process leading to the Single European

Act was set in motion at the European Council held in Milan (June 1985). The Intergovernmental Conference resulting in the Maastricht Treaty on the European Union was initiated in Rome (Autumn 1990). Finally, the Intergovernmental Conference that has led to the Amsterdam Treaty was formally opened in Turin (Spring 1996). See F. R. Willis, *Italy Chooses Europe* (New York, Oxford University Press, 1971); A. Rizzo, *l'Italia in Europa tra Maastricht e l'Africa* (Roma-Bari, Laterza, 1996).

2 Cf. R. Ranieri, *Italy and the Schuman Plan Negotiations* (Florence, EUI, 1986).

3 See especially F. Francioni (ed.), *Italy and EC Membership Evaluated* (London, Pinter, 1992).

4 Cf. I. Poggiolini, 'Europeismo degasperiano e politica estera dell'Italia: un'ipotesi interpretativa (1947–1949)', *Storia delle Relazioni Internazionali*, I (1985), No. 1, pp. 161–181; F. Romero, 'L'Europa come strumento di nation-building: storia e storici dell'Italia repubblicana', *Passato e presente*, XIII (1995), No. 1–2, pp. 46–54; A. Varsori, *l'Italia nelle Relazioni Internazionali dal 1943 al 1992* (Roma, Laterza, 1998).

5 See N. Kogan, *The Politics of Italian Foreign Policy* (New York, Praeger, 1963); P. Vannicelli, 'Italy, NATO and the European Community: the interplay of foreign policy and domestic politics', *Harvard Studies in International Affairs*, (1974), No. 31; D. Sassoon, 'The making of Italian foreign policy', in W. Wallace and W. E. Paterson (eds), *Foreign Policy Making in Western Europe: A Comparative Approach* (Westmead, Saxon House, 1978), pp. 83–105; A. Panebianco, 'Le cause interne del basso profilo', *Politica Internazionale*, X (1982), No. 2, pp. 15–21; S. Silvestri, 'L'Italia: partner fedele ma di basso profilo', in L. Caligaris (a cura di), *La Difesa Europea – Proposte e Sfide* (Milano, Edizioni di Comunità), pp. 185–202. For a comparative overview see also A. Panebianco, *Guerrieri Democratici. Le Democrazie e la Politica di Potenza* (Bologna, Il Mulino, 1997), especially p. 227.

6 The three 'circles' – a clear hint at Winston Churchill's famous speech in the House of Commons – were first mentioned by Ludovico Garruccio (a.k.a. Ludovico Incisa di Camerana), 'Le scelte di fondo e il retroterra culturale', *Politica Internazionale*, X (1982), No. 2, pp. 7–14.

7 Italy's only source of embarassment coincided with the outbreak of the Falklands War between Britain and Argentina in 1982: only after weeks of wavering did the government in Rome eventually join its EC partners, take sides with London, and enforce the embargo against Buenos Aires. See S. Nuttall, *European Political Cooperation* (Oxford, Clarendon Press, 1992); S. Stavridis and C. Hill (eds), *Domestic Sources of Foreign Policy: Western European Reactions to the Falklands Conflict* (Oxford, Berg, 1996). Similarly, a typical (and topical) detour on Middle East issues occurred with the 'Achille Lauro'-Sigonella affair, in 1985, that resulted in a major clash with the Reagan administration: see G. Calchi Novati, 'The case of the Achille Lauro hijacking and the Italo-Arab relations: one policy, too many policies, no policy', *Journal of Arab Affairs*, X (1991), No. 2, pp. 153–179.

8 See, respectively, B. Schoch, *Die internationale Politik der italienischen Kommunisten* (Frankfurt-New York, Campus, 1988); the special issue of *Limes*, 'Le citta' di Dio', *Limes* I (1993), No. 3, as well as S. Picciaredda, 'Quanto e' italiana la Chiesa universale', *Limes*, VI (1998), No. 1, pp. 35–43;

and G. Sapelli, *Uno Sviluppo tra Politica e Strategia: ENI (1953–1983)* (Milano, Angeli, 1992). The main area on which such plurality of actors and approaches impinged upon was, of course, the *Ostpolitik*; cf. C. Alix de Montclos, 'Monseigneur Casaroli et l'Ostpolitik', *Relations internationales*, XXVIII (1981), pp. 427–442; M. Dassu, 'Italo-Soviet relations: the changing domestic agenda', in G. Flynn (ed.), *The West and the Soviet Union: Politics and Policy* (New York, St. Martin's Press, 1990), pp. 109–155.

9   Cf. A. Missiroli, 'La PESC e la politica estera italiana: vincoli, problemi e scenari', in G.Bonvicini et al. (eds), *Italia Senza Europa ? Il Costo della non Partecipazione alle Politiche dell'Unione Europea* (Milano, Angeli, 1997), pp. 37–61.

10 With possibly one or two exceptions – Altiero Spinelli and Antonio Giolitti – Italian EC Commissioners have never enjoyed a particularly high political profile at home. With the exception of Spinelli, Italy has tended to avoid appointing members of the (left-wing) opposition to the Commission. See R. E. M. Irving, 'Italy's Christian democrats and European integration', *International Affairs*, LII (1976), pp. 400–416; B. Olivi, *L'Europa Difficile. Storia Politica della Comunita' Europea* (Bologna, Il Mulino, 1993); L. Bardi and G. Pasquino, *Euroministri. Il Governo dell'Europa* (Milano, Il Saggiatore, 1994).

11 Not *all* Italian regions, however, acted like that: cf. R. Leonardi (ed.), *The Regions and the European Community: The Regional Response to 1992 in the Underdeveloped Areas* (London, Frank Cass, 1993); R. Leonardi, *Convergence, Cohesion and Integration in the European Union* (London, Macmillan, 1995).

12 See F. Pocar et al., 'Italy', in H. Siedentopf, J. Ziller (eds), *Making European Policies Work: The Implementation of Community Legislation in the Member States* (Bruxelles-London, Bruylant-Sage, 1988), pp. 449–517; S. Cassese, 'Poteri divisi: amministrazione europea e amministrazioni nazionali', in G. Amato and M. L. Salvadori (a cura di), *Europa Conviene?* , (Bari, Laterza, 1990), pp. 70–81; M. V. Agostini, 'Italy and its community policy', *The International Spectator*, XXV (1995), No. 4, pp. 87–97; M. Giuliani, 'Italy', in D. Rometsch and W. Wessels (eds), *The European Union and Member States: Towards Institutional Fusion?* (Manchester, Manchester University Press, 1996), pp. 105–133. For a wider picture of the institutional system cf. D. Hine, *Governing Italy: The Politics of Bargained Pluralism* (Oxford, Clarendon Press, 1993).

13 Cf. the essays in A. Cassese (ed.), *Parliamentary Foreign Affairs Committees: The National Setting* (New York-Padua: Oceana-Cedam, 1982). See also F. Cazzola, *Governo e Opposizione nel Parlamento Italiano* (Milano, Giuffre, 1974).

14 For an overview G. Bonvicini, 'Italy: an integrationist perspective', in C. Hill (ed.), *National Foreign Policies and European Political Cooperation* (London, Allen & Unwin, 1983), pp. 71–82; E. Noel, 'Italia/CEE – Vizi e virtu' di un membro fondatore', *Relazioni Internazionali*, LIV (1990), No. 2, pp. 15–21; F. Romero, *Emigrazione e Integrazione Europea 1945–1973* (Roma, Edizioni Lavoro, 1991); A. Sbragia, 'Italia/CEE – Un partner sotto-valutato', *Relazioni Internazionali*, LVI (1992), No. 2, pp. 78–87; M. Neri

Gualdesi, *L'Italia e la CE. La Partecipazione Italiana alla Politica d'Integrazione Europea 1980–1991* (Pisa, ETS, 1992); M. Dassu and A. Missiroli, 'L'Italia in Europa: i primi cinquant'anni', *Rassegna di sociologia*, XL (1996), No. 12, pp. 18–36.

15 See R.Walker, *Dal Confronto al Consenso. I Partiti Politici Italiani e l'Integrazione Europea* (Bologna, Il Mulino, 1976); A. Missiroli, 'Il "guado" europeo della sinistra', *Il Mulino*, XLIV (1995), pp. 715–726. Both Alleanza Nazionale (heir to the neo-fascist MSI) and Rifondazione Comunista (a splinter of the former PCI) voted against the ratification of the Maastricht Treaty, yet neither opposed European integration per se. See also C. M. Radaelli, 'Europeismo tricolore', *Relazioni Internazionali*, LII (1988), No. 4, pp. 92–98; F. Battistelli, P. Isernia, 'Dove gli angeli non osano mettere piede. Opinione pubblica e politica internazionale in Italia', *Teoria Politica*, VII (1991), No. 1, pp. 81–119.

16 Cf. P. Pastorelli, *La Politica Estera Italiana del Dopoguerra* (Bologna, Il Mulino, 1987); C. M. Santoro, *La Politica Estera di una Media Potenza. L'Italia dall'Unita' ad Oggi* (Bologna, Il Mulino, 1991); L. V. Ferraris (a cura di), *Manuale della Politica Estera Italiana 1947–1993* (Bari, Laterza, 1996).

17 Cf. Francioni (ed.), *Italy and EC Membership Evaluated*; G. Amato, 'The impact of Europe on national policies: Italian anti-trust policy', in Y. Meny et al. (eds), *Adjusting to Europe: The Impact of the European Union on National Institutions and Policies* (London-New York, Routledge, 1996), pp. 157–174. The same applies to environmental regulations and to consumers' protection.

18 See M. Artis, 'The Maastricht road to monetary union', *Journal of Common Market Studies*, XXX (1992), No. 3, pp. 299–310; J. Story, M. De Cecco, 'The politics and diplomacy of monetary union: 1985–1991', in J. Story (ed.), *The New Europe: Politics, Government and Economy Since 1945* (Oxford, Blackwell, 1993), pp. 328–354; P. Daniels, 'L'Italia e il trattato di Maastricht', in S. Hellman, G. Pasquino (eds), *Politica in Italia* (Bologna: Il Mulino, 1993), pp. 199–218.

19 On the interplay of financial and political crisis see P. McCarthy, *The Crisis of the Italian State: From the Origins of the Cold War to the Fall of Berlusconi* (New York, St. Martin's Press, 1995); D. Hine, 'Italian political reform in comparative perspective', in S. Gundle, S. Parker (eds), *The New Italian Republic: From the Fall of the Berlin Wall to Berlusconi*, (London-New York, Routledge, 1996), pp. 311–325.

20 Relations with Slovenia, in particular, were long affected by bilateral issues: cf. E. Greco, 'Italy, the Yugoslav crisis and the Osimo agreements', *The International Spectator*, XXIX (1994), 1, pp. 13–31; L. Caputo, 'Il puzzle jugoslavo e l'Italia', *Affari Esteri*, XXVII, No. 106, pp. 338–350; T. Favaretto, E. Greco (a cura di), *Il Confine Riscoperto. Beni Degli Esuli, Minoranze e Cooperazione Economica nei Rapporti dell'Italia con Croazia e Slovenia* (Milano, Angeli, 1997). Italy eventually lifted its veto on the European Agreement to be signed with Slovenia – a veto that made the country unpopular with many EU partners – in the spring of 1996. On the historical background see M. Galeazzi (a cura di), *Roma-Belgrado. Gli Anni della Guerra Fredda* (Ravenna, Longo, 1995).

21   Cf. M. Dassu', 'Perche' l'Italia ha fallito nella ex Jugoslavia', *Limes*, II (1994),
     No. 3, pp. 219–228; E. Greco, 'L'Italia e la crisi balcanica', in AA.VV.,
     L'Italia nella Politica Internazionale (Roma, Sipi, 1994), pp. 107–128; A.
     Nativi (a cura di), *Bosnia: l'Intervento Militare Italiano* (Genova, Publi-Rid,
     1996); P. Donatucci and S. Lucarelli, *Il Contributo dell'Italia all'Intervento
     Internazionale per la Pacificazione e la Ricostruzione della Bosnia-
     Erzegovina* (Roma, IAI-R9831, 1998). The combined effect of *Tangentopoli*
     and the breakdown of Former Yugoslavia killed also one of the most inter-
     esting *autonomous* foreign policy initiatives of Italian diplomacy, notably the
     'Pentagonale': as a forum for post-1989 subregional cooperation, it involved
     also Austria, Hungary, Czechoslovakia, Poland, and Yugoslavia. Only years
     later did it resurface, albeit in a different format, as Central European
     Initiative (CEI). See V. Mastny (ed.), *Italy and East-Central Europe:
     Dimensions of the Regional Relationship* (Boulder, Westview, 1995);
     L. Troiani, 'Un caso di cooperazione intergovernativa per lo sviluppo; l'inizia-
     tiva centro-europea', *Politica Internazionale*, XXII (1994), No. 3, pp.
     93–104.
22   Cf. J.-L. Rhi-Sausi (a cura di), *La Crisi della Cooperazione Italiana* (Roma,
     Edizioni Associate, 1994); P. Isernia, *La Cooperazione allo Sviluppo*
     (Bologna, Il Mulino, 1995). As a result, in 1995, Italy increased its share in
     the European Development Fund from 12.03 to 12.57 per cent, thus compen-
     sating for the reductions demanded by Britain, Germany and the Netherlands.
23   The temporary, relative decline in Euro-enthusiasm is detectable among both
     citizens (as showed by Eurobarometer) and opinion leaders, as the polls taken
     by Pragma since 1990 show: cf. *L'Europa degli italiani*, I (1992)–VIII (1999).
     See E. Rogati, 'Il governo Berlusconi fra nazionalismo e federalismo', *Politica
     Internazionale*, XXIII (1995), No. 1–2, pp. 46–54; P. Neal, 'La "nuova"
     politica estera italiana', in P. Ignazi, R. S. Katz (eds), *Politica in Italia*
     (Bologna, Il Mulino, 1995), pp. 185–195; M. Dassu, A. Missiroli (a cura di),
     'L'Italia nell'Europa di fine secolo', special issue, *Europa Europe*, V (1996),
     No. 1.
24   See e.g. E. Galli della Loggia et al., 'Alla ricerca dell'interesse nazionale',
     Limes, I (1993), No. 1–2, pp. 13–26 (the periodical *Limes* has become the
     main vehicle and target of such controversy); G. E. Rusconi, 'Il ruolo inter-
     nazionale dell'Italia: la necessita' di essere una nazione', *Il Mulino*, XLII
     (1993), No. 5, pp. 892–897; AA.VV., *Il Sistema Italia. Gli Interessi Nazionali
     Italiani nel Nuovo Scenario Internazionale* (Milano, Angeli, 1997); F. Corsico
     (a cura di), *Interessi Nazionali e Identita' Italiana* (Milano, Angeli, 1998). For
     an evaluation cf. R. Aliboni and E. Greco, 'Foreign policy renationalisation
     and internationalism in the Italian debate', *International Affairs*, LXXII
     (1996), pp. 43–51.
25   Operation 'Alba' was run by a mixed 'coalition of the willing' – Italy as
     'framework nation', France, Spain, Greece, Romania, Slovenia, Turkey,
     plus minor contributions by Denmark, Austria and Belgium – with a
     UN/OSCE humanitarian mandate, but without a specifically European one:
     cf. S. Silvestri, 'The Albanian test case', *The International Spectator*, XXXII
     (1997), No. 3–4, pp. 87–98; E. Foster, 'Ad hoc in Albania: did Europe fail?',
     Security Dialogue, (1998), No. 29, pp. 201–212; A. De Guttry and F. Pagani

(a cura di), *La Crisi Albanese del 1997*, (Milano, Angeli, 1999). As such, 'Alba' represented an important boost for Italy's role in international peace-keeping missions, especially after the shocking and disappointing experience made with the 1993 UN Operation 'Restore Hope' in Somalia (see M. C. Ercolessi, 'L'Italia e l'intervento dell'ONU in Somalia', in AA.VV., *L'Italia*, 134–154). On the specific (also domestic) impact of the Albanian crisis on Italy see F. Pastore, *Conflicts and Migrations: A Case Study on Albania* (CeSPI Occasional Papers, Rome, 1998). It is worth noting here that in the Italian Parliament 'Alba' was supported by the centre-right opposition but not by Rifondazione Comunista, that was part of the majority and backed the effort to join EMU.

26 On Italy's EU enlargement policy cf. CeSPI (a cura di), *L'Italia e l'Allargamento dell'Unione Europea ai PECO* (Roma, MAE, 1997); A. Missiroli, 'Verso una piu' larga Unione Europea', in S. Bianchini and M. Dassu (eds), *Annali dell'Europa Centrale, Orientale e Balcanica* (Bologna, Guerini, 1998), pp. 57–70. Surprisingly enough, Italy is the second largest EU trade partner and investor (after Germany) in the ten central European appli-cant countries. Such economic interests do not significantly affect, however, official foreign policy formulation. A possible explanation lies in the different geographical origin and self-perception of Italian business (North) and bureaucratic elites (South).

27 Italy, specifically, canvassed Slovenia and, to a lesser extent, Romania as additional candidates for membership. On the occasion of the parliamentary ratification of NATO enlargement, again, the centre-right opposition supported the decision and Rifondazione Comunista did not – further evidence of the fact that Prodi's majority (the 'Olive Tree' coalition plus Rifondazione) was united on European/EMU policy, but not on foreign policy at large. Cf. M. Dassu and R. Menotti, 'Italy and NATO enlargement', *The International Spectator*, XXXII (1997), No. 3–4, pp. 65–86.

28 For a critical overview cf. F. Andreatta, C. Hill, 'Italy', in J. Howorth and A. Menon (eds), *The European Union and National Defence Policy* (London and New York, Routledge, 1997), pp. 66–86. On the 'new model' see C. M. Santoro, *L'Elmo di Scipio. Studi sul Modello di Difesa Italiano* (Bologna, Il Mulino, 1992); A. Casu, 'Italie: vers un nouveau modèle de défense', in P. Buffotot (dir.), *La Défense en Europe. De la Guerre du Golfe au Conflit Yugoslave* (Paris, La documentation Française, 1995), pp. 107–116; and the contributions by M. Cremasco, S. Silvestri and A. Politi in AA.VV., *L'Italia*, pp. 63–104.

29 The old CSCM blueprint – that included four European countries (France, Italy, Spain, and Portugal) and five Arab countries, all members of the Maghreb Union (Algeria, Libya, Mauritania, Morocco, and Tunisia) – was formally presented by Italy and Spain at the Mediterranean Environment Conference of the CSCE in September 1990. The idea was to extend the logic of cooperation to the whole Mediterranean area, using the rules and princi-ples adopted in Europe within the CSCE framework. American opposition and lack of enthusiasm on the part of EC partners brought the project to a dead end. On Italy's Mediterranean policy, see J. Holmes, 'Italy: in the mediterranean, but *of* it?', *Mediterranean Politics*, I (1996), No. 2, pp.

176–192; R. Aliboni, 'Italy and the Mediterranean in the 1990s', in S. Stavridis et al. (eds), *The Foreign Policies of the European Union's Mediterranean States and Applicant Countries in the 1990s* (Basingstoke and London, Macmillan, 1999), pp. 73–97. For an overall assessment cf. M. Dassu', M. De Andreis, 'International institutions and European security: the Italian debate', in M. Carnovale (ed.), *European Security and International Institutions after the Cold War* (New York, St. Martin's Press, 1995), pp. 215–232; G. Bonvicini, 'Regional reassertion: the dilemmas of Italy', in C. Hill (ed.), *The Actors in Europe's Foreign Policy* (London, Routledge, 1996), pp. 91–107; A. Missiroli, 'Italiens aussenpolitik vor und nach Masstricht. Europa als herausforderung und reformzwang', *Aus Politik und Zeitgeschichte*, (1998), No. 28, pp. 27–36.

30 Such economic dynamism and global reach, however, are rarely matched by an adequate public action to safeguard and promote specific interests. For a critical overview see M. Dassu and R. Menotti, 'Made in Italy – il sistema che non c'e'', *Limes*, VI (1998), No. 1, pp. 45–63.

31 On all these points see M. Monti, *Intervista sull'Italia in Europa* (a cura di F. Rampini) (Bari, Laterza, 1998).

32 See e.g. S. Silvestri, 'L'Italia e la difesa comune europea', *Il Mulino/Europa*, II (1995), pp. 76–83; R. Romano, 'La difesa europea e l'impatto sulla politica e sull'industria della difesa italiana', in Bonvicini et al. (eds), *Italia senza Europa?* quot., pp. 62–80; and especially G. Gasparini, 'Politica di sicurezza e nuovo modello di difesa', *IAI Quaderni*, 9, (1999). On the Defence Ministry in specific cf. C. Jean, *Il Ministero della Difesa* (Roma, NIS, 1992); V. Ilari, *Storia Militare della Prima Repubblica 1943–1993* (Ancona, Nuove Ricerche, 1994).

33 See A. Casu (a cura di), *Parlamento e Sicurezza Nazionale* (Ancona, Nuove Ricerche, 1995); *Informazioni AREL*, special issue, (1997), No. 2; A. De Guttry, *Le Missioni delle Forze Armate Italiane Fuori Area* (Milano, Angeli, 1997).

34 See C. Caggiula, R. Benedetti, *Il Ministero degli Affari Esteri* (Roma, NIS, 1992). On the reform proposals see R. Palmieri (a cura di), *Rapporto Preliminare sulle Strutture della Politica Estera Italiana* (Roma, Effepi, 1995).

35 For a summary of the European debate on the issue see A. Missiroli, 'Flexibility and enhanced cooperation after Amsterdam – the prospects for CFSP and the WEU', *The International Spectator*, XXXIII (1998), No. 3, pp. 101–118.

36 Cf. A. Riccardi, *Sant'Egidio, Rome et le Monde* (Paris, Beauchesne, 1996); M. Giro, 'The community of St. Egidio and its peace-making activities', *The International Spectator*, XXXIII (1998), No. 3, pp. 85–100.

6

Spain

Paul Kennedy

Introduction: from 'neutrality' to 'post-neutrality'

The nature of General Franco's regime hindered all Spanish diplomatic efforts aimed at putting a definitive end to Spain's pariah status within the international community. Despite closer ties with the United States, following a 1953 agreement which allowed the US to possess several military, naval and air bases on Spanish soil, and the country's much-trumpeted 'special relationships' with Latin America and the Arab world, which contained little of genuine substance, Spain remained isolated. Although the European Community (EC) deigned to sign a Preferential Trade Agreement with the Franco regime in 1970, full membership, sought by Spain from the early-1960s, was never a realistic prospect before the death of the Dictator in November 1975.

Although some progress was made by the Democratic Centre Union (*Unión de Centro Democrático* (UCD)) government, which governed Spain from 1977 to 1982 – for example, negotiations to join the EC got underway, after some delay, in 1979 – foreign affairs under the UCD always remained subordinate to the priority task of steering the country through its transition to democracy.

Furthermore, UCD foreign policy makers had little practical experience of international affairs, which contributed towards the elaboration of a somewhat quirky foreign policy stance under Adolfo Suárez, the Prime Minister until 1981. Seeking to build on the unpromising legacy of the previous dictatorial regime, Suárez fashioned a neutralist policy that saw Spain participate in the Conference of Non-Aligned Countries in Havana in 1979.

Security concerns were also relegated to a secondary plane before they were given an unexpected prominence by Suárez's UCD successor as Prime Minister, Leopoldo Calvo Sotelo, who hastily secured Spain's membership of North Atlantic Treaty Organisation (NATO) months before losing power at the October 1982 general election.

It was therefore only with the election of the Socialist Party (*Partido Socialista Obrero Español ol* (PSOE)) to office in 1982 that a coherent foreign and security orientation was established. In its manifesto for the election, the PSOE described the UCD's failure to establish and implement a comprehensive and rigorous foreign policy as 'one of Spanish democracy's main shortcomings'.[1] Armed with a convincing electoral mandate the PSOE had a historic opportunity to reshape Spain's external relations and enhance the country's international profile.

The PSOE's own foreign and security policy orientations had evolved somewhat during the transition. Although the neutralist, anti-imperialist tone which had characterised the PSOE's pronouncements during the years immediately after Felipe González's appointment as party leader in 1974 had been moderated by the time that the party reached office, certain vestiges of radicalism remained.

Without doubt the most significant of these elements was the party's opposition to NATO membership. A watershed in this process of de-radicalisation was reached when the party leadership controversially reversed this stance during the PSOE's first term in office (1982–1986). Significantly, European integration was a key factor in the PSOE's *volte-face* on the issue and references to 'Europeanisation'/'modernisation' were a constant refrain in the government's campaign in support of Spain remaining in the Alliance at the referendum which backed the government's stance in March 1986. During the referendum campaign, the government placed little emphasis on defence and security policy concerns, preferring to emphasise the potential political and economic costs of Spanish withdrawal.[2]

Henceforth, the imperatives of European integration established the parameters of the PSOE's foreign and security policy orientation until the party was defeated at the 1996 general election. Key policy aims included efforts aimed at reorientating EC attention towards the two areas of traditional foreign policy concern, the Mediterranean and Latin America; maintaining the flow of European Union (EU) financial transfers to Spain via sources such as the Structural and Cohesion Funds in the context of prospective EU enlargement; and providing support for EU initiatives such as the Common Foreign and Security Policy (CFSP) and the reinforcing of the European pillar of the Atlantic Alliance based on a rejuvenated Western European Union (WEU).

This European-oriented foreign and security policy has continued without major reorientation under the Socialists' Popular Party (*Partido Popular* (PP)) successors in government.

Foreign policy change – adaptation and socialisation

Adaptation through membership

European imperatives provided the PSOE with the ideal justification for policies in both the domestic and foreign policy spheres. However, whereas the tough economic policies applied by the Socialists following their sweeping 1982 general election victory were presented as being necessary if Spain were to gain admission to the EC, any appeal to a link between NATO and EC membership proved far more problematic for the PSOE. The Socialists' apparent opposition to Spanish membership of NATO was one of the chief features of the party's manifesto for the election. Indeed, it has been estimated that the PSOE's pledge to hold a referendum on NATO membership earned the party over a million votes.[3]

However, once in government, the Socialists realised that NATO membership and the fate of Spanish negotiations to join the EC were inextricably linked and, from 1984, the Socialists backed Spain's continued membership of the Alliance, albeit outside the military structure. It may therefore be argued that the prospect of EC membership had a direct impact on the Socialist leadership's stance on NATO. The evolution of the PSOE's position on the issue is studied below.

The end of the Cold War has done much to neutralise anti-NATO feeling and in November 1996, Parliament, including the Socialist opposition, voted overwhelmingly in favour of Spain joining the military structure. Ten years after the referendum, the most controversial foreign policy issue during the Socialists' period in office – the question of Spanish membership of NATO – received relatively scant coverage in the Spanish press, indicating that Spanish membership of the Alliance was no longer a major issue of national debate. The appointment of the Spanish Socialist, Javier Solana, as NATO Secretary-General in December 1995 illustrated the extent to which Spain's position on the Alliance had changed over the decade.

Another important change in Spanish foreign policy, to bring it in line with the EC, was the Socialist government's establishment of diplomatic relations with Israel in 1986, shortly after Spain's entry into the EC. Under Franco, Spanish policy, although lacking in real substance, had been unambiguously pro-Arab, a stance continued by the UCD following the establishment of democracy – for instance, Yasser Arafat visited Adolfo Suárez in Madrid in 1979. During Spain's EC negotiations, the Dutch insisted that a condition of Spain's entry into the EC was an exchange of ambassadors with Israel.

Spain was, in fact, able to remain on good terms with both Arabs and Israelis – as was shown by the choice of Madrid in 1991 to host the Peace Conference on the Middle East which marked the start of the current peace process. Spain has established itself as one of the leading advocates of a more active EU role in the Middle East and it was a Spaniard, Miguel Ángel Moratinos, formerly in charge of the country's Directorate for North African Affairs, who was appointed as the EU's Special Envoy to the Middle East in October 1996.

A further instance in which the Spanish government was able to redefine its stance in a controversial area was on the question of the Western Saharan conflict. Whilst the PSOE had traditionally been a supporter of the Polisario Front, in government the Socialists were able, with the help of the EC's first political declarations on the conflict, to adopt a more moderate stance, thereby enabling Spain to improve relations with Morocco. As Barbé argues, 'European obligations . . . were an excuse for distancing policy from the Polisario Front. Thus the *realpolitik* of the Spanish government, finds in the "European commitment" an excellent alibi before Spanish public opinion [which was favourable to the Polisario Front]'.[4]

In both these areas – Israel and the Western Sahara – the Europeanisation of Spanish policy enabled the government to bring Spanish policy in line with European norms. However, the most glaring example in which EU membership has failed to provide the context for improved relations concerns the thorny question of Gibraltar and British–Spanish relations. Britain had even been prepared to veto Spain's entry into the EC over the question of the blockade of the Rock, which dated back to 1969. The British Foreign Secretary, Robin Cook, threatened to block Spain's military incorporation into NATO in July 1997 on account of Spanish airspace restrictions over Gibraltar. Britain's objections were finally withdrawn at the end of 1998, thereby enabling Spain to become a part of NATO's military structure – fifteen years after Spain joined the Alliance. Bilateral relations therefore retained their capacity to spill over into such a major question as the reform of NATO's military structure.

The British colony's continuing capacity to provoke controversy was once again illustrated by a dispute – ostensibly over Spanish fishing rights in Gibraltarian waters – in early 1999. The stand-off, which led to the temporary closure of the border between the British colony and Spain and the imposition of strict (and extremely time-consuming) border checks on Gibraltarians seeking to enter Spain, brought Anglo-Spanish relations to their lowest point in recent years. Months later, the Aznar government again displayed Spanish sensitivities over the sovereignty of the British colony when it invoked the so-called Luxembourg Compromise, by which an EU Member State can block legislation if it believes its national interests will be threatened. The move came in response to an EU directive that recognised independent Gibraltar authorities.

With respect to the Spanish response to changes in the treaty base of the EU, it is noteworthy that PSOE party documents had long since sought to counterbalance the 'Atlanticist' elements in Spain's security situation by formulating security policy in European terms. In its manifesto for the 1986 general election, the PSOE pledged to 'reinforce the European pillar of security, contributing towards providing Europe with appropriate and agreed mechanisms for the best defence of its interests and specific needs', whilst support was given to moves to provide 'a greater degree of European autonomy in the defence field'.[5] The following year, Felipe González pledged to 'do everything possible in order to reinforce Europe's identity in the field of security'.[6]

As Barbé has commented, the end of the Cold War served to facilitate Spain's participation in the debate on European security,[7] and the PSOE gave its full support to the CFSP as agreed at Maastricht. A year after the Treaty was signed, the PSOE's manifesto for the 1993 general election supported moves to 'progressively endow the European Union with its own identity in the field of security and defence'.[8] The party also argued that:

> 'the WEU after Maastricht is no longer just a European political forum on security matters, but rather is charged by the Treaty on European Union with the elaboration and execution of those decisions of the European Union which have military implications. This will require the strengthening of those structures which will allow the WEU's operational dimension to develop'.[9]

Before leaving office in 1996, the party's 1996 general election manifesto similarly maintained, 'the process of European construction is incomplete until it has a defence dimension. We therefore support the WEU's progressive integration into the European Union'.[10]

In response to a series of written questions prepared by the author in May 1999, Felipe Gonzalez explained his support for a CFSP in the following terms:

> There is no sense in the idea of a purely national foreign policy in the twenty-first century. This is particularly so with regard to security policy. Our frustration with regard to what has happened in the former Yugoslavia allows us to draw the conclusion that we have failed due to a 'lack' of Europe, rather than the opposite. I am aware that our history prevents us from moving rapidly and in unison towards the implementation of the CFSP, and that is why I frequently emphasise the need to adopt specific actions that will allow us to act together, and Yugoslavia, unfortunately, offers us a good example of that type of experience. The solution lies in more Europe, and not, as could be gathered from the Berlin Summit in March 1999, less Europe.

The degree of bi-partisanship on Spanish security policy was illustrated by the PP's manifesto for the 1996 general election, which followed the main lines of policy established by the Socialists. The party argued that:

> 'it is necessary to transform the Western European Union into the European Union's operational defence instrument. In order to bring this about it, is

expedient to draw up a plan which envisages the gradual integration of the WEU into the European Union as it establishes itself as the European pillar of the Atlantic Alliance'.[11]

The major regional parties, most notably the Catalan nationalist Convergence and Union (*Convergència i Unió* (CiU)), echoed this pro-European line. Indeed, the latter provided crucial parliamentary support to the PSOE government of 1993–96; its backing is also required to maintain the current PP government in power. In contrast, the Communist-dominated United Left (*Izquierda Unida* (IU)) upheld its opposition to NATO and opposed the development of the WEU and the creation of armed bodies such as the Eurocorps.[12]

The failure of European states to generate alternative strategies to those of NATO has nevertheless undermined the ability of the WEU to develop into a competitor to the Alliance.[13] Spain nevertheless established itself as being amongst those countries most in favour of a stronger European defence identity.[14]

Socialisation of foreign policy makers

When the Socialists gained office in 1982, their foreign policy stance may be characterised as having two main components – the desire to take the country into the EC and an apparently unequivocal opposition to continued Spanish membership of NATO.[15]

The Socialists' stance on the NATO issue must be viewed in the context of the PSOE's relatively recent clandestine past and the marked anti-Americanism which had been a feature of party rhetoric since the 1953 Madrid Pacts cast the United States in the role of saviour of the Franco regime.

The PSOE had no monopoly in anti-Americanism, which spread 'right across the political spectrum short only of the unreconstructed right'.[16] The PSOE's uncompromising stance on the United States must therefore be viewed as being in line with national sentiment. The majority feeling in Spain, which had been conditioned by resentment at the Franco-sanctioned presence of US military bases on Spanish soil, was that the threat of a Soviet military strike on Spain was non-existent and that membership of the Alliance would actually make the country more, rather than less, vulnerable to attack. In actual fact, anti-Americanism was a more significant factor in Spanish public opinion than anxiety about Soviet military intentions. It affected Spanish attitudes towards international affairs and shaped the public's stance on the question of Spain's membership of NATO. Therefore, whilst all major political forces in Spain had backed European integration, the question of the country's membership of the Alliance proved to be deeply divisive.

However, once in power, the Socialists were persuaded by their European and Alliance partners that, irrespective of the dominance of the

United States, the continent's security depended on NATO. If Spain were to abandon the Alliance, it would also effectively be washing its hands of the key organisation responsible for the EC's security. Within two years of coming to office, Felipe González's U-turn on the issue was well under-way when he argued that, 'if one shares the political, economic and institutional destiny of a group of peoples, logic suggests that one also has to share the destiny of its collective security'.[17] Security issues were there-fore viewed by González as being an essential component in his government's policy of Europeanisation and in the Europe of the mid-1980s that component was based on NATO.

The evolution of the PSOE's security policy was explained in a party document commissioned by the party's Federal Executive Committee. Entitled *Propuesta de una Política de Paz y Seguridad* (Proposal for a Policy of Peace and Security) and issued in December 1985, just three months before the NATO Referendum, the document makes interesting reading. The identification with Europe is striking as the party considers the implications of Spain's departure from NATO:

> Our overall project of European construction would be compromised in all areas, political, economic and as regards matters or, in other words, our acceptance of all the consequences of being in Europe. European countries would view our departure from the Alliance as an unfriendly gesture showing a lack of solidarity.[18]

Socialisation at the hands of Spain's EC and NATO partners had brought about a new appreciation on the part of the Socialist leadership that rights were accompanied by responsibilities, specifically the duty of participating in the EC's security arrangements via NATO. As Marks argues, 'The more Spain became integrated in international organisational frameworks, the more likely its leaders would be exposed to information about the norms and agreements that underpin these organisations, perhaps challenging previous foreign policy beliefs'.[19]

As Felipe González has commented:

> There has never existed any formal link between the two [NATO and EC membership], but it was clear even before we entered the Community that if we wished to be members of the European family in the creation of an economic space it was very difficult not to be similarly engaged in the defence of Europe, which at that time basically centred around NATO; our problem was not one of imposition, but rather one of conviction, of coherence, which became clearer the more we advanced in the integration process and the more the scope of integration grew.[20]

This process of 'Europeanisation' continued to develop after the water-shed year of 1986, during which Spain joined the EC and the Spanish population endorsed the government's stance on NATO in the referen-dum on the issue. In essence, Spain's Socialist government acknowledged that the tension between national and EC interests was a false one. National interest could best be defended by presenting Spanish interests as being in harmony with the interests of the EC as a whole.

The Socialist government therefore gave its support to the Economic and Monetary Union (EMU) project set out in the Maastricht Treaty signed in 1992, albeit with the proviso that financial support be awarded to the Community's poorer members (considered as those countries with a per capita gross domestic product (GDP) of less than 90 per cent of the Community average). González was the main figure behind the establishment of the resulting 'Cohesion Fund' agreed at the Edinburgh Summit in December 1992. Over half of the 15 billion European Currency Units (ECUs) provided for the Fund between 1993 and 1999 went to Spain, with the balance going to Greece, Portugal and Ireland.

The Spanish leadership again took pains to stress that it was in the Community's interest to reduce the regional differences and structural handicaps of the poorer states. Indeed, it was argued that all Member States would benefit in the long-term since economic growth in the poorer Member States would offer improved investment opportunities in expanding markets.

González's stance at Edinburgh marked a defining moment in the Socialists' attitude towards European integration. Whereas Spain had, until that point, been prepared to pursue national interests within the framework of the interests of the Community as a whole, the Socialists' final period in office was notable for a more naked defence of national interests. Concerned that EU expansion would harm Spanish national interests by shifting EU resources away from Southern Europe, González was even prepared to engineer an unlikely alliance with John Major in 1994 on the question of qualified majority voting. As Gillespie argues, 'the fact that Spain stood together with an anti-federalist member like the UK on the issue showed how the defence of national interest now over-shadowed the commitment to European federalism'.[21] Yet this change in tone must not be over-estimated. Despite the considerable strains placed on the Spanish economy by the EMU project, the Socialists never wavered in their commitment to the necessary austerity measures before their defeat at the March 1996 general election.

Despite the fact that, when in opposition, José María Aznar's PP criticised González for going 'cap in hand' to the EU, since becoming Prime Minister in 1996, Aznar has proven himself to be as tenacious in his defence of continued EU financial transfers to Spain as his Socialist predecessor – indeed Spain's position at the 1996 Intergovernmental Conference (IGC) was dominated by the issue. In defending the Spanish stance, Aznar has adopted González's strategy of presenting Spanish demands within the context of overall EU interest. For instance, he defended the deal reached on EU finance at the Berlin Summit in March 1999 as being 'positive for the European Union and for Spain'.[22]

Foreign policy process – domestic and bureaucratic

Domestic factors in the policy process

Since the PP succeeded the PSOE in government, there has been no radical redrawing of Spanish policy, although there has been a change of emphasis in several areas. As we have already seen, the PP took Spain into the military structure within months of gaining office – with the support of the Socialist opposition. This development helped counterbalance the Socialists' European-oriented foreign policy with a more overtly Atlanticist component.

In addition to closer relations with Washington, José María Aznar has also developed a close working relationship with Tony Blair that has caused some chagrin in Spanish Socialist circles.[23] Indeed, both Prime Ministers signed a joint declaration on employment and economic reform at Chequers in April 1999. Whether Blair and Aznar seek to forge an alliance based on the Anglo Saxon-style labour market 'flexibility', which underpins the so-called Third Way as an alternative to the European social market paradigm, remains to be seen.

A second area in which there has been a discontinuation between Socialist and PP policy has concerned relations with Cuba. Following his election victory, José María Aznar attempted to distance his government from the Socialists' relatively close relationship with the island, instead adopting a confrontational stance which led him to propose that the EU exert more pressure on the Castro regime. This change in emphasis led to a diplomatic impasse at the end of 1996 when the Cubans withdrew the Spanish ambassador's credentials.

Despite the PP government's critical stance on Cuba, Aznar nevertheless took pains to stress that not only did he oppose the US Helms–Burton legislation but his government was actually responsible for achieving the EU's joint action against the US proposal.[24] Nevertheless, Aznar's claim that the EU common position on Cuba was due to a Spanish initiative sat rather uncomfortably with the obvious deterioration in Madrid's relations with Havana.

Although relations have since improved, the government was charged with threatening Spain's considerable commercial interests in Cuba as well as compromising Spain's capacity to encourage the Castro regime towards democratic reforms.

It has also been argued that the PP has given less emphasis to Mediterranean policy than the Socialists, for whom the area was a particular concern.[25] The region nevertheless remains an area of strategic importance to Spain.

Finally, the PP government has adopted a far more forthright policy on Gibraltar, as noted above. The former PSOE Foreign Minister, Fernando Morán, shortly before the PP came to power in 1996, predicted that a PP government would pursue a more aggressive policy with regard to the Rock.[26] In the light of the 1999 stand-off, his forecast appears to have been sound.

As regards the impact of non-state actors on policy, the stance of Spain's biggest employers' association, the *Confederación Española de Organizacion es Empresariales* (CEOE) during Spain's EC accession negotiations is worthy of note. Throughout the negotiations, the CEOE's attitude was one of critical support for the government, expressed in the phrase '*si a la adhesión, pero no a cualquier precio*' ('yes to membership, but not at any price'). Despite the CEOE's criticisms of the conditions negotiated by the Socialist government for EC membership, including warnings about the impact of membership on both the industrial and agricultural sectors, it ultimately had little influence on the negotiations. The impact of employers' organisations on foreign policy has since remained no more than marginal.

A greater influence has been exerted by the banking and commercial sectors, which have played an important role in increasing Spain's international presence abroad, particularly in Latin America. Foreign acquisitions in the region by Spanish companies more than tripled in value to US$6.3 billion in 1996; Latin America accounted for 61 per cent of the total investment abroad in the first half of 1997 compared with 34 per cent in the same period of 1996.[27] Following the merger in 1999 between the *Banco Santander* and the *Banco Central Hispano*, the resulting *Banco Santander Central Hispano* (BSCH), Spain's largest bank, became the leading financial group in Latin America.

It may therefore be argued that the banking sector in Spain, generally viewed as being a relatively small-scale player in European terms, has been at the forefront of efforts to establish a higher Spanish profile in the region. Moreover, the sector's efforts have been particularly important given the relative failure of Spanish efforts to promote a more pro-active EU role in the region, as we will see in the final section of this chapter.

Trade unions have generally had little influence on the foreign policy-making process. Both the Socialist Union *General de Trabajadores* (UGT) and the Communist-dominated *Comisiones Obreras* (CCOO) have given their broad support to Spanish European integration, and both have departments responsible for EU affairs. However, the criticism levelled by both trade unions at the possible deflationary aspects of the EMU project have had little tangible effect on government policy.

With respect to Spain's seventeen autonomous communities, it has been argued that Spain's entry into the EC has facilitated the participation of the autonomous communities in the development of foreign policy.[28] It is to be noted that Article 149 of the Constitution awards the central state exclusive competence over several areas, including foreign and security policy. Regional governments nevertheless seek to influence Community decisions both at the domestic and EC level using formal as well as informal channels.[29] The formal opposition of central authorities nevertheless remained strong, and Felipe González stressed that Madrid retained responsibility for foreign affairs throughout his period in office.

García stresses that the participation of the autonomous communities in the decision-making process is not institutionalised and that instruments of collaboration between the state and the autonomous communities have been created more as a response to the external activity of the autonomous communities than as a result of the state's readiness to allow them to participate in the development of foreign policy.[30] The PSOE's reliance on the Catalan nationalists to retain their parliamentary majority between 1993 and 1996, and the PP government's similar dependence after 1996, is nevertheless likely to have strengthened the hand of the autonomous communities at the expense of the centre. Indeed, following the PP's narrow victory, the Catalan Nationalist Party, CiU were able to obtain a representative for the autonomous regions of Spain at the Spanish Permanent Representation in Brussels. Whether moves towards a Europe of the regions also offer the autonomous communities the possibility of a more independent role in international affairs remains to be seen.

Bureaucratic politics in the policy process

The Prime Minister has played a particularly prominent role in the evolution of foreign policy since the death of General Franco. Heywood argues that, as Prime Minister, Adolfo Suárez tended to take the initiative on international matters rather than his foreign affairs minister, Marcelino Oreja.[31] Suárez's UCD successor as Prime Minister, Calvo Sotelo was able to rush through NATO membership during 1981, despite major crises within the ruling party and opposition misgivings, whilst Felipe González further illustrated the political dominance of the Prime Minister when he reversed his own position on the Alliance.[32]

González's particular interest in foreign policy, and in particular European affairs, further reinforced the importance of the Prime Minister in the foreign policy-making process. González's dominance was also underpinned by the fact that the PSOE maintained an absolute majority in Parliament until 1993.

Little criticism of policy was levelled by the PSOE itself, whose role in parliament was more that of a cipher rather than an effective vehicle for critical debate.

Parliamentary opposition to the PSOE was relatively ineffective and in any case muted by the fact that the major political parties were pro-

European. The boom experienced by the Spanish economy between 1986 and 1992 also served to invalidate criticism of further Spanish European integration. Although the deflationary effects of the EMU project were criticised by the leadership of the Communist-dominated *Izquierda Unida* (IU), even that party tempered its disapproval by stressing its overall support for Spanish membership of the EU. Overall, parliamentary scrutiny of European policy making has been negligible.

José María Aznar's role during the diplomatic *imbroglio* with Cuba within months of the PP's general election victory suggest that the power of the Prime Minister in the reassessment of foreign policy positions still remains considerable.

Foreign policy is carried out by the Ministry of Foreign Affairs, under mandate from the Prime Minister, whose control over external affairs is facilitated by his specialised policy staff.[33] Although nearly all the ministries have units dealing with European affairs, the greatest number are located within the Ministry of Foreign Affairs.[34] The Ministry holds meetings with other ministries and seeks to ensure that no single ministry defends its own interests rather than the interests of the country as a whole.[35] The department within this Ministry responsible for coordinating state action in Community institutions is the Secretariat of State for the European Union, which was renamed as the Secretariat of State for Foreign Policy and the EU (SSEU) by the incoming PP government in May 1996. The effect was to widen its remit to include foreign policy as well as the coordination of EU affairs.

The SSEU has a number of working groups, not formally institutionalised, which discuss issues raised at the Council of Ministers at EU level.[36] Officials have been recruited from different ministries, a practice which facilitates coordination due to their direct experience of departments and personal contacts. *Ad hoc*, informal meetings are held with ministerial representatives in the Secretariat, although the formal convocation of coordination meetings is within the framework of the Interministerial Committee for Economic Affairs related to the European Communities chaired by the SSEU.

The Interministerial Committee seeks to achieve a consensus on the issues which have caused conflict between ministries in the working groups, and reach a united policy line to be passed to the EU level, although it has less power than the government's cabinet committees and can only make recommendations. The cabinet always has the last word on controversial issues. The final decision becomes an instruction communicated to the Permanent Representation in Brussels (SPR).

This SPR was set up in 1986 and has the sole right in Brussels to represent Spain and ensure that its interests are defended in all areas of European policy, as well as ensuring that the domestic arena is informed of developments at EU level. The presence of Spanish administrators in

Brussels permits close monitoring of EU policy developments and the establishment of contacts with a wide range of actors. The SPR therefore enjoys a fairly high degree of autonomy in its formulation of the Spanish position. Contact with the International Department of the Prime Minister's Office (*Presidencia del Gobierno*) is essential for the formulation of a strong Spanish position in the most controversial areas. The Prime Minister plays a key coordinating role in the preparation of European Council meetings and high-level policy decisions remain the domain of a small team of expert officials.

Whilst the SSEU has sought to centralise the EU policy-making process as far as possible, ministries active in EU policy have, for their part, attempted to increase their autonomy by maintaining regular contact with sectoral and regional interest groups prior to and during the drafting of directives, and during the formulation of the ministry's position. Although most of the central ministries are involved in EU policies, the most active players in the EU arena include, in addition to the Ministry of Foreign Affairs, the ministries of Economy and Financial Affairs; Industry and Energy; Public Works; Transport and Environment; Agriculture, and Health and Consumer Affairs.[37]

It is nevertheless important to stress the continued centralisation of the policy process around the Prime Minister, who remains the key figure in the field of foreign affairs. Even so, the relative importance of the SSEU is indicated by the fact that Carlos Westendorp, Foreign Minister in Felipe González's last cabinet, had previously been Secretary of State for European Affairs, whilst a previous incumbent, Pedro Solbes, was Finance Minister in the same cabinet. Even before Spanish accession was agreed, Leopoldo Calvo Sotelo, Prime Minister between 1981 and 1982, had previously served as Minister for EC relations under Adolfo Suárez.

Foreign policy actions – with or without the EU?

With the EU: constriction or opportunity?

The presentation of difficult foreign and security policy issues in terms of European commitments suggests that the Spanish leadership considered this 'Europeanist' approach as an opportunity of retaining the support of the population. The anti-Americanism referred to above is of interest here. Spanish public opinion favoured a 'European identity' in the foreign and security field so as to reduce reliance on the US. A Eurobarometer poll in 1993 indicated that 71 per cent of Spaniards favoured the creation of a European defence system.[38]

The public's endorsement of such an identity was useful to the government during the Gulf War when it is recalled that public opinion was broadly opposed to direct Spanish involvement in the Gulf War, with polls indicating that over two-thirds of the population were against the conflict.[39] Spain's long history of international isolation and general pro-Arab feeling in Spain were also important factors. Only after the War ended were the Spanish people informed that Spain had been the single most important European platform for the launch of US bombing raids on Iraq. The 'Europeanisation' of Spanish foreign and security policy therefore facilitated the government's task of 'selling' difficult policy decisions to the Spanish public.

The government therefore chose to present its participation in the conflict as an aspect of Spain's European obligations, much as the PSOE had defended Spain's continued membership of NATO during the referendum campaign in 1986. The strategy appeared to work: at the end of the Gulf War, an opinion poll indicated that 62 per cent of the public supported the government's role during the conflict.[40] Once again, European integration provided the PSOE with the ideal means with which to present controversial policy options to a public with a distinctively isolationist viewpoint which nevertheless identified with the PSOE's key policy of using the European integration project to modernise the country. As Marks argues, 'similar to the way that González defended his decision to support continued membership of NATO, his analysis of the Gulf War situation was framed by the wider process of European integration in its many aspects'.[41]

European integration therefore provided the PSOE with the ideal framework on which to elaborate a more coherent national security policy. As the Socialist government's perception of Spain's relationship to European security developed, it advocated Spain's remaining in NATO, and involved itself in those institutional developments which favoured a European security policy identity, the WEU and the CFSP. This institutional progression brought about a policy more in line with European security norms which was also capable of satisfying Spain's international obligations, as well as maintaining public support.

However, despite the presentation of Spanish military action abroad as being a function of its obligations to the EU, and, during the Kosovo conflict, to NATO, policy still remains constrained by a general mood of public reluctance to get involved in international conflicts. Opinion polls during NATO's bombing raids against Yugoslavia during the Kosovo conflict indicated that less than a third of Spaniards supported the campaign. Although a small number of Spanish military aircraft were involved in the NATO operation, José María Aznar was just as relieved to see an end to the military campaign as Felipe González had been during the Gulf War.

Spain's participation in UN peace-keeping operations have found far greater favour with the public and have also served to enhance the country's international standing, which has also been underpinned by Spain's enthusiastic support for the more integrationist aspects of the

European project. Spanish enthusiasm has enabled Spain to steal a march on Italy (more concerned with its own domestic political crisis during the first half of the 1990s) in recent years with regard to areas of interest such as the Mediterranean. Indeed, Barbé suggests that 'the high-profile role of Spain in the Middle East and as lobbyist for the Euro-Mediterranean Partnership, leads one to wonder if the EU–Mediterranean lobby has a leader, playing a similar role to that of Germany in its support of Central and Eastern Europe'.[42] Indeed, throughout the 1990s, Spain has arguably been the most prominent member of the EU's Mediterranean lobby, which also includes France and Italy.

However, as has already been noted, the PP under José María Aznar has chosen to adopt a far lower profile in the region than its Socialist prede-cessor, and it remains to be seen whether the Euro-Mediterranean Conference of 1995 will prove to be the high-water mark of Spanish diplomacy in the Mediterranean.

Spanish success in promoting greater EU interest in the other tradi-tional area of Spanish foreign policy interest, Latin America, has been more limited as we will see in the following section. Spanish disap-pointment at the relatively modest improvements in the EU's relationship with Latin America was exacerbated by the fact that, when Spain joined, the European Commission had highlighted Spanish ties with the region as being one of the most valuable aspects of the 1986 enlargement. Indeed, Spain's Accession Treaty contained a protocol recognising Spain's particular interest in Latin America as well as a clear declaration on the need to intensify the relationship between the Community and Latin America.[43]

Spain has also established itself as being the most influential of the four Member States in receipt of EU transfers via the Cohesion Fund, itself created on the initiative of Felipe González. Spain's championing of the rights of the four poorest Member States has continued under José María Aznar.

The ability of a middle-ranking country like Spain to 'punch above its economic weight' in the field of foreign affairs has found expression in the number of Spaniards appointed to leading roles in international organisations in recent years: Javier Solana – NATO Secretary-General prior to taking up his post in charge of the EU's CFSP at the end of 1999; Carlos Westendorp – International High Representative for Bosnia; Felipe González – Special Representative of the Organisation for Security and Cooperation in Europe (OSCE) and the EU for Yugoslavia; Miguel Ángel Moratinos – Special EU Envoy for the Middle East; and José María Gil Robles – President of the European Parliament from 1997 to 1999.

Without the EU: special relationships and special interests

Latin America and the Mediterranean are the two traditional areas of Spanish foreign and security policy concern. Although the Franco regime made much of its links with these two regions, the substance of these ties was more rhetorical than real. UCD governments made little progress in altering this situation. The Socialists' strategy on both regions was to foster bilateral and EU-based links and during Spain's two Presidencies of the EU (in 1989 and 1995), Spain endeavoured to place both areas more firmly on the EU agenda, albeit with mixed success.

Spain attaches particular importance to the Maghreb and it is no coincidence that both Felipe González and his successor as Prime Minister, José María Aznar, chose to visit Morocco as their first official overseas visit. Although relations between Spain and Morocco have never been easy, Spain has a significant economic interest in the country. Spain's exports to Morocco represented just over 4 per cent of Spanish total exports in 1994 – about the same as Spain's total exports to the whole of Latin America.

In addition, Spanish advocacy of increased EU financial aid to Morocco, and the other Maghreb countries, at a time when the EU was switching its attention to Central and Eastern Europe, has been much appreciated by the Moroccan authorities. In this respect, Spain's appeal from within the EU for greater European commitment to the region has contributed to improved relations between Spain and Morocco in recent years.

Spain and other Southern European countries view the Mediterranean as an area of strategic concern not just to the southern flank of the continent, but also to the EU as a whole. Concerns about demographic pressures and possible mass immigration are particularly acute. The fact that unemployment on the Southern shore of the Mediterranean has risen by around 50 per cent in the last decade, against an average rise of just 9 per cent inside the EU during the same period, has done little to soothe European anxieties.

Spain's emergence as an influential player in the Mediterranean became particularly apparent at the start of the 1990s when, together with Italy, Spain proposed a Conference on Security and Co-operation in the Mediterranean. The initiative floundered in the context of the outbreak of the Gulf War. Spain nevertheless maintained its profile in the region by successfully hosting the Middle East Peace Conference in 1991, which marked the start of the current peace process.

The Euro–Mediterranean Conference held in Barcelona during Spain's Presidency of the EU in 1995 underlined Spain's role as an advocate for EU engagement in the region. Felipe González himself considered that the process of cooperation in the Mediterranean that emerged at Barcelona marked the high point of Spain's contribution towards an improved

EU–Mediterranean relationship.[44] Generally considered to be a success, the Conference enabled an agreement to be reached on the gradual introduction of a free trade area in industrial goods by the year 2010.

Developments since the Conference nevertheless suggest that there has been a failure to maintain the momentum provided by Barcelona. The Second Euro-Mediterranean Conference held in Malta in April 1997, which failed to produce a Final Declaration and the Third Conference, held in Stuttgart in April 1999, reinforced the impression that the Mediterranean had started to slip down the agendas of both the EU and Spain.

As for Spain's handling of the Presidency as a whole, the country's international projection was undoubtedly enhanced.[45] Speaking in the debate on the Spanish Presidency in the European Parliament in January 1996, the leader of the Socialist Group stated:

> For the last six months the talk has not been of a closed and shuttered European Union worrying about threats, threatening exclusions and closing borders, but rather a European Union looking to work with our neighbours, helping to sustain, to develop and to encourage and it is the Spanish Presidency which has developed that approach and which deserves our thanks.[46]

More generally, during the 1990s, Spain was able, in the context of the end of the Cold War, to secure an influential role within the EU's pro-Mediterranean lobby and to promote a more effective EU strategy towards the region that would address the concerns of Spanish foreign and security policy. This strategy had two components: first, to convince its EU colleagues that the socio-economic security of the EU's southern flank depends on the fostering of economic prosperity in the region, and secondly, to encourage the EU to acknowledge that the problems posed by the region have broader implications for the EU as a whole.

The Socialists were therefore able to make use of the EU as a 'vehicle' for their policy aims which was many times more effective than any unilateral Spanish initiative could realistically hope to be. The EU provided the means to support Spanish regional foreign policy aims which Spain could not effectively implement on its own. This 'Europeanisation' of Spanish policy in the region nevertheless did not preclude the cultivation of existing bilateral relations with countries of the region. Most notably, throughout the Gulf War, Spanish diplomacy maintained a close dialogue with the countries of the Maghreb in an effort to explain Spanish policy and avoid deterioration in bilateral relations.

This development, the intensification of existing relations with the Arab nations of the region, and Spain's increasing awareness of its key geo-strategic position in the Western Mediterranean all contributed towards Spain's emergence as an influential player in the region capable of shaping

EU policy during the 1990s. In its programme for the 1982 general election, the PSOE had ambitiously proposed 'a Mediterranean policy which will enable Spain, as a top-ranking power in the region, to play an active role in harmonising the interests of countries on both rims of the Mediterranean'.[47] Thirteen and a half years later, when the Socialists left office, they could justifiably claim to have achieved considerable success in realising this aim, having given Spain a more assertive profile within the EU as one of the most innovative countries on Mediterranean foreign policy and security issues.

Whilst the PP government has adopted a less prominent stance with regard to the Mediterranean, it has nevertheless allied itself with Spain, France, Italy and Portugal against the proposal made by Germany, the United Kingdom and Belgium that the meetings of EU and Mediterranean Foreign Ministers, agreed at the Barcelona Conference in 1995, be held every two years rather than annually. The tension between the Mediterranean lobby and those Member States whose policy positions focus on Eastern Europe will doubtless remain a key issue as enlargement to the East approaches.

The Spanish position on Latin America has been more equivocal. Despite the Socialist government's undoubted interest in Central America, particularly during the early 1980s, it must nevertheless be noted that Spanish policy towards the region always remained subordinate to what was viewed as being the more important foreign and security policy goals defined by the Euro-Atlantic system. This stance required the Socialists to make a realistic appraisal of US hegemony in the region, whilst accepting the limitations of the EC as an independent international actor. Strident Socialist criticism of US policy in the region therefore gave way to a more muted attitude, a process that was facilitated by the lessening of tension in the region during the 1990s. Overly ambitious hopes of employing the EU as a more effective surrogate for Spanish policy aims were scaled down as the Socialists recognised that whilst the Community had an interest in institutionalising relations with the countries of the region, its financial commitment remained modest.

It was a pattern that would be repeated with regard to EC policy to Latin America as a whole. The Socialists left office in 1996 having gained a far more realistic appreciation of their capacity to shape EU policy towards a region of the world that did not feature amongst the Union's priority areas of concern.[48] Although the Socialists lobbied for increased political and economic dialogue between the EU and Latin America, with Spain contributing towards the achievement of a number of measures advantageous to Latin America, the EU's commitment to the region remained limited.

Whilst the Socialists enjoyed a significant input into the elaboration of EU policy towards the Mediterranean, a region considered as a key area of economic and strategic concern to the EU, their efforts to do the same in Latin America were frustrated by the EU's marginal interest in the region. As Hazel Smith has argued, despite predictions by some sectors of European and Latin American opinion, Spain has not evolved as a significant political interlocutor for Latin America.[49] In this context, European policy was an inadequate instrument for the implementation of Spanish foreign policy aims in the region.

This situation nevertheless did not preclude significant bilateral action outside the framework provided by the EU. Indeed, it can be argued that, having accepted the limitations of the EU as an actor in the region, the Socialists had some success in pursuing a more autonomous policy in the region that more adequately served Spanish policy aims. Conscious that Spain's own interests in Latin America could only be met by significantly increasing its economic presence in the region, the Socialists enjoyed considerable success in raising Spain's profile as the country emerged as the second largest investor in Latin America between 1990 and 1994 and the highest in 1995 and 1996, according to the Inter-American Development Bank.[50]

Outside the framework provided by the EU, the Spain has played a key role in the Latin American Community of Nations (Comunidad Iberoamericana de Naciones) which groups together the twenty-one Spanish- and Portuguese-speaking countries of the American continent, in addition to Spain and Portugal. Annual Community Summits attended by Heads of State and Government began in 1991. Although the summits have failed to obtain much of real significance, they have nevertheless provided a forum for the exchange of views between Member States on difficult issues such as Cuba.

It is nevertheless important not to overemphasise the importance of the Spanish–Latin American relationship. Just as the Socialists and their PP successors in government have not viewed Latin America as being the main focus of foreign policy, neither did Latin America view the EU as being a priority concern, and even less so Spain itself. Spain's foreign policy imperatives remained within the framework set by Spain's European orientation, just as Latin American countries concentrated on regional integration initiatives such as the Common Market of the Southern Cone (Argentina, Brazil, Paraguay, Uruguay) (MERCOSUR) (with whom the EU signed a trade and economic cooperation agreement in December 1995 during the Spanish Presidency of the EU)[51] and the retention of strong links with the region's key trading partner, the United States.

Spain's development of links with Latin America – whether within the framework of the EU or on a more autonomous basis – did not alter the basic fact that the country's future lay within the parameters set by Europe, thereby effectively relegating the Latin American element within

Spanish foreign policy to a secondary plane. We might conclude that a more realistic policy towards the region has been developed, based on national rather than European policy.

Conclusion

European integration had a decisive influence on Spanish foreign and security policy orientations, providing Spanish governments with the ideal template with which to provide Spain with a coherent national foreign and security policy more in line with that of the EU as a whole. Certainly, 'Europeanisation' effectively put the final nail in the coffin of the patronising notion of Spain being 'different', a concept fostered by the Franco regime. European integration therefore enabled the foreign and security component of Spain's transition to democracy to be completed.

This approach gained the support of the vast majority of the Spanish people, who identified with the utilisation of European integration as the key element in the all-embracing policy/*leitmotif* of 'modernisation' that has been a feature of post-Francoist Spain

In the security field the PSOE's Europeanist strategy entailed the party's embrace of the NATO Alliance, and the integration of Spain into the other chief instruments of European defence, the WEU and EPC/CFSP. Having formalised the country's security situation, the Socialists then chose to present Spain's controversial involvement in the Gulf War in terms of its European security obligations, a strategy viewed as being the best means of retaining the support of a sceptical public.

With regard to foreign policy, the priority awarded by the PSOE to European imperatives effectively subordinated the two traditional regions of Spanish policy concern, the Mediterranean and Latin America. Whilst European integration provided the PSOE with the opportunity to place both regions more firmly on the EU agenda, results were mixed. With respect to the Mediterranean, the effectiveness of the Socialists' advocacy of a more pro-active EU role in the region was enhanced by the fact that they were able to combine their efforts with those of an already existing Mediterranean lobby within the EU. The utilisation of the EU as a vehicle for Spanish policy aims in the region was therefore a realistic strategy. No similar Latin American lobby existed within the EU, forcing the PSOE to make a pragmatic appraisal of its limited capacity to influence EU policy in a region considered to be of secondary importance to the Union. The Socialists' response was to place more emphasis on the development of bilateral relations, a strategy that met with some success as Spain established itself as a major source of investment in the subcontinent.

Foreign policy under the Socialists' PP successors, whilst retaining its European focus, has been notably less dramatic, with less emphasis on ostentatious initiatives such as the Euro-Mediterranean Conference and a greater concentration on the protection of Spanish interests in the context of EU enlargement towards Central and Eastern Europe. Policy since 1996 has therefore been notable for being both more low-key, with regard to Spain's position on the world stage, and more pragmatic, with respect to the Aznar government's greater readiness to present its positions in terms of Spanish national interests.

Overall, democratic Spain has proven itself to be a relatively quick learner in the field of foreign and security policy. Its significant contribution and commitment to the general development of European integration has left the country well-positioned for the challenges of the new millennium. A quarter of a century after the death of General Franco, Spain can consider itself as an established middle-ranking power which enjoys considerable international prestige. More than any other factor, European integration provided the catalyst for this remarkable transformation.

Notes

1 PSOE, *Programa Electoral* (Madrid, PSOE, 1982), p. 45.
2 P. Heywood, *The Government and Politics of Spain* (Houndmills, Macmillan, 1995), p. 267.
3 Heywood, *Government and Politics*, p. 266.
4 E. Barbé, 'Spain: The uses of foreign policy cooperation' in C. Hill (ed.), *The Actors in Europe's Foreign Policy* (London, Routledge, 1996), p. 122.
5 PSOE, *Programa Electoral* (Madrid, PSOE, 1986), p. 113.
6 F. González, 'A new international role for a modernizing Spain' in R. Clark and M. Haltzel (eds), *Spain in the 1980s: The Democratic Transition and a New International Role* (Cambridge Mass, Ballinger, 1987), p. 187.
7 Barbé, 'Spain', p. 120.
8 PSOE, *Programa Electoral* (Madrid, PSOE, 1993), p. 93.
9 PSOE, *33 Congreso. Resoluciones* (Madrid, PSOE, 1994), pp. 120–121.
10 PSOE, *Programa Electoral* (Madrid, PSOE, 1996), p. 203.
11 Partido Popular, *Programa Electoral* (Madrid, Partido Popular, 1996), p. 229.
12 Izquierda Unida, *Programa Elecciones Generales* (Madrid, Izquierda Unida, 1996), p. 279.
13 W. Rees, *The Western European Union at the Crossroads* (Oxford, Westview, 1998), p. 81.
14 In response to a series of written questions sent by the author in May 1999, Felipe González commented that he did not envisage a WEU independent of the EU in the medium term.
15 C. del Arenal and F. Aldecoa (eds), *España y la OTAN. Textos y Documentes* (Madrid, Tecnos, 1986), pp. 315–316.
16 G. Treverton, 'Spain, the United States, and NATO: strategic facts and political realities' in F. Gil and J. Tulchin (eds), *Spain's Entry into NATO* (Boulder, Lynne Reiner, 1988), p. 126.
17 J. Yáñez-Barnuevo and A. Viñas, 'Diez Años de política exterior del gobierno socialista (1982–1992)' in A. Guerra and J. Tezanos (eds), *La Década del*

   Cambio. Diez Años de Gobierno Socialista, 1982–1992 (Madrid, Sistema, 1992), p. 98.

18 del Arenal & Aldecoa (eds), *España y la OTAN*, p. 360.

19 M. Marks, *The Formation of European Policy in Post-Franco Spain* (Aldershot, Avebury, 1997), p. 33.

20 Comments in response to a series of written questions submitted by the author in May 1999.

21 R. Gillespie, 'The Spanish socialists' in R. Gillespie, F. Rodrigo and J. Story (eds) *Democratic Spain: Reshaping external relations in a changing world* (London, Routledge, 1995), p. 163.

22 *El País* (International Edition), 30 March 1999, p. 23.

23 See Will Hutton, 'Now Spanish socialists know how British socialists feel', *The Observer*, 18 April 1999.

24 Quoted in *El País* (International Edition), 25 November 1996, p. 11.

25 R. Gillespie, 'Spanish protagonismo and the Euro-Med partnership initiative', *Mediterranean Politics*, 2:1 (1997), p. 45; *Anuario El País 1998*, p. 96.

26 Interview with the author.

27 W. Chislett, *The Central Hispano Handbook: Spain 1998* (Madrid, Banco Central Hispano, 1998), p. 59.

28 C. García, 'The autonomous communities and External Relations' in R. Gillespie, F. Rodrigo and J. Story (eds), *Democratic Spain*, p. 138.

29 F. Morata, 'Spain' in D. Rometsch and W. Wessels (eds), *The European Union and Member States* (Manchester, Manchester University Press, 1996), p. 145.

30 C. García, 'The autonomous communities', p. 128.

31 Heywood, *Government and Politics*, p. 262.

32 P. Heywood, 'Governing a new democracy: the power of the prime minister in Spain', *West European Politics*, 14:2 (1991), p. 112.

33 Gillespie, Rodrigo and Story (eds), *Democratic Spain*, p. 204.

34 M. Newton with P. Donaghy, *Institutions of Modern Spain* (Cambridge, Cambridge University Press, 1996), p. 329.

35 Newton with Donaghy, *Institutions of Modern Spain*, p. 330.

36 For the following section on the Secretariat of State for Foreign Policy and the EU (SSEU), the Interministerial Committee and the Spanish Permanent Representation, I owe a special debt to Rachel Jones' *An Analysis of State Autonomy in Spanish European Policy-Making during EC Accession Negotiations and EC/EU Membership*, unpublished PhD thesis, Loughborough University, 1999.

37 Morata, 'Spain', p. 145.

38 E. Barbé, 'European political cooperation. The upgrading of Spanish foreign policy' in Gillespie, Rodrigo and Story (eds), *Democratic Spain*, p. 119.

39 J. Hooper, *The New Spaniards* (Harmondsworth, Penguin, 1995), p. 105.

40 C. Alonso Zaldívar and M. Castells, *España, Fin de Siglo* (Madrid, Alianza, 1992), p. 215.

41 Marks, *Formation*, p. 109.

42 E. Barbé, 'Balancing Europe's eastern and southern dimensions' in J. Zielonka (ed.), *Paradoxes of European Foreign Policy* (The Hague, Kluwer Law International, 1998), p. 124.

43 Juan Pablo de Laiglesia, 'Las relaciones entre la Europa de los doce y América Latina. Un proceso de cambio acelerado' *Pensamiento Ibérico*, 13 (1988) p. 139.

44 Comments in response to a series of written questions submitted by the author in May 1999.

45 For an analysis of Spain's Presidency of the EU, see P. Kennedy, 'Spanish European policy and the 1995 presidency', *CMS Occasional Paper*, No. 17 (Bristol, Centre for Mediterranean Studies, 1998).

46 Quoted in Kennedy, 'Spanish European policy', p. 11.

47 PSOE, *Programa Electoral* (Madrid, PSOE, 1982), p. 46.

48 Felipe González has argued that, 'Today it can be clearly stated that the European Union has a distinct policy with regard to Latin America, about which we can be rightly satisfied, even though there still remain several areas which might be improved'. Comments in response to a series of written questions submitted by the author in May 1999.

49 H. Smith, 'Actually existing foreign policy – or not? The EU in Latin and Central America' in J. Peterson and H. Sjursen (eds), *A Common Foreign Policy for Europe* (London, Routledge, 1998), p. 166.

50 W. Chislett, *The Central Hispano Handbook 1997* (Banco Central Hispano, Madrid, 1997), p. 62.

51 Argentinean President Carlos Menem acknowledged the key role played by the Spanish government in the brokering of the deal, *El País* (International Edition), 18 December 1995, p. 9.

7

Belgium and the Netherlands

Rik Coolsaet and Ben Soetendorp

Introduction

The support of Belgium and the Netherlands for European cooperation efforts goes back as far as the inter-war period. From the 1950s onwards, they have been two small European countries at the core of European integration. Both countries thus have a long record of active support for supranational arrangements within the European Economic Community (EEC), the European Community (EC) and the European Union (EU). One should therefore expect that the two countries would be quite happy to adapt their foreign policy to that of the EU as a whole – whether through the former European Political Cooperation (EPC) and the current Common Foreign and Security Policy (CFSP) – even if this means the loss of national autonomy in the conduct of their own foreign policy. Indeed whether such an impact on the foreign and security policy of the two countries has transpired is the central question which we address in this chapter from two different national perspectives.

Foreign policy change – adaptation and socialisation

Before the Netherlands and Belgium joined the EEC as two of the six founding Member States, the Atlantic Alliance, and the North Atlantic Treaty Organisation (NATO) in particular, was for both countries the main point of reference in the conduct of their foreign policy. Dutch and Belgian EEC membership, and their participation in the EPC, have not really changed this fundamental pattern of the foreign policy behaviour of both countries. For many years successive governments in Belgium and the Netherlands managed to reconcile the two conflicting loyalties to NATO and the EEC by making a distinction between the countries' membership of the EC and their participation in NATO. While the EC membership served their economic interests, NATO membership provided the countries the necessary security. In this way support for the ultimate goal of a federal Europe had never to be at the expense of being a faithful ally within the Atlantic Alliance.

When the EC members started to deal with foreign policy issues in the early 1970s within the EPC framework, Dutch foreign policy makers insisted on keeping security matters out of the EPC agenda to avoid any conflict of interest between the EC and NATO. The Dutch attempt to integrate the CFSP into the institutional framework of the EU during the intergovernmental negotiations on the Maastricht Treaty represents, therefore, on first sight, a basic change in the former Dutch foreign policy pattern. However, closer examination of the Dutch endeavour illustrates that it simply originated from the Dutch conviction that the creation of the EU offered a unique opportunity to bring about a merger between the EC's economic external relations and the EPC. This would have caused a unitary institutional structure instead of two separate institutional frameworks for the external economic relations and the EPC. Moreover, the Dutch support for the revival of the Western European Union (WEU), to serve as the defence arm of the EU and the building of a European Security and Defence Identity (ESDI), has more to do with the removal of the Soviet threat which has changed the entire European security environment. A revised NATO remains the cornerstone of Dutch security, as the most recent 'policy paper' on Dutch defence policy indicates.[1]

Compared to the Netherlands, at the end of the 1960s and the beginning of the 1970s, Belgium was much more outspoken in its pursuit of détente between the East and West. One of the arguments used at the time was that détente would provide for a more favourable environment for a more autonomous European role in world affairs. The latter, in turn, was considered necessary in view of the American involvement in Vietnam and the unilateral American dollar policy that led to the demise of the Bretton Woods system between 1971 and 1973.

The Treaty of Maastricht, as well as the expected enlargement of the EU, brought some modifications in the traditional policies of both countries towards the EU itself and towards other Member States. These modifications were somewhat different in both countries. The Netherlands, like Belgium, has traditionally resisted tendencies within the EU to establish institutional structures that would erode the principle of supranationality. The Netherlands, as mentioned above, campaigned for a supranational Union when it presided over the last stage of the intergovernmental negotiations concerning the Maastricht Treaty. But it took a more realistic attitude towards the basically intergovernmental decision-making structure of the CFSP, when it chaired, as President-in-office, the final intergovernmental negotiations over the Treaty of Amsterdam in 1997. Particularly significant in this connection is the fact that the Dutch government has actually given up its traditional strategy of arguing in favour of supranationalism to escape a *directoire* of the larger states and accommodated itself to the coalition building realities that operate within the EU. In an enlarged EU the Netherlands clearly wants to be part of the core, grouped around the French–German tandem. This has the consequence that the Netherlands pursues a good understanding with the French–German axis instead of ganging up against it, even if this is at the expense of the traditional support for Anglo-American positions.

Belgium has remained quite 'orthodox' and rather unswerving in its original European orientation. Despite the fact that the end of the 1980s saw an adherence to diverging opinions among the Belgian political elite, the government positioned itself as a advocate of a more forceful European player in defence matters, even if that were to be realised at the expense of NATO primacy. This was demonstrated both in the discussions concerning the second pillar in the Maastricht Treaty (and its WEU annex), and in the Belgian advocacy of a WEU-led operation in the Yugoslavian civil war. In the event, the latter was cancelled in September 1991 as a result of the opposition of a rather small number of more Atlantic-oriented countries, including the Netherlands and the UK.[2]

After nearly thirty years of cooperating with the other EU Member States within the EPC and CFSP frameworks, Dutch and Belgian foreign policy makers have fully internalised the habits of working together. This relates not only to the practice of informing and consulting each other on international issues, but also to the definition of Dutch and Belgian foreign policy positions in terms of agreed European common positions. Dutch and Belgian foreign policy makers still try to convince their partners to accept their views on certain foreign policy issues during the political decision-making process leading to such a common position. But once agreement on a common position has been reached both governments will adopt it as their own national position. Any attempt of 'going alone', where preference is given to a national position over a common European position, is out of the question.

In this respect it should be mentioned that Dutch foreign policy makers have always been reluctant to argue in terms of 'egoistic' narrow national interests.[3] They prefer to define the national interest in a broader sense and to see it as serving a greater good. Thus, promoting an international legal order is a declared long-term crucial foreign policy goal, while the preservation of the national level of prosperity is considered to be a short-term vital national interest. Being a small trading nation Dutch policy makers have actually always regarded a stable international legal order a basic precondition for achieving prosperity. This notion is re-emphasised in a recent review of Dutch foreign policy that says that promoting such a global interest does not imply that the government has lost sight of its own national interests and its duty to represent the concrete interests of individuals and companies abroad.[4] European integration, for example, has advanced peace and stability in Europe but also serves Dutch interests

both in Europe as worldwide. It has boosted Dutch trade with its EU partners and has strengthened the economic role of the country as an
international transit and distribution centre.

Enlightened self-interest was a primary source for the original European
orientation of Belgium during the inter-war years. This also continued to
be the driving force in the current definition of the Belgian position on
European matters. Membership of the EC/EU is seen as a means of reducing the power and influence of the great Member States over the smaller
states, thus enhancing the relative weight of the smaller Member States in
the decision-making process. In the economic as well as in the CFSP
domain, Belgium uses its EU membership as a means of levelling the
playing field. This explains the outspoken Belgian hostility towards the
idea of 'Contact Groups' or *directoires* of the greater Member States,
which hollows out CFSP policy making.[5] Belgium has endorsed, reluctantly, the possible future concept of a core Europe, since this might be
the only alternative to a Europe *à la carte*. The latter form of European
construction is considered to be detrimental to the influence the smaller
states acquired laboriously through the institutional set-up of the EC/EU.
The renewed 'agressive bilateralism', which seems to be growing lately in
the external commercial and economic policies of some countries, is still
largely absent in Belgium.

In contemporary Belgium, and as a consequence of domestic political
and constitutional rearrangements, with the advocation of an increased
role for the sub-state units (Flanders, Wallonia and Brussels), Europe is
considered a convenient and comfortable terminal station for the successive state reform efforts in Belgium. As Europe takes over many of the
functions of the central Belgian state, and others are being devolved to the
sub-state political actors, an ideal scenario is thus presented for coping
with tensions rising from the perceived diverging interests and policies of
the constituent communities. According to opinion polls[6] and academic
research[7] this scenario, however, is a view held by a minority of the public
at large, both in Flanders and in Wallonia; among political elite on the
other hand, especially at the (sub-)state level, it is endorsed quite strongly.

The foreign policy process – domestic and bureaucratic

Although European integration in general, and the CFSP in particular, is
still an undisputed issue in domestic Dutch political debate, in recent years
some Dutch politicians have become much more reluctant to transfer
national sovereignty in the area of foreign policy to the EU.[8] These political leaders have began to express some second thoughts about how far
European integration should go, especially in an enlarged Union where
the Netherlands is one of the twenty to twenty-six members. The cautious
attitude is echoed in the reluctance of some Dutch political leaders to give

up veto power in CFSP matters. It is also reflected in their opposition to replace the Presidency by a directorate which would secure the involvement of the larger states in CFSP matters. Since this would probably imply that the Netherlands would have to rotate with the other two Benelux countries in such a directorate, the Netherlands would not always be present at the making of decisions that might touch upon vital Dutch interests.[9]

The Dutch government, for its part, has not openly adopted such a position, and basically holds the view that the only way to defend Dutch interests is to be present when decisions are taken. It realises that institutional innovations, that would lead to more efficiency in EU decision making in an enlarged Union, are inescapable. However, in an attempt to limit the extension of the powers of the large states at the expense of the smaller members, the Dutch government has suggested to replace the Presidency by a team of Member States so that both large and smaller Member States will have more opportunities to sit behind the 'driving wheel' of the Union. In a Union of twenty members each Member State would have to wait under the current system ten years before it can act as President-in-office. The government also believes that qualified majority voting contributes to the effectiveness of decision making and has to be applied to most policy areas, including at some point the CFSP, before the round of enlargement. To appease its domestic opponents, the government demands a larger number of votes in the event a reallocation of votes takes place. The Dutch government has already tried to do so during the intergovernmental negotiations over the Treaty of Amsterdam and it will certainly repeat its demand for a larger number of votes during the next revision of the current institutional arrangements within the EU.

One of the most basic institutional changes Belgium seeks in the European integration process is the substitution of the unanimous decision making in the Council for qualified majority voting. This includes the CFSP, where Belgium hopes to gradually achieve the same decision-making procedures as in the first pillar. This emphasis follows from the original Belgian objective of European integration, namely reducing the power of the larger neighbouring states, even at the expense of one's own right of veto.

Dutch membership of the EC/EU had almost no impact on the way the making of Dutch foreign policy making is organised. The two basic principles underlying governmental policy making in the Netherlands, namely, departmental autonomy and collective decision making in the Dutch Council of Ministers, have determined the making of the country's foreign policy throughout the long period of membership. As a consequence of the Dutch adherence to the principle of departmental autonomy, it is not the foreign ministry but the responsible ministry that deals with the relevant issue in the EU or any other international organisation. In 1972 the foreign ministry was given the leading role in the preparation and formulation of the national negotiation position on EC/EU matters in the Council of Ministers. It is also the State Secretary for European Affairs, located in the foreign ministry and supported by its officials, who chairs the crucial meetings of the inter-ministerial Coordination Committee for European Integration where the negotiation positions are drafted. But the preparation of these drafts actually remains within the specialised ministry. This means that in practice the foreign ministry, besides its overall responsibility for the preparation of a coherent Dutch negotiation position, carries the sole responsibility only for CFSP issues. But even here it has to share this responsibility with the ministry of defence when the concerned issue involves security matters. Despite the increased involvement of the Prime Minister in the framing of the CFSP, as a consequence of the Prime Minister's participation in the European Council, the foreign ministry has kept its primary responsibility for the formulation of Dutch positions regarding the CFSP. However, the decisions taken by the European Council with respect to CFSP issues, have become the main points of reference for Dutch foreign policy makers. Departmental autonomy nevertheless ends at the cabinet level where every negotiation position taken by a Dutch minister or prime minister, at the EU or any other international organisation, is decided collectively in cabinet.

The Dutch foreign ministry has recently been subjected to a rigorous reorganisation, but this had more to do with domestic politics than with EU membership or with the introduction of the CFSP. Moreover, the department within the foreign ministry which is responsible for the coordination of a Dutch negotiation position in the Council of Ministers, was not touched by the reorganisation. Also the decision-making procedures which regulate the preparation of such a negotiation position have not been affected by the reorganisation.

In Belgium, historical research supports the view, paraphrasing von Clausewitz, that foreign policy is the continuation of domestic policy by other means.[10] The Belgian elite's original choice for European cooperation (and even integration) in the inter-war period followed naturally from its economic and ideological interests. First, the neighbouring countries' markets have always constituted the necessary foundation for the commercial and industrial interests of the Belgian social elite. Secondly, a multilaterally organised Europe (from the 1920s onwards) offered a more stable and predictable international environment for those interests. Thirdly, the degree to which the larger neighbouring countries were linked by international arrangements, was considered commensurate to the freedom of movement available to the smaller countries in the commercial, economic and also diplomatic fields. Fourthly, the supranational *economic* organisation of Europe from the 1950s onwards made it possible (for the centre-right wing of the political elite) to pursue the classical liberal policy of limited political interference in economics. Finally, and from the 1970s onwards, the supranational *political* organisation of Europe provided the political elite (and especially its centre-left wing) with regulatory mechanisms with regard to issues of which the distinction between domestic and foreign dimensions had become blurred.

In its narrow sense, CFSP has been virtually untouched by domestic variables. Security and foreign policy (as distinct from commercial diplomacy) never ranked as a high priority in Belgian foreign policy since independence in 1830. Moreover, there exists a rather strong consensus on the CFSP in the Belgian political elite as a result of the broadly accepted view (since the mid-1950s) that supranationality strengthens the influence of small states in foreign policy making. Moreover, even most adherents of a enhanced importance for the sub-state actors, still generally accept that 'high politics' remain the competence of the national government. This has preserved the major role of the (federal) Ministry of Foreign Affairs, and the Prime Ministers office, in the CFSP field.

As a result, however, of the continuous constitutional reforms since 1970 policy areas other than the strict CFSP domain have required a much more systematic adaptation. The sub-state actors, called the 'federated entities' (Communities and Regions), acquired in this process far-reaching 'sovereign' powers, some of which include an important international dimension. Since, contrary to other federal states, there exists no legal hierarchy between the national and the sub-state levels, the federated entities now retain exclusive rights in specific domains. As a consequence, the Communities and Regions in 1993 acquired international treaty-making power over matters in which they have exclusive competence. Only in very specific, and clearly defined circumstances, may the central state act temporarily in lieu of the bodies of the Communities and the Regions.

This necessarily led to new *sui generis* arrangements for policy and decision making in a number of fields, such as culture, education, industry and research, environmental and health policies, energy, agriculture and even the internal market. Partly in contrast with the Netherlands, Belgian policy positions on European matters are defined in a two-fold process. They are first prepared in the so-called 'European coordination', a consultative body set up at the European desk of the Ministry of Foreign Affairs. The final decision then lies with the so-called 'Interministerial Conference on Foreign Policy'. Both bodies meet regularly and comprise all departments with a stake in European matters, including the sub-state actors. Decisions concerning the Belgian position have to be reached by consensus. It is important to note that representatives of the Communities and Regions are always invited, even if the subject at hand deals with federal competencies (such as the agenda of the General Affairs Council or Ecofin). This original set-up (which includes more bodies than the ones listed above and which is now legally codified) makes it possible for Belgium to arrive at European Council meetings with a position which has been dealt with on beforehand by all relevant departments (thus in accordance with Article 146 of the Treaty of Maastricht stating that 'the Council is comprised of a representative of each Member State'). If such a domestically negotiated position needs urgent adjustment, the Belgian representative will either consult with the relevant federal or federated authorities, or he/she can, exceptionally and *ad referendum*, take a provisional line, which has then to be confirmed or invalidated within three days.

This institutional set-up also makes it possible for Belgium to be represented in the Council by a sub-state Minister. In order to do this, the configurations in which the Council meets have been classified into four categories according to whether the subject-matter falls entirely or mainly under the federal jurisdiction and entirely or mainly under the jurisdiction of the federated entities. After some initial difficulties, this set-up has been working rather smoothly. This is above all due to the goodwill and the pragmatism of all the partners concerned. It also implies, however, a rather small foundation for Belgian foreign policy in terms of the long-term sustainability of its decision-making mechanisms. It is open to reasonable doubt whether the goodwill displayed by the various entities so far will remain available in the future, in the event that the different government levels would be directed by governmental coalitions of a different composition. Domestic tensions could easily translate into a deadlock in the foreign policy field, since all partners involved have *de facto* the right of veto. Especially in the so-called 'mixed treaties', where competencies of both national and sub-state actors are involved, decision making could become hostage to purely domestic policy calculations.

Moreover (but this is not typical for Belgium alone) foreign policy decision making in European matters will probably come under increased pressure in the years ahead, since European policy can no longer be called 'foreign' while it cannot be labelled entirely domestic either. European decision making carries important domestic consequences. A first obvious result is that the role of the heads of state and government on the diplomatic scene has increased significantly following from their role as core referees in domestic affairs and the increasing transnational nature of domestic affairs. A second consequence is that the influence of the Ministry of Foreign Affairs decreases in proportion to the increasing autonomy of other, so-called technical, ministries. Within the European context, this evolution expresses itself institutionally in the decreasing role of the General Affairs Council. A possible result of these changes could be the reduction of the Ministry of Foreign Affairs to a sheer technical ministry accepted by other ministries at best in the role of an 'escort service': Foreign Affairs puts its international infrastructure at the disposal of other ministries which otherwise develop their own autonomous diplomacy. This evolution seems inescapable as the border line between domestic and foreign policy will undoubtedly continue to wane, at least in European affairs.

Foreign policy actions – with or without the EU?

As the CFSP still has a voluntary character, the extent to which the CFSP really presents a limit to the freedom of a Member State to make its own foreign policy choices, depends upon how seriously a Member State takes the obligations under the CFSP provisions. Some Member States do not hesitate to pursue their own interests, independently of the CFSP. Other members simply obstruct further decision making on a common position or a joint action. Since the Netherlands is very committed in its obligations under the EU Treaty, the CFSP provides, from time to time, a constriction on foreign policy choices. As common positions and joint actions can only be taken by consensus, it repeatedly faces situations where it has little other choice but to line up with its European partners along the lowest common denominator, although the government would have preferred another outcome.

A good example of such a dilemma is the implementation of human rights norms, which is given a high priority in Dutch foreign policy. The Dutch government has had the experience on several occasions that, in spite of the CFSP rhetoric about the respect for human rights and fundamental freedoms, most of its partners are not willing to subordinate the common foreign policy to the promotion of human rights when the protection of human rights clashes with economic interests. When the government tried to use its Presidency to conduct a more assertive common policy towards countries that violate human rights, it was forced by its partners to back down on the question of human rights. The main argument was that such a position interfered with the economic relations of some Member States with the country concerned. The Dutch foreign minister was, for instance, heavily criticised by France when he made some remarks during the Dutch presidency in 1997 about the violation of human rights in China.

But the need to conduct a foreign policy in agreement with the CFSP may also offer an opportunity for policy action. It is obvious that Dutch diplomacy has much more leverage when it acts in name of the EU as such, especially when the country occupies the Presidency. This applies of course to every other small Member State as well, but it is much more relevant for the Dutch who are eager to play an active role on the international stage. Thanks to its EU Presidency in 1991 Dutch diplomacy, for example, was able to leave its fingerprints on the EC involvement in the crisis in Former Yugoslavia. The Netherlands initiated the EC Conference on Yugoslavia in The Hague, and set up the EC Monitoring Mission which was a novelty in the EPC practice.

On several occasions the Dutch government has used its participation in the EPC (which has been replaced by the CFSP) to legitimise a modification in its traditional foreign policy pattern. The common position towards the Arab–Israeli conflict agreed upon within the EPC framework, after the October war of 1973, served as a perfect cover to overcome the domestic uneasiness concerning the shift in the Dutch position towards that conflict in the mid-1970s. In the 1970s the Dutch government had to change its one-sided pro-Israel image to appease the Arabs and to protect the Dutch economic interests in the Middle East. The CFSP also offered the Dutch government the opportunity to hide behind the EU common positions when it wanted to escape difficult choices on controversial issues. The initial inability of the EPC partners to agree on severe economic measures against South Africa, to support the international anti-apartheid campaign, was used by successive Dutch governments to legitimise its policy at that time of reluctance towards the implementation of full scale economic sanctions against South Africa. The most important argument the government used in the domestic debate over the implementation of such measures, which would have damaged the economic relations between the two countries, was that the implementation of full scale economic sanctions would make sense only when they were taken by all EC members.

In Belgium, the CFSP is largely seen as a 'multiplicator' for Belgian foreign policy possibilities and influence. Until now, the CFSP has not been a major constriction for the foreign and security policy making of Belgium. In positive terms, participation in the CFSP has made it possible for Belgian foreign policy makers to be involved in foreign policy issues without having to elaborate a national position, where such a position would have been of insignificant value (Albania, Cambodia, the Western Sahara provide good examples). More importantly, the CFSP enables a small country such as Belgium to pursue foreign policy objectives, which it would be unable to achieve on its own. For instance, during the crisis preceding the Gulf War (1990–1991) Belgium consistently insisted upon a European framework in order to achieve the joint European playing-down of an exclusively military option – considered to be the preferred American, but not the preferred Belgian, option. By positioning its effort inside the EC (and the WEU) framework, and by trying to forge a distinctive European approach, the Belgian government believed it could pursue a broader political agenda.[11] This agenda included recognition of the political nature of the Palestinian question and the maintenance of a European–Arab dialogue – both traditional Belgian objectives. Through the EC framework Belgium was able to liaise with like-minded countries, including the larger Member States such as France and Germany and thus to increase the efficacy of its effort. As a small country in a military coalition (NATO), it would have been much more difficult for Belgium to raise these points.

Another example is the issue of European defence. In the run up to the Maastricht Treaty, Belgium stressed its preference for a more autonomous European defence, with the strengthening of the WEU as a first step towards its realisation. This would have provided an alternative to NATO, which at that time was seen as a Cold War relic. Reinforcing the French and German view of the WEU as primarily the military arm of the European construction, Belgium helped to define the terms of the formulation of the 'WEU-compromise' in the annex to the Maastricht Treaty, defining the WEU both as an integral part of the European construction and simultaneously as a European pillar of NATO, thus leaving both options open. Belgium was also an active participant in the drafting of Article J.4.1. of the same Treaty which states the goal of 'a common defence policy, which might in time lead to a common defence'.[12]

From the beginning of the 1990s, Belgian foreign policy makers have additionally used the CFSP, along with other multilateral and bilateral channels, to increase the effectiveness of its own foreign policy towards Central Africa. This has been done especially through the Council Working Group on Africa and the Council meetings themselves. Working from the general principle of keeping Central Africa on the agenda of the EU, Belgium has succeeded on several occasions in rallying the EC/EU behind its own position. This was the case, for instance, at the end of 1994, when Belgium pursued an active bi/multilateral diplomatic exercise organised around four key issues. First, organising the return of the refugees; secondly, encouraging national reconciliation and establishing the rule of law in Rwanda; thirdly, maintaining stability in Burundi and fourthly, promoting international coordination (as opposed to the then fragmented approach of the international community towards this region). The General Affairs Council of November 1994, and the subsequent Essen Summit in December, endorsed the Belgian policy, thus giving it a much broader international base. However, it is obvious that the so-called 'Europeanisation' or multilateralisation of the Belgian Africa policy also implies the possibility of 'dumping' the intricate and intractable situation in Central Africa into a more anonymous European decision-making process. This offers a Belgian government, if it should wish to do so, the opportunity of pretending to search for a broad supporting base, while in reality the Europeanisation is a screen for non-activity.

Besides the largely advantageous character of CFSP for Belgium, there are some, albeit minor, examples of what might be called 'constriction', examples which demonstrate how Belgian foreign policy was forced in a direction which it did not want. This was the case in the 1980s, when Belgium was forced to endorse the trade sanctions against South Africa.

Until then, Belgian foreign policy makers had maintained that trade sanctions against South Africa were not in the best interest of the black majority. From the moment that a majority within the EC chose the opposite view, Belgian foreign policy makers could no longer argue that unilateral trade sanctions would be of no avail and contrary to Belgium's national interests. As a result of its EC membership Belgium had thus to abandon its implicit pro-South African diplomatic stance.

It can be expected that the CFSP extending to 'hard' military matters in the future will increase the instances of constriction. Since Belgium champions European decision making in foreign affairs, including defence, it will be impossible to withdraw from participating in operations decided under the CFSP. This has already happened in the case of Former Yugoslavia. In the past, Belgium has demonstrated a conspicuous lack of interest in Eastern and Central Europe. It has always abstained from any concrete engagement in the region, which was never considered relevant to Belgian national interests. However, as Yugoslavia entered European decision making in 1990, Belgium has become increasingly militarily involved in this region for the first time in its history.

Tiers of exclusivity

Within the Union, no tiers of exclusivity exist as far as the Netherlands and Belgium are concerned that are comparable to the Bonn–Paris axis. The actual absence of tiers of exclusivity within the EU reflects a long-standing Belgian and Dutch habit of eschewing any such relationship with their large neighbours. This would not only hinder relations with the other neighbouring countries, but would also result in a form of dependency of a small country upon a larger neighbour.

Some observers of EU politics, however, consider the Benelux as a privileged relationship or a 'sub-system' between three small EU Member States. But for quite some time, reality has shown a rather different picture. The Benelux started during the Second World War (after some initial hesitation in both the Dutch and Belgian governments in exile) as a reaction to the pending marginalisation of small countries in the post-war organisation of Europe. In the early years the Benelux functioned both as a laboratory for economic multilateralism and a coordination mechanism for the three Member States in multilateral negotiations in order to defend their position more effectively. This was the case in the negotiations on the Marshall Plan of 1947 and in the Conference of London of 1948, which gave birth to the Federal Republic of Germany. In the 1950s however, the former function was taken over by the trade liberalisation effort within the General Agreement on Tariffs and Trade (GATT) as well as the EEC frameworks, whereas the latter function gradually disappeared.

From then on, the Benelux merely offered an irregular and informal meeting place, without a specific agenda or objectives. However, the mere fact that it exists offers the Member States, on specific occasions, a ready starting point for political coordination and common initiatives, if they wish to do so. Irregular formal Benelux *demarches* are undertaken within the EU, such as in the run up to the negotiations on the Treaty of Amsterdam, especially when the position of smaller states within the Union are being marginalised.

However more recently, as a result of such more or less successful attempts to heighten the visibility and efficacy of the three small countries' common position, the Benelux has tended to become a more permanent preparatory decision-making level for the countries evolved. Meetings in order to agree joint positions have become far more regular at the level of the ministers involved as well as at the level of officials. Even high level summits at the level of Prime Ministers have become more institutionalised than was the case before. This is no guarantee of success, as the attempts in forging a common Benelux position in the IGC leading to the Amsterdam Treaty of 1997 demonstrates. Important divergences on institutional reform, especially a Dutch proposal for a re-weighting of Council votes, which would have favoured the Dutch, prevented the Benelux countries from acting together during the endgame.[13]

The Netherlands has no special relations with other countries or regions outside the EU. Until the end of the Cold War successive Dutch governments considered the Atlantic relationship to be a cornerstone of its foreign policy. The Atlantic Alliance, led by the United States, provided the country with the security it needed. This has very much affected the relationship with France and the Dutch unwillingness to follow the French ambition to make the common European foreign policy independent of the United States. Although the Dutch supported the French effort to flesh out the process of European integration, the major orientation in the foreign and security policy remained an Anglo-American one. The Netherlands, for example, responded to the French veto of British accession to the EC, with a veto over the French ambition in the 1960s to create a political union, the so-called Fouchet plan. In the continuous clashes between France and the United States, the Dutch openly side with the United States. With Germany, the Netherlands has had to repeatedly balance between the conflicting foreign policy views of the United States and France, seeking a European middle road, usually along the lowest common denominator. However, the intensity of these conflicts has been reduced with the end of the Cold War that has placed the American–European relationship on a new footing.

In the commercial tradition of the golden age, the Dutch have sought a good relationship with almost any country that offers the Netherlands new markets to extend its trade. This was, for instance, clearly proven when the Dutch did not hesitate to shift the balance in its special relationship with Israel in the 1970s in favour of the Arab world. At that time the oil exporting Arab countries offered enormous opportunities for trade and investment, given their newly acquired oil wealth. Nonetheless the Netherlands continues to feel a special obligation towards the less developed countries. Like the other colonial powers, the Netherlands feels a special responsibility towards its former colonies, Indonesia and Surinam. But generally speaking, one may say that successive Dutch governments have considered it their obligation to offer all kinds of development aid to the less developed countries without any discrimination between their location in Africa, Asia or Latin America. The real criteria for development help has actually been their poverty.

As far as Belgium is concerned, the only really distinctive 'special relationship' concerns its former colonies. As far as the link between the CFSP and this relationship is concerned, the Belgian view can be summarily described as follows: within the CFSP if possible, without the CFSP if necessary. Until the end of the 1980s, the Belgian Africa policy was largely seen through bilateral eyes. Inside this bilateral relationship the commercial dimension prevailed. From the end of the Cold War onwards, however, Belgium deliberately opted for a more multilateral and political approach. The first channel was the troika formula (United States–France–Belgium) which was, at times, rather effective in its decision making concerning the specifics of the former Zaire. At the beginning of the 1990s however, the troika formula became somewhat vacuous because of the divergent views held by France on the one hand, and the United States and Belgium on the other. The EC/EU then constituted the second channel, which was, however, less specific and more declamatory. In short, and dependent on the situation, Belgium used alternatively a bilateral CFSP or a troika framework to pursue its objectives in Central Africa.

To a lesser degree, Belgium also cherishes a special relationship with the Middle East in general, and Algeria in particular. Initially (in the 1970s) Belgian–Algerian relations were influenced by the discourse on the new international economic order, securing for both countries a predictable relationship in the energy field. This relationship explains the efforts of the Belgian EC presidency in 1986 to strengthen again the EPC role in the Middle East conflict. It also marked the Belgian attitude during the Gulf War.

Conclusion

By way of conclusion we may say that both the Netherlands and Belgium can be categorised as states with an extensive network of external relations outside the EU. Both are active members of the UN, NATO and a large number of other international organisations. At the same time however, both the Netherlands and Belgium represent the type of Member States that act in concert with the EU. Especially after the end of the Cold War both countries consider the CFSP as their main point of reference. Even NATO had initially lost its exclusivity, as the two countries were ready to consider new institutional arrangements for the organisation of a common European defence within the EU framework. This has, of course, to do with the fact that the two countries realise very well that their foreign policy gains more effect when it is exercised as part of an overall EU foreign policy. But it has also to do with a basic commitment of the two countries to the European integration process. As the EU promotes collaboration and cooperation in new policy areas, the two countries are ready to shift their bilateral and multilateral cooperation arrangements towards the EU. The Netherlands, for example, that ranks as a large financial contributor to the Third World, used to channel its aid and help programmes through bilateral and multilateral channels. Since the Treaty on European Union has intensified the common development and cooperation policy of the Member States within the first pillar, the Dutch government has also increased its participation in this common policy. Like the German–French tandem, the Benelux considers itself the motor behind the European integration process, including the CFSP. It was therefore not surprising that the two countries were the only ones, during the intergovernmental negotiation on the Treaty on a European Union, who supported an EU institutional structure where the CFSP was integrated into the EC. The two countries still, in principle, support the merger of the first and second pillars, although the Netherlands, more than Belgium, have learned to live with the intergovernmental nature of the CFSP. Belgium, however, still thinks of itself as the ultimate supporter of the post-war supranational European integration effort, as launched by Robert Schuman and Jean Monnet in the early 1950s.

Notes

1 Based on the Ministry of Defence Policy Paper: Ministry of Defence, *Hoofdlijnennotitie voor de Defensienota 2000* (The Hague, Ministry of Defence, January, 1999).
2 Based on direct participation in military decision making as deputy chief of cabinet at the Ministry of Defence from 1988 until 1992.
3 This observation is based on the yearly debate on Dutch foreign policy in the Dutch Parliament.
4 Ministry of Foreign Affairs, *The Foreign Policy of the Netherlands: A Review* (The Hague, Ministry of Foreign Affairs, 1995).
5 Since 1997 this frustration has been regularly expressed by Foreign Minister Erik Derycke, most recently at his 1999 annual press conference (8 February 1999). For an official statement, see the common Benelux letter of 27 April 1998.

6 An opinion poll by Marketing Unit (1996), published in *Humo*, 24 September 1996.
7 B. Kerremans, 'The Flemish identity: nascent or existent ?', *Res Publica*, 39:2 (1997), pp. 303–314.
8 These views were clearly expressed on several occassions in recent years by the leaders of the Liberal and Labour faction in Dutch Parliament. See also A. G. Harryvan and J. van der Harst, 'Verschuivingen in het Nederlandse Europa beleid', *Transaktie*, 26:3 (1997), pp. 356–377.
9 Based on own interviews.
10 R. Coolsaet, *België en Zijn Buitenlandse Politiek 1830–1990* (Leuven, Van Halewyck, 1998).
11 On the attitude of the Belgian government in the Gulf War, see R. Coolsaet, *Chronique d'une Politique Étrangère. Les Relations Extérieures de la Belgique (1988–1992)* (Brussels, EVO, 1992), pp. 27–38.
12 Coolsaet, *Chronique d'une Politique Étrangère*, p. 47.
13 Y. Devuyst, 'Treaty reform in the European Union: the Amsterdam process', *Journal of European Public Policy*, 5:4 (December 1998), p. 622.

8

Greece

Dimitrios Kavakas

Introduction

This chapter deals with a unique case among the European Union (EU)
Member States. It is unique because Greece has been the only Member
State that does not share a border with any other EU state. Greece has
been surrounded by countries with which it has either had hostile relations or those neighbouring states were on the opposite side during the
Cold War. Greece is also historically 'different' from the other Member
States. It has had cultural and religious differences that have shaped Greek
politics throughout its history as a Greek state.[1] Greece is the only
Member State that participates in two cultural formations, the western
liberal tradition and the eastern orthodox tradition.[2] Greece is situated in
the south-eastern corner of Europe in a very unstable environment. The
instability that characterises the Balkans region, and the immense sense of
threat to the Greek territorial integrity by a neighbouring country, create
a very fragile security environment for Greece.

This chapter looks at Greek foreign policy in three sections. The first
examines Greek foreign policy change as a consequence of membership of
the EU. It studies the issues of adaptation (and lack of adaptation) of
Greek foreign policy, as well as the degree of Europeanisation occurring
in three levels: the system of policy formation; the foreign policy makers;
and the policies themselves. The second section looks at the foreign policy
process. In this section the impact of domestic factors which influence
Greek foreign policy are discussed. The nature and design of the Greek
political system, the development of the Greek national issues and the
non-state actors, like the Greek Orthodox Church (and the traditional
culture that the Church enforces within the society), are all factors that
have a direct impact upon the foreign policy decision-making process. The
section also looks at the bureaucratic politics involved in decision making
as the foreign policy administration reflects the general political culture of
Greece. The final section deals with foreign policy actions. It looks at the

impact of participation in the Common Foreign and Security Policy (CFSP) on Greek foreign policy. Furthermore, it also looks at Greek foreign policy outside the CFSP in order to determine when, how, and why, Greece chooses to act outside the institutions of the CFSP on a foreign policy issue.

The main argument that is advanced throughout the chapter is that membership of the EU has had an important impact upon Greek foreign policy. The argument is that this impact is not limited to the areas in which adaptation has occurred and that the foreign policy process has been Europeanised. Furthermore, this Europeanisation has extended to areas in which adaptation has not occurred. Even in these non-adapted areas membership of the EU influences both the foreign policy-making process and the outcome.

Foreign policy change – adaptation and socialisation

Adaptation through membership

The impact of EU membership on Greek foreign policy can be examined in three areas: the changes in the administration of foreign policy; the changes in national foreign policy capabilities; and the changes in the policies themselves. EU membership has brought significant changes to the administrative structure of the foreign ministry. In Greece, the overall coordination and representation of Greek European policy was shifted from the Ministry of Coordination (later to be renamed the Ministry of National Economy), to the Ministry of Foreign Affairs (MFA). The MFA became responsible for the functions of forming, coordinating and presenting Greek policy in the European Community (EC) institutions. The structure of the MFA has undergone significant changes on several occasions since the accession of Greece into the EC in 1981. The last time such a restructuring was undertaken was with the Presidential Decree No. 230 of 28 July 1998.[3] The new structure of the ministry makes a separation between issues of the first and third pillar of the EU and those of the second pillar. Directorate General (DG-C) is responsible for issues of pillars one and three while Directorate General A is responsible for pillar two. The DG-C for EU affairs is responsible, among other EU issues, for EU external relations that are not subjects of the CFSP. The C1 Directorate deals with European external relations, which are the subject of the first pillar of the EU, while the C4 Directorate is concerned with the third pillar, including the Schengen agreement. DG-C is headed by the General Secretary for European affairs and is under the supervision of the Alternate Minister. The issues of the CFSP are subjects of the A11 Directorate, which is part of the DG-A for Political Affairs. This Directorate General is headed by the General Secretary for Political Affairs who has the grade of a Political Director. However, inside DG-A there is a separation of Directorates into two, each one the subject of a different deputy General Director. A11 is subject to the first Director, who is responsible for all issues of foreign policy except those of Cyprus (A2), the Balkans (A3) and Turkey (A4). The second deputy General Director is under the direct leadership of the Deputy Foreign Minister, who is responsible for Greece's 'national issues', that is Cyprus, Turkey and the Balkans. Despite the coordination between the different Directorates, this separation of the Greek national issues can create problems of coordination when these issues are discussed in the CFSP. For instance, in a case where economic aid and humanitarian assistance to the Balkans are discussed as a joint action in the CFSP, there are three different offices that deal with the issue. The subject obviously becomes an issue of A11 as it is discussed in the CFSP. It also becomes an issue of A3 on south-east Europe, which is directly linked to the Deputy Foreign Minister, and a subject of C1 on European external relations which is linked to the Alternate Minister. Another area of possible administrative problems can be the fact that DG-A is responsible for the coordination of political issues, subjects of other DGs, but not of DG-C. That means, for example, that when Directorate C1-III on EU–Turkish relations deals with the issue of the fourth financial protocol to Turkey there is a problem of coordination and representation with A4 on Turkey and A11 on the CFSP, as this issue is a highly politicised issue of foreign policy in Greece and is linked with the Greek position on Turkey in the CFSP.

The MFA has taken the role of the gatekeeper of European policy, and as the Permanent Representation in Brussels is subject to it, and any interaction between other ministries and the Brussels representation has to go through the MFA. Another innovation that resulted from membership of the EU was the creation of the post of the Alternate Minister of Foreign Affairs who was to be exclusively responsible for all issues of the EC/EU, and therefore responsible for the work of the General Secretariat of European Affairs.

EU membership also brought significant changes in Greek foreign policy capabilities. Both the resources of the foreign ministry and the areas of Greek interest were very limited before accession. EU membership has affected Greece's access to information, the know-how of its diplomatic force and the negotiating skills. The management of information has been important for the achievement of efficiency in the management of issues of the CFSP. Greece took advantage of the large amount of information available through the COREU system (the telex network used by the Member States for the transmission of CFSP matters) receiving information from the Member States more experienced in foreign policy and with more extensive networks. This information was used in order to familiarise itself with the foreign policy making process and to gain additional political importance in international relations.

Thus, Greece has gained access to information that is available to EU members and which Greece was not otherwise in a position to have. This gave Greece both the interest, and the tools, to deal with issues of foreign policy that were not traditionally on its agenda. It also provided Greece with the opportunity to improve the know-how of its diplomacy and to increase its negotiating skills. This was, in fact, one of the most important benefits of EU membership for foreign policy. Indeed, Greece has used its status as an EU member in order to increase its negotiating position in its relations towards third countries. Greece managed to halt the recognition of the 'Turkish Republic of Northern Cyprus' by Pakistan by threatening to block its economic agreements with the EU. Given the fact that Greek foreign policy is part of a large network of cooperation in which national administrations come into direct interaction with each other, the European experience has been a learning process for the increase of the negotiating skills of Greek diplomats.

Finally, EU membership signified changes in Greek foreign policy. As Theodoros Couloumbis puts it:

'Greece found herself, like modern Ulysses, tied to the pole of the European Union that allowed its to resist the Sirens of atavistic irredentism and offensive nationalism. Without that 'pole', the Greek boat could have slipped from its path and would have faced the deadly traps of a Balkan war'.[4]

This has been particularly true during the crisis in the Balkans of the last nine years. Greece could have easily slipped into the conflict if it was left at the influence of nationalistic elements. However, EU membership offered a European orientation that finally overshadowed any nationalist influences. Although Greek foreign policy in the region has been differentiated from that of the other Member States and this has caused tension, particularly with regard to Turkey, EU membership has helped in containing excessive nationalistic elements in Greek foreign policy. Historical evidence suggests that without such a curtailment Greece could have been drawn into regional conflicts. The development of the framework of the CFSP developed a need for common position and common actions for the EU Member States and, despite the fact that the policy area has not always been the most successful, it has had an impact on Greek foreign policy. The need to fall in line with a common position has caused Greek policies to develop in directions that would not otherwise have been the case. An example of this is the Greek position on Yugoslavia. Greece has traditionally had friendly relations with Serbia and has been more reluctant to condemn Milosevic than any other Member State. However, particularly in the 1999 crisis in Kosovo, Greece adopted the common position concerning the Serb aggression in the province.[5] Greece agreed on the common position of 14 December 1998 in which the Council imposed restrictions against officials of Yugoslavia that act against the independence of the press.[6] The Greek agreement, and implementation of this position, would have been unthinkable if Greece was not a part of the CFSP. The argument that EU membership has had an important impact on Greek foreign policy and helped in containing extreme elements within it is more evident after the end of the Cold War, particularly in the Balkans. The rise of nationalism and the questioning of the borders in the Balkans could have resulted in the Greek engagement in the conflict. However, despite the awkward behaviour of Greece during the Yugoslavian crisis on the Macedonian question, EU membership offered a vital tool for avoiding the escalation of the conflict to that analogous to the beginning of the century, when the Macedonian issue was the subject of two Balkan wars. It is not an exaggeration to argue that EU membership helped Greece to avoid an engagement in a regional conflict for borders.

Socialisation of foreign policy makers

The important impact of membership on Greek foreign policy has been the gradual change of attitude of its foreign policy makers in their dealings with their fellow Europeans. The European policy making process has not only been a learning process for the administration and the diplomats, as seen above, but also for the policy makers. The habits of working together have gradually altered the way that Greek foreign ministers behave in the Council meetings and the manner with which they pursue their interests.[7] This is evident in three aspects. First, there is an increasing level of pre-consultation between Greek and other ministers. This has been developed gradually and was totally absent during the first few years after Greece's accession. The practice then was to go to the meetings with a determined position in order to defend it in any way. This attitude has been transformed today into a more flexible approach. Although this does not mean that Greece does not appear inflexible in specific cases, its inflexibility has decreased significantly over the recent years. A second aspect is that of compromise. Greek foreign policy makers appear more familiarised with the process of compromises and trade-offs that dominate EU negotiations. This means that Greek policy makers are more flexible in making compromises in one area in exchange for benefits in another. An example of this has been the Greek agreement to the EU–Turkey custom union in exchange for the start of negotiations for the accession of Cyprus to the EU. The third aspect is that of building a common position. It is not argued that Greece has achieved a sufficient level in any of these aspects, however, membership has made significant changes. In the aspect of common positions, socialisation of foreign policy makers has brought a tendency to reach agreements in the Council. Greece has gradually left behind its strategy of blocking the common positions and started to develop an attitude of trying to influence them. The most prominent example of this has been the Luxembourg European Council of 1997 on the naming of the candidate states for accession to the EU. Greece did not block Turkey from being a candidate state but rather managed to influence a common position imposing conditions on the Turkish candidature.[8]

As a member of the EU, the Europeanisation process that can be found primarily in the economic field affected Greek foreign policy. Greece has developed a European orientation in its policy making that has to a degree transformed the traditional identity of Greek foreign policy. By participating in European foreign policy cooperation, Greece has widened its areas of interest. Areas such as the Baltic would otherwise have never have been important issues on the Greek agenda. Europeanisation has created new interests but also new policies. Despite the traditional description of Greek 'national issues' and its policies towards Turkey and Cyprus, the feeling of belonging to the EU brings a sense of security that has implications for the other policies of Greece. Despite the criticisms that there have not been enough changes of the Greek positions in this area, it is clear that Europeanisation has brought some effect. Greek policy makers have gradually abandoned the attitude of trying to impose their position on their fellow members and are now trying to adopt a more constructive approach of explanation and comprehension of the issues under consideration. The 1999 conflict in Kosovo offers an example of such a change of the Greek policy makers' attitudes. Despite the widespread opposition among the Greek public to NATO involvement in Kosovo, the Greek government supported the campaign against President Milosevic. In the CFSP, Greece took initiatives to develop a consensus for a common response to the crisis on the basis of humanitarian assistance and post-conflict reconstruction arrangements.[9] This attitude is adopted as a consequence of the fact that the practice in the Council meetings is one of partnership and not of an adversarial nature. Europeanisation has also affected the Greek image in foreign policy, particularly in the region, and the definition of national interest. The EU became, for Greek foreign policy, the main priority for its national interest. Despite the tensions that have been created by particularities in its foreign policy, nothing can be balanced against the benefits to Greece of belonging to the EU. This process of Europeanisation has gradually become more evident in Greek foreign policy. In particular the benefits can be demonstrated in Greek relations with third parties.

Foreign policy process – domestic and bureaucratic

Domestic factors

Foreign policy in Greece is linked with domestic political debate. This means that the government uses foreign policy to claim successes and national victories for electoral purposes. An important aspect of this has been the separation of foreign policy into two spheres. The first, which is the normal foreign policy, is concerned with all issues that do not affect Greek interests directly, such as the Arab–Israeli conflict and Iraq. The second includes issues of national importance, which are Turkey, Cyprus and the Balkans. This sphere of foreign policy has taken the name of 'national issues', particularly after the end of the Cold War. The new security landscape that was created in the 1990s, and the turmoil in the Balkans with the disintegration of Yugoslavia, led to the development of a nationalist element in Greek foreign policy. Ever since the outbreak of the conflict with Macedonia in 1991, the problem was considered by Greek politicians, and the Greek press, as a national issue for Greece. Soon after the notion of 'national issues' dominated the domestic political debate and included all issues of Greek foreign policy that are regarded as important because of proximity or historical reasons. These are the Greco-Turkish conflict, Cyprus, and the Balkans. The latter includes the Macedonian question and the Greek-speaking minority in Albania.[10] It is the argument of this chapter that this separation and renaming is not accidental and has important implications for Greek foreign policy and its relationship to the domestic arena.

There are three significant results from the Greek renaming of foreign policy to 'national issues'. Greece 'securitises' its foreign policy issues under the name 'national issues'.[11] 'Securitisation' means that the specific issues of foreign policy are being brought out of party political debate. They become issues of national importance for which disagreement between political parties, or within the society, is unacceptable. This also implies the development of a nationalist foreign policy which shapes public opinion and vice versa. With this inter-relationship it is impossible for the government, or a political party, to advocate a policy different from the one that is accepted as national policy, without a significant electoral cost or the fear of being criticised as a traitor. As Buzan et al[12] argue, a 'securitisation' attempt can be fully successful, partially, or not successful. The Greek dispute with Turkey has been successfully 'securitised' as an issue. The validity of the Greek position is beyond any public debate. The issue of Macedonia can be described as partially successful since it became 'securitised' for a limited time period, with the exemption of the Communist Party which has always been against the policy consensus on Macedonia.

The second result of 'national issues' is that foreign policy is made for domestic consumption. Foreign policy issues take national importance and, thus, achieve widespread publicity, which is then used by the government to make a foreign policy decision on the basis of either seeking to improve its electoral image or to distract public attention from a difficult issue in domestic politics. Public opinion also becomes a foreign policy maker. During the early 1990s, when the issue of Macedonia was in the spotlight, two big rallies in Thessaloniki and Athens each attracted one million people.[13] Also, the term Macedonia or Macedonian came to be added to a large number of Greek companies or institutions as a demonstration of the validity of the Greek claims. In the case of Turkey, the issue is rooted in the Greek society through education, where the notion of the 'enemy of Greece' is developed. A simplified example, but with a lot of significance for the case of public opinion as foreign policy maker, is when, in the 1980s, coffee shops decided unilaterally to rename 'Turkish coffee', which had been so known for centuries, into 'Greek coffee'.

Finally, 'national issues' give a perception of a threat to the territorial integrity of the Greek state. Regardless of whether there is a real threat or not, the fact that the issue takes on such huge proportions, serves as a tool for the government to justify policies such as extra military spending or measures like the economic embargo on Macedonia of 1994.[14] Both examples have had negative implications for the Greek economy, and the embargo on Macedonia damaged the image of Greece both in the EU and in the Balkan region. Greek defence uses a significant part of the resources of the Greek economy with the result of less investments of capital in several sectors of production and a worsening level of social services.[15] However, the 'securitisation' of the issue of Turkey in Greece makes decision making inevitable which is not in the Greek interest but which is driven by a nationalistic and militaristic sentiment.

The impact of the domestic political debate on Greek foreign policy is concentrated mainly in the above-mentioned 'national issues'. On the rest of foreign policy issues the political debate does not significantly affect the government position, with the government free to pursue its own objectives. For instance, during the Gulf War in 1990–91, the Greek conservative government contributed a frigate to the international force. This decision brought disagreement and criticism from the opposition parties. However, the political debate did not change the government position or bring any political cost. On the contrary, 'national issues' have been exploited by the opposition, which has invested in popular support for nationalist sentiments and this has brought significant problems for the government. Two examples of such a development, related to Turkey, are the Imia crisis and the S-300 missiles that Cyprus ordered from Russia. During the Imia crisis in January 1996, the Greek and Turkish navy came to the point of war over a group of islets that both sides claimed as their territory.[16] The eventual disengagement, with the aid of US diplomacy, brought furious opposition by the opposition parties, particularly due to the fact that Greece agreed to remove its national flag from one of the islets in order to avoid any provocation. The reasonable and peaceful resolution of the Imia crisis was characterised in the Greek political discourse as a national defeat and the government was considered responsible. A similar kind of response, but in a different context, resulted after the backing-off of the Cypriot government on its commitment to install on the island S-300 missiles, which had been ordered from Russia.[17] This incident gained wide publicity during the last months of 1998 and the beginning of 1999. The Greek government was held responsible by the opposition and the press for influencing the Cypriot decision to avoid the escalation of the crisis, since Turkey made clear that the installation of the missiles in Cyprus was a prime threat and it would not hesitate to strike at them.

It is not only the political parties that have an impact on foreign policy in the context of Greece's 'national issues' but society in general. Greek society has developed a very sensitive approach to issues of foreign policy, particularly when they concern perceived threats to Greece's national integrity. For this reason the societal sentiments have been exploited in several cases, as seen before, by political parties, organisations or the press. A particular case of a non-state actor that has an important influence on the society, and that has used that influence to promote nationalistic sentiments, is that of the Greek Orthodox Church. The Church maintains a significant level of influence in the Greek political system. This creates tensions in Greek foreign policy making for a special relationship with countries with major orthodox populations. During the Yugoslav crisis in the early 1990s, these circles favoured open support of Yugoslavia.[18] However, despite some evidence of its existence, this never became official Greek policy. These tensions can be attributed to a general conflict in Greek society between Europeanists and Traditionalists. The former favour total integration of Greece in the EU, while the latter sees integration as a threat to Greek traditional values and religion and sees Greece as part of the East European group of orthodox countries. However, Traditionalists have not managed to achieve high posts in government and thus their influence in the policy process is kept to the minimum.

Despite the failure of the Traditionalists, and the Greek Church, which is their main mechanism for achieving direct influence in government, their influence in the society has functioned as a tool to pressure for nationalist policies. The newly elected head of the Greek Orthodox Church Archbishop Christodoulos has, on many occasions, expressed political views with a nationalist and irredentist tenor, and has caused discomfort among the political leadership.[19] It is worth noting that in recent polls on popular ratings for leaders, Archbishop Christodoulos is situated in first place enjoying more popular support than any political leader. The change of leadership of the Greek Orthodox Church in 1998 signified a change in the way that the traditional nationalistic ideals were transmitted to the public. The new leadership is developing a kind of a Greek orthodox fundamentalist movement. This is manifested in three ways: involvement in politics; mass public support; and a nationalist message. The Church, and particularly the new leadership, has been involved in Greek politics by commenting on political developments and using its influence to apply pressure. In the recent crisis in Kosovo the Archbishop of the Greek Church used religious meetings to transmit anti-NATO and anti-Western messages. He has also been active in giving interviews to the press expressing the Church's political opinions. The message that the Church transmits to the public has been that the Catholic and Protestant West is fighting against the orthodox people and their traditions in Yugoslavia.

The second manifestation has been the Church's success in getting its message across. The orthodox Churches that were almost empty before are now starting to fill up with people from all age groups.[20] The characteristic of this development is the fact that these people are attracted not by a plain religious message but by a message of reviving their 'lost' national identity. This is linked to the third manifestation, which has been the Church's involvement in promoting Greek nationalism. There have been several occasions when Church delegations or social and political groups, influenced by the Church's ideals, have visited Belgrade using the Kosovo crisis in order to demonstrate their solidarity with the Serbian people. The nationalist messages that the Church transmits take an anti-European character. The EU, according to the Church, is responsible for the loss of the traditional Greek orthodox culture. Greece is seen by the Church as closer to the 'Orthodox brotherhood' of Eastern Europe than to the Catholic–Protestant dominated EU. These arguments found fertile ground during the NATO intervention in Kosovo.

Bureaucratic politics

The Greek bureaucracy is totally controlled by the government. In Greece, the tradition of having an independent civil service that works for the state and not for a specific government and can influence government policy, as in the US or British model, is totally absent. The government controls the administration, and appoints to the senior posts using appointments as a tool for the implementation of the government's programme.[21] The problem, as many scholars observe, is the problematic relationship between the state and the political parties. As Dimitris Sotiropoulos argues,[22] the Greek bureaucracy has been unable to shape policy output the way it has in other Western democracies because of the problem of clientelism in the recruitment process. Because of the clientelist culture the administration is characterised by weak organisation. The personnel are selected on political criteria and not on qualifications and expertise. This weak organisation strengthens the way political parties dominate the state to forward their own needs. It is a custom in the Greek administration that each time the governing party arrives in government, it changes all the high posts of the administration in order to place people of ideological allegiance to the party. This creates the contradiction that 'the Greek State is top-heavy, mismanaged, overburdened with excess labour but understaffed in terms of technical expertise'.[23] This is a general observation of the Greek political culture, which impacts on the MFA as well. However, the impact of clientelism, which poses a serious problem in the representation of Greece in the EU, is less marked in foreign policy because of the diplomatic force, which is permanent. The control of the government, though, is a problem in the foreign policy decision-making process since the bureaucracy does not have the adequate means to challenge the direction of the political leadership, or to act as a mechanism to provide consistency. The MFA has been criticised for failing to advise the political leadership on the issue of the two huge popular rallies organised in Greece in 1992 on Macedonia. These rallies had been fuelled, and supported, by the political leadership of the MFA. Criticism has been levelled at senior diplomats for their failure to explain the consequences of such activities to the political leadership.[24]

Foreign policy actions – with and without the EU?

With the EU

Membership of the EU has had an important impact on Greek foreign policy and, as argued above, it transformed the orientation and process of decision-making. In the first five years of its membership of the EC Greece followed an odd attitude in European foreign policy, mainly for ideological reasons, under the PASOK government of Andreas Papandreou. However, soon the process of adaptation, and the comprehension of how to gain benefits, slowly changed Greek foreign policy behaviour in European Political Cooperation and later in the CFSP. Greek foreign policy actions within the EU faced a number of constrictions of which the majority has been positive. Greece has also been presented with a number of opportunities that have transformed the orientation and the scope of Greek foreign policy. Furthermore, the EU policy process has created some tiers of exclusivity, which have had an impact on Greek foreign policy.

It seems that for Greece EU membership has helped in answering the founding question for the Greek state – does Greece belong to the East or to the West? Despite the continuing arguments in Greek society that Greece belongs to the East, membership of the EU has irreversibly oriented Greece towards the West. This development has had important implications for foreign policy. It has placed a limitation on the development of nationalistic policies by the Greek state. Although nationalist preoccupations have not been totally eliminated, membership has helped to contain them to a minimum level. Despite the fact that this can be seen as a constriction on the development of independent Greek foreign policy, it is a positive development that has spared Greece from engaging in dangerous rivalries in the region. Another observation is of the limitation that membership caused to the development of traditional links in foreign policy. This issue can be illustrated with the case of Serbia. Greece has enjoyed traditional friendly relations with Yugoslavia and the Serbs throughout the century, they have been on the same side during the two Balkan and the two World Wars, and they share similar cultural and religious customs.[25] However, despite the limited divergence of Greece from the common European perspective on Serbia, Greece has been forced to agree and enforce common agreements against its traditional friend.

In the vast majority of cases, however, membership of the EU has provided opportunities for Greek foreign policy, although these opportunities have not always taken. Greece has widened the scope of its foreign policy through participation in the CFSP. The information received from the diplomatic services of its fellow members, as well as its participation in the institutions of European foreign policy making and EU external relations, gave Greece both the interest and the ability to pursue a more extensive network of external relations, both political and economic. This development has enhanced Greece's international status, which is now perceived not as a small state in the south-eastern Mediterranean but as one of the fifteen members of the EU.[26] Perhaps the most significant effect was the enhancement of its foreign policy in the Balkan region, in the sense that Greek foreign policy has the weight of a member of the EU.

The question here is how this weight has been used and it is the argument of this chapter that Greece has failed to use it constructively until 1996, since when Greek foreign policy in the region has undergone a remarkable change. The pre-1996 failure can be seen particularly in the case of Macedonia, which was the first 'test' of Greek foreign policy in the new framework of the CFSP. In a period of increased nationalism in the Balkans, Greece, instead of demonstrating a constructive approach as an EU member in the region, engaged in nationalist policies that turned Greece into a part of the problem. Greece used the consensus rule in the CFSP in order to avoid an EU recognition of Macedonia, and tried to transform the Greek position into an EU one, by working through the institutions of the CFSP and trying to influence the outcome of decisions.[27] It was not only the case of Macedonia but also the Greek relations with Albania and Bulgaria that were also damaged. However, during the last three years Greece has been following a foreign political and economic policy in the region that has strengthened Greece's relations with its northern neighbours. Greece has become the channel of EU aid to the Balkan states, particularly Bulgaria and Albania, but is also acting as a representative of the Balkan region in the EU, encouraging the development of the region and the prospects for EU membership.

As mentioned at the beginning of this chapter, Greece has a strong perception of threat to its territorial integrity. This perception has been the reason why Greece has been trying to accommodate its security concerns by becoming a member of security alliances. The particularity of Greece has been that the NATO alliance could not solve its concerns since the threat was perceived as emanating from another member of the alliance. Integration in the EC was seen in the 1970s primarily as a security decision. This is the reason why even the anti-integrationist government of Papandreou in the beginning of the 1980s was in favour of the development of a European common defence structure. It was clear that Turkey would not be a member of this structure. The primary concern of the Greek government during the Maastricht negotiations was Greece's integration as a full member in the Western European Union (WEU).[28] The WEU was a security alliance, unlike the EU, and in which Turkey was not a member. This development was considered then as an objective to be pursued at any cost. An extension to this objective has been the Greek promotion of WEU integration in the CFSP and the development of the idea of securing the EU's external borders that dominated Greece's negotiation strategy during the 1996 Intergovernmental Conference (IGC) that resulted in the Treaty of Amsterdam.[29]

As a consequence of the different tiers of exclusivity that the EU policy process created, Greece is a part of groups of states in different policy areas that have had an impact on the Union's foreign policy. Greece is part of the so-called cohesion group. Although it is mainly concerned with economic development, the forthcoming enlargement gives it significance in foreign policy, since the members of the cohesion group of states are concerned by the threat of cohesion fund redirection to the forthcoming members. This in turn influences their behaviour during the accession negotiations. Greece is also part of a group of the geographically small states. This group has been particularly active during the last IGC negotiations on issues of institutional change that affect the representation of smaller states, and it seems that it will continue to be alert as enlargement brings the need for the restructuring of representation in the EU institutions.[30] Small states are hostile to the idea of revising the number of Commissioners and the sharing between them of a limited number of posts. Another group of which Greece is a member is that of the Mediterranean Member States. This has been the least active group for two reasons. First, although all its members belong to the South of Europe, they have many differences that prevent them acting together, and secondly, they can be described as having an individualist character that characterises Mediterranean populations. It can be argued that Southern Europe lacks the cooperative culture of, for example, the Nordic countries. The Spanish initiative in 1991 for the development of a Conference for the Security and Cooperation in the Mediterranean failed, not because of the disagreement of Northern European states but, because of the dispute on the origination and leadership of the initiative from other Mediterranean Member States, particularly Italy. However, on the issue of Mediterranean security that affects all Southern Member States, the group has managed to promote the Euro-Mediterranean partnership initiative, under the leading role of Spain. Despite success, disagreement on the origination still exists. Although Spain has implemented it, Greece claims the right of initiator.[31] It is not surprising that during a recent visit of the Greek Prime Minister Constantinos Simitis to Madrid, he made a reference to the development of a front of Southern Member States.[32] This 'front' can take the form of pressure group against the changes proposed to the structural funds as well as the institutional arrangements. Being part of this group has an impact on Greek foreign policy as alliances between Member States are formed, which have spill-over effects in other policy areas. They also influence Greece's relations with third countries, as in this case the Central and Eastern Europeans. Apart from these three groups, there are issues of institutional reform that bring together Member States and have an impact on foreign policy. For Greece, security is a vital issue and it is one that Greece would like to be developed as an EU security structure. The incorporation of the WEU into the CFSP, therefore, has been developed as a prime objective of Greek foreign policy together with the issue of external borders. The objective is to achieve an EU common foreign and defence policy that will recognise the Union's external borders and will be willing to guarantee their inviolability.[33]

Without the EU

Apart from the impact that EU membership has on Greek foreign policy inside the CFSP, there are issues which Greece has retained as matters of national importance and therefore the influence of the CFSP on these issues is not desirable. However, there is a contradiction in the Greek behaviour that is very interesting. This contradiction can be identified in two areas. Greece has separated the areas of national importance from the rest of foreign policy areas in order to keep them 'national' and to avoid any European influence from the CFSP on its policies. On the other hand, Greece wants to use its membership and its participation in the CFSP in order to persuade its partners of the validity of its arguments on these issues and has used the CFSP process in order to pursue these national objectives. In other words Greece wants its partners to support its national policies without having the right to express their opinion on them. The second area of contradiction is that Greece, during the two last IGCs, has supported the development of the CFSP, campaigning as well for its defence dimension. However, Greece objects to the abolition of the right to a veto in the CFSP and wants to keep the CFSP intergovernmental in nature, although integrated in the EU policy process. This contradiction is linked to the previous one because Greece understands the benefits of an institutionalised CFSP that can develop a common policy for the whole of the EU, but is reluctant to accept the possibility of its opinion being in a minority.

The Balkans has been an area of Greek interest in foreign policy and is an area which at times is kept outside the CFSP framework. This has been the case because Greece has either not been able to pursue an initiative through the institutions of the CFSP, or was afraid of the influence of the positions of the other Member States. An example of such an issue has been the Balkan Cooperation initiative. The Balkan Conference, which started in Crete in 1997 and continued in Antalya in 1998, has been a successful initiative that once a year brings together the Heads of States of eight Balkan states. It is a process that seeks to enforce stability and co-operation in the region, and although formally the Greek–Turkish dispute is not discussed, the meetings between the two countries in the Conference leads to a more structured dialogue. However, Greece has not tried to link the Balkan initiative to the CFSP, and although the Royaumont process also deals with South-east Europe, there is no link between the two.[34] The Greek decision to exclude the issue from the CFSP agenda, and thus to follow an independent initiative, can be seen as a product of the limited adaptation of Greek foreign policy. Because of Greece's behaviour, and the Greek interest that it promotes, its partners in the EU are very sceptical about Greek initiatives for the Balkans region in the CFSP. Even if the other Member States agree on the priorities and objectives of the initiative, they always prefer a system of institutional control in order to safeguard the exclusion of nationalistic elements and any secret agenda that Greece might promote. From the perspective of Greece, the institutionalisation of special links between the Balkan states and the EU, including Turkey, goes against the principle objective of Greek national foreign policy, which is to maintain control over the EU–Turkish relations. To accept and promote a CFSP initiative for the Balkans could mean that Greece would no longer have the leading role and that the views of other Member States, particularly on Turkey, would take on greater significance in the process.

Conclusion

As analysed in this chapter, EU membership has had a significant impact on Greek foreign policy. This impact can be found in the policy spheres that have been Europeanised as well as those kept as strictly national. As regards foreign policy change, the impact has been at different levels. The administration of foreign policy has been adapted in order to function under the requirements of membership. It has also been affected by the increase of resources and information that widened the scope and the potential of Greek foreign policy. The socialisation of policy makers and diplomats has helped in building interpersonal relations and processes that were bound to change national decision making. The increasing number of common positions and the gradual convergence of Greek foreign policies to these demonstrate, to a large extent, the familiarisation of policy makers due to the socialisation process. Although divergence still exists, membership has had an impact on the volume and intensity of these differentiations. Outside the EU, Greek foreign policy would have been different as membership has helped to contain Greek nationalist elements.

In the foreign policy process, EU membership has an impact on the domestic factors that influence foreign policy. Indeed, membership and all its benefits are rooted in the domestic political process. The Europeanisation process in Greece has been facilitated by the success of European integration. The main obstacle to the progress of Europeanisation of national foreign policy is the perception of threat. As integration progresses to the political and defence areas this perception is due to decrease. Despite the setbacks, Europeanisation and modernisation have progressed in many areas of domestic political life and there are signs of their extension in others. Finally, in the area of foreign policy actions, membership has altered the character of Greek foreign policy both in political and economic external relations. Participation in the CFSP has contributed to the raised international status of Greece but also, as an EU member, Greece has increased its potential for economic relations with third countries, through the EU's external relations. Although the existence of the 'national issues' creates tensions between Greece and its fellow members, the divergence has been limited and there is hope that eventually EU membership can contribute to the elimination of Greece's nationalist considerations. This hope is derived from the fact that although the policies on 'national issues' remain the same, the Greek attitude as regards the promotion of them in the EU institutions has changed.

Notes

1 Greece became a state for the first time after the War of Independence of 1821.
2 M. Christakis, 'Greece: competing with regional priorities' in K. Hanf and B. Soetendorp, *Adapting to European Integration* (Harlow, Longman, 1998), p. 85.
3 *Official Journal of the Government of the Hellenic Republic*, n. 177, (1), pp. 2761–82, 28/07/98.
4 Th. Couloumbis and S. Dalis, *Greek Foreign Policy in the Threshold of the 21st Century* (Athens, Papazisis, 1997), p. 88.
5 Interview with senior official in the Permanent Representation of Greece, Brussels, 11 January 1999.

6 *Official Journal of the European Communities*, L345/1, 98/725/CFSP, 19/12/98.

7 M. T. Johnston, *The European Council* (Oxford, Westview Press, 1994), p. 70. This provides a good explanation of how socialisation affects country positions and policies.

8 Interview with senior official in the Political Committee, Brussels, January 1998.

9 These initiatives were taken before the extraordinary summit in Brussels in April 1999, and are recorded in both the Greek and the European Press.

10 Three 'National Issues Councils' took place on the issue of Macedonia between 1991 and 1993. These are informal meetings of the leaders of all major political parties under the chair of the President of the Republic. There is no legal basis for them and they only serve the purpose of uniting Greek political forces and society at times of 'national emergency'.

11 For 'Securitisation' see B. Buzan, O. Wæver and J. de Wilde, *Security: a New Framework for Analysis* (London, Lynne Rienner, 1998).

12 Buzan, Wæver, de Wilde, *Security*, p. 39.

13 J. Pettifer, 'Greek political culture and foreign policy' in K. Featherstone and K. Ifantis, *Greece in a Changing Europe* (Manchester, Manchester University Press, 1996), p. 22.

14 Th. Veremis, 'A Greek view of Balkan developments' in K. Featherstone and K. Ifantis (eds), *Greece in a Changing Europe* (Manchester, Manchester University Press, 1996), p. 139.

15 N. Antonakis (1990), 'The impact of military spending on the development of the Greek economy', *Epilogi*, special issue October 1990, pp. 34–36.

16 E. Athanassopoulou, 'Greece, Turkey, Europe: Constantinos Simitis in premiership waters' in *Mediterranean Politics*, 1:1 (Summer 1996), pp. 113–117.

17 Interview with Greek senior official in the Foreign Ministry, January 1999.

18 Pettifer, 'Greek political culture', pp. 21–22.

19 See the newspaper *To Vima*, Athens, 11 April 1999, p. A16. I. K. Pretenderis, 'The Party of Orthodoxy'.

20 See the newspaper *To Vima*, Athens, 8 April 1999, p. A24–25. Report by D. Galanis and N. Karagiannis on 'Why the young are returning to the Church?'.

21 Interview with senior official in the Greek Permanent Representation, Brussels, 11 January 1999.

22 D. Sotiropoulos, 'A colossus with feet of clay: the state in post-authoritarian Greece', in H. J. Psomiades and S. B. Thomadakis, *Greece, the New Europe, and the Changing International Order* (New York, Pella, 1993).

23 Sotiropoulos 'A colossus', p. 54.

24 Off-the-record interviews with senior Greek diplomatic official in Athens and Brussels, March 1998 and January 1999.

25 S. E. Forester, *A Short History of Modern Greece* (London, Methuen, 1941). See particularly Chapter 4 on the Balkan Wars; p. 52 on the first Balkan War; p. 57 on the Greco-Serbian Treaty in the second Balkan War; Chapter 8 on the First World War; p. 75 on Greek support to Serbia; and Chapter 10 on Greece's obligations towards Serbia.

26 Th. Veremis, 'A Greek view of Balkan developments and the implications for CFSP', *CFSP Paper No. 52* (Brussels, Centre for European Policy Studies, 1994), p. 7.

27 Greece blocked the recognition of Macedonia in several ministerial meetings in 1992. See conclusions of the Council of Foreign Ministers of Lisbon, 17 February, Luxembourg, 6 April, Guimarraes, 5 May, and the European Council of Lisbon, 26–27 June.

28 Y. Valinakis, 'Security policy' and in P. Kazakos and P. C. Ioakimidis, *Greece and EC Membership Evaluated* (London, Pinter, 1994), p. 208.

29 Greek Memorandum on the 1996 IGC, Greek Foreign Ministry's Web page, http://www.mfa.gr/foreign/euro_union/ddceng.htm, 17 September 1996.

30 G. Friden, 'The objectives of the small and medium, in respect of population, Member States for the IGC of 1996' in S. Perrakis (ed.), *The EU after the IGC in 1996: the Role and the Position of the Small and Medium, in Respect of Population, Member States* (Athens, Livani, 1996), p. 235.

31 Interview with senior official in the Greek MFA, Athens, March 1998.

32 See interview of Mr Simitis at the newspaper *El Pais*, 14 January 1999, p. 4.

33 Greece has already managed to achieve the inclusion of a mention on external borders of the EU in the Amsterdam Treaty, in the preamble of the CFSP provisions.

34 The Royaumont process has been a French initiative in the CFSP, which started in Paris on 13 December 1995 and aimed at the improvement of relations between the countries of Southeast Europe.

9

Portugal

José Magone

Introduction

Portuguese foreign policy has undergone a considerable transformation since the collapse of its authoritarian regime on 25 April 1974. The breakdown of the regime put an end to the Portuguese empire which had colonies in Africa and Asia and led to a general crisis of identity amongst the population. Portugal became a small country overnight which had to adjust its economic and political structures accordingly. Portugal became the first country undergoing a process of democratisation labelled by Samuel Huntington as the Third Wave of Democratization.[1] From the very start the European Community (EC) worked as a monitoring mechanism of this process of evolution towards a liberal West European democracy. During the pre-accession period, the European integration process became the main motivation among the Portuguese elite to strengthen this emerging new democracy. European integration was regarded as the best way to ensure democratic stability in Portugal. The pre-accession period was important in the restructuring of the foreign policy priorities of Portugal. The period of reconstruction of Portuguese foreign policy ended only in the mid-1990s with the creation of the *lusophone* community of Portuguese-speaking countries – the *Comunidade de Paises de Lingua Portuguesa* (CPLP). Within European Political Cooperation (EPC) and the Common Foreign and Security Policy (CFSP) Portugal has remained a supporter of the Portuguese-speaking countries, particularly on the question of East Timor. This chapter intends to illustrate this transformation of Portuguese foreign policy by discussing its adaptation through EU membership, domestic and bureaucratic processes and Portuguese foreign policy actions.

Foreign policy change – adaptation and socialisation

*Adaptation through membership: from participatory
observer to active participant*

The collapse of the Portuguese authoritarian regime on 25 April 1974, during a period of restructuring of East–West relations, became a central issue for the United States. Portuguese domestic political events very soon gained international significance, when the military Movement of Armed Forces (*Movimento das Forcas Armadas* (MFA)), the new government, wanted to introduce a vague form of pluralist Socialism in the country and establish stronger relations with countries in the Third World, Central and Eastern European people's democracies and the Soviet Union.[2] For the United States and the other members of NATO this was regarded as a danger for the balance of power between West and East. For one and a half years, until 25 November 1975, revolutionary Portugal was perceived by most commentators as dangerous for the ongoing process of detente carried out in the Conference of Security and Cooperation in Europe (CSCE) in Helsinki.[3]

The collapse of the authoritarian regime was intrinsically related to the colonial wars in Guinea-Bissau, Angola and Mozambique that had been going on since 1961. The members of the MFA were middle-ranking officers who were fighting in Africa and felt that the colonial wars could not be won militarily and a political solution had to be found. Instead of changing its strategy, the authoritarian regime was pushed by the ultra right-wing faction under the leadership of Admiral Américo Tomás to reinforce its military efforts. At the same time the career prospects of the middle-ranking officers were undermined by last-minute policies of recruitment by the authoritarian regime, leading to more discontent among these officers.[4] A further factor accounted for the motivation of the MFA to organise the *coup d'etat* against the authoritarian regime. This confrontation and contact with the liberation movements and their ideologies in the colonies led to a general feeling among these middle-ranking officers that Portugal itself needed to be freed from the authoritarian regime and establish a more just and democratic system.[5]

During the revolutionary period, the military decided to speed up the decolonisation process by granting independence to Angola (11 November 1975), Mozambique (25 June 1975), Guinea-Bissau (10 September 1975), Sao Tomé and Principe (12 July 1975) and Cape Verde (5 July 1975) in a very short period of time. East Timor was also to be granted independence but a civil war between the main parties in the territory, and the illegal annexation by the Indonesian army during this period of revolutionary turmoil in Portugal, made this impossible.

After 25 November 1975, the military dominance within the new Portuguese democracy was gradually reduced. In spite of this, civilian governments had to deal with the supervisory institution created by the MFA called the 'Council of the Revolution', which made it possible for the military to watch over the Portuguese democracy for a five year period after approval of the constitution. Only after the revision of the constitution in 1982, abolishing the Council of the Republic and creating a civilian Constitutional Court, the adoption of the National Defense Law in 1982, and the election of the civilian Mário Soares as President of the Republic in early 1986, could one speak of a completed process of civilianisation of the new political system.[6]

In this sense, the first decade of the new Portuguese democracy was characterised by a strong commitment to European integration as the only viable option to strengthen its democratic regime. The poor economic situation after the revolutionary period leading to the implementation of two International Monetary Fund (IMF) austerity programmes in 1978/79 and 1983/84, the political instability due to ideological differences between right and left, the lack of an overall national design in foreign policy and national defence and the growing impatience with the EC negotiations, further undermined the search for a new identity in the international order. It is only after the entry to the EC on 1 January 1986 that we can speak of a reconstruction of Portuguese foreign and defence policy.

The most peculiar element of adaptation through membership was, and is, Portugal's relationship with Spain. For centuries the two countries lived back-to-back, but with European integration both countries were going in the same direction in terms of their identity in general, and foreign and defence policy in particular. Both countries had to abandon the isolationist standpoints of their authoritarian regimes and move towards a European defence identity.[7]

There is some evidence to suggest that Portuguese foreign policy has become more 'Mediterraneanised' since the early 1990s. Although Portugal does not participate actively in the Eurocorps and is, at present, an observer, the same cannot be about said about the Mediterranean. Portugal has become an important country in the Euro-Mediterranean partnership established after the Barcelona Conference in November 1995 and militarily it takes part in the Eurofor and Euromarfor, two military forces of rapid intervention of the WEU and with their command centre based in Florence.

In general terms, one may suggest that the end of the Cold War liberated Portugal from an American defined foreign and security policy through membership of NATO and created a richer post-Cold War policy, in which dialogue with other Member States, on equal terms, has led to a reconstruction of Portuguese defence and foreign policy and the strengthening of Portuguese diplomacy in the world. Following Kenneth Hanf's and Ben Soetendorp's framework of analysis of the adaptation of small states to European integration, administrative and political adaptation did not differ substantially.[8] Instead the consensual support for foreign policy within European integration parameters has been a major feature since 1986. Therefore strategic adaptation was characterised by continuity as a reflection of the consensual political support achieved among the two main parties, the Socialist Party (*Partido Socialista* (PS)) and the liberal Social Democratic Party (*Partido Socialdemocrata* (PSD)).

The socialisation into EPC procedures took six years from accession. In terms of positions adopted during the first period, the question of East Timor ranks among the most salient one. In 1989, Portugal was able to achieve a common position of the Member States in relation to the dominance of Indonesia over East Timor. This was put forward by the Presidency of the EC to the General Assembly of the United Nations (UN) in New York and the Human Rights Commission in Geneva. Furthermore, Portugal suspended all bilateral contacts with China after the 1989 Tiananmen incident in Beijing. Indeed, this seemed to affect the relationship of Portugal and the EU on the question of the enclave of Macau.[9]

The East Timor question remains the single most important issue raised by Portugal within the EPC and CFSP, resulting again in 1995 in a common position of the EU in the context of the CFSP. This was backed by the European Parliament in 1996.[10]

After 1992, the socialisation into the EU structures led to a more assertive position by Portugal on matters related to the peace process in Angola, to the Africa policy of the EU, to EU–Mercosur relations and to the Euro–Mediterranean partnership. According to the yearly reports of the Portuguese *Ministerio dos Negocios Estrangeiros* (MNE) on the role of Portugal in the EU which are prepared to inform the Committee on European Affairs (*Comissao de Assuntos Europeus*) of the Portuguese parliament, Portugal wholeheartedly supports a Europe speaking with one voice to the outside world and is interested in seeking a strong congruence or convergence of positions. In spite of this position, Portugal has transfered its 'observer' stance of the second half of the 1980s into one of an active participant in the second half of the 1990s, particularly on questions related to the Portuguese-speaking countries around the world.[11]

Socialisation of foreign policy makers: the Europeanisation of foreign policy making

On 28 February 1977, the Portuguese Prime Minister Mário Soares submitted the Portuguese application for EU membership. Both the Council of Ministers and the Commission reacted both quickly and positively to the intentions of this young democracy. The positive opinion of the Commission was produced on 19 May 1978 and the first negotiations for accession were started in autumn 1978 with the real negotiations commencing in 1980.[12]

Since 1976, the MNE has embarked upon a major restructuring of foreign policy towards European integration which has required the socialisation of civil servants, as well as diplomats, into the policy-making structures of the EU. This process of socialisation and training of diplomats and civil servants was constrained by three main aspects. The first one was of an economic nature. The economic austerity to which the Portuguese administration was subject between 1978 and 1985 did not allow for too much investment in this area. The second reason was related to the fact that the longer the negotiations were continuing, the more insecure Portuguese governments and Portuguese diplomacy became in relation to the accession date. The third reason was that governmental instability prevented any profound changes of the Portuguese MNE.

A major restructuring only took place in 1985 by Jaime Gama, shortly before the accession to the EC and then finally in 1994 by José Durao Barroso. In both cases there was a reinforcement of the policy makers dealing with EU affairs. Between 1980 and 1985 the Portuguese government sent some civil servants to Community institutions for training. It was only in the last year before the accession that the Portuguese government made major efforts to strengthen the number of civil servants and diplomats dealing with European affairs. In 1986 the MNE began to seriously train its personnel in EPC procedures. Inside the MNE restructuring took place to adjust the different departments to the EPC structure. Moreover the COREU telegraphic system was installed and gradually permanent personnel were allocated to its operation. The Portuguese Permanent Representation was also used to socialise foreign policy makers into the procedures of EPC.[13]

It is important to bear in mind, that while in domestic policy matters institutional and personnel resources only began to be massively invested when there was a stronger demand coming from Brussels, the staff dedicated to European foreign policy did not change as dramatically. The latter continued merely to send a permanent delegation to the headquarters of NATO. Moreover when Portugal became a member of the WEU in 1988, the responsibilities of the ambassador to NATO were extended to the WEU, thereby reinforcing the Portuguese interpretation that the WEU was merely the European pillar of NATO. Between 1986 and 1992 there was a continuing increase in the training of civil servants and diplomats in the Ministry of Foreign Affairs.[14] The Presidency of the EC, held by Portugal in the first half of 1992, became an important catalyst to improve knowledge about European institutions and to do a good job during these six months. Such an effort was made both in aspects related to domestic affairs as well as matters of European security. Every year civil servants and diplomats were sent to Community institutions for training, or to special programmes offered by different institutes and universities in the United Kingdom, France and in the Netherlands. The main objective was to prepare Portuguese personnel for the forthcoming presidency in the first half of 1992. Training and updating courses continue to be provided to Portuguese civil servants and diplomats, not only in different international institutions but also domestically by the National Institute of Administration (*Instituto Nacional de Administracao* (INA)).[15] The breakthrough towards adjustment happened during the first Portuguese EU presidency when Portugal had to deal with the Yugoslav crisis, the peace process in the Middle East, relations with countries of Central and South America, the situation in Central and Eastern Europe as well as in the former USSR, the situation in the Southern part of Africa and the CSCE process. During the Portuguese presidency over a hundred meetings of twenty-one working groups, six ordinary meetings and nine extradionary meetings of the Political Committee took place and seventy-six EPC declarations were issued.[16]

Foreign policy process – domestic and bureaucratic

Foreign policy process: the emphasis of continuity and consensus
This very programmatic definition of the international relations of the Portuguese Republic clearly shows that foreign policy has become firmly interlinked with the European integration process. Looking back to before 1989, after the first revision of the constitution in 1982, the European integration process was not mentioned at all. Article 7 of the 1982 version ends with a reference to the privileged relationship of Portugal with its former colonies. Only after the second revision of the constitution in 1989 did the constitution include a section on the strengthening of European identity. But it is only during the third revision of the constitution that the major parties adjusted it to new requirements to comply with the Treaty on the European Union (TEU). In the revision of 1992, the construction of the EU became the overarching project for the Portuguese foreign policy of the 1990s.[17]

Portuguese foreign policy became synergetic with the European foreign policy decided intergovernmentally at a supranational level through EPC, now within the CFSP. According to the governmental programme of the present Socialist government elected on 1 October 1995, Portugal was very interested in taking advantage of the synergies of policies created through the CFSP in the relations with third countries.[18]

During and after the adoption of TEU, the small Christian Democratic Party (CDS), under the leadership of Manuel Monteiro, pursued an anti-Maastricht position. A campaign for a referendum was conducted throughout 1992 which was largely ignored by the two major parties. The

CDS shifted its position from wholehearted support for European integration and conformity with the position of the European People's Party
in the European Parliament to a more reluctant 'Europe of Fatherlands'
approach, advocating European integration, but not if it constrained
aspects of national sovereignty. This policy shift led not only to splits
within the CDS, but to the expulsion of the CDS from the EPP. The other
major opposition party, the Communist Party (*Partido Comunista
Portugues* (PCP)), also opposed European integration, because it is seen to
be dominated by economic interests. The so-called 'Europe of the
Monopolies' was rejected during and after the TEU was adopted. The
close relationship of the EU to NATO also led to opposition from the
PCP.[19]

Despite of this opposition, these two parties on the right and left of the
spectrum have not been able to play a major role in the overall design of
Portuguese foreign policy. On the contrary, the share of the vote of these
two parties in relation to the two larger parties has been declining since
the 1980s, lowering their possibility of taking part in government. While
the two main parties were able to increase their share of the vote from
59.26 per cent in 1976 to almost 80 per cent in the 1990s, the smaller
parties decreased their share from 30 per cent in 1976 to 13–16 per cent
in the 1990s. Therefore European policy making is dominated by the two
large parties, which with or without the support of the smaller parties
shape Portuguese foreign policy.[20]

Another institutional-political aspect that has changed since the 1980s
is the relationship between the presidency and the government. The original definition of the directly-elected presidency was to make the political
system more stable. Therefore, the President was allocated strong powers
in foreign policy and defence matters. Due to the fact that the governments were very unstable between 1976 and 1983, President Ramalho
Eanes, strongly supportive of the MFA, was able to influence foreign and
defence policy until 1982. Until the early 1980s the constitution had both
a political, as well as a military, realm.[21]

This changed only after the revision of the constitution in 1982, when
the main revolutionary-military institution, the 'Council of Revolution',
was abolished and the political system completed its civilianisation in
constitutional terms. After adoption of the National Defence Law in the
same year, and the election of Mário Soares as new President in 1986, the
civilianisation process was finally completed. From then on, the implicit
semi-presidential nature of the political system became more domesticated
by the civilian politicians.

During the presidency of Mário Soares between 1986 and 1995, most
of the disputes with Prime Minister Anibal Cavaco Silva were about
domestic politics. The semi-presidentialist system in Portugal, which
allows the direct election of the President, led to a so-called 'institutional

guerilla war' after 1991 between President Mário Soares and Prime Minister Anibal Cavaco Silva, instead of cohabitation as has been common practice in France. The President and Prime Minister belonged to different parties and they were driven by a mutual dislike of one another, so that the conflict had its sources in personal rather than real policy differences in Portuguese foreign policy.[22]

The decision-making process in Portuguese foreign policy remains simple because, apart from consensualism and continuity at the elite level, the Portuguese system continues to be highly centralised, so that no other territorial units exist which may challenge or shape Portuguese foreign policy. The referendum on 8 November 1998 overwhelmingly rejected regionalisation of the country into eight units. Despite a low turnout of slightly above 50 per cent, two thirds of the population were against regionalisation, while one third were for it.[23]

This shows that referenda are regarded as a risky business for the Portuguese elite. For that reason, the PS, the PSD and the CDS decided to give up on the idea of a referendum in Portugal related to the introduction of Economic and Monetary Union (EMU) and the new Treaty of Amsterdam. The decision-making process on European integration has, until now, directly excluded the participation of the population in referenda, fearful that the population may vote against integration. In spite of the fact that the Portuguese population is among the most pro-European population in the EU, the population has a perception that it actually has a low level of knowledge on EU matters. There is always the possibility that better information may lead to a more sceptical, or a more divided, public opinion. This is a risk that the Portuguese political elites have been able to avoid to date.[24]

Bureaucratic politics in the policy process: the restructuring of the MNE
Since 1982, the MNE has steadily gained in prestige and power within the governmental system. All matters related to European affairs are now dealt with by the Secretariat-General of European Affairs (*Secretariado-Geral de Assuntos Europeus* (SGAE)) which is supported by a General-Directorate for Community Affairs (*Direccao-Geral de Assuntos Comunitarios* (DGCE)) which before 1985 was split between the Council of Ministers and the Ministry of Finances. The centralisation of the coordinating administration for EU affairs in the Ministry of Foreign Affairs was accepted without problem by the internal bureaucracy. An Interministerial Committee on Community Affairs (*Comissao Interministerial de Assuntos Comunitarios* (CIAC)) meets every friday morning to discuss all major decisions related to issues brought forward in COREPER and the working committees of the Council. The work of DGCE and CIAC gained a reputation within the government services as being well-prepared to deal with the coordination of policy. Parallel to

this centralisation of the coordination of EU affairs in the MNE, the Ministry was also subject to major restructuring of its other services in 1985 and 1994 and replacing the structure that was taken over from the former authoritarian regime. Shortly before integration into the EC in 1984 several services within the MNE were restructured leading partly to centralisation. In the 1994 reform the emphasis was on decentralisation but with better coordination. Several coordinating inter-departmental committees within the MNE, as well as inter-ministerial committees comprising other ministries, were created to strengthen the coherence of Portuguese foreign policy. While the DGCE was able to gain a monopoly over most EU matters in terms of its coordination, the MNE as a whole strengthened its coordination structures with a view to achieving better coherence between multilateral relations within international organisations and bilaterateral relations with other countries. These two departments were reinforced by a further coordinating department which was in charge of keeping an overview of the whole picture of Portuguese foreign relations. Within the DGCE three departments deal specifically with bilateral or multilateral relations within or without the EU. One can also observe that the matters related to the CFSP discussed within Pillar II are a matter for the DGCE. It constitutes the largest group within the permanent representation in Brussels.[25] In sum, one can assert that since 1985, the MNE has been under pressure to restructure its very fragmented foreign policy through the introduction of more efficient forms of coordination inside the MNE.

Foreign policy action – with the EU and beyond

With the EU: the dignity of a small state restored

Since the Portuguese presidency of the first half of 1992, Portuguese diplomacy and foreign policy restored its importance in the world. For six months the Portuguese MNE was able to coordinate most of the external relations of the EC as well as prepare the major policy areas related to the further development of the European integration process. The Portuguese presidency was evaluated as being well-organised and very efficient, in spite of the pressures that it was exposed to, such as an agreement on the reform of the Common Agriculture Policy (CAP), the process towards the ratification of the TEU by the Member States, as well as the growing role of the EU in external relations. It was during the Portuguese presidency that the crisis in Bosnia-Herzegovina broke out. The Portuguese ambassador José Cutileiro tried to bring the different parties involved to a conference in Lisbon but with limited success. Moreover, during the Portuguese presidency the first Danish referendum on the TEU in June 1992 led to its rejection by a slight majority creating a crisis in most other countries. A climax of the presidency was when the Portuguese Prime

Minister Anibal Cavaco represented the EU in the UN Rio Conference on the environment and development. This event actually changed the whole perception of Portuguese foreign policy makers concerning their involvement in the external relations of the EU. Instead of presenting a contradictory position to that of Portugal, the event demonstrated the strengthening of a national position if there is a synthesis of the Member States' positions.[26]

The case of East Timor is illustrative of the strengthening of a national position through common action with the other Member States of the EU. Since its accession to the EC Portugal has always tried to influence through the EPC, and later in the CFSP, the position of the other Member States on this issue. This resulted in a common position in relation to East Timor during the Greek presidency in 1989.[27] East Timor, part of one of the islands in south-east Asia, became independent during the decolonisation process in 1974 and 1975. During 1975, several parties emerged in East Timor which presented themselves as the legitimate representatives of the Timorese people. A three-month civil war led to the dominance of the Liberation National Timor Front (*Frente Timorense de Libertacao Nacional-Fretilin*), which declared independence for East Timor, but decided to withdraw this declaration until Portugal would announce it. Meanwhile, on 7 December 1975, Indonesian troops invaded East Timor and annexed the territory to Indonesia. Since then, Portuguese diplomacy has been very keen to restore to the East Timorese people the right to choose for themselves which kind of political solution they would like for the future. Portugal was able to achieve such a common position of the EU in 1989, thereby reinforcing the Portuguese position.[28]

Since its accession to the EC Portugal has always tried to influence in the EPC, and later on the CFSP, the position of the other Member States towards a common position in relation to East Timor and the condemnation of Indonesia. Such an effort was successful during the Greek presidency in 1989.[29] A condemnation of the annexation of East Timor by Indonesia was achieved in 1996. The recent events in Indonesia have led again to conflicts between the Indonesian army and the East Timorense movement for independence. Indeed, the main leader of the independence movement, Xanana Gusmao, called for supporters to protect themselves against the new aggression and killing of pro-independence supporters by the Indonesian army. The Portuguese government plays an important role in trying to give an opportunity to the population of East Timor to freely choose their future path.

The growing 'Mediterraneanisation' of Portuguese foreign and security policy is illustrated in its participation in two major forces for rapid intervention in the Mediterranean region. Eurofor and Euromarfor, founded in 1995, consist of Spanish, Italian, French and Portuguese troops, which may be used rapidly as a part of WEU Petersberg missions. The Eurofor consists of 10,000 soldiers, who are deployable in a very short period of time. The Euromarfor is a maritime force with airforce facilities to be used in conjuction, or independently, from the Eurofor. These two forces can be used by NATO, the UN and the EU. These forces are under a permanent command based in Florence and are – along with Eurocorps (France, Germany, Benelux and Spain forces) founded in 1992, the British–Dutch Amphibious division and the Central Multinational Division of NATO (United Kingdom, Belgium, Germany and Netherlands forces) – the first signs of emerging European military forces, which are a response to a growing need to use multi-national forces for peacekeeping and peace re-establishment missions. The Portuguese government also has observer status in the Eurocorps. Furthermore, Portugal is engaged in several peacekeeping and monitoring missions around the world under the auspices of the UN.[30]

The Mediterraneanisation of Portuguese foreign policy does not only have a military aspect. Indeed, the most important aspect has so far been the cooperation between the northern and southern fringe of the Mediterranean through the '5+5 dialogue', which is envisaged as a continuing dialogue between the northern and southern fringe of the Mediterranean. By far the most important initiative was organised by Spain in November 1995. The Barcelona Conference, during the Spanish presidency, initiated what is now called the Euro-Mediterranean partnership, which intends to create a Mediterranean Free Trade Area (MEFTA) by the year 2010. For this purpose the EU is allocating ECU 4.7 billion, with additional projected funding of ECU 5 billion coming from the European Investment Bank. These funds are intended to improve the living conditions of the population in the southern rim of the Mediterranean and bring these countries closer to the level of economic development of the northern rim EU Member States. Twenty-seven governments in the north (fifteen) and south (twelve) have signed up to MEFTA and its completion by 2010. Portugal is one of the members interested in making this initiative a success, so that the Mediterranean region becomes less volatile and emigration to the EU from Africa can be stopped. Portugal has, in recent years, intensified its contacts with Morocco in this respect. In this sense, the policies of the Portuguese government clearly are synergetic with the policies of the EU. This issue was less important to Portugal than to Spain and Italy, but it strengthened the role of Portugal in the Mediterranean.[31]

Portugal has also been extremely interested in strengthening a Euro-African dialogue. Indeed, the Portuguese government was a major force in shaping the dialogue between the EU and the South African Development Community (SADC) to which South Africa, Angola, Botswana, Lesotho, Malawi, Mozambique, Namibia, Swaziland, Tanzania, Zambia and Zimbabwe belong. The SADC was founded in 1980 and clearly intends to

raise the level of economic development of these countries. As a consequence of Angola and Mozambique's membership of SADC, one of the
speaking languages of the organisation is Portuguese.[32]

Beyond but within EU parameters: Lusophony and Hispanidad

Since 1992 there has been a narrowing of the gap between EU and
Portuguese foreign policy. This is due to a growing expansion of multilateral relations of the EU with third parties. The European integration
process is being exported to other parts of the world. The Community-
building method has become a way of overcoming regional tensions and
fostering democratic behaviour and economic cooperation. Portuguese
foreign policy is the foreign policy of a small state, which has had to learn
to be realistic and pragmatic in terms of its aims and objectives. There is
no longer a contradiction between Portuguese foreign policy from within
and without European parameters. The main reason is that the EU is
extremely committed to the UN's principles of peace, democracy and
human rights.

The traumatic events during and after the decolonisation of the large
Portuguese colonial empire has led to a will, on the part of the Portuguese
political class, to keep in touch with the developments of the new independent Portuguese-speaking countries. The symbolic dimension of what
has been called lusophony (lusofonia) has played a role in the definition
of Portuguese foreign policy since 1976. However, the instability of
government and the adjustment to the European integration process made
it difficult for Portuguese foreign policy to reconstruct its linkages to the
former colonies. Indeed, in some of these countries (Mozambique and
Angola) civil wars between different political factions broke out, which
are today still a major impediment of the economic and social development of these countries. A reconstruction of the network of the
relationships of Portugal with other Portuguese speaking countries started
in the 1990s leading in 1996 to the creation of the Community of
Portuguese-speaking countries (*Comunidade de Paises de Lingua
Portuguesa* (CPLP)) in 1996. This new international organisation has its
seat in Lisbon and consists of seven members (Mozambique, Angola,
Cape Verde, Sao Tome and Principe, Guinea-Bissau, Portugal and Brazil).
East Timor has an observer status, due to the fact that its international
role is still not defined. Similar to the French Community (*Communauté
Francaise*) and the British Commonwealth, it intends to foster political,
economic, social and cultural cooperation between the different countries.
Since 1997 the meetings between the governments of the Community have
been intensified.

This reconstruction of the Portuguese-speaking community may be
regarded as a major success of the Portuguese foreign policy of the 1990s.
It was after many years of political-diplomatic negotiations that such a

joint enterprise became reality. An important event celebrating the international role of Portugal was the Expo '98 which devoted some attention to the newly found lusophony. In spite of this the CPLP is a small enterprise in comparison to the French Community and the Commonwealth.

Nevertheless, it is an important new step in Portuguese diplomacy, because it may lead to a strengthening of these fragile democracies in an international context. The five African countries can be regarded as among the poorest in terms of gross domestic product (GDP) per capita, so that the CPLP may be a way of increasing international solidarity among the Portuguese speaking countries. In this context, Brazil was always a promoter of South–South relations in the past.

Apart from lusophony, Portugal has increased its commitment to Ibero-American cooperation jointly with Spain. The Ibero-American summits (*Cumbres Iberoamericanas*) were originally a project of Spanish foreign policy established in July 1991 in Guadalajara in Mexico. The summits are an annual meeting of the Heads of State and Prime Ministers of the Iberian countries with Latin American countries. The summits are designed for the exchange of information on questions related to poverty, external debt, economic, social, technological and cultural development, childhood, health, drug trafficking, marginalisation, underdevelopment and cooperation. One of the most notable issues of the summit has been Cuba, including the condemnation of the introduction of the US Helms–Burton Act in 1996. The summits are an opportunity to strengthen the bilateral and multilateral relations between the Iberian countries and Latin and Central America. In the first half of the 1990s, the Portuguese political elite viewed the role of Spain in promoting the summits with suspicion, but since 1995 cooperation between Portugal and Spain in synergetic foreign policy issues has increased considerably. Portuguese and Spanish are the two languages of the Common Market of the Southern Cone (MERCOSUR) and this may reinforce the bridge function of Portugal and Spain in a future more well-defined EU CFSP.[33]

In Asia and the Pacific, Portugal is now completing its process of decolonisation. Macau will be handed over to China by the end of 2000, and preparations are under way to make this happen as smoothly as possible. Due to the commitment to democratisation on the part of the Indonesian government, there is also the hope that East Timor may soon be able to choose its own destiny. The recent release of opposition leader Xanana Gusmao from prison is leading to contacts between the different parties of East Timor to find a consensual path towards democratisation and possible independence from Indonesia. Portuguese foreign policy continues to be a major player in drawing public attention to the question of East Timor as well as a negotiator on behalf of East Timor with the Indonesian government.

On the whole, Portuguese special relationships are no longer conducted without the EU. On the contrary, the initiatives of the Portuguese foreign policy complement the CFSP. Synergies have been created since Portugal became a member of the EC in 1986. The integration into a larger role through EU membership strengthened Portuguese foreign policy. This is in part because Portugal was under pressure to adjust to the EU CFSP machinery, which is also itself in a condition of permanent restructuring. This double process of restructuring led to synergies, which made Portuguese foreign policy less fragmented and ideological, but more integrated, efficient and pragmatic. Instead of a constructivist approach towards foreign policy, we may assert that Portuguese foreign policy adopted a reconstructivist approach based on the experience that Portuguese diplomacy has accummulated over centuries of international relations.

Conclusion

After the collapse of the Portuguese colonial empire during the revolutionary process of 1974–75, Portuguese foreign policy lost its credibility. The rapid decolonisation created more instability in Africa and Asia. The main priority became the accession to the EC, mainly to strengthen the structures of the new fragile democracy. Foreign policy was very much oriented towards Europe. Only after 1986 did Portuguese foreign policy begin to reconstruct its past linkages to the new Portuguese-speaking countries. Portuguese diplomacy became quite successful during the 1990s in pursuing this aim. After twenty-five years of democracy and thirteen years of EU membership, Portuguese influence in the world has increased substantially. But this influence is that of a small country which subscribes to the principles of the UN and the EU. The colonial wars of the 1960s and 1970s shaped the mentality of the new democratic Portugal. Peaceful settlement of conflicts, diplomatic-political solutions, peacekeeping and peace re-establishment missions, as well as the protection of human rights, became the main elements of Portuguese foreign policy. More than ever, Portuguese foreign policy is attempting to put into practice the lessons that were learned from mistakes made in dealing with Portugal's own colonial problems.

Notes

1 S. P. Huntington, *The Third Wave: Democratization in the Late Twentieth Century* (Norman, University of Oklahoma Press, 1991).
2 Three major factions emerged in the summer of 1975 within the MFA with three different constitutional designs for the future of Portugal. The *Goncalvists* supported Prime Minister Vasco Goncalves in his intention to transform Portugal into a People's Democracy close to the Soviet Union; the

Otelists supported Otelo Saraiva de Carvalho, who wanted the establishment of a grass roots democracy and gained its inspiration from the liberation movements of Third World countries. The third group, under Melo Antunes, were moderate and tended towards social democracy with some elements of the ideology of Third World liberation movements. In the end, the latter was able to prevail and work with the main political parties towards a liberal-democratic model. Meanwhile several studies were written on these struggles between the different factions of the MFA. See for example R. Eisfeld, *Der Pluralistischer Sozialismus in Europa. Ansaetze und Scheitern am Beispiel Portugal* (Cologne, Verlag Wissenschaft und Politik, 1984); D. Porch, *The Portuguese Armed Forces and the Revolution* (London, Croom Helm, 1977), pp. 124–153.

3   The danger of a domino theory, as was perceived to have occurred in Indochina, was a scenario considered by Henry Kissinger during this period. See J. F. Antunes, *Os Americanos e e Portugal* (Lisboa, Publicacoes Europa-America, 1985), pp. 348–353. During the revolutionary period Portugal was excluded from the nuclear planning group of NATO; see K. Maxwell, 'The thorns of the Portuguese revolution', *Foreign Affairs*, 54:2 (January 1976), pp. 250–271.

4   Porch, *The Portuguese*, p. 65.

5   V. Alves, 'Colonialismo e descolonizaca', *Revista Critica de Ciencias Sociais*, 15–17, pp. 559–567, particularly p. 561; O. S. de Carvalho, *Alvorada em Abril* (Lisboa, Alvim, 1986), pp. 92–108.

6   On civilianisation and democratisation see the excellent study by F. Aguero, 'Democratic consolidation and the military in southern Europe and South America' in R. Gunther, P. N. Diamandouros, H-J. Puhle (eds), *The Politics of Democratic Consolidation. Southern Europe in Comparative Perspective* (Baltimore, John Hopkins University Press, 1995), pp. 124–165, particularly pp. 131, 144.

7   In spite of all that the Portuguese feared that a stronger commitment of Spain in NATO and in the EC would swallow Portuguese foreign policy and defence interests. To date, the Portuguese have been successful in resisting Portuguese troops in NATO's Iberlant command being commanded by a Spanish officer and have been able to use the special relationship with the United States, which they had created since the foundation of NATO in 1949, against the steady integration of Spain and France into the military structures of NATO during the 1980s and 1990s. The ambiguous position of these countries in relation to NATO gave even more significance to the membership of Portugal which did not question its military integration into NATO structures. Portugal was able to ensure that both Spain and Portugal would not be in the same territorial command. While Spain remained integrated in the European command SACEUR, Portugal continued to be part of SACLANT which had its military headquarters in Norfolk, Virginia. (A. Vasconcelos, 'Portuguese defence policy: internal politics and defence commitments' in J. Chipman (ed.), *NATO's Southern Allies: Internal and External Challenges* (London, N.Y., Routledge, 1988), pp. 86–139, pp. 117–118.)

8   K. Hanf and B. Soetendorp, *Adapting to European Integration: Small States and the European Union* (London, Longman, 1998).

9 Ministerio dos Negocios Estrangeiros, Portugal na Comunidade Europeia, 4 ano, 1989 (Lisboa, MNE, 1990), pp. 361–362.

10 F. S. Costa, 'Introducao' in Ministerio dos Negocios Estrangeiros, *Portugal na Uniao Europeia*, 10 ano, 1995 (Lisboa, MNE, 1996), I–XXVIII, XXIV; Ministerio dos Negocios Estrangeiros, *Portugal na Uniao Europeia*, 11 ano, 1996 (Lisboa, MNE, 1997), pp. 18–19.

11 Ministerio dos Negocios Estrangeiros, *Portugal na Uniao Europeia*, 10 ano,1995, pp. XXI–XXIV.

12 J. Magone, 'A integracao Europeia e a construcao da democracia portuguesa' in *Penelope*, 18 (1998), pp. 123–163, pp. 139–141.

13 P. S. da Costa Pereira, 'Portugal: public administration and EPC/CFSP – a fruitful adaptation process' in E. Regelsberger and F. Algieri (eds), *Synergy at Work: Spain and Portugal in European Foreign Policy* (Bonn, Europa Union Verlag, 1996), pp. 207–229, particularly pp. 378 and 386.

14 In contrast, in June 1985, after signing the Treaty of Accession to the European Community in Belém, the government was bombarded by the institutions of the EC to send representatives to several internal and external committees. According to the figures provided by the Portuguese MNE the Portuguese government was requested to nominate overnight representatives to the different structures of the EC, as well as 250 committees and 500 expert groups, which work in the Commission. In the first year Portuguese representatives had taken place in over 2500 meetings. (Ministero dos Negocios Estrangeiros, *Portugal nas Comunidades Europeias. Primeiro Ano 1986* (Lisboa, MNE, 1987), pp. 181–182.)

15 Ministerio de Negocios Estrangeiros, *Portugal nas Comunidades Europeias. Terceiro Ano, 1987* (Lisboa, MNE, 1989), pp. 331–333; Ministerio dos Negocios Estrangeiros, *Portugal nas Comunidades Europeias, Quarto Ano, 1989* (Lisboa, MNE, 1990), pp. 351–353; Ministerio dos Negocios Estrangeiros, *Portugal nas Comunidades Europeias, Quinto Ano, 1990* (Lisboa, MNE, 1991), pp. 381–386.

16 Ministerio dos Negocios Estrangeiros, *Portugal na Comunidade Europeia, 7 ano, 1992,* (Lisboa, MNE, 1993), pp. 378 and 386.

17 *Constituicao da Republica Portuguesa. As 3 versoes apos 25 de Abril* (Lisboa, Porto Editora, 1989), pp. 26, 132, 215.

18 Assembleia da Republica, *Programa do XII Governo Constitucional. Apresentacao e Debate* (Lisboa, Assembleia da Republica, 1996), pp. 35–41.

19 J. Magone, 'Portugal', in J. Lodge, *The 1994 Election to the European Parliament* (London, Pinter, 1996), pp. 147–156, particularly p. 150; J. Magone and M. J. Stock, 'Portugal' in European Political Data Yearbook, 1997, *European Journal for Political Research*, 4 (1999).

20 J. Magone, *European Portugal. The Difficult Road to Sustainable Democracy* (Basingstoke, Macmillan, 1997), p. 85.

21 On the Portuguese semi-presidentialism before the first revision see E. da Veiga Domingos, *Portugal Politico. Analise das Instituicoes* (Lisbon, Rolim, 1980), pp. 115–132.

22 M. Frain, 'Relacoes entre o presidente e o primeiro ministro em Portugal: 1985–1995' *Analise Social*, XXX:133 (1995), pp. 653–678, pp. 673–675. Particularly in 1995 there were different positions held by the President of the

Republic Mario Soares and Prime Minister Anibal Cavaco Silva in relation to Angola.

23 *Diario de Noticias*, 9 November 1998.

24 See *Eurobarometer*, 49 (1998), pp. 2–3; p. 33.

25 Ministerio dos Negocios Estrangeiros, *A Reestruturacao do Ministerio dos Negocios Estrangeiros* (Lisboa, MNE, 1995), pp. 11–22.

26 On the Portuguese presidency see J. Magone, *European Portugal*, pp. 164–170.

27 Ministerio dos Negocios Estrangeiros, *Portugal nas Comunidades Europeias, 1 Ano, 1986* (Lisboa, MNE, 1987), p. 200; Ministerio dos Negocios Estrangeiros, *Portugal nas Comunidades Europeias, 3 Ano, 1988* (Lisboa, MNE, 1989), p. 342.

28 P. G. Teles, 'O estatuto juridico de Timor-Leste: Um case study sobre as rela-coes entre os conceitos de autodeterminacao e soberania' *Politica Internacional*, 1:15/16 (Outubro-Inverno 1997), pp. 195–202.

29 Ministerio dos Negocios Estrangeiros, *Portugal nas Comunidades Europeias, 1 Ano, 1986* (Lisboa, MNE, 1987), p. 200; Ministerio dos Negocios Estrangeiros, *Portugal nas Comunidade Europeias, 3 Ano, 1988* (Lisboa, MNE, 1989), p. 342.

30 C. Antunes, 'A insercao portuguesa nas organizacoes militares e de seguranca' in *Janus 98, Anuario de Relacoes Exteriores* (Lisboa, Publico e Universidade Autonoma de Lisboa, 1997), pp. 32–33. In March 1997, Portugal had deployed 411 military staff to the 23,861 strong military force of the UN. It occupied the twenty-fifth place in terms of its strength within joint multina-tional forces. These UN troops were based in Bosnia-Herzegovina, in the Western Sahara during the referendum monitored by the UN and the moni-toring mission of the UN in Angola. *Dictionnaire de l'Union Europeenne, Politiques, Institutions, Programmes* (Brussels, DeBoeck University, 1998), pp. 315–316; 'Mediterraneanisation' was coined by M. Frain, 'A peninsula Iberica e a Europa: uma convergencia nas politicas de defesa espanhola e portuguesa no pos-guerra fria?' *Politica Internacional*, 1:15/16 (Outono-Inverno 1997), pp. 249–282, particularly p. 267.

31 On the Euro-Mediterranean Partnership see R. Gillespie (ed.), *The Euro-Mediterranean Partnership. Political and Economic Perspectives* (London, Frank Cass, 1997). For a first assessment see J. Calabrese, 'Beyond Barcelona: the politics of the Euro-Mediterranean partnership', *European Security*, 6:4 (Winter 1997), pp. 86–100.

32 J. J. M. da Gama, 'Cooperacao Europa-Africa e Politica Portuguesa para a Africa Austral'. Intervencao na Reuniao Ministerial UE/SADC em Windhoek, 14 October 1996 (http://www.mne.gov.pt).

33 N. Gomes, 'As relacoes externas da America-Latina' in *Janus 98, Anuario de Relacoes Exteriores* (Lisboa, UAL e Publico, 1997), pp. 130–131.

III

The (post-)neutral states?

10

Sweden and Finland

Lee Miles

Introduction: from 'neutrality' to 'post-neutrality'

Sweden and Finland have long been regarded as countries maintaining relatively distinct foreign policies – principally built around a commitment to neutrality, and more recently, to a more flexible definition of 'non-alignment'. For this reason the two Nordic neutrals are often grouped together. Nevertheless, despite obvious similarities, the commonalties between these two states should not be over-emphasised. Miles, for example, has argued elsewhere that despite Swedish and Finnish neutrality being seen as a common grouping of 'asymmetrical neutrals', there have always been subtle differences between the two.[1] Sweden's neutral status was almost entirely voluntary (non-mandatory) and active. Finland's version was 'semi-mandatory', embodied in the 1948 Fenno-Soviet Treaty of Friendship, Cooperation and Mutual Assistance (FCMA), and passive, having been borne out of the experience of two military defeats (1939–40 and 1941–44) at the hands of the Soviets.

However, the challenges confronting these two Nordic neutrals remained (more or less) the same in the 1990s. First, both states' foreign policies have responded to the strategic changes affecting Eastern Europe since 1989, which led ultimately to the disintegration of bloc politics in Europe, and more specifically, the abolition of one of the two superpowers, when the Soviet Union dissolved in 1991. Secondly, and riding on the back of this, Sweden and Finland have dealt with the demands emanating from a more dynamic European Community/Union (EC/EU). Their governments eventually sought full EU membership (which they achieved in January 1995). Thirdly, and reinforcing the attractiveness of EU accession in the eyes of governing elites, both states have experienced economic difficulties (including severe recessions between 1990 and 1993), suggesting to their governing elites that distinct Nordic-style social-democratic inspired approaches to economic management were increasingly ineffective in the 1990s.[2] Sweden and Finland's image as two of Europe's most successful post-industrialised states was now tarnished, prompting calls from domestic quarters for economic-based priorities to have a greater influence in shaping each government's foreign policy.

It was clear for all sides to see that traditional doctrines of neutrality would no longer be appropriate in a post-Cold War Europe. More flexible foreign policies were needed by Sweden and Finland that would be compatible with their dual intentions of attaining full EC/EU membership and satisfying the changing security parameters and pressures operating in Europe. To all intents and purposes, the overriding question for their policy makers was not whether these states should adapt to, and/or become 'socialised' with, the new European security and EU environments, but rather how, in what ways and to what extent.[3] In one sense, the size of adaptation affecting Swedish and Finnish foreign policies is more marked precisely because they had tried previously to remain aloof from Cold War security frameworks. As Carlsnaes has commented Swedish (and Finnish) neutrality was not a 'doctrine' in the first instance, 'but a policy aimed at sustaining and, hence *ipso facto* constituting a particular form of "power relationship" defined in terms of a specific contextual structure' – namely a Cold War derived, bloc-based Europe.[4]

As Europe's 'contextual structure' altered, Sweden and Finland operated with 'post-neutral' foreign policies. 'Security threats' and 'opposing actors' could no longer be identified for certain and in the language of Hakovirta,[5] neutrality policy would not be effective when its outcomes were neither credible nor predictable in an increasingly vacuous Europe. Thus, the first step was that traditional terms such as neutrality were replaced by narrower, but more flexible, definitions of 'non-alignment', with Swedish and Finnish foreign policies both using the official title of 'non-participation in military alliances'. The second step (and one that is still taking place) was that elements of the Swedish and Finnish elite embarked on serious 'psychological' domestic debates (involving larger number of political actors and even the Nordic publics) on whether it was appropriate for their countries to join European military alliances sometime in the future. For these 'Nordic post-neutrals', it was not a case of merely adapting within an existing Western security alliance or framework (be it the North Atlantic Treaty Organisation (NATO) or the Western European Union (WEU)) – as it was for the 'NATO Nordics' of Denmark, Iceland and Norway.[6] In short, these states now have to consider whether they should drop the language of 'non-alignment' altogether and become firmly associated with Western European military alliances either through some kind of 'semi-alignment', an active military role in the EU's Common Foreign and Security Policy (CFSP), and/or membership of NATO and the WEU. The objective of this chapter is to ascertain the degree of foreign policy change and whether the Sweden and Finland are now conducting an 'EU foreign policy' with the Union's emerging CFSP at its core. For brevity, and to reflect the differences in the size of the two nations, this chapter will concentrate on Sweden, and draw out any useful comparisons for Finland.

Swedish and Finnish changes in foreign policy

Sweden

The start of the substantial changes in Swedish foreign policy can be traced back to 1990. During the summer of that year, the Swedish press played its traditional role as a forum for the views of leading party and public figures and the main subject for discussion was the prospects for Swedish EU accession. Later, in that October, Prime Minister Ingvar Carlsson outlined his vision at the opening of the Swedish Parliament (Riksdag) of an evolving Europe, free from division into superpower-led blocs and under this scenario, EU membership would be compatible with Swedish neutrality.[7] This marked a notable reversal in his official view when compared to those outlined previously in the Swedish press during May 1990.[8] The path was thus laid for the same Prime Minister to announce shortly afterwards (26 October 1990) that Swedish membership of the (then) EC was now in the national interest and full membership application was submitted in July 1991. However, the process was controversial, attracting criticism from within the Social Democratic Cabinet, the SAP party and amongst other key political and public actors.

Under the succeeding non-socialist administration led by Carl Bildt (1991–94), further alterations in official Swedish foreign policy began, for the most part, in earnest when the language of neutrality was replaced with that of 'a security policy with a European identity'.[9] Bildt's more openly pro-Western foreign policy was not to be devoid of domestic criticism, with the Centre Party (a government coalition partner) and the Social Democrats (now in opposition since October 1991) advocating the maintenance of non-alignment. Indeed, the restraining influence of the Centre Party on their moderate and liberal colleagues, and the continuing attachment of the majority of the public to Sweden's non-aligned status, largely ensured that non-alignment continued as the foundation of Swedish foreign policy. Nonetheless, during the Bildt years in government, Swedish foreign policy became more assertive, going beyond what would have previously been acceptable in Sweden. The Bildt years were also the time when Sweden's accession terms for entry into the EU were being negotiated and agreed. As Bildt noted in a flagship speech (16 September 1993) in Brussels 'we look upon the European Union . . . as the hub of the new European security order'.[10]

The next phase in Sweden's foreign policy adjustment, it could be argued, began in 1994 with the return of the Social Democrats to office. Although the Social Democrats were to relieve the non-socialists of power

in 1994 and thus it was Ingvar Carlsson who was to be at the helm when
the country acceded to the Union in January 1995, Swedish foreign policy
became (at least at the official level) less openly 'European'. Certainly,
Bildt's official security policy 'with a European identity' was pursued
more subtly and replaced in official statements by an emphasis on 'non-
participation in military alliances' as the core of Swedish foreign policy.
This is not to say that Carlsson or his successor as Prime Minister, Göran
Persson, have not followed a 'Europeanised' foreign policy – for clearly
EU membership and participation in its CFSP are central elements of
government policy. Rather the language of Swedish foreign policy has
been more cagey given that substantial numbers of the SAP's party faithful and the public at large prefer the continuation of the country's
non-aligned status. In short: 'sixty years of indoctrination has its price'.[11]

Yet, over the years since 1994, and in spite of the Social Democrats
retaining power in the 1998 general election, Swedish foreign policy has
continued to 'soften' as regards its non-alignment to the point where even
'non-participation in military alliances' has been interpreted liberally by
the Swedes. Their commitment to 'non-participation' has, for example,
not prevented the Swedish Defence Minister, Björn von Sydow from
permitting Swedish forces to be placed under NATO command structures
in Bosnia (sanctioned as part of UN mandates) or allowing for 'Gripen'
jets from participating in NATO manoeuvres since 1997. To a large
degree, the Social Democratic government has slowly been down-grading
even this official commitment to 'non-participation in military alliances'
in practice. However, the subject of formal Swedish membership of
NATO is still controversial and successive Swedish governments have
been careful to cloak closer cooperation with NATO powers under the
broader banner of the UN and/or the auspices of crisis management (see
below). The Swedes have been careful throughout to stress that there still
remains a substantial 'internationalist' streak within their foreign policy
and they continue to seek an active role in promoting peace and human
rights on the global stage.

Finland

A similar process also took place in Finland. The country, now free from
the shackles of the 1948 FCMA Treaty (which was declared void by the
Finnish and Russian governments on 20 January 1992 and replaced by a
looser free trade agreement), was for the first time able to ally itself more
closer with the West, and pursue a foreign policy that was no longer
'semi-mandatory' nor necessarily passive. Indeed, the Finns, even more
than the Swedes, perceived that their security needs required them to be
rooted firmly in the expanding Western European security architecture.
To a degree, this derives from the realisation amongst Finns that the
country's prior neutrality policy had always been an essential practical

component guaranteeing the Finnish nation state's independence from its larger Soviet neighbour.[12] Since the Soviet Union's disintegration in 1991, and once it was clear that Russian democratic reforms would continue, Finnish policy makers acknowledged that changes in Finland's foreign policy were appropriate within a post-1989 security order. Hence, once the Swedes indicated they were pursuing the fast track to EU membership, 'the Finns were not far behind'.[13] In fact, the Finnish government moved from a commitment to seeing out the protracted European Economic Area (EEA) negotiations to submitting a full EU membership application within a year (lodging their application in March 1992) – some eight months after the Swedes had done so.

The Finnish government placed even greater emphasis than their Swedish counterparts on security considerations in their reasons for joining the (then) EC. On top of Austrian and Swedish-derived arguments that neutrality was no longer an obstacle to EC accession, the Finnish elite were also concerned that if Finland remained outside the Community, it could well be squeezed between an increasingly important Community and a rather politically unstable Russia.[14] The Centrist government of Esko Arho, for example, claimed repeatedly that in the post-Cold War Europe, there was 'no longer ground for a broadly applied policy of neutrality'.[15] By 1993, the Finns abandoned, to all intents and purposes, any pretext to 'hard-line neutrality' and were advocating their readiness to accept the Maastricht Treaty and its embryonic CFSP. As Arter noted, the Finnish government, political parties and even the public approved EU membership in their (16 October 1994) referendum (by 57 per cent) as much on the grounds of being a vote for the West and the CFSP, than as a specific 'Yes' for the economic aspects of the Maastricht Treaty.[16]

However, successive Finnish governments have also so far been reluctant to come out in favour of Finland joining formally any European or Atlanticist security framework. The need to maintain friendly bilateral relations with the Russian Federation, which remains wary of NATO enlargement, is still a primary consideration for Finnish policy makers. 'Finlandisation' may have effectively disappeared along with the Soviet Union, but Finland will always need to accommodate the security concerns of its larger neighbour if its foreign policy is to be successful. Hence, despite a fairly open debate in Finland in 1995–96 on the merits of Finnish membership of NATO, the Lipponen government maintains that Finland is better served by cooperation with NATO powers under the auspices of peacekeeping and crisis management, rather than formal membership of NATO for the present. However, Finland is further along the road to NATO membership than Sweden is, given that the Finns have at least engaged in detailed public debate on the prospect of NATO membership. The cumulative effect of these gradual shifts in Swedish and Finnish foreign policy has been that the leading policy makers in each country have followed a tentative line on future EU development in the foreign and security policy areas. The Nordic 'post-neutrals' have been drawn more tightly into the complex multi-purpose, Western security architecture (as part of their obligations under the CFSP and 'peacekeeping'), but have shied away from fully joining security organisations that require a commitment on the part of its members to WEU/NATO Article V style collective security guarantees.

Foreign policy change – adaptation and socialisation

Adaptation through EU membership

The intention of this section is to examine general themes affecting Swedish and Finnish membership of the Union, which are useful to the detailed examinations undertaken later. If Swedish and Finnish aspects are placed within the key elements of adaptation through membership as outlined by Manners and Whitman, then a number of general themes are clearly evident.

First, the impact of membership on the political debates in Sweden and Finland has been sizable and is continuing. To a degree, this is not surprising given that the question of EU membership was 'sold' by their respective elites to their populations as part of a wider economic solution to some of their countries economic difficulties in the 1990s. As Jerneck and Sundelius argue, the seismic changes in these countries' international orientations are best understood by models which incorporate 'external shocks' and 'domestic restructuring' as key sources of foreign policy change.[17]

Secondly, it is arguable that the end of the Cold War removed the 'psychological' obstacle of neutrality from the issue of EU membership and allowed for a freer debate to take place on the merits of EU accession in both countries. Sundelius makes the interesting point in his analysis of Sweden's decision to join the Community that, in spite of major alterations in the objectives and fundamental premise underpinning Swedish foreign policy, this transformation was accompanied by a 'remarkable lack of any sense of failure' on the part of the country's foreign policy makers.[18] This was due to the fact that the new pro-EC policy line was regarded by most key figures in the governmental apparatus as the logical consequence of a new situation. Accordingly, the 1994 referendum campaigns in these countries, for instance, were largely fought on economic issues and on the political implications of the Union on Swedish and Finnish democracy, rather than on security related questions. Hence, the impact of the end of the Cold War on Nordic foreign policy should not be perceived in isolation. It was part of a wider picture and reinforced the general feeling in these states that the time was ripe for fundamental changes across most of government policy.

Thirdly, the process of adaptation to EU membership has been slower in the Swedish case than the Finnish one, with substantial elements of Sweden's population remaining sceptical about the benefits of EU accession since 1995. The narrower victory of the 'Yes' camp (by 53 per cent), when compared to the Finnish result, is indicative that the Swedes were not convinced wholesale of the merits of the Union right from the start. This is important, for as Kjell Goldmann has argued, changes in foreign policy are best analysed through a detailed depiction of the 'policy-making system' and in addition, changes can only be comprehended adequately within wider concepts of general foreign policy stability (including 'stabilizers').[19] Indeed, the notion of Goldmann's 'stabilizers' may explain why, for example, the Swedes and Finns have not dropped the notion of non-alignment completely. These countries are, after all, still the same societies and their governments are restricted by elite and public attachments to traditional concepts of how foreign policy is conducted which grew out of their neutrality policies.

Hence, Swedish and to a much lesser extent, Finnish governmental policies have been largely based on 'defensive strategies' directed, for instance, at initiating improvements in EU competencies in those areas especially deemed as deficient by the anti-EU sections of the elites and populations, such as transparency and openness in EU decision making. To a large degree, these strategies have been successful to date, and the EU treaty base now incorporates large areas of specific Nordic interest. For instance, greater transparency measures, an employment chapter and improved articles dealing with social and environmental issues were included in the 1997 Amsterdam Treaty, which were, albeit to a limited extent, prompted by Nordic initiatives.[20] While this does not necessarily place a constraint on foreign policy harmonisation at the EU level, it does nevertheless ensure that Swedish and Finnish EU policy is directed as much towards the respective domestic audience as to the international community.

This has also been the case in relationship to Swedish and Finnish policy on the Union's CFSP. Sweden and Finland's input into the EU security dimension has generally been a positive one, and the Swedes and Finns have viewed the CFSP as an 'opportunity' to consolidate their EU credentials. The 1997 Amsterdam Treaty – which was after all, the first major Intergovernmental Conference (IGC) where Swedish and Finnish pressure could be brought to bear – accommodated the concerns of the Nordic 'post-neutrals' in the crisis management area and has allowed for flexible definitions of 'non-alignment' to coexist alongside an evolving CFSP (see below). Hence, it can be argued that Swedish and Finnish foreign policies have contained a substantial EU element because they have been geared in recent years to achieving concessions at the EU level that would ensure that national policies and EU competencies mirror each other more closely.

Socialisation of foreign policy makers

The 'socialisation' of Swedish and Finnish foreign-makers to 'European' questions is well-established. Not only have their foreign policy procedures been 'internationalized' for a long time,[21] but Swedish and Finnish policy makers were dealing continually with their EU colleagues prior to accession as part of the post-1984 'Luxembourg' process and later EEA negotiations. As Ekengren has argued, the EEA negotiations established 'a contact zone' between Swedish (and Finnish) officials and diplomats from the EU institutions.[22] Nordic national officials were consequently versed in the EU's operational procedures as part of multilateral negotiations in the EC/EU environment prior to membership. However, to a large degree, the socialisation of Swedish and Finnish national officials has been facilitated by the fact that the EU's operational dynamics fit nicely alongside Swedish and Finnish traditions of Nordic cooperation and an active role in UN forums. To be successful in the EU environment, national officials coalesce with like-minded officials from others states and EU institutions. This usually requires firm action on the part of national officials and the proposing of formal discussion papers at an early stage if their points are to be heard loudest at the EU level. These are taken as normal procedure by Nordic concepts of 'integrative democracy'. Moreover, since most national officials in Sweden and Finland believed that there were few alternatives for small states outside European integration in the 1990s, the emphasis within their new found 'Europeanised' psychosis was to be adaptable as applicant countries and (then later) as new Member States.[23]

By the time these countries joined the Union then, a high degree of elite socialisation was present between the national and supranational levels. Swedish and Finnish foreign policy already had substantial EU overtones. As a Swedish official report noted in 1996 on Swedish experiences of its first year of EU membership: 'the overall picture is that the (Swedish) administration functions relatively well in the EU'.[24] However, as Ekengren and Sundelius argue there has been a limited clash of administrative cultures between Swedish and EU officials at times, which perhaps illustrates that their 'socialisation' into the EU operations only goes so far.[25]

At the risk of over-simplification it would seem that the Finns have been slightly more successful than the Swedes in integrating into the EU system. To some extent, this may be due to the fact that the Finnish diplomatic service has a reputation for 'skillful diplomacy'. As Dörfer comments, Finnish decisions are usually taken by 'a small, close-knit elite, probably the most able group in Northern Europe', using well practiced techniques that were honed by Finnish officials during the forty or so years of incorporating Soviet, Nordic and EFTA concerns into Finnish foreign policy.[26] In short, Finnish diplomats have been accustomed to accommodating external influences procedurally into their policies for a long time. Since 1995, they just happen to be labelled EU, rather than Soviet, Nordic or EFTA considerations.

Nevertheless, from a general perspective, it would seem that the Swedish and Finnish governments have been 'constructivist' in the sense that, at least within the governing elite, there has been a further incorporation of a 'European' identity and priorities into government thinking. Lipponen's 'rainbow coalition' administrations (1995–99; 1999–) may, for instance, have included parties from all sides of the Finnish political spectrum, but his governments are clearly identified as being proactively 'European' and have steered the country's participation in the third stage of Economic and Monetary Union (EMU). Even in Sweden, the governing Social Democratic elite is pro-EU membership and sees the country's future lying within the EU.

A corresponding process of 'elite socialiation' has taken place at the parliamentary level between the mainstream political parties and their opposite numbers in other Member States and through participation in transnational party alliances in the European Parliament.[27] During the EEA and application processes, cooperation began between the transnational party (con)federations and the Swedish and Finnish parties gained observer status in most of the EP political groups. In addition, Swedish and Finnish parliamentary structures have been revised to reflect the need for parliamentary actors to influence government EU policy – something that will only largely take place if the respective Parliament speaks with 'one voice'.

Foreign policy process – domestic and bureaucratic

Domestic factors in the policy process

Swedish and Finnish foreign policy makers have been careful to incorporate the views of domestic actors precisely because EU accession is comparatively recent and individual domestic actors are still in the process of refocusing their interests. Nonetheless, it is also equally important to stress that the 'constitutional design' of these 'consensual democracies' and their policy-making procedures include high degrees of interest group participation in governmental policy. Although foreign and security questions have been perhaps less open areas of government decision making, this does not mean that Nordic traditions of policy making can be ignored out of hand. Indeed, Ingebritsen, for example, has stressed national attributes such as domestic structures and their close-knit elite networks, in influencing the redirection of Nordic foreign policy by altering the national capacity to act. According to Ingebritsen, the critical domestic structures supporting the traditional foreign policy line of Swedish and Finnish autonomy, were eroded in favour of a new constellation of interests promoting a pro-EC membership solution to the challenges of economic interdependence.[28]

Sweden for example, has long experienced stable, minority governments in which the ruling Social Democrats have accommodated the chief interests of their parliamentary and interest group allies (and even adversaries) into government policy. Parliamentary actors have been more assertive of late in influencing Swedish and Finnish foreign policy. Persson's ruling Social Democrats (initially) accommodated the concerns of its Centre Party parliamentary allies (1996–98) and since the SAP's dismal performance at the September 1998 general election, they now rely upon the parliamentary support of the anti-EU Left Party and Greens who are reluctant to see any movement towards a more defence orientated EU and CFSP. Hence, Persson's Social Democrats have concluded a 'selective deal' securing parliamentary cooperation with the EU-sceptic Left Party and Greens on domestic issues. This agreement does not extend to areas of foreign, security or EU policy and in these areas, Persson will seek *ad hoc* parliamentary alliances with the 'non-socialists' in order to protect the existing 'Europeanisation' of government policy. However, given that it is commonly acknowledged that the scope of the EU impact is wide, and that the distinction between domestic and foreign policy remits is especially blurred when it comes to EU policy mandates, the practical viability of this agreement must surely be in question. Moreover, differences between the Social Democratic government and key interest groups (such as the LO trade union congress), on EU-related questions has been notable, whilst in general the pro-EU stance of Swedish 'big business' has ensured that the Social Democrats probably follow more accommodating EU policies than the unions would prefer.[29]

Changes in the constitutional design of foreign policy in these two countries also features here. In particular, the EU remit has been at the forefront of the debate on the future role of the Finnish President and his powerful constitutional powers over the formulation of foreign policy. One of the first decisions made after Finnish EU accession in 1995 was, for instance, that the overall responsibility for Finnish EU policy would be shared between the President and Prime Minister. In practice, this means that the Finnish Prime Minister has assumed a greater role in shaping Finnish foreign policy and this process will be given even further credence once Finland's new constitution is approved by the Parliament in 1999. Similarly, in the Swedish example, Swedish policy makers have been (albeit to a limited extent) constricted by the insistence of the Swedish Riksdag that its Advisory Committee on EU Affairs (ACEUA) is regularly consulted on Swedish policy positions in the run-up to European summits. Indeed, given the continuing controversy in Sweden over EU-related matters, the government has gone to great lengths in practice to ensure that the Parliament is regularly informed on EU developments. Hence, the 'domestication' of Swedish and Finnish foreign policy continues, even if the respective foreign ministries largely maintain their roles as the primary 'gatekeepers' between the EU and national levels.

However, domestic circumstances have also ensured that the respective governments can no longer rely on subservient publics willing to accept foreign policy lines without censure. The previous 'unflinching' support of mainstream political parties and public at large for the existing 'non-aligned' security policies[30] is now long gone, while the activities of the foreign ministries are now the subject of greater scrutiny from non-governmental actors. This more flexible environment has allowed for some of the party elites to begin campaigns aimed at slowly persuading the sceptical public of the benefits of dropping 'non-alignment' and introducing the potential for WEU and NATO membership. Indeed, the 'economic profile' of EU membership within Nordic domestic debates, combined with the fragile performances of the Swedish and Finnish economies, have also compounded arguments in favour of using foreign policy changes to grasp the potential economic benefits of a 'peace dividend', and instigate large scale reviews of their existing defence commitments.

Taking a more conceptual approach, it could be argued that the impact of domestic forces on Swedish and Finnish EU policies has been sizable and has increased over the time since accession. Certainly, in terms of Putnam's 'two-level games' analogy, the prioritising of Swedish interest in EU negotiations, such as transparency and openness at the 1997 Amsterdam IGC, reflects the constraints imposed on Swedish policy makers by domestic actors and more specifically, the continuing popularity of the 'anti-EU' voice in Swedish politics. The Swedish and Finnish governments have stated in international negotiations that the achievement of these prioritised policy interests is critical to their continuing campaigns aimed at making the EU popular back home and thus, reduce the future potential problems of ratifying new EU treaties (Putnam's 'win-set').[31]

Nonetheless, the Finnish elite has been more successful than its Swedish counterpart in quelling domestic concerns on EU policies. In short, its 'win-set' is easier to achieve than that of Sweden. Eurobarometer figures since 1995, and domestic public opinion polls, regularly indicate that scepticism towards the EU is lower in Finland than in Sweden and thus the 'problem' is smaller. To some extent this can be explained by the fact that Finland is a 'war-fighting nation' and the experience of several defeats this century means that it is not necessary for the elite to outline the importance of the security dimension to the public, nor the potential opportunities that EU membership provides for Finland. Indeed, public opinion has not traditionally played a major role in foreign and security policy in the post-war era and it has only been in recent years that this has altered. Moreover, the make-up of Lipponen's governing 'rainbow coalitions' (1995–99; 1999–) also ensured that the majority of Finnish parties supports involvement in key EU policies, and enabled even Finnish NATO membership to be discussed publicly.[32] Sweden is different for, first, the 'anti-EU voice' has been kept alive by the revived Left Party and Swedish Greens and secondly, discussion of Swedish NATO membership is more controversial and thus the elite are less willing to encourage such a public debate.

In general, domestic actors are critical to formulation of EU foreign policy in new Member States given that levels of adaptation to the Union is uneven within the respective states. With some simplification, the respective policy makers have become Europeanised to a high degree, the political parties slightly less so (and in the Swedish case far from uniformly) petering down to limited socialisation at the 'grass roots' party levels and amongst the population. There is also a geographic bias to this 'Europeanisation', with the rural, conservative and sparsely populated northern communities in Finland and Sweden displaying greater resistance to the whole concept of European integration.

Bureaucratic politics in the policy process

Bureaucratic politics plays, in general, an important role in the formulation of Swedish and Finnish foreign policies. As t'Hart, Stern and Sundelius have emphasised, 'many important decisions and developments in foreign policy are shaped by relatively small groups and informal face-to-face interaction' and there is clear evidence that these countries' reorientation towards the EU have been elite-led and driven by small coalitions of policy makers intent on ensuring that policy takes a specific path.[33] As Gustavsson argues in the Swedish case, the change in orientation of the Social Democratic government on EU membership in 1990 was due largely to a coalition between the Prime Minister and Finance Minister, Allan Larsson, who jointly spear-headed the initiative through the Swedish Cabinet.[34] Indeed, Gustavsson, asserts that foreign policy change is the result of a three-step procedure in which decision makers act as key 'mediators'.[35] Whilst this latter interpretation is convincing, it tends, like most others, to be most useful in analysing 'flagship' changes in foreign policy. They are less handy when analysing the longer-term adjustment and influences on policy and in particular, the impact of continuous, but also dynamic structural factors such as participation in the EU, which generally falls short of instilling 'crisis situations' on domestic foreign policy makers. After all, the influence of the EU on Swedish and Finnish foreign policy tends to be ever present, yet simultaneously rather unpredictable.

Moreover, the fact that bureaucratic or cabinet political struggles – at all levels of government – can be a driving dynamic behind aspects of foreign policy making is also illustrated by Nordic examples. It was, for instance, cooperation between the moderate and liberal elites in the Bildt administration that facilitated the later alterations in Swedish policy and largely negated the demands of their Centre Party coalition partners of retaining the basic tenets of neutrality.

The responsibility for directing Swedish and Finnish EU policy has remained within a number of 'firm hands' since accession. In the Swedish example the Prime Minster, Göran Persson, is now responsible for coordinating EU policy (with the support of the Prime Minister's Office and the Foreign Ministry). In Finland, the Prime Minister, Paivo Lipponen, has assumed a greater role in formulating Finnish EU policy, and given his pro-EU and EMU stances he has proved a natural compliment to the equally enthusiastic Finnish President, Martti Ahtisaari. Indeed, the role of central figures in coordinating Nordic EU policy provides an effective (and speedy) counterweight to the Nordic countries' deliberative and often cumbersome 'consensual' approaches to policy making. This is particularly important in the EU context, where key decisions at the EU level are often made between Heads of State and/government at the meetings of the European Council ('institutionalised summitry') and information dispersal back to the domestic audience can be rather slow. As Carlsnaes argues, the intentional behaviour of political actors, the impact of structural conditions and the significance of the time dimension in shaping Swedish and Finnish approaches are of critical importance (especially within the general discussion of 'agency–structure' problems).[36] After all, the conduct of Swedish and Finnish foreign policy requires future orientated (rather than just reactive) behaviour on the part of key policy makers. They are making further commitments to an EU of which they have neither full control over, and/or are uncertain of which direction its evolution will take.[37]

Nonetheless, the respective Foreign Ministries have also remained central players in EU policy, acting as the primary (if no longer exclusive) 'gatekeepers' between the EU and national levels and in spite of the Union's general impact requiring more ministries being involved in the formulation of EU policy. In the Swedish case, the Foreign Ministry's influence continues through, for example, the State Secretary for European Affairs (from the Foreign Ministry) holding the chair of the government's Coordinating Group for EU relations (EU-beredningen). Moreover, recent government reforms in 1999 have retained the central role of the Foreign Ministry. A new Department for EU Affairs, an EU Information Section, and a specialist 2001 Secretariat have been established within the Foreign Ministry to further improve coordination of government structures on general EU policy and prepare specifically for Sweden taking over the EU Council Presidency in 2001. As the Foreign Minister Anna Lindh noted, 'This new order creates a dynamic organization for EU matters at the Foreign Ministry, which will ensure that we make an effective contribution to work in the EU and safeguard Swedish interests within the Community'.[38]

However, there have also been measures aimed at reflecting the increasing 'domestication' of foreign policy and recognising the global impact of EU decision-making on work of government ministries. One of the first decisions by the new Swedish Premier Göran Persson upon taking up the position of Prime Minister in March 1996 was to abolish a separate Ministry for European Affairs, as an acknowledgment that EU influence embraced all policy areas, involving all the major ministries.

To a large degree, these bureaucratic arrangements allow government ministries to work closely together in formulating policy positions in time for EU summits. A recent study by the author suggests that, to a large degree, the coordination functions of the Swedish ministries were successful in facilitating the speedy tabling of proposals in time for the 1997 Amsterdam Summit.[39] However, as Allison argued in his landmark study in the 1970s, people's behaviour is moulded by the offices they hold and there is some evidence in the Swedish and Finnish cases of 'pulling and hauling' as key figures in ministries assert control of their respective 'turfs', and adopt strategies to persuade and manipulate others to accept a new political situation.[40] In the Swedish case, for example, there has been some friction between the Foreign Affairs and Finance ministries over the direction of governmental policy towards the 'Euro'.

Furthermore, the importance of elite groups in general is accentuated in the Nordic countries precisely because their political systems operate on the principles of 'technocracy'.[41] There is a long tradition of Nordic governments using Royal Commissions of Enquiry and/or investigatory parliamentary committees in order to investigate the merits of potential foreign policy options. In practice, these bodies act, on the one hand, as a source of information for interested parties and on the other, enable the respective governments to use detailed policy arguments to legitimise preferred policy choices. On EU-related issues, the Swedish and Finnish governments have regularly used these elite bodies as means of farming out controversial areas for investigation in order to allow time for opposition to foreign policy change to dissipate and/or be neutralised by the merits of detailed arguments of the investigatory committees. In short, both the Swedish and Finnish elites have used these elite 'think tanks' and bureaucratic techniques in order to legitimise unsavoury policy choices and thereby persuade or 'by-pass' a disapproving public.

Foreign policy actions – with or without the EU?

With the EU: constriction or opportunity?

The Finnish and Swedish governments were quick to acknowledge that they would become active and full members of the CFSP as part of their wider acceptance of the Union's *acquis communautaire* during the accession process. They were, of course, able to state that this was the case precisely because of the primarily intergovernmental character of the 'second pillar' and that the CFSP was still in its immaturity. Yet, at first glance, it would seem initially that the EU's developing CFSP would be a sizable constraint on Swedish and Finnish foreign policy even within the more fluid background of post-1989 Europe. The European Commission for example, in its opinions on the Swedish and Finnish membership applications, drew attention to the need to gain 'concrete assurances' from these non-aligned states on their commitment to the CFSP. Given that both countries persist with their non-aligned status, the central question for their governments has been how to enable Finland and Sweden to participate in CFSP 'second pillar' development, without compromising their official non-alignment and, at the same time, also not being seen by other Member States as obstructing European integration in this area.

Even today, there are still fundamental concerns in both countries over the future evolution of the CFSP and in particular, whether a military dimension requiring states to commit themselves to a system of collective defence guarantees will be incorporated into the CFSP. However, the governments of Sweden and Finland have adopted similar approaches – something that has been facilitated by a mutual understanding between the governments that initiatives on CFSP development have more credence if they are proposed jointly by the two Nordic 'post-neutrals'.

First, both states tried initially to segregate the foreign policy segment of the emerging CFSP from those elements associated with any future CFSP defence organ. To a degree, these policies have been helped by the fact that the CFSP is, at present, concerned primarily with common foreign policy action, with any military developments sub-contracted to the WEU under the articles of the Maastricht Treaty. This enables Finland and Sweden to participate in the existing CFSP, whilst maintaining their reservations about formal commitments to military alliances by only taking up WEU observer status (in 1995). In a sense then, Finnish and Swedish foreign policy makers restricted the scope of the CFSP's impact on their security policies by prioritising the rhetoric of 'non-alignment' over the nebulous ambitions of the CFSP.

Secondly, while Finland and Sweden are generally content with the overarching intergovernmental nature of the CFSP, and oppose the merging of the EU pillars I and II, their governments have been constructive in pushing forward European foreign policy cooperation. The Swedes, for instance, proposed, at various times, extensions to qualified majority voting rules associated with the CFSP which would allow quicker CFSP-related decisions in areas of 'minor national interest'. In addition, the Swedes and Finns have stated openly they would not obstruct the evolution of a military dimension of the CFSP provided it is done through the WEU avenue and thus will not impinge on their 'selective' interpretation of the CFSP.

Moreover, both countries have recognised (increasingly since accession) that the CFSP is an 'opportunity' to further their general goals of 'internationalism' and for Europe to play an interventionist, collective role in human rights and peacekeeping questions. In short, the Finns and Swedes have been at the forefront of strengthening the CFSP's capabilities in crisis management. It was for example a joint Swedo-Finnish memorandum (April 1996) that proposed the incorporation of the 'Petersberg tasks' into the Amsterdam Treaty (which was ultimately successful) and thus formally expanded the CFSP's remit into peace-making, peace shaping and crisis management. The incorporation of the 'Petersberg tasks' suits perfectly the objectives of Finnish and Swedish policy makers. By legitimising common action under the umbrella of peace-keeping (which is an area where Nordic states have been prominent on the international stage), the Finnish and Swedish governments are more comfortable with involvement in European foreign policy cooperation. The post-Amsterdam CFSP has a much stronger foreign policy element and where Member States cooperate militarily this can now be rationalised under the banner of 'crisis-management' (rather under the guise of formal collective defence arrangements), which is far more acceptable to states articulating the rhetoric of 'non-alignment'. As Anna Lindh commented recently, 'it is vital that the distinction between military crisis management and territorial defence is upheld'.[42] Thus, Swedish and Finnish forces are now able to participate in NATO maneouvres and in Bosnia and Macedonia, even be placed under NATO command (on the proviso that there was a UN mandate sanctioning such military operations), without risking substantial public opposition or raising the immediate question of Swedish and Finnish full membership of NATO.

It would seem that there has been a gradual shift of perspective in Swedish and Finnish foreign policy towards the EU and particularly the CFSP since the signing of the Amsterdam Treaty. The CFSP is no longer seen as primarily a 'constraint' on their non-aligned policies, but increasingly as a policy 'opportunity', given that the post-Amsterdam CFSP is largely about common foreign policy action at this stage, remains essentially intergovernmental and has a strengthened, but still rather flexible, remit in European crisis management.

Given Sweden's larger size and proportionate influence compared to Finland, it would have been logical to argue some years ago that Sweden would have been the leading Nordic 'post-neutral' inside the EU. However, it can be argued today, with a fair level of conviction, that the Finns have been more successful in grasping the opportunities offered by the EU. The Lipponen government has, for example, committed Finland to being the first Nordic member of the 'Euro' and is at the forefront of enlargement debates by promoting the Estonian cause for early EU accession. Finland is also a leader in the developing 'EU Northern Dimension' (see below) and will also be the first Nordic 'post-neutral' to hold the EU's Council Presidency. However, the reality in the late 1990s has been that a 'Nordic bloc' has not developed as a distinct identity inside the Union and, if anything, Finland, rather than Sweden has been closer to the hub of EU policy making. In the language of Manners and Whitman's 'tiers of exclusivity' it would seem that Finland has been more centrally involved in EU decision making than Sweden in spite of its more peripheral status on the eastern boundaries of Europe.

Without the EU: special relations and special interests

It should not, however, be forgotten that Sweden and Finland also have substantial bilateral relationships with other states that they are also keen to protect and foster as part of their general foreign policy approaches. For the Finns, the need to keep cordial relations with Russia remains an ever present concern, and may explain partly why they have resisted NATO membership. Sweden and Finland have also been keen to further their prospering relations with the three Baltic Republics (Estonia, Latvia and Lithuania). In the Swedish case, the Persson government has committed substantial financial and political resources in order to promote Swedish objectives in the Baltic Sea region and strengthen relations with the three new Republics, Poland and Russia in particular.[43] It has, for instance, launched a new 'flagship' initiative in 1999 aimed at deepening bilateral cooperation with Poland.[44] Indeed, there is still a degree of rivalry between these two states as to who will play the leading role in the Eastern Baltic. Hence, the Swedes and Finns have been active recently in re-establishing and developing special bilateral interests with key states in Central and Eastern Europe (most of whom are not presently EU members).

However, since the Nordic 'post-neutrals' are small states in the Union, any special interests such as Nordic, Baltic, Barents and/or Arctic ties, which may be perceived to be, more or less, as 'special relationships' have not been 'ring-fenced' out of the EU's policy process. Indeed, the opposite view is closer to the truth. The Union is viewed by the Swedes and Finns as a vehicle to provide additional collective weight to their governments' objectives, and especially as a forum to articulate the support of the larger EU states for Swedish and Finnish policy initiatives. Hence, their EU memberships have complimented their existing roles in, amongst others, the Council of Baltic Sea States, the Euro-Arctic Barents Council and the Arctic Council.

The Swedes and Finns have largely viewed the EU then as an 'opportunity' to strengthen existing regional initiatives in which they are leading players, and thereby reinforce their bilateral contacts with key states. The Finnish Lipponen government has for instance, argued that the EU has been of special use for 'soft security' reasons.[45] Given the growing political instability within its larger Eastern neighbour, and continuing fears about the levels of environmental degradation and public health questions in Russia (such as rising levels of tuberculosis in the St Petersberg area), the Finns have sought to use the EU as vehicle to remove Russian concerns about being marginalised by the West and promote EU–Russian cooperation on environmental, energy and transit issues. In 1997, for instance, the Finnish government was responsible for initiating the establishment of a formal EU 'Northern Dimension' policy, whose chief aim is 'confidence-building' with the Russians by increasing their involvement in selective EU policies.

Similarly, the Swedish and Finnish governments have invested considerable political effort into playing a leading role in Baltic cooperation[46] and principally in the Council of Baltic Sea States. Both countries have also sought (on the basis of ever-growing bilateral contacts) to champion the Baltic Republics' cases as EU applicants, although there have been tensions between the two countries on which strategy would be the more appropriate. The Lipponen government, for instance, broke ranks in 1997–98 with its Danish and Swedish counterparts (the latter two preferred to deal with the three 'Balts' as a bloc'), and prioritised Estonia as the Baltic front-runner to be 'fast-tracked' into EU membership. However, a qualification needs to be made here. In the case of Swedish domestic politics, Baltic concepts are often more popular than EU-related ones with the electorate. So for essentially this reason, Baltic questions, along with bilateral contacts, often assume at least as high as importance as more general EU ones in Swedish debates.

This is perhaps less of a case when the specific aspects of Nordic cooperation is considered. Once the last vestiges of the foreign policies of the Nordic states, and even though still important, the Nordic concept has been largely subsumed into wider Baltic and more recently EU contexts. Even relations between the Nordic EU (Denmark, Finland and Sweden) and non-EU states (Norway and Iceland) maintain a wider European context as these contacts are now governed to some extent by the wider framework of the EEA.

Probably the only areas where Sweden and Finland continue to maintain a semi-independent stance is of course, in their roles in the UN, for it is this forum that both countries have, albeit to differing degrees, stressed their individual 'internationalist' credentials as part of their non-aligned foreign policies. Sweden for instance recently held a seat on the UN Security Council and developed some foreign policy lines that were to some extent distinct from the EU colleagues holding permanent Security Council Seats (France and the UK). However, to a large degree, this difference is mostly a question of emphasis, for if Swedish ideas are to be pushed forward at the UN level, the Swedish delegation needs to coalesce with their Nordic, Baltic and European counterparts to secure success.

Conclusion: a case of 'semi-alignment'?

It is perhaps too early to draw concrete conclusions for the Swedish and Finnish cases to the questions posed by the editors of this book given that their accessions are so recent. The influence of the Union on their foreign policies is unclear because the impact of EU membership on the residual elements of their foreign policies happened, more or less, alongside fundamental changes to these residual elements in response to wider strategic changes in Europe. Hence, it is not so much the case that Sweden and Finland altered radically as the fact that Europe started to change around them. There was no place left for their pre-1989 neutrality policies which were premised on European structures remaining largely constant. Yet, as small states perched on the northern tip of Europe, their foreign policies were always 'internationalised' in the sense of being highly susceptible to external pressures. Nevertheless, from a policy-making perspective, it is true to say that in the Swedish and Finnish case, the periods up to 1989 were noted by the dominance of elite thinking on foreign policy questions and the lack of any substantial public debate on the future of their foreign policies.

However, as part of the process of closer European integration marked by their accessions in January 1995, a number of trends associated with the evolution of an 'EU foreign policy' are appearing. First, the trends towards a more pluralistic approach to the formulation of foreign policy is well under way in both states. In a sense the corporatist and consensual democracy traditions of these two states have tried to accommodate EU-related matters and the universal impact of EU membership on national policy making, which necessarily means that larger numbers of government ministries and key political actors participate in Nordic EU policy making. In this sense, Nordic versions of democracy accelerate the creation of an 'EU foreign policy', even if ultimately the respective foreign ministries continue to be the primary 'gatekeepers' between the national and EU levels.

Secondly, as Member States, Finland (1999) and Sweden (2001) will hold the EU Council Presidency and be responsible for the future direction of EU common foreign policy action during those times. For small states like Sweden and Finland, this imposes new burdens, but also provides opportunities for these states to impact on the general consciousness of the Union. New institutional structures have been, and are being, put in place to maximise the ability of their respective ministries to coordinate EU policies. Perhaps the test of whether Sweden and Finland are following an 'EU foreign policy' will be the 'imprint' of these structures on their foreign policy making machinery after their EU Council presidential terms come to an end.

Thirdly, Swedish and Finnish cooperation with NATO EU powers is so close that it is now dubious that the phrase 'non-alignment' and/or 'non-participation in military alliances' is an accurate description of Swedish and Finnish foreign policies. Indeed, since the onset of the 1999 Kosovan crisis, the Swedes and Finns are confronted with the increasing dilemma of whether to cooperate further with NATO powers (which their governments may like to do) even when there are no over-arching UN mandates sanctioning such military operations on the part of NATO. Thus, although the Swedish and Finnish governments are committed to taking action on 'internationalist', humanitarian grounds in these cases, the usual legalistic sanction from the UN allowing indirectly Swedish and Finnish forces to work closely with NATO counterparts does not (as yet) apply to the Kosovan example – perhaps indicating that there is even further room for flexibility within Swedish and Finnish 'non-alignment' in the future.[47]

In effect the two Nordic 'post-neutrals' are now practicing selective, ill-defined forms of 'semi-alignment' in which the only item that remains contentious is cooperating with their EU and NATO counterparts in Article V-related collective security. Probably then, Swedish and Finnish 'post-neutral' foreign policies should be formally re-named with 'non-participation in collective security guarantees' as their even narrower central cores in the years beyond 2000. Indeed, it is likely that whatever the terminology adopted in the near future, Sweden (and to a lesser extent, Finland) will continue using these 'twilight' phrases until domestic opinion alters and the long shadow of neutrality disappears from the consciousness of the Swedish and Finnish people.

Notes

1 See L. Miles, 'Sweden and security' in J. Redmond (ed.), *The 1995 Enlargement of the European Union* (Aldershot, Ashgate, 1997), pp. 86–124.

2 J. Gustavsson, *The Politics of Foreign Policy Change: Explaining the Swedish Reorientation on EC Membership* (Lund, Lund University Press, 1997), pp. 135–139.

3 For more detailed theories of 'EU adaptation' in relation to the Nordic small states see H. Mouritzen, *External Danger and Democracy: Old Nordic Lessons and New European Challenges* (Aldershot, Dartmouth, 1997).

4 W. Carlsnaes, 'Sweden facing the new Europe: whither neutrality?' *European Security*, 2:1 (Spring 1993), p. 76.

5 H. Hakovirta, *East–West Conflict and European Neutrality* (Oxford, Clarendon Press, 1988).

6 C. Archer, 'The NATO Nordics and the CFSP' in L. Miles (ed.), *The European Union and the Nordic Countries* (London, Routledge, 1996), pp. 260–72.

7 L. Miles, *Sweden and European Integration* (Aldershot, Ashgate, 1997).

8   C. Ingebritsen, *The Nordic States and European Unity* (Cornell, Cornell University Press, 1998), pp. 96–98.

9   This phrase was introduced in Bildt's first prime ministerial speech to the Riksdag on 4 October 1991.

10 Address by Prime Minister Carl Bildt to La Fondation Paul-Henri Spaak, Palais des Académies, Brussels, 16 September 1993, p. 15.

11 I. Dörfer, *The Nordic Nations in the New Western Security Regime* (Washington D.C., The Woodrow Wilson Center Press, 1997), p. 4.

12 T. Tiilikainen, *Europe and Finland: Defining the Political Identity of Finland in Western Europe* (Aldershot, Ashgate, 1998), pp. 141–168.

13 C. Ingebritsen, *The Nordic States and European Unity* (Cornell, Cornell University Press, 1998), p. 99.

14 It should not be forgotten that the Russian political situation enabled right-wing nationalists such as Zhironovsky to come to the fore, who often called for Russia to re-emphasise its traditional interests in Finland.

15 Taken from 'Finnish foreign policy and EC membership' *Finnish Features* (Helsinki, Ministry for Foreign Affairs, October 1992), p. 2.

16 D. Arter, 'The EU referendum in Finland on 16 October 1994: a vote for the west, not for Maastricht' *Journal of Common Market Studies*, 33:3 (September 1995), pp. 361–387.

17 Both authors prefer to use Charles Hermann's 'foreign policy change' model – see M. Jerneck, 'Sweden – the reluctant European?' in T. Tiilikainen and I. Damgaard Petersen (eds), *The Nordic Countries and the EC* (Copenhagen, Copenhagen Political Studies Press, 1993), pp. 23–42, and B. Sundelius, 'Changing course: when neutral Sweden chose to join the European Community' in W. Carlsnaes and S. Smith (eds), *European Foreign Policy: The EC and Changing Perspectives in Europe* (London, Sage, 1994), pp. 177–201.

18 Sundelius, (1994), p. 198.

19 Goldmann's primary contribution is the notion of 'stabilisers', which largely determine whether an input into the 'policy-making system' will set a process of policy change in motion. These 'stabilisers' can take the form of four types – political and administrative (both actor-specific) and international and cognitive (both universal) – see K. Goldmann, *Change and Stability in the International System. The Problems and Possibilities of Detente* (London, Harvester Wheatsheaf, 1988).

20 L. Miles, 'Sweden and the IGC: testing the "membership diamond"', *Cooperation and Conflict*, 33:4 (December 1998), pp. 339–366.

21 L. Karvonen and B. Sundelius, *Internationalization and Foreign Policy Management* (Aldershot, Gower, 1987).

22 M. Ekengren, 'The Europeanization of state administration: adding the time dimension', *Cooperation and Conflict*, 31: 4 (1996), pp. 387–415.

23 Ekengren, Europeanization, p. 399.

24 SOU, 6 *Ett år Med EU-Svenska Statsjänstemäns Erfarenheter av Arbetet I EU* (Stockholm, Government Printing Office, 1996).

25 M. Ekengren and B. Sundelius, 'Sweden: the state joins the European Union' in K. Hanf and B. Soetendorp (eds), *Adapting to European Integration: Small States and the European Union* (London, Longman, 1998), pp. 130–148.

26 I. Dörfer, *The Nordic Nations in the New Western Security Regime* (Washington D.C., The Woodrow Wilson Center Press, 1997), p. 5.

27 K. M. Johansson, *Transnational Party Alliances* (Lund, Lund University Press, 1997).

28 C. Ingebritsen, *The Nordic States and European Unity* (Cornell, Cornell University Press, 1998).

29 A. Bieler, 'Globalization, Swedish trade unions and European integration: from europhobia to conditional support', *Cooperation and Conflict*, 34:1 (March 1999), pp. 21–46.

30 See K. Goldmann, 'The Swedish model of security policy' in J-E. Lane (ed.), *Understanding the Swedish Model* (London, Frank Cass & Co, 1991), pp. 122–143. (The article first appeared in a special issue on 'Understanding the Swedish model', *West European Politics*, 14:3 (July 1991).)

31 For a more detailed assessment see L. Miles, 'Sweden and the IGC: testing the "membership diamond"', *Cooperation and Conflict*, 33:4 (December 1998).

32 D. Arter, 'Finland: from neutrality to NATO', *European Security*, 5:4 (Winter 1996), pp. 614–32.

33 P. t'Hart, E. K. Stern and B. Sundelius, 'Foreign policy-making at the top: political group dynamics' in P. t'Hart, E. K. Stern and B. Sundelius (eds), *Beyond Groupthink: Political Group Dynamics and Foreign Policy-Making* (Ann Arbor, The University of Michigan Press, 1997), pp. 3–34 (quotation from pp. 4–5).

34 J. Gustavsson, *The Politics of Foreign Policy Change: Explaining the Swedish Reorientation on EC Membership* (Lund, Lund University Press, 1997), pp. 170–187.

35 According to Gustavsson, this three-step procedure equates to: (1) there are a number of 'sources' (domestic and international factors) that are (2) mediated by 'individual decision makers' who act (3) within the 'decision-making process' in order to bring about a change in policy – see J. Gustavsson, 'How should we study foreign policy change?' *Cooperation and Conflict*, 34:1 (March 1999), pp. 73–95.

36 Carlsnaes argues that 'methodological individualism' (in which decision makers' preferences, and causal statements on how these preferences were shaped by underlying values, previous steps, and prevailing structural and institutional conditions, are all important) provides an effective means of explaining foreign policy change – see W. Carlsnaes, 'The agency–structure problem in foreign policy analysis', *International Studies Quarterly*, 36 (1992), pp. 245–70.

37 W. Carlsnaes, 'On analyzing the dynamics of foreign policy change: a critique and reconceptualization', *Cooperation and Conflict*, 28:1 (1993), pp. 5–30.

38 Taken from MFA, *Press Release* 'New organization for EU affairs at the ministry for foreign affairs', Stockholm, MFA, 19 February 1999.

39 L. Miles, 'Sweden and the IGC: testing the "membership diamond"', *Cooperation and Conflict*, 33: 4 (December 1998).

40 G. Allison, *Essence of Decision; Explaining the Cuban Missile Crisis* (Boston, MA, Little, Brown, 1971), p. 171.

41 O. Petersson, *Swedish Government and Politics* (Stockholm, Publica, 1994), p. 40.

42 Taken from an address by the Minister of Foreign Affairs, Anna Lindh, at the Swedish Institute of International Affairs, Stockholm, 16 December 1998.

43 Swedish financial support (through bilateral and EU aid programmes) to Estonia, Latvia, Lithuania, and Poland amounted to SEK 500–600 million in 1998 – see Ministry of Foreign Affairs, 'Swedish Support to the European Integration of Northern Europe', *UD Info*, No. 1, (Stockholm, Ministry of Foreign Affairs, 1998), p. 1.

44 The new programme is entitled 'Sweden–Poland: Baltic neighbours in the new Europe'. The Persson government is aiming to build bilateral contacts with key EU candidate countries in the Baltic, which will also strengthen Swedish influence in the Baltic region and the EU as a whole – see Ministry of Foreign Affairs, 'Statement of Government Policy in the Parliamentary Debate on Foreign Affairs, 10 February 1999' (Stockholm, Ministry of Foreign Affairs, 1999), p. 3.

45 *European Security Development and Finnish Defence: Report by the Council of State to Parliament on 17 March 1997* (Helsinki, Oy Edita Ab, 1997, 2nd revised edition), p. 48.

46 C. Archer 'Nordic swans and Baltic signets', *Cooperation and Conflict* 34:1 (March 1999), pp. 47–71.

47 At the same time, the Kosovan crisis also illustrates how the continued existence of 'non-alignment' as the official policies of Sweden and Finland can also benefit these small nations. Due to the maintenance of their countries' non-aligned' status, prominent Swedish and Finnish officials, such as Carl Bildt and Martti Ahtisaari are nicely placed to play important diplomatic roles in defusing the crisis. It also allows these two countries to be acceptable and maintain cordial relations with both NATO powers and the Russia.

11

Austria

David Phinnemore

Introduction

During Austria's long courtship with the European Community (EC) prior to the early 1990s, membership was ruled out primarily because it would act as a constraint on foreign policy and thus undermine the country's status as a neutral. Since joining the European Union (EU) in 1995, however, Austria has appeared, in terms of its foreign policy, to adapt to membership without too many problems. Indeed the adaptation has generally been very smooth. As this chapter argues, this is due primarily to the fact that Austria's adaptation was taking place well before EU membership. Moreover, changes in Austria's foreign policy priorities and needs have coincided with the establishment and gradual development of the EU's Common Foreign and Security Policy (CFSP). This has facilitated further Austrian adaptation since 1995.

Various factors explain the apparent ease of adaptation. Notable among these is the changing security situation in post-Cold War Europe. This has pushed Austrians into reconsidering the value of neutrality and seeking full integration into structures which either do or have the potential to promote the country's security. A further factor that explains the adaptation is the domestic situation in Austria where coalition politics and concern for popular sentiments, notably over neutrality, make the EU the most attractive and viable security option. The adaptation process has also been assisted by the fact that EU membership has provided Austria with opportunities to promote its own interests, most notably through holding the Presidency in the second half of 1998. Whether membership will always be viewed positively in foreign policy terms remains, however, to be seen.

Foreign policy adaptation on the road to membership

For the majority of Member States, the EU's impact on national foreign and security policies has come during membership. They joined the EU before the CFSP was created and before the Single European Act formalised procedures for European Political Cooperation (EPC). Austria has found itself in a different situation. Rather than adapting its foreign policy to that of the EU after accession, changes in foreign and security policy in the early 1990s were bringing it in line with the EU prior to 1995. For the most part, these were brought about by the end of the Cold War. With the relative stability of a divided Europe being replaced by political and economic instability in neighbouring Central and Eastern Europe, neutrality on its own was no longer viewed as a viable guarantor of Austria's security. The reassessment of neutrality coincided with a desire to join the EC. The coincidence was welcome as the EC at this time was keen to bolster foreign policy cooperation and establish the CFSP. There were fears within the EC, however, that moves towards the CFSP could be hampered by neutral states becoming members. Hence, in an attempt to secure membership, particularly at a time when an unprecedented number of non-Member States were seeking accession to the EC membership, the significance of neutrality within Austrian foreign and security policy had to be played down.[1]

It is easy to forget that when Austria applied for membership, the Berlin Wall was still standing and there was only limited evidence that the Cold War was about to come to an end. On 17 July 1989, when the Austrian government forwarded its membership application to the Council of Ministers, the Soviet Union still dominated Central and Eastern Europe. In Hungary and Poland reform processes were underway, but there were few if any signs portending the collapse of communist regimes throughout much of the eastern bloc by the end of the year. With Europe still divided, and with the policy having served the country's interests well since its adoption in 1955, neutrality remained the central element of Austrian foreign policy. When applying for membership, the Austrian government made clear its position. It declared that the application was being submitted:

> on the understanding that its internationally recognised status of permanent neutrality ... will be maintained and that, as a member of the European Communities by virtue of the Treaty of Accession, it will be able to fulfil its legal obligations arising out of its status as a permanently neutral State and to continue its policy of neutrality as a specific contribution to the maintenance of peace and security in Europe.[2]

Subsequently, however, this stance was rapidly revised so that by the time Austria acceded to the EU in 1995 it was able to identify itself clearly with, and offer its full support to, the CFSP. As indicated, two forces were at play here. The first was the changing external environment. With the Cold War coming to an end in 1989–90, question marks were raised over the relevance of neutrality as an appropriate and viable central pillar of

Austrian foreign policy. Political and economic instability in neighbouring countries and a security vacuum existing in Central and Eastern Europe raised serious concerns about Austria's security. Fears intensified once war broke out in Yugoslavia. With Sarejevo closer to Vienna than the Swiss border, the vulnerability of Austria was exposed. In addition, there were fears that the days when Austria could effectively count on assistance from the West, should its territorial integrity be violated, had gone. Neutrality could no longer guarantee the country's security.

In reaction to the changing threats, the Austrian government began to rely less heavily on neutrality and pursued an active policy in favour of establishing mechanisms to promote a common European security system. This included support for building up the pan-European Conference on Security and Cooperation in Europe (CSCE), and for a more active role for the United Nations (UN).[3] It was recognised, however, that there were limits on how successful these organisations could be given their size and limited resources. As a consequence, the Austrian government was also looking elsewhere for mechanisms to guarantee the country's security. Links with Europe's defence organisations – the North Atlantic Treaty Organisation (NATO) and the Western European Union (WEU) – were considered. Yet membership would have required the abandonment of the country's cherished neutrality. The solution was the EU. With its objectives of common foreign, security and defence policies, the EU was seen by the Austrians as an embryonic European security system. As such it could provide Austria with security without requiring membership, at least in the short-term, of a military alliance. Given the desire to retain neutrality, the EU provided the most realistic security option for the Austrians.[4]

The second factor leading to a revision of the Austrian government's stance on neutrality was the position of the EC and Austria's desire to ensure its accession. Eager in the late 1980s, and the early 1990s, to see the EC develop foreign policy cooperation and establish a CFSP, several of the more integrationist Member States, alongside the Commission, were expressing reservations about admitting neutral states fearing that they may act as a brake on the EC's ambitions.[5] If Austria wished to ensure inclusion in the next round of enlargement the significance of neutrality had to be down-played. This was made clear in the Commission's 1991 *avis* on Austria's application for membership. It noted that the country's policy of neutrality would raise certain problems were Austria to accede to the EC. If the EC, as anticipated, were to move ahead towards the development of a common foreign and security policy, specific assurances would have to be obtained from the Austrian government concerning its legal capacity to undertake obligations resulting from such a policy.[6] Such reservations were echoed in the Commission's 1992 Report *Europe and the Challenges of Enlargement*. This stated clearly that: 'An applicant country whose constitutional status, or stance in international affairs, renders it unable to pursue the project [of a common foreign and security policy] . . . could not be satisfactorily integrated into the Union.'[7] The Report also made it clear that future Member States would have to subscribe 'in principle and in practice' to the provisions of the Treaty on the European Union (TEU) concerning the definition and implementation of the CFSP and questions related to the eventual framing of a common defence policy. Applicant states would be left with no doubts in this respect. The Commission concluded by stating that it considered the question of neutrality and its compatibility with the CFSP a particular concern in the context of accession.

In response to such statements, the Austrian government began to de-emphasise the significance of neutrality through *aide memoires* stressing its commitment to the EC's goals regarding the development of foreign policy cooperation. Indeed, a declaration issued on the second anniversary of the 1989 application failed to mention neutrality at all.[8] At the same time, the Austrian government was also reinterpreting neutrality, reducing it to three basic elements: non-participation in a war, non-participation in a military alliance, and no foreign bases on Austrian soil. This more differential concept of neutrality meant that Austria participated in economic sanctions against Iraq following the invasion of Kuwait and in 1991–92 allowed the US-led alliance against Saddam Hussein to transport war materials across Austria.[9] It was also accompanied by a keen interest in the EC's efforts to move beyond EPC and develop a common foreign and security policy. In a later *aide memoire* circulated prior to the European Council's Lisbon Summit in June 1992, the Austrian government identified itself fully with the objectives of the CFSP and promised active participation in its 'dynamic development'.[10] This de-emphasising of neutrality would continue to the point where it appeared that the government had almost forgotten the neutrality reservations submitted with the 1989 application. The effect was to reduce uncertainties among existing Member States about admitting Austria to the EU. Hence, at the start of the accession negotiations, the Austrian Foreign Minister, Alois Mock, stressed Austria's attachment to the fulfilment of CFSP aims and the development of the EU's security structures.[11] Later, in his opening statement on the CFSP chapter of the accession negotiations, Mock declared that the CFSP was 'an important step in strengthening the Community's international capacity to act' and that Austria proceeded from the assumption that 'the active and solidaristic participation in the [CFSP] will be compatible with its constitutional rules'. Mock failed to mention neutrality.[12] Austria was adapting itself to the requirements of membership before actually joining the EU.

The outcome of the accession negotiations bears this out. Not only were the negotiations on the CFSP chapter concluded almost as soon as they were opened, Austria, along with the other applicant countries, agreed to accept the provisions of the TEU relating to the CFSP and its development without reservation. In a joint declaration with Sweden and Finland, Austria agreed to 'participate fully and actively' in the CFSP and to 'take on in their entirety and without reservation' the EU's objectives relating to common foreign, security and defence policies, including the possibility of a common defence.[13] On joining the EU, the Austrian government reiterated this stance noting that Austria was committed to exhausting the opportunities created by the TEU for developing the EU as a community of solidarity and contributing to security in a pragmatic way through cooperation and partnership. Although no coherent strategy for membership was spelt out, the government's *Weißbuch* (White Book) on membership went on to note Austria's particular support for the European Stability Pact, closer ties with Ukraine, the EU's role in the administration of Mostar; and the development of a human rights policy. It also contained declarations to the effect that Austria would apply for observer status with the WEU, seek closer cooperation with NATO via the Partnership for Peace (PfP) programme, and support the early admission of applicant states, notably those in Central and Eastern Europe, to the EU.[14] The commitment to the CFSP was also reflected in the constitutional amendment adopted at the time the accession treaty under went parliamentary ratification. This resulted in a series of articles concerning the EU being added to the constitution. Of particular significance was the new Article 23f that noted Austria's participation in the CFSP on the basis of Title V of the TEU, and that such participation could involve measures under the EC pillar where economic relations with one or more non-Member States are interrupted, restricted or completely cut-off. The implication of this last point was clear: neutrality would be overruled by EC law concerning sanctions. As for the CFSP, participation would be full although the intergovernmental nature of pillar two decisions did provide the Austrian government with the opportunity to veto measures where neutrality was threatened. On acceding to the EU Austria appeared to accept fully the EU's foreign policy mechanisms, ambitions and priorities.

That Austria welcomed the existence and development of the CFSP clearly suggested that adaptation to membership would be smooth. The situation was also enhanced by the extent to which Austria had already been aligning itself with the EU positions. Austria's position on security matters dealt with in the UN was moving closer to that of the EU majority. Its record in some years was actually better than that of France and the United Kingdom.[15] In the 1994 *Weißbuch* on EU membership, the Austrian government was able to claim that Austrian foreign policy positions had in the last few years been significantly in line with those adopted under EPC and the CFSP. Furthermore Austrian assessments of security policy questions corresponded closely with those of the EU.[16]

Foreign policy adaptation through membership

At the time of its accession in 1995, Austria's foreign policy interests were clearly coinciding with those of the EU. With Austria as a security *demandeur* the development of the CFSP was welcome since it signalled the emergence of the EU as a security community.[17] Also, the limited defence dimension to the CFSP raised no serious problems for the maintenance of the strict interpretation of neutrality now adopted by the Austrian government. The fact too that Austrian foreign policy positions had increasingly coincided with those of the EU suggested few problems in adapting to membership. Indeed, early analyses of Austria's EU membership suggest a trouble-free integration into the CFSP. Austrian officials were as involved as might be expected.[18] Furthermore, annual foreign policy reports note increased degrees of convergence in European voting behaviour in the UN.[19]

Membership has, however, obviously involved some adaptation. Generally, the requirements have been limited. In terms of foreign trade, Austria's 1972 free trade agreement, alongside participation in the European Economic Area during 1994, meant that there were already only very few restrictions on trade with other EU Member States. Austria's alignment with the EC's Common External Tariff and Common Commercial Policy did result, though, in a slightly less liberal trade policy overall. Trade arrangements with Central and Eastern European (CEE) states changed little, however, since the free trade agreements that the European Free Trade Association (EFTA) states had concluded tended to follow the provisions of the Europe agreements. Beyond trade, accession to the EU has seen an increase in Austrian contributions to overseas development aid. In 1995, multilateral assistance increased from AS 1.4 billion to AS 2.1 billion. This was partly due to the AS 850 million which Austria had to contribute to the European Development Fund.[20] One further adjustment of note resulted in Austria recognising Russia as the successor to the Soviet Union and therefore as a party to the 1955 State Treaty. In exchange, Russia recognised that Austria alone was to determine the future of its neutrality policy.[21]

The limited adaptation in terms of foreign policy can obviously be explained by the adaptation that took place prior to membership and the coincidence between the aims of Austrian foreign policy and those of the EU. When Austria joined it was supportive of the EU developing into a security community. This support has remained consistent since and can be seen in the position Austria adopted with regard to the 1996 Intergovernmental Conference (IGC) and its response to the Treaty of Amsterdam. Although Austria has retained its policy of neutrality, this has not prevented support for the CFSP and further integration. In the lead up to the 1996 IGC, the government openly supported increasing the role of the EU as a stability factor in Europe by making the CFSP more efficient and workable. In its position paper, the Austrian government identified four priority tasks: strengthening the coherence of external relations across the EU pillars; developing joint planning and analysis capacities; improving the efficiency of decision making (including a smooth transition to majority voting except for military security decisions) and the way in which decisions are implemented; and making progress in the development of a common security and defence policy by enhancing the capacity for action in the areas of conflict prevention, crisis management, peacekeeping, disaster relief and humanitarian action. The government also noted that it would advocate the WEU being mandated by the EU to carry out Petersberg tasks.[22] Reference was, however, made to the Irish formula in Article J.4.4 on the CFSP not prejudicing 'the specific character of the security and defence policy of certain Member States'. For domestic reasons (see below), the IGC could not result in the abandonment of neutrality.

Given the IGC met these priorities, the Treaty of Amsterdam was welcomed by the Austrian government. Its ratification in the *Nationalrat* on 18 June 1998 was supported by both the two government parties, the Austrian Peoples Party (ÖVP) and Social Democrats (SPÖ), as well as the Liberal Forum. At the same time, Article 23f of the constitution was amended to allow Austrian participation, in a spirit of solidarity, in 'peace-keeping tasks and tasks of combat forces in crisis-management including peace-making' on the basis of either an EU joint action or a UN mandate. Despite the retention of neutrality, Austria was in a position to be fully involved in the CFSP and the mandated activities of the WEU.

Austria's willing involvement in the development of the CFSP has been accompanied by closer relations with other organisations. On joining the EU, Austria sought and obtained observer status of the WEU. Such a status has since been extended to meetings of the WEU-based Western European Armaments Group. Austrian voices have also been heard advocating the eventual integration of the WEU into the EU.[23] Relations with NATO have also been intensified. In 1995 a PfP was signed. Since then Austria has contributed transport and logistical contingents of approximately 240 personnel and 100 military vehicles to the Stabilisation Force for Bosnia-Herzegovina. Austria is also represented in the Euro-Atlantic Partnership Council established in May 1997. In November 1997 the Austrian government upgraded its diplomatic links with NATO replacing the existing 'liaison office' with a full diplomatic representation via its ambassador to Belgium. Austria has also agreed to participate in NATO-led peacekeeping activities via the 'Enhanced Partnership for Peace' (PfP-plus). In November 1998, the Austrian government announced that this would include active steps in peace enforcement, albeit based on the principle of 'self-differentiation'. Austria would not be obliged to participate in any specific NATO activity. The Austrian parliament would still be required to approve the use of Austrian soldiers in any mission.

These developments highlight the extent to which the changing security situation in Europe since the end of the Cold War has affected Austria's foreign policy priorities. Neutrality can no longer guarantee the country's security. Hence, Austria willingly participates in the CFSP. It has not, however, followed many of its immediate neighbours in seeking NATO membership, despite the fact that for many policy makers the Atlantic Alliance is the most obvious guarantor of security in Europe. Also, at the 1996 IGC the Austrian government was not among those Member States advocating integration of the WEU into the EU. This is not to say that such developments do not attract support within the Austrian government. Rather, domestic differences over foreign policy prevent official advocacy. Although at the moment the main focus of debate is the question of whether Austria should seek NATO membership, the repercussions of this debate and the positions adopted by those involved facilitate understanding of Austria's position within the EU. Divisions over NATO and the desire to retain neutrality encourage Austria to seek the development of the CFSP.

Domestic factors in the policy process

Austria being a federal state certainly suggests that the domestic dimension should be a factor in foreign policy. The federal structure was changed in 1992 to compensate the provinces for a loss of competencies following membership. With membership, the Austrian government is obliged to inform the provinces of all plans that touch on their interests.[24] Where the provinces agree on an *einheitliche Stellungnahme* (common position) the federal government and its representative in the EU Council are bound by this. It is, however, possible for the government to deviate from the common position for 'compelling reasons concerning foreign or integration policy'. As far as influence over foreign policy is concerned, this places the provinces in a similar position to that of the *Länder* in Germany. As regards the Federal Parliament, it too can bind the government representative within the Council. This it initially sought to do via tight *Stellungnahme*. More flexibility has since become evident. In 1997, for example, only four parliamentary positions were established. These covered EU–Iran relations, the IGC, the conference of EU transport ministers, and biotechnology. Even where the *Stellungnahme* is restrictive, deviation is possible for 'compelling reasons of foreign and integration policy'. What is meant by 'compelling reasons' is not stated. Legally, interpretation lies with the Constitutional Court.

Given the limited constraints so far imposed on the Austrian government, plus the possibility of deviation, policy is defined very much at the governmental level. Here, the nature of coalitions in Austria is important. The Chancellor, although formally head of the government, is only *primus inter pares*. Power resides firmly in the ministries which are allocated proportionately to each of the coalition parties. Of significance here is that both the Foreign and the Defence Ministries are in the hands of the ÖVP, the more pro-integration of the coalition parties. It was the ÖVP that led the bid for EC membership in the 1980s and which has since played a central role in challenging the sanctity of Austria's neutrality policy and advocating NATO membership. This does not mean that the ÖVP has free reign in determining policy. Foreign policy positions within the EC and CFSP are determined by the Foreign Ministry and Chancellery in line with the agreed aims of foreign and security policy. On these there is broad agreement. The 1996 coalition agreement gives prominence to the notion of solidarity through participation in both the EU and the UN. The two parties support the goal of establishing a pan-European security architecture in which a collective European security system guarantees that Europe can meet the challenges of the post-Cold War world. There is further agreement on the desirability of such a system developing within the EU.[25] This and earlier coalition agreements do not necessarily ensure agreement on policy. During the initial years of EU membership, differences between the ÖVP and SPÖ led to some fierce disputes over policy making and representation.[26] Policy positions advocated by the ÖVP have also been checked by the SPÖ. One early example was the decision to await EU membership before seeking observer status with the WEU. The ÖVP had advocated following the Swedish and Finnish governments and applying as early as May 1994.

The clear differences which exist between the SPÖ and ÖVP are evident in their positions on neutrality and NATO membership. Both accept that neutrality alone no longer provides an adequate means of ensuring Austria's security. The ÖVP goes further and argues that neutrality is redundant. Moreover, in its present form, the EU does not constitute a fully functioning security system. Nor, given its slow progress in developing the CFSP, is it likely to become such a system for several years to come. Even with the EU and WEU moving closer, the EU is unlikely to be able provide an adequate security guarantee for Austria. It is further argued that with so many EU Member States looking to NATO as the guarantor of European security, the likelihood of the EU developing into a fully functioning security system is limited and there is no point waiting for such an event when it may not happen and when nobody outside Austria really believes in it. Moreover, a military attack cannot be ruled out, and by not joining NATO Austria risks alienating other states who may well argue that through their membership of the Alliance they are paying for Austrian security. Consequently, the ÖVP fully supports the idea that Austria joins NATO and abandons neutrality. There is also support for WEU membership and its full integration into the EU.

The SPÖ rejects the ÖVP's analysis and argues that Austria's security is adequately met via neutrality, membership of the UN, Organisation for Security and Cooperation in Europe (OSCE) and EU, observer status in the WEU, and the PfP with NATO. Although neutrality no longer affords the same security as during the Cold War, there is no reason to abandon it, at least not until a Europe-wide system of collective security is in place. Until such a time, the emphasis of foreign policy should be placed on building up pan-European security organisations, promoting confidence-building measures, and pursuing balanced disarmament in terms of both conventional and nuclear weapons. Participation in Petersburg tasks is to be encouraged, however, provided it is compatible with a strict definition of neutrality. Similarly, cooperation with NATO through the PfP is not ruled out. Yet NATO membership should not be sought. Austria is at present not threatened with attack, nor is it likely to be threatened within the foreseeable future. And with NATO having enlarged to include the Czech Republic and Hungary, Austria is almost surrounded by NATO states. As for non-military threats to security, it is argued that these can be dealt with via the above organisations.[27]

Such differences within the SPÖ–ÖVP coalition over NATO membership were rarely more apparent than in early 1998 when the government failed to agree on the text of a report concerning Austria's security options. A commitment to producing the report had been contained in the agreement establishing the coalition in March 1996.[28] Its proposed publication was designed to ensure that the direction of security policy could be determined before Austria assumed the Presidency of the EU Council on 1 July 1998. The key reason behind the non-appearance of an official report was division within the coalition over whether the report should include NATO membership as a policy option. Whereas the ÖVP openly advocated its inclusion, the SPÖ was unwilling to countenance the idea. Although the SPÖ leader and Chancellor, Viktor Klima, is supposed to have been willing not to rule out NATO membership, the majority within the SPÖ ensured that he identified with the anti-membership view.[29] Disagreements over NATO were accompanied by differences over how far the EU should be involved in defence matters. Whereas the ÖVP favoured Austrian participation in realising a common defence policy and a common defence, the SPÖ was unconvinced of the need.[30]

The differences within the coalition, highlighted by the failure to produce the policy options report, have since been sustained as the ÖVP has intensified its support for NATO and heavily criticised the SPÖ for avoiding even a discussion of the question. The indecision has been criticised outside Austria too. This has caused concern within the ÖVP and among other supporters of NATO membership. As NATO enlarges and seeks to set out its strategy for future enlargement, Austrian indecision means that it is unlikely to be included. This is unlikely to change the position of the SPÖ. Hence a bid for NATO membership from the current coalition is certainly unlikely. An alternative ÖVP-led coalition would, however, be in a position to apply if such a coalition could be established. Among the opposition parties, only the Greens oppose NATO membership outright. They are determined to maintain neutrality and actually advocate the disbanding of both the WEU and NATO. By contrast, the Liberal Forum argues that neutrality is obsolete and is not opposed to NATO membership although there is a clear preference for WEU membership since the former is seen to be dominated by the US. The Populist Freedom Party (FPÖ) is also supportive of joining NATO, albeit subject to popular endorsement through a referendum. Under the populist leadership of Jörg Haider, however, the FPÖ remains unacceptable to the ÖVP as a potential coalition partner. In many respects it is Haider and the FPÖ which requires the existing coalition to remain viable. Indeed, it was due to fears that the governing coalition would split that the ÖVP rejected calls from the FPÖ in April 1998 for a vote on submitting a membership application.

If a pro-NATO coalition did emerge, NATO membership would only be possible if it received popular support via a referendum. Hence, Austrian foreign and security policy is not just determined by the politics of coalition government, key decisions will also be affected by the views of the electorate. At present, there is no convincing evidence that NATO membership and the abandonment of neutrality would receive popular approval. Indeed, the SPÖ has rejected ÖVP calls to initiate a nationwide debate on the future of Austrian foreign policy on the grounds that there is no popular support for such a debate. They would appear to be right in their assessment. The SPÖ's opposition to NATO membership certainly appears to reflect popular reluctance to abandon neutrality and join NATO. Opinion polls in February 1995 suggested that 80 per cent of Austrians wished to keep neutrality with 55 per cent stating in March 1995 that neutrality was 'topical and up-to-date'. Only 25 per cent of Austrians thought that neutrality was obsolete.[31] Such findings were similar to those from earlier in the decade. Since Austria joined the EU, attitudes have been changing, albeit without consistency, particularly with regard to joining NATO. In 1997 only 37 per cent of Austrians said they opposed NATO membership. More (45 per cent) were either undecided or had no opinion. Only 18 per cent of respondents were in favour of joining, although the figure rose to 28 per cent if CEE states were included.[32] A year later, the indecision was equally evident. In one 1998 poll 73 per cent of respondents said they opposed Austria joining NATO either immediately or some time soon. An earlier poll in September 1998 suggested that opposition stood at 57 per cent, although 58 per cent of respondents believed that Austria would join NATO within the next five years. The percentage in favour of membership had, however, risen to 38 per cent. Indeed, a further poll in November 1998 suggested that 49 per cent of Austrians favoured joining NATO with only 40 per cent opposed. The trend was reversed though once NATO launched air-strikes against Serbia in March 1999. Opposition to NATO membership rose to over 65 per cent with one poll registering opposition at 73 per cent.[33] The lack of consensus had already been underlined by the finding that although 68 per cent of Austrians wanted to keep neutrality, 51 per cent of respondents believed that neutrality would not guarantee Austria's security in the event of a threatened military attack.[34]

The fact that popular opinion influences Austrian foreign policy has already become evident in the EU context. Popular concerns have led to government enthusiasm for EU enlargement to wane. Traditionally, Austrian governments have strongly supported widening the EU to admit CEE countries. Indeed, it is regarded within the Foreign Ministry as one of Austria's key policy interests.[35] Yet public opinion is more cautious. Fears of low-cost competition, job losses, immigration and increased crime have led to opinion poll results showing majorities against the accession of the Czech Republic, Estonia, and Poland as well as those CEE states not involved currently in negotiations. Only Hungarian membership enjoys majority support (53 per cent). Slovenia has the support of 44 per cent of the population.[36] Popular reservations alone would not normally force a government to alter a key foreign policy goal. In Austria, however, the existence of the populist FPÖ means that the coalition government risks further decreases in popularity if it does not respond. The rise in support for the FPÖ, as witnessed in the provincial elections in March 1999 where the party made significant gains in Carinthia and the Tyrol, did not go unnoticed. Even before these, partly in response to pressure from the country's eastern most provinces, the government was toning down its support for enlargement and arguing strongly within EU fora that the costs of enlargement should not disproportionately affect Austria. New members should be subject to long transitional periods. Indeed, in January 1998, the government requested that the Commission proposed a special programme for those regions bordering on membership applicants. The Commission replied in the negative. The influence of domestic concerns on policy can also be seen in the government's support for EU demands that Hungary impose visas on Romanians as a sign of the country's determination to police what will be the EU's south-eastern border.[37]

With or without the EU – constriction or opportunity?

The lack of domestic consensus over NATO membership, and the future of neutrality alongside the desire of the coalition parties to remain in power, certainly enhances the attractiveness of the EU as the organisation through which Austria is to promote its security. In general, the EU is therefore not regarded as a constraint on foreign policy. Indeed, membership has consistently been viewed as providing opportunities. This is not to say that any sense of distinctiveness has been abandoned. In advance of Austria's Presidency of the EU Council in 1998, State Secretary for Foreign Affairs, Benita Ferrero-Waldner, stressed that 'although the EU presidency will focus Austria's foreign policy, . . . [Austria's] forthcoming leadership of the EU neither dominates nor defines that policy'.[38] This has already been proven. There have been several examples of the government openly delaying the conclusion of agreements in order to ensure Austrian interests were taken fully into account, notably over alpine transit. This is the one area where Austria claims a special and almost unique interest. In its accession negotiations, Austria fought hard for environmental reasons to ensure that increases in transit traffic as a consequence of membership would be kept to a minimum.[39] As a member, Austria has sought to ensure that transit traffic does not increase. Such a position has led Austria to hold up initialling of the Europe Agreement with Slovenia in May 1995. Austria was also forthright in ensuring its interests were protected in the context of EU negotiations with Switzerland. At various points Austrian officials were critical of the EU position believing that it provided better treatment to the Swiss. Moreover, it is clear that Austria's foreign policy interests are not entirely dominated by the EU and its agenda, although there is considerable overlap. Key interests do include strengthening the EU as a security, prosperity and value community and EU enlargement.[40] Yet, Austria is equally intent on contributing via other fora to the development of effective European security structures and the promotion of peace in Former Yugoslavia. Clearly such interests coincide with those of the EU and other EU Member States. The same is true of interests beyond Europe. Here, the Austrians are keen to see transatlantic relations developed and the UN strengthened. The official view is that the EU does not constrain Austrian policy.

In terms of promoting foreign policy interests, EU membership has certainly been welcomed. As the Foreign Minister, Wolfgang Schüssel, observed in 1997, Austria's status as an EU member has given the country 'a real opportunity to play an equal part in shaping the issues which are most decisive for the future of Europe'. Schüssel also noted 'the extent to which [Austria's] international activity has gained in breadth and depth through membership'.[41] In 1998, the government's official position was unchanged:

> As a member of the European Union Austria has the opportunity to play an active part in the further development of the Common Foreign and Security Policy and to assist in realising the perspective of a common defence system in a spirit of European solidarity . . . Today, Austria can also help extend the

pacifying and stabilising power of European integration to the Greater Europe.[42]

Schüssel noted that in contrast to the widely expressed apprehension that Austrian foreign policy would become 'euro-centric', the exact opposite had been the case. The EU–US transatlantic dialogue had proved beneficial and relations with countries in the Asian–Pacific region, Africa and Latin America had 'developed a good deal more dynamically than would have been possible if [Austria] had still been acting alone'. The 'EU bonus' had also helped consolidate Vienna's position as a seat for international organisations – the technical secretariat of the Comprehensive Nuclear Test Ban Treaty Organisation was located in the Austrian capital, and facilitated the conclusion of the Convention on a Total Ban on Anti-Personnel Mines in December 1997.[43] Attention was also drawn to the increased flow of information and the opportunities for the joint formulation of policy which membership creates.[44]

As well as providing Austria with a voice within decision making, membership is also seen as providing opportunities, via the CFSP, to promote specific national foreign policy interests. For example, in 1996, the Austrians initiated the proposal that led to the establishment of an EU presence in Pristina in Kosovo in an attempt to defuse tension in what was rightly regarded as a potentially explosive situation. On the environment too, Austria has sought successfully to use the EU to promote its interests. Developments within the UN Environment Programme in 1996 depended very much on Austrian prepared contributions from the EU. The Austrians also claim responsibility for initiating the EU's joint action of 1 October 1996 on landmines and for promoting international measures concerning the protection of children. Outside the CFSP, membership has also afforded Austria the opportunity to consolidate relations with Italy. This is seen as important given the Austrian government's interest in protecting the interests of the German-speaking minority in the South Tyrol.

The major event which facilitates an assessment of the impact of EU membership on Austrian foreign policy is the Austrian Presidency of the Council in the second half of 1998. For the government, this was clearly seen as providing an opportunity to pursue national foreign policy interests. State Secretary Ferrero-Waldner noted in early 1997 that it: 'is the visible expression of a foreign policy which pursues a series of medium- and long-term goals defined by the federal government goals which may well receive more attention and be realised sooner as a result of our presidency'. Progress towards Eastern enlargement, increased stability in South-east Europe, human rights and anti-personnel mines were noted.[45] Officially, the Austrian government recognised that the role it had to play as the Presidency was very much the honest broker. All the same, the six months did provided a clear opportunity to use the EU to promote foreign policy interests. The opportunity was openly acknowledged.

In terms of foreign policy, the main goal of the Austrian Presidency was to launch the EU's enlargement process.[46] In addition, there was a clear wish to establish an active role for the EU in conflict prevention ending the bloodshed in Kosovo, monitor the situation in Bosnia and Middle East, and support human rights as a factor international politics. Other areas noted in the Presidency's programme included further trade liberalisation through the World Trade Organisation (WTO); improved relations with Turkey; the conclusion of negotiations with Switzerland; consolidation of multilateral and bilateral dialogue with the EU's Mediterranean partners; implementation of the New Transatlantic Agenda; and new negotiations with the Lomé countries.[47] Each of the main goals fitted in with ongoing concerns of the EU. They were, however, of particular interest to Austria. And on three of them the Presidency did deliver. Accession negotiations with Cyprus, the Czech Republic, Estonia, Hungary, Poland and Slovenia were launched; the Vienna European Council adopted common foreign policy strategies for the Middle East Peace Process and the Western Balkans; and the EU adopted a human rights declaration in December 1998 to celebrate fifty years of UN Declaration of Human Rights. At the time, the Austrian Chancellor, Viktor Klima, asserted Austria's role as a 'motor' in human rights questions. Also of note was the EU's decision to allocate 40 million Euro in aid for refugees in Kosovo. With the Austrian government fearful of the possible implications of further refugees entering Austria, this was seen as a significant success. Earlier in the year the fear of refugees had led to Austrian calls for the EU to develop a European security and defence identity.

Beyond these issues, the Austrians also managed to use the Presidency to ensure progress in other areas of particular interest. These included the long-awaited conclusion of bilateral treaties with Switzerland. For Austria the agreement on Alpine transit was most welcome. Secondly, the Austrians exhibited a keenness to promote EU activities in combating international crime. Further development of Europol was supported. A third example was the environment. In a speech to the European Parliament, Foreign Minister Wolfgang Schüssel seized the opportunity to promote a particular Austrian concern: nuclear safety standards in Central and Eastern Europe. Deviating from his original text at a meeting in July 1998, Schüssel demanded the immediate closure of the Bohunice nuclear power station in Slovakia and a further review of safety at the Mochovce nuclear power station. The Presidency also provided the Austrians with the opportunity to promote closer economic cooperation with the USA and Asia, and with developing countries via the launching of the new round of Lomé negotiations. The establishment of political dialogue within EU–South Africa relations was welcomed too.

With regard to the CFSP, the Austrians willingly used the Presidency to promote their interests. Success was not, however, guaranteed. Certainly, the Presidency failed to prevent bloodshed in Kosovo. The Vienna summit of the European Council also failed to agree on who should be Mr/Ms CFSP and on the establishment of policy planning and early warning unit. Yet the Presidency did seek to use the CFSP to promote conflict prevention. In September 1998 it advocated using Article J.4 to call on the WEU to send 600 additional police to Albania. And, although no agreement could be reached on the appointment of a High Representative for Kosovo, a special envoy, by coincidence an Austrian, Wolfgang Petritsch, was appointed to cooperate with the US envoy in Kosovo. The Austrian government was also able to push forward the adoption at the Vienna European Council of the first CFSP strategies, as provided for in the Treaty of Amsterdam. These cover Russia, Ukraine, the Mediterranean, the Middle East Peace Process and the Western Balkans.

Austria's interest in the CFSP was also reflected in the efforts made to develop it further. The Austrians used the informal summit of EU leaders at Pörtschach in October 1998 to promote discussion of the EU's security role with Chancellor Klima advocating a stronger external and security policy for the EU. The Austrians also announced support for the UK proposal that the political functions of the WEU be merged with the EU.[48] Of particular significance was that the first meeting of EU defence ministers and the first informal meeting between the Presidency of the EU Council and the NATO Secretary-General took place during the Austrian Presidency.[49] For the government of a neutral state divided over the question of NATO membership, such contacts were significant. The EU was taking one further step towards becoming the security community sought by the Austrians.

Conclusion

In terms of foreign policy, Austria's adaptation to EU membership has progressed smoothly. This was certainly helped by the adaptation already under way prior to accession. With the Cold War coming to an end and new security threats emerging as the communist regimes in Central and Eastern Europe collapsed, Austria found itself in a position where neutrality could no longer be relied upon as a guarantee for the country's security. Inclusion was therefore sought in new security arrangements which would not require the abandonment of neutrality. With the then EC developing the CFSP and eschewing a defence identity in the short term at least, the attraction of the EU as an emerging security community was obvious. This perception of the EU has since been sustained. Hence, Austria has welcomed the Treaty of Amsterdam's reforms of the CFSP and adopted the requisite amendments to the country's constitution to enable full participation in the policy.

Further proof of the smooth adaptation of Austrian foreign policy to EU membership can be found in the positive statements issued by government ministers. Far from acting as a constraint on foreign policy, EU membership is seen as providing opportunities to promote national interests. In most cases, notably concerning enlargement and efforts to promote stability in Central and Eastern Europe, these coincide with the interests of other Member States and the EU. This facilitates the adaptation process. Austria has, however, held out on various occasions to protect its interests in negotiations with non-Member States, notably where the proposed agreement would have implications for transit traffic. It has also reacted cautiously, although not negatively, to proposed developments in EU–WEU relations. Such behaviour undoubtedly reflects the need to accommodate domestic influences on foreign policy. Differences within the governing coalition, the nature of coalition politics and the need to respond to popular concerns can and do impact on the government's position towards developments and policy at the EU level. Hence, there are constraints on the extent to which Austrian foreign policy is able to adapt to the EU. So far, however, adaptation has been smooth. Provided the EU continues to be regarded as a source of security and opportunity, and moves only cautiously on the development of a defence identity, this is likely to remain the case.

Notes

1 On Austria's adaptation prior to membership generally, see Paul Luif, 'Austria: adaptation through anticipation' in K. Hanf and B. Soetendorp (eds), *Adapting to European Integration: Small States and the European Union* (London, Longman, 1998), pp. 118–124.

2 EC Commission, 'The challenge of enlargement: commission opinion on Austria's application for membership', *Bulletin of the European Communities*, Supplement 4/92, p. 6.

3 P. Jankowitsch and H. Porias, 'The process of European integration and neutral Austria' in S. Harden (ed.), *Neutral States and the European Community* (London, Brassey's, 1994), pp. 42–45.

4 K. Koch, 'Austria: The economic logic of accession' in J. Redmond (ed.), *Prospective Europeans: New Members for the European Union*, (Hemel Hempstead, Harvester Wheatsheaf, 1994), pp. 45–46; H. Neuhold, 'EFTA-erweiterung der Europäischen Union: eine österreichische Sichtweise', *Integration*, 17:2 (1994), pp. 110–111.

5 See, for example the position of the Belgian government as described in P. Luif, 'Austria' in H. Wallace (ed.), *The Wider Western Europe: Reshaping the EC/EFTA Relationship*, (London, RIIA/Pinter, 1991), p. 133.

6 EC commission, 'The challenge of enlargement: commission opinion on Austria's application for membership', *Bulletin of the European Communities*, Supplement 4/92, pp. 15–18.

7 EC Commission, Europe and the challenge of enlargement, *Bulletin of the European Communities*, Supplement 3/92, p. 11.

8   A. Mock, *Declaration on the Occasion of the 2nd Anniversary of Austria's EC Membership Application* (London, Austrian Embassy, 17 July 1991). See also the *aide-memoire* of November 1991 as discussed in R. Rack, 'Österreich: "D'rum prüfe, wer sich ewig bindet . . ."', *EG Magazin*, 1–2/92, pp. 24–26.

9   H. Kramer, 'Austrian foreign policy from the state treaty to European Union membership (1955–1995)' in K. R. Luther and P. Pulzer (eds), *Austria 1945–95: Fifty Years of the Second Republic* (Aldershot, Ashgate, 1998), p. 173.

10 P. Luif, 'EPC/CFSP and Austria's Neutrality', *EPC/CFSP Forum – Newsletter of the Institut für Europäische Politik (IEP)*, July 1993, pp. 2–3.

11 A. Mock, *Erklärung Anläßlich der Eröffnung der Beitrittsverhandlungen mit der Europäischen Gemeinschaft* (Wien, Bundeskanzleramt, 01 Februar 1993).

12 Cited in P. Luif, *On the Road to Brussels: The Political Dimension of Austria's, Finland's and Sweden's Accession to the European Union* (Vienna, Wilhelm Braumüller, 1995), p. 307.

13 Treaty of Accession – Joint Declaration on Common Foreign and Security Policy, reproduced in OJC 241, 29 August 1994.

14 Bundesregiurung Österreich, *Wießbuch der Bundesregierung* (Wien, Bundesregierung, December 1994), V.3 and V.4.

15 P. Luif, *On the Road to Brussels: The Political Dimension of Austria's, Finland's and Sweden's Accession to the European Union* (Vienna, Wilhelm Braumüller, 1995), pp. 286–302; H. Neuhold, 'Austria and European security: the question of neutrality' in F. Algieri et al (eds), *Managing Security in Europe: The European Union and the Challenge of Enlargement* (Gütersöh, Bertelsmann Foundation, 1996), p. 31 and Table 10 on p. 255.

16 Bundesregiurung Österreich, *Wießbuch der Bundesregierung* (Wien, Bundesregierung, December 1994), V.2.3-V.2.4

17 H. Neuhold, 'Austria and European security: the question of neutrality' in F. Algieri et al (eds), *Managing Security in Europe: The European Union and the Challenge of Enlargement* (Gütersöh, Bertelsmann Foundation, 1996).

18 A. Skuhra, 'Österreich und die Gemeinsame Außen- und Sicherheits-politik der EU (GASP)', *Österreichische Zeitschrift für Politikwissenschaft*, 25:4 (1996), pp. 443–454.

19 The government was not, however, wholly successful in coordinating its own position with that of the EU on arms control and arms reductions. See Federal Ministry for Foreign Affairs, *Austrian Foreign Policy Yearbook 1996* (Vienna, Federal Ministry for Foreign Affairs, 1997) via Federal Ministry for Foreign Affairs at http://www.bmaa.gv.at accessed on 27 February 1998.

20 Federal Ministry for Foreign Affairs, *Austrian Foreign Policy Yearbook 1996*, (Vienna, Federal Ministry for Foreign Affairs, 1997) via Federal Ministry for Foreign Affairs at http://www.bmaa.gv.at accessed on 27 February 1998.

21 H. Neuhold, 'The national interests of Austria' in W. Wessels (ed.), *National vs. EU-Foreign Policy Interests: Mapping 'Important' National Interests* (Cologne/Brussels, Trans European Policy Studies Association, 1998), p. 123.

22 See F. Laursen 'The EU "neutrals", the CFSP and defence policy', *TKI Working Papers on European Integration and Regime Formation*, No. 26 (Esjberg, South Jutland University Press, 1998), pp. 22–23; *Austria's Positions*

of Principle on the Intergovernmental Conference: Austrian Government Document of 26 March 1996, via European Parliament Intergovernmental Conference task Force at http://europa.eu.int /en/agenda/igc-home/eu-doc/parlment/peen2.htm#a2 created on 15 November 1996.

23 Österreichische Volkspartei, (*Untitled Report on Security Policy Options*) (Wien, Österreichische Volkspartei, 1998), p. 82 via Österreichische Volkspartei at http://www.oevp.or.at accessed on 20 April 1998. Indeed, Chancellor Viktor Klima (SPÖ) stated in April 1998 that he was convinced that the WEU and EU would eventually be merged. See 'Amsterdam-Ratifizierung: Schritt zur gemeinsamen Sicherheitspolitik', *Die Presse*, 16 April 1998 via Die Presse Online at http://www. diepresse.at/ accessed on 21 April 1998.

24 For fuller details, see P. Luif, 'Austria: adaptation through anticipation', pp. 118–124.

25 *Koalitionsuebereinkommen zwischen der Sozialdemokratischen Partei Oesterreichs und der Oesterreichischen Volkspartei* (Wien, 11 Maerz 1996) via SPÖ at http://www.spoe.or.at/ accessed on 18 March 1999.

26 H. Kramer, 'Austrian foreign policy from the state treaty to European Union membership (1955–1995)' in K. R. Luther and P. Pulzer (eds), *Austria 1945–95: Fifty Years of the Second Republic* (Aldershot, Ashgate, 1998), p. 175.

27 See H. Neuhold, 'Austria in search of its place in a changing world: from between the blocs to full western integration' in K. R. Luther and P. Pulzer (eds), *Austria 1945–95: Fifty Years of the Second Republic* (Aldershot, Ashgate, 1998), pp. 217–218.

28 *Koalitionsuebereinkommen zwischen der Sozialdemokratischen Partei Oesterreichs und der Oesterreichischen Volkspartei* (Wien, 11 Maerz 1996) via SPÖ at http://www.spoe.or.at/index1.htm accessed on 18 March 1999.

29 'Wiens Berührungsängste gegenüber der Nato', *Neue Zürcher Zeitung*, 2 April 1998.

30 Österreichische Volkspartei, (*Untitled Report on Security Policy Options*) (Wien, Österreichische Volkspartei, 1998), p. 82 via Österreichische Volkspartei at http://www.oevp.or.at accessed on 20 April 1998; and 'Das gescheiterte Bericht', *Die Presse*, 20 April 1998 via Die Presse Online at http://www.diepresse.at/ accessed on 21 April 1998.

31 Cited in H. Neuhold, 'Austria and European security: the question of neutrality' in F. Algieri et al. (eds), *Managing Security in Europe: The European Union and the Challenge of Enlargement* (Gütersloh, Bertelsmann Foundation, 1996), p. 33.

32 *Die Presse*, 12 September 1997, cited in H. Neuhold, 'Austria in search of its place in a changing world: from between the blocs to full western integration' in K. R. Luther and P. Pulzer (eds), *Austria 1945–95: Fifty Years of the Second Republic* (Aldershot, Ashgate, 1998), p. 218.

33 See 'Krieg belebt Nato-Debatte', *Der Standard*, 3 April 1999 via Der Standard at http://derstandard.at/ accessed on 1 June 1999.

34 See 'Mehrheit schätzt Neutralität, spricht ihr aber Schutzfunktion ab' *Die Presse*, 25 November 1998 via Die Presse Online at http://www.diepresse.at/ accessed on 18 March 1999.

35 See H. Neuhold, 'The national interests of Austria' in W. Wessels (ed.), *National vs. EU-Foreign Policy Interests: Mapping 'Important' National Interests* (Cologne/Brussels, Trans European Policy Studies Association, 1998), p. 121–122.

36 EC Commission, *Eurobarometer 49* (Brussels, EC Commission, Spring 1998), B.145; see also the earlier survey reported in 'Austrians oppose large EU', *Financial Times*, 26 March 1998, p. 3.

37 'Austria and its eastern neighbours', *The Economist*, 9 May 1998, p. 53.

38 Federal Ministry for Foreign Affairs, *Austrian Foreign Policy Yearbook 1997* (Vienna, Federal Ministry for Foreign Affairs, 1998) via Federal Ministry for Foreign Affairs at http://www.bmaa.gv.at/ApBericht/ index.html.en accessed on 12 March 1999.

39 D. Phinnemore, 'Austria, transit and the environment' in J. Redmond (ed.), *The 1995 Enlargement of the European Union* (Aldershot, Ashgate, 1997), pp. 64–85.

40 On Austria's foreign policy interests, see H. Neuhold, 'The national interests of Austria' in W. Wessels (ed.), *National vs. EU-Foreign Policy Interests: Mapping 'Important' National Interests* (Cologne and Brussels, Trans European Policy Studies Association, 1998), p. 118–126.

41 Federal Ministry for Foreign Affairs, *Austrian Foreign Policy Yearbook 1996* (Vienna, Federal Ministry for Foreign Affairs, 1997) via Federal Ministry for Foreign Affairs at http://www.bmaa.gv.at accessed on 27 February 1998.

42 Federal Ministry for Foreign Affairs, *Austrian Foreign Policy Yearbook 1997* (Vienna, Federal Ministry for Foreign Affairs, 1998) via Federal Ministry for Foreign Affairs at http://www.bmaa.gv.at/ApBericht/ index.html.en accessed on 12 March 1999.

43 Federal Ministry for Foreign Affairs, *Austrian Foreign Policy Yearbook 1997* (Vienna, Federal Ministry for Foreign Affairs, 1998) via Federal Ministry for Foreign Affairs at http://www.bmaa.gv.at/ApBericht/ index.html.en accessed on 12 March 1999.

44 Annual Yearbooks make a point of noting how many COREU communications are transmitted each year.

45 Federal Ministry for Foreign Affairs, *Austrian Foreign Policy Yearbook 1997* (Vienna, Federal Ministry for Foreign Affairs, 1998) via Federal Ministry for Foreign Affairs at http://www.bmaa.gv.at/ApBericht/ index.html.en accessed on 12 March 1999.

46 W. Schüssel, 'The priorities of the Austrian presidency' in K. R. Luther and I. Ogilvie (eds), *Austria and the European Union Presidency: Background and Perspectives* (Keele, Keele European Research Centre, 1998), pp. 87–101.

47 *Programme of the Austrian Presidency of the EU Council 1998* via Austrian EU Presidency site at http://eu.presidency.gv.at/programm/arbeitsprogram-mindex.html.en updated 19 October 1998.

48 'EU shows broad consensus', *Financial Times*, 26 October 1998, p. 2.

49 The meeting also helped overcome a sense of frustration in some Austrian circles that, as a result of non-membership of the WEU, the country's EU Presidency could not be coupled with the WEU Presidency. This had to be given over to the Italians.

12

Denmark and Ireland

Ben Tonra

Introduction

On the face of it, one would expect an analysis of Danish and Irish foreign policy to provide limited insights to the study of comparative European foreign policy. As a rule, smaller states are seen as the flotsam and jetsam of the international system or as 'make-weights' for realist-inspired band-wagoning coalitions. If a unique model of transformatory Foreign Policy Analysis (FPA) is to be identified, however, its utility is likely to be most evident in an analysis of the more adaptable, less institutionalised and necessarily more open structures and practices of smaller EU Member States.

It is especially useful to pursue a comparative analysis of Danish and Irish foreign policy within the European Union (EU). First, both are smaller Member States sharing problematic historical relationships with much larger neighbours. Secondly, both states joined the then European Communities (EC) at the same time and for much the same reason – the economic imperatives occasioned by British membership – and neither was initially inspired by the political logic of integration. Subsequently, however, Irish policy makers have traded upon a self-characterisation as 'good Europeans' while Danish elites have struggled with a significantly sceptical public. Thirdly, each state has had a somewhat unique perspective on issues related to security and defence that has set them apart from the European mainstream. As a result, albeit for different reasons, each has had significant difficulties with moves towards a substantive Common Foreign and Security Policy (CFSP). Finally, both states share a self-perception of being principled foreign policy actors making a progressive and positive contribution to the international system. Their ambitions for that system are also similar, seeing it based upon the rule of law, international justice and the pacific settlement of international disputes.

Based upon these common threads, it is therefore interesting to note that in the cases of Denmark and Ireland there is evidence of 'Europeanisation' in national foreign policy. This does not represent a transfer of loyalty on the part of policy makers but instead a significant change in the context of policy formation and a consequent internalisation of norms and expectations arising from a complex, collective policy making system.

Foreign policy change

The external environment

The external context within which Danish and Irish foreign policies operate is both regional and global. Undoubtedly, the regional context is dominated by Danish and Irish membership of the EU while the global context has been transformed as a result of the end of the Cold War.

Both Denmark and Ireland are long-standing members of the EU, joining the then EC in January 1973. Membership was presented as offering significant material benefits to key national constituencies and, at least in part, was seen as a necessary consequence of decisions being taken in other European capitals – most notably in London. For Denmark, membership was politically challenging. Danish elites that favoured a 'yes' vote in the referendum made a point of insisting that membership was based upon the material gains which would accrue from access to a large, wealthy single market. Moreover, many of these same elites insisted that membership entailed no dedication to political integration in Europe and that it would have no impact upon Denmark's Atlantic-centred security identity or Nordic-centred political identity.[1]

In Ireland, the material benefits of membership were more tangible as financial transfers from the Community budget were promised and delivered. The political aspirations of integration were also seen in a positive light as a means of freeing Ireland from an overwhelming bilateral relationship with Britain. Membership broadened the range of Ireland's relationships and promised to reduce its asymmetrical economic dependence. The major obsessive point in Irish membership was related to neutrality. On accession, European interlocutors were assured that neutrality would not preclude Ireland's participation in an agreed European defence structure that developed as a result of political unification. However, Irish elites simultaneously promised their domestic constituencies that this was not a consequence of EC membership and that any such eventuality would have to be agreed by a future Irish government.[2]

By the late 1980s and early 1990s Danish policy makers had accepted the integrative logic of proposals for Economic and Monetary Union (EMU) and a CFSP. The Danish Government's 1990 position paper on proposed treaty change (which had been agreed with six mainstream political parties) argued that the future of the EC was as '. . . the foundation for the political and economic unity of all of Europe'.[3]

The resulting Treaty of European Union (TEU) agreed at Maastricht in December 1991 was, however, narrowly rejected by the Danish people in the subsequent June referendum. Opposition centred upon the unacceptable politicisation of what had been promised to be an economic endeavour. Provisions on an EU citizenship, EMU, and the development of a defence aspect to the CFSP were seen to be especially problematic. Only after four specific treaty opt-outs had been agreed at the 1992 Edinburgh Summit was the treaty presented to the Danish electorate in a second (and successful) ratification attempt. One of these opt-outs included all defence-related aspects of the CFSP.

For the Irish Government, the focus of attention in the run-up to the 1990–91 Intergovernmental Conference (IGC) was on the economic implications of the EMU. Proposals for European security also excited some early official unease. By June of 1990, however, the Taoiseach (Prime Minister) could report his confidence that no mutual defence commitment would be forthcoming in the treaty negotiations and that therefore the government's position on neutrality would be unaffected.[4] The Maastricht Treaty provoked little public debate on foreign/security policy with most media and popular attention fixed on the promise of a six billion pound European budget payoff and a political crisis surrounding abortion. In the event, the referendum was carried by a two to one majority.

When the EU Member States came to begin their discussions on another round of treaty revision in 1996 the Danish government found itself obliged to restate its adherence to the four previously agreed opt-outs. This was despite the fact that government ministers publicly insisted that the opt-outs were limiting Danish influence in key policy areas.[5] The government focused upon the means by which the Danish public might be reattached to the European project. As a result, there was considerable Danish attention devoted to issues such as employment and consumer rights. Based upon their existing opt-outs, Danish negotiators did not fully engage in debates surrounding a strengthened security and defence identity for the Union. However, they did support efforts to make the CFSP a more efficient and effective intergovernmental bureaucracy. The Amsterdam Treaty was ratified in Denmark by the referendum of May 1998 with – in a Danish context – a comfortable majority of 55 per cent.

The 1996 treaty negotiations were more problematic for the Irish government. The focus of Irish attention was directed towards defending existing institutional balances and restricting the scope of any 'variable geometry' within the Union. Irish negotiators had also to monitor closely the broader debate surrounding the evolution of a European Security and Defence Identity (ESDI). It soon became clear, as result of decisions taken in the North Atlantic Treaty Organisation (NATO), that such an entity would be centred within the Atlantic Alliance. Subsequent Finnish/ Swedish proposals for the Western European Union (WEU) to act on behalf of the EU in specified military contexts had the merit of being proposed by two other neutrals and of focusing upon areas such as peace-keeping, which had a positive domestic resonance. Nonetheless, ratification was achieved by the narrowest margin to date in a European referendum, securing just a 60 per cent majority (compared with 66 per cent at Maastricht, 70 per cent for the Single European Act and an 83 per cent vote for membership in 1972).

For both Danish and Irish foreign policies the impact of EU member-ship has been to challenge preferred national security and defence policies. It has forced these governments to make policy choices they would not otherwise have had to face and have raised significant domestic opposi-tion to membership. Denmark and Ireland have also had to expend some political capital in their efforts to limit the evolution of the EU's capacity in this area or, as in the case of Denmark, have had formally to opt out of treaty provisions.

While the evolution of the EU has had a significant impact on national foreign policies, the end of the Cold War has transformed the context within which these foreign policies operate. Denmark is no longer a 'front-line' state in terms of any conceivable military confrontation and NATO's evolution – to which Denmark has contributed significantly – has created a European security/defence system which closely reflects traditional Danish concerns.[6]

This system is firmly Atlantic-centred, relies more heavily upon politi-cal frameworks than military strategy and defines security more broadly than that of defence of territorial boundaries. NATO is the lynchpin of this new system. Its strategic doctrine is now less nuclear-centred, is no longer based on 'forward defence', underlines its commitment to no 'first-use' of force and places a priority upon the development of multinational conventional forces in support of crisis management operations mandated by the UN and/or the Organisation for Security and Cooperation in Europe (OSCE). This multilateral, multinational and multifaceted secu-rity/defence system has opened pathways to a more proactive Danish foreign policy.

Denmark's new 'active internationalism',[7] based upon a rejuvenated Atlantic Alliance, contrasts with its traditional ambivalence towards a Euro-centric model such as that offered by the EU and WEU. Danish fears that the 'four corners' of its foreign policy (NATO, UN, EU, Nordic) would be thrown out of balance by a weakening NATO and an overly ambitious EU have been set to rest. Danish foreign policy has thus been liberated from its worst fear – that of having to make a choice between the Atlantic and Europe. Confident in the underlying stability and strength of the Atlantic Alliance (and being vigorous advocates of its enlargement to the Baltic states), Danish foreign policy makers pursue more assertively the norms that underpin Danish foreign policy: collective security, the rule of law and self-determination.[8]

For Irish foreign policy makers, by contrast, the end of the Cold War has laid bare a difficult and unresolved question at the heart of Irish foreign and security policy. Since Irish neutrality was neither ideological nor strategic, the revolutionised political and strategic context of the post-Cold War era has not – in the public mind – drawn Irish neutrality into question. At the same time, Irish policy makers are acutely conscious of the fact that Ireland's arguably peripheral position within the evolving European security system threatens it with substantive marginalisation.[9] Moreover, the fact that this system is centred upon NATO poses special difficulties. The hook upon which an Irish contribution to European security and defence was traditionally promised (European political unification) remains distant. Meanwhile, the emerging European security system offers only marginal benefits to Irish policy makers (in terms of access to new modes of peacekeeping) while NATO continues to be held in popular suspicion.

Irish policy makers have grappled with these issues. In 1996 the government published its first White Paper comprehensively reviewing Irish foreign policy. While a remarkably participative process contributed to its drafting and the report itself is detailed and analytically rigorous, the White Paper did not offer any clear direction on security issues. Its contribution was to delimit Irish participation in the WEU (ruling out a contribution to crisis management operations) and to open a debate on participation in Partnership for Peace (PfP). This latter possibility was immediately denounced by the largest political party in the state (then in opposition) as a betrayal of Irish neutrality and was also opposed by the smallest of the then three government parties.

The impact upon Irish foreign policy of the end of the Cold War has thus been to light a long and slow fuse to the debate surrounding Ireland's contribution to European security. It has also served to highlight the potential marginalisation of Irish foreign and security policy. This is raised by the relative success to date of NATO-sponsored peace-keeping operations and the consequent sidelining of traditional UN-style operations to which Ireland has made a modest but significant contribution. Limited Irish participation in the Bosnian Stabilisation Force (SFOR) operation and the government's declared intention in 1999 to pursue PfP membership (which entailed a reversal of declared policy on the part of the largest political party in the state) all signify a determined effort to bring Ireland closer to the European security mainstream.

The internal environment

While membership of the EU may most obviously be perceived as an external context to national foreign policy, it may also be seen as part of the construction of that policy and thus part of the internal environment. The question that arises is the extent to which, if at all, one can speak here in terms of 'Europeanisation'. This is defined here as a transformation in the way in which national foreign policies are constructed, in the ways in which professional roles are defined and pursued and in the consequent internalisation of norms and expectations arising from a complex system of collective European policy making.

In the first instance both Danish and Irish policy makers value the international weight that EU membership provides. For one senior member of the Danish Socialist People's Party, this provided a 'higher profile' and a greater substance to Danish foreign policy than previously.[10] Danish policy makers speak of a stronger 'voice', greater 'influence' and a seat at the 'big table' where '. . . you have the possibility [of influence] which you do not have if you are not at the table'. Interestingly, influence at that table is also seen to be transferable. Another Danish official insisted that '. . . your influence [elsewhere] is also dependent upon your influence in that central [European] forum'. Irish policy makers speak in similar terms about Ireland's 'voice', 'impact' and 'weight' having been augmented. They also note that their position within the EU gives them access to policy makers in third countries and to other international institutions that would not otherwise be open to them.

Secondly, policy makers in Copenhagen and Dublin note the impact that collectively shared information has upon internal foreign policy discussions. The sheer scope and wealth of information has meant that the 'cognitive reach' of Danish and Irish foreign policy is greater than before. This informational base is also seen to be central to the delineation of at least some national foreign policy positions. One Danish political advisor made this point with respect to Latin America that was '. . . in the second or third line . . .' of foreign policy concerns. Policy makers in Copenhagen thus constructed their national position on issues in Latin America largely from analyses provided by their EU partners. Irish officials speak in similar terms with one mid-ranking official noting that this information provides much '. . . ready made briefing material . . .' while a more senior figure noted that it provided '. . . the kind of information [that] as a country entirely on our own we would never get . . .' and which was fed directly into the Department's analyses.

This raises questions such as where information is coming from, whose concerns it might reflect and to what extent officials are capable of analysing it. As one senior Danish foreign office official notes, '. . . we certainly do not have the resources to *analyse* all [COREU telex] information but I would say that to *process* the information we do pretty well' (author's emphasis). A similarly placed Irish official concurred, noting that the priority was to process and distribute incoming information to the appropriate officials and adding that these flows of information made it easier '. . . to be a real player' in terms of Irish foreign policy.

Thirdly, the structures of collective European policy making have made themselves felt. For at least one Danish foreign ministry official his work 'is geared by standard operating procedures to feed into these [CFSP] structures'. A senior Irish official noted that participation in the structures of the collective policy making machinery 'meant interacting with part-ners whose diplomatic organisation had a certain kind of structure [that] meant that you had to adapt to some extent to that'. Thus, a common 'work set' might serve to contribute to a common 'mind set'.

Fourthly, policy makers in both countries insist that this process of collective policy making has gone a long way towards establishing the substantive parameters of their foreign policy. Thus, according to an Irish official '[w]ith that [information] goes a structuring of the agenda'. This is most often presented as a 'broadening' or a deepening of the Member State's foreign policy interest. In other words, foreign policy makers contribute to the formulation of policies in which they would not other-wise engage. More broadly another Irish official insists that '. . . yes, to a very great extent the agenda that you get involved in is to a degree set by our involvement [in CFSP]'. This highlights the way in which both sets of foreign policy makers see themselves as developing national positions through a European context – as opposed to bargaining pre-established national interests at an intergovernmental negotiating table.

Fifthly, and crucially, a degree of collective identification among foreign policy makers in Denmark and Ireland does appear to exist. One Irish diplomat noted that 'there is a lot of soul searching all the time about our profile, that is [the Union's] profile, at the UN'. This is not deemed to be a dramatic shift but an evolutionary process that occurs at least in part as a result of constitutive rule-making. Thus, another Irish diplomat notes that the Maastricht Treaty was designed to 'create habits of thinking' within the CFSP. For a Danish colleague this leads CFSP participants to 'try and rally round the common view'. For another Danish diplomat this also entails the fact that '. . . more and more [we] take into consideration the views of our partners' in formulating policy. This, the official went on to say, has been a sensitive shift as 'there has certainly, gradually, over the years been a move which has been recognised and accepted by most polit-ical parties . . . towards giving more weight to [EU foreign policy coordination].'

What conclusions might one draw from the analysis above? First, that institutional coordination – common work practices and structures, a shared information base and the establishment of a common substantive agenda – set up a truly collective context through which a large proportion of 'national' foreign policy is being formulated and pursued. That does not eliminate the role of unique national perspectives, concerns and even of declared 'interests'. It does, however, underline the degree to which a substantial portion of these two states' national foreign policies are being translated and formulated through a European context before it hits the intergovernmental negotiating table. Moreover, there is also evidence for the construction of some collective identification – whether it is the ambition to put forward a united front at the UN, efforts made to internalise the aims of collective foreign policy making or even the simple urge to 'rally round' a united European position. What is also crucial here is to note that its participants do not see this process as a zero-sum game: setting the pursuit of 'national interests' against a defined EU interest. It is a means by which the two are defined together.

Foreign policy process – domestic and bureaucratic

Domestic factors in the policy process

In looking at domestic factors that impinge upon the foreign policy process, the first point of departure is a consideration of the constitutional framework. At the heart of the Danish constitution is the fact that the government acts in all external matters, but is simultaneously constrained by specific provisions relating to the Folketing's (parliament's) ratification of international treaties, the delegation of sovereignty to international organisations and sending Danish troops overseas. The Irish constitution similarly vests ultimate control over foreign policy in the executive branch but gives the Oireachtas (parliament) the right to declare war, states of emergency in time of war, and to ratify international treaties.

Both the Folketing and the Oireachtas have traditional constitutional and political powers over foreign policy to be found in most Western democracies.[11] The Folketing, however, has been rather more advanced in the matter of parliamentary scrutiny. As early as 1923, the Folketing had established a permanent consultative Foreign Affairs Committee, the provision for which was strengthened in the 1953 Danish constitution.[12] This has had the effect of bringing a number of parliamentarians into the heart of the policy process – but has also provoked the criticism that it established a 'golden mousetrap' for the few rather than open access for the many.[13]

On European issues, however, the Folketing has been firmly in the driving seat. The Committee on Europe plays a significant role in the formulation of Danish EU policy. The politicisation of Danish EC membership coupled with a culture of coalition (and often minority) government gives that committee a high profile and an unparalleled role.[14] Indeed, it is not exceptional for this committee to issue instructions to ministers related to their European portfolio and to demand detailed explanations from those ministers on their success or failure in fulfilling such mandates.[15]

In Ireland, by contrast, a select joint committee on foreign policy was only established in 1993 and a new joint committee on European affairs in 1995. Today these two committees listen to expert witnesses, quiz civil servants, hold open meetings and scrutinise proposed legislation. They do not, however, systematically publish their deliberations or regularly draw up detailed reports. Press reports of their activity are also sporadic. They can be said, at best, only to have a very modest policy influence.[16]

At the executive level in both states, neither foreign minister operates in isolation. Foreign policy is established at the cabinet table with input from a wide variety of ministers. Overseeing all government policy, of course, is the Danish Prime Minister and the Irish Taoiseach. While 'first among equals' in a constitutional sense, both now usually operate within the exigencies of a coalition government. The high profile of foreign affairs often means that the leader of a coalition partner holds the office of Foreign Minister. This may lead to political tensions that may or may not relate to policy issues. Exacerbating this is the fact that, partly as a function of their EU roles, prime ministers in both states have increasingly taken on foreign policy functions – either through the European Council or in leading national policies towards the Union itself.

In sum, the impact of constitutional frameworks in Denmark and Ireland are quite different. In the case of Denmark, parliamentary scrutiny is close and sustained and, in matters related to European issues, may be determining. Moreover, the nature of coalition and minority government in Denmark serves to augment the role of the Folketing *vis-à-vis* the government. In the case of Ireland, by contrast, the executive retains considerable latitude in the formulation of foreign policy. Serious parliamentary scrutiny is both a recent and comparatively weak innovation.

In assessing domestic factors it is also useful to consider the way in which policy makers play their domestic and international responsibilities off against one another. The first point of departure is to consider how policy makers employ their domestic bases. For Danish policy makers it is clear that close parliamentary supervision tightly circumscribes their freedom of manoeuvre. These limitations are especially crucial in EU affairs. Here, Denmark's partners are usually aware of the terms of any parliamentary mandate and they know that Danish negotiators must seek agreement within those parameters. For some policy makers this has the advantage of making Danish 'bottom lines' more explicit than those of their partners. At the same time, it reduces their capacity to agree the trade-offs, side payments and package deals that are all core features of EU negotiations.

Irish policy makers are under far less constraint. Parliamentary supervision of EU policy is almost always a *post hoc* affair in which ministers and/or the Taoiseach report to the Dáil (lower house of parliament) only after major decisions have been taken. At the same time, there is much more capacity for Irish policy makers to trade off various domestic interests in package deals and side payments which are then deemed to have been in the 'national interest'. Since the government is not obliged to declare such interests (or have them defined by the Oireachtas) in advance, there are no measurable criteria of 'success'. The scope for *ex post facto* rationalisation of the 'national interest' is more than significant.

Beyond the EU, significant freedom is accorded both Danish and Irish foreign policy makers. Since the EU is the context through which many international welfare issues are decided, national foreign and security policies rest comparatively more often upon principle than material interest. Here, both states face a quandary. As minor states they have fewer direct 'interests' than those of their larger partners. This is clearly seen as a weakness in the coordination of foreign policy at EU level where the discourse of 'national interests' has significant power. One Irish diplomat, for example, noted ruefully that in EU foreign policy discussions 'you are very vulnerable where you are seen to be speaking on principle. Other people are very quick to say, 'Where are your interests here?'"

Both Danish and Irish policy makers thus speak of the importance of public opinion as a means of strengthening their hand. A well-organised and mobilised domestic constituency can have a significant impact. Public demonstrations, boycotts, parliamentary debates and even letter writing campaigns can all be used as evidence by Danish and Irish foreign policy makers to underline the extent of a national 'interest'. Irish policy makers, for example, took an interest in Cambodia in the early 1990s. They could 'say truthfully that the [foreign] minister had received ... thousands of letters on Cambodia. So [they] could say that this was a matter of great concern to public opinion'. Similarly, Danish policy makers pointed to public concern with the plight of the Baltic states as justification for the Danish government's taking the lead (following Iceland) in the recognition of Baltic independence.

However, just as governments need to rely upon their domestic base to underpin the strength of their international position, so too may they rely upon their international responsibilities to shield them from domestic political pressures. Both states have frequently invoked the need for 'consultation' and a coordinated European position as a means of fending off pressure for foreign policy action or to justify (or to shield) a shift in a long-held foreign policy orientation. In Ireland during the late 1970s and 1980s, for example, consecutive Irish governments had fended off demands for unilateral Irish sanctions against apartheid South Africa. They insisted that such action would undermine collective EU measures and strengthen the hand of those opposed to sanctions in principle. Only a major industrial dispute in Ireland's largest supermarket chain – over a trade union directive not to handle South African produce – led the Government to invoke an International Labour Organisation (ILO) regulation and thus institute a unilateral ban on the importation of South African fruit and vegetables.

Similarly, within a collective European policy position, Danish policy makers pursued a significant shift in Danish policy towards the Middle East. One senior political figure noted that 'Traditional Danish policy was absolutely and unilaterally pro-Israeli … this has been gradually corrected after our having joined the EC'. Meanwhile a senior Danish diplomat is even more explicit noting that 'it is often helpful to have the group [of EU foreign ministers] because then you can justify your stand by saying we have consulted our partners and that is the result so we use this to justify our position'.

Foreign policy actors in both Denmark and Ireland clearly employ their participation in this two-level game to maximise their own field of political and diplomatic manoeuvre. Crucially, however, a threshold at which national concerns and/or 'interests' may predominate over the previously mentioned 'Europeanisation' of national foreign policy does exist. Interesting questions are then raised: to what extent (if at all) has that threshold risen over time? What are the conditions which must exist if either government is to break an established policy position or pre-empt efforts at forging the same?

It is evident that a European shield is used to deflect domestic political pressure on foreign policy issues. While parliament offers some kind of vehicle for political parties, non-state actors such as non-governmental organisations (NGOs) and other sectoral interests must pursue other channels.

In Denmark, there is significant activism on the issue of EU membership itself. The June Movement and the People's Movement Against the EU see foreign policy cooperation as eliminating a truly Danish foreign policy. As one senior campaigner noted 'The voice of 350 millions is no longer our voice – it is the voice of others'. More broadly, foreign policy interest groups are said to be 'not really important' to Danish foreign policy, according to at least one former senior minister. This contrasts with the period of the early 1980s when the same minister noted that anti-nuclear and peace movements could mobilise tens of thousands and could tie the hands of Danish governments within NATO. Both the Danish Labour Federation and the Federation of Danish Industries have campaigned on EU membership and have taken part in foreign policy debates on issues such as apartheid. The Danish government also supports a significant network of foreign policy research centres.

In Ireland several organisations have grown up to oppose Irish EU membership. A major focus of these groups (such as the Peace and

Neutrality Alliance (PANA)) has been the perceived threat to Irish neutrality posed by EU membership. This is perhaps the single foreign policy issue that raises any sustained level of public debate. Foreign policy interest groups tend to be small, poorly funded voluntary organisations that campaign on a single issue. Only rarely do such groups succeed in winning for themselves a central place in policy debates. Larger organisations such as Amnesty International and some development NGOs have established regular, two-way communication with government. By further contrast with Denmark, there is no significant foreign policy research community in Ireland. One senior Irish policy maker describes the state of national debate on foreign policy as simply 'sad'.

It may thus be argued that the role of non-state actors in both Denmark and Ireland is limited. While active debates surrounding EU membership exist – and NGOs critical of membership make some (or, in the case of Ireland, considerable) use of foreign policy arguments to sustain their case – a broader and deeper foreign policy community is missing. In neither country do foreign policy interest groups succeed in mobilising public opinion on any sustained basis. However, where and when they do tap into significant public concern they have the capacity to contribute significantly to the outline of national foreign policy priorities.

Bureaucratic factors in the policy process

Bureaucratic politics plays an interesting role in both the Danish and Irish foreign policy processes. Structural adaptation of the foreign ministries to the exigencies of EU membership has been significant. For Denmark this has perhaps been most graphically illustrated by the 1991 restructuring of the economic and political departments into geographic units.[17] This was in explicit response to post-Maastricht developments in the EU that saw the bureaucratic fusion of the CFSP and EU 'External Relations'. In the case of Ireland, adaptation entailed an early substantial increase in budgets and personnel as well as a modest structural re-organisation within the political division towards a geographic 'desk' system.[18]

For both foreign ministries, limited size and resources have had an impact upon the way in which they relate to the rest of the world. Danish diplomats accept that theirs is a limited international profile but insist that 'when we identify an issue that we find of basic interest to us we are certainly not [reactive]'. Moreover, once effective foreign policy priorities are established, limited resources are then dedicated to core interests/ concerns. This has the unfortunate effect of leaving out 'those things we would like to do [but for which] we do not have resources'. For Ireland, with a diplomatic corps and overseas representation that is about half the size of their Danish counterparts, this problem is even more acute. Irish policy makers see themselves as occupying a 'modestly significant – or even just modest' position in world affairs. Moreover, between the pursuit of peace in Northern Ireland and Irish interests in the EU there is 'less energy for striding up and down the world stage'.

As regards bureaucratic tensions, there appears to be only limited evidence. The one area of tension is that between the offices of Prime Minister and Minister for Foreign Affairs. For a former advisor to the Danish Prime Minister, European Council meetings 'give the Prime Minister an excellent chance at least twice a year to get very close to [foreign] affairs'. This is valued at least in part for the often positive and extensive media coverage such a role endows so that 'Prime Ministers as a general rule want to become more generally involved in foreign policy and European co-operation offers them that opportunity'. On the other side of this fence, a senior foreign ministry official noted that 'the difficulty in the Danish case is that the Prime Minister's office is not [properly] equipped' to take on such a role and that there is therefore 'a certain balance to be struck' between these offices of state. The centre of gravity in that balance, however, is clearly moving. In 1993, the incoming Prime Minister appointed several top-ranking foreign ministry officials to his department to offer an in-house advisory and policy-making capacity.[19]

In Ireland, the scope for even this kind of turf battle is limited. The small size of the Irish civil service and the reliance upon *ad hoc* policy-making structures means that foreign policy making tends to be less structured. According to one mid-level Irish diplomat 'we tend to have very good communications between people working in our service – you tend to know the other person . . . and there is no great suspicion or rivalries of one great office of state dealing with one another'. As regards the role of the Taoiseach's Department, a civil servant there insists that '. . . there is no question of rivalry . . .'. At the Department of Foreign Affairs, however, there is some sensitivity evident when a senior diplomat notes that '. . . we work very hard to ensure that there are no crossed wires and that the Taoiseach's office has all the material that it requires'.

The final issue that should be noted in this context is the extent to which, through their access to EU technical councils, domestic ministries are now conducting their own 'foreign policies'. It has been noted for example, that within Danish ministries teams of civil servants are responsible for handling EU affairs and for factoring the 'European' aspect of policy making into domestic decision making. In this context the Foreign Ministry's role has become that of a 'transverse' policy coordinator.[20] In Ireland too, it is recognised that 'foreign policy' has exceeded the capacity of the Foreign Ministry to govern. While vertical policy responsibility is the province of individual ministries, the Department of Foreign Affairs concentrates on those policy 'packages' where the need for interdepartmental coordination is at a premium or within 'horizontal' policy dossiers.[21]

It would therefore appear that the impact of bureaucratic politics upon respective national foreign policies in Denmark and Ireland is limited. This is largely a function of the fact that the size of their foreign ministries and associated domestic political structures prioritises flexibility and adaptability over structure and hierarchy. Where bureaucratic politics may be seen to be significant is in the fact that organisational change in both foreign ministries has been towards a perceived European 'norm'. Moreover, there is also clear evidence that much of what was thought of as 'foreign policy' has in fact been domesticated to functional ministries, with the augmented role of the Prime Minister's office as the best illustration of the fact that foreign policy is no longer quite so 'foreign'.

Foreign policy actions – with or without the EU?

With the EU: constriction or opportunity?

Among Danish and Irish policy makers there appears to be a clear consensus that participation in EU foreign policy cooperation has broadened the range, deepened the analysis and strengthened the impact of what they see to be their national foreign policies. The constrictions imposed by the CFSP are deemed to be marginal. For one Danish diplomat this is an obvious point since 'we are not giving up any sovereignty because we have very little to start with'. For this official, foreign policy cooperation at the EU level is a win-win scenario and, moreover, 'it is logical [for a small state] to be a member of a stronger co-operation'. For a senior Irish diplomat this logic is also clear since 'if you are a small country you want to see the system work according to rules because that is your best protection'. Better, in other words, the (constrictive) rule of law than the (permissive) law of force. For a mid-level Irish diplomat the costs of such cooperation are perhaps more evident. Rather than argue that there has been no loss, this official insists instead that 'we haven't really had to sacrifice more than some others have had to sacrifice'. and that in any event this amounts only to having to 'trim your sails'. Over time, however, this same diplomat worries that this raises the question as to whether 'your principles might get dulled through too much compromise'. Finally, policy makers in both capitals are quicker to welcome restrictions on the ambitions of larger Member States than they are to bemoan the same limitations being placed on themselves.

As regards foreign economic policy much of the same psychology applies. So long as the rules are applied and so long as largely the same criteria apply to all Member States then, in principle, there is no distinction between the CFSP and 'External Relations'. The key issue here, of course, is that *different rule sets apply*. It is to this one should look to understand why it is that policy coordination within the CFSP is deemed to be more problematic than in the realm of foreign economic policy. The tensions that exist appear to be precisely the same.

Neither Danish nor Irish foreign policy makers distinguish between their commitment to 'national interest' in the CFSP as opposed to External Relations. There is no hint either that EU 'interests' predominate in foreign economic relations or that national interests are in some way easier to reconcile in this field as opposed to the foreign policy realm. What does clearly emerge, however, is that differing decision-making processes lead to differing kinds of policy outputs. Indeed, some policy makers recognise the potential need to move along the road of a unified decision making framework in both realms.

The Danish and Irish governments remain unwilling to apply the standard Community-based decision-making model to the CFSP. In other words, the point at which a CFSP becomes a key national foreign policy interest has not yet been reached. By contrast, this principle was accepted in foreign economic relations some time ago. The value of foreign policy cooperation has been that it improves the effectiveness, range and capabilities of national foreign policy making, while imposing significant, but acceptable, constraints on foreign policy output.

At least one reason for hesitancy on decision making reform is the fear/expectation that any such collective policy process will necessarily be dominated by the larger Member States. Tiers of exclusivity are clearly evident from the perspective of both Member States. While both are happy to exploit the resources and global reach of these larger Member States both oppose a condominium of these interests determining the shape of a collective policy. One might expect, in such circumstances, an effort either to create a counter-coalition or to pursue the development of a truly communautaire foreign policy machinery through the Commission. Neither is advocated nor seen as being realistic.

Instead, policy makers in both states are satisfied with the development of a CFSP that gradually transforms the process of national foreign policy formulation, which slowly constitutes a complex, cooperative system of policy formulation but which, in the final analysis, is subject to national vetoes. This may be seen as partly due to a second 'tier of exclusivity'. In addition to the fact that they are small Member States, both are also marginalised from the substantive heart of the CFSP. Denmark, with its defence opt-outs and Ireland, with its neutrality, lay outside the consensus upon which the CFSP has been founded.

The effect of these two 'tiers of exclusivity' is to make policy makers in both states conservative and cautious towards the development of the CFSP, its decision-making procedures and the development of any significant defence capacity. The foreign policies of both states are thus placed upon the defensive – sometimes demanding exceptions and exclusions.

Without the EU: special relations and interests

The realm of 'special' relationships for Denmark and Ireland is an intriguing one. In the Danish case three such relationships might be identified. Throughout the post-war period – and despite the difficulties occasioned by a strong neutralist/pacifist tradition – the United States has been the key referent of Danish security policy. This has qualified and compromised Danish policy towards a European security and defence identity and has meant that the Atlantic Alliance remains a founding stone of Danish foreign policy.[22]

Similarly, Nordic cooperation has been a key relationship beyond that of the EU. For many years, opponents of EU membership presented Nordic cooperation as a more natural framework for political and economic cooperation. Indeed, the first reflex of Danish policy makers in the post-war era was to seek out some system of Nordic security. The failure of that initiative led to the establishment of the so-called 'Nordic Balance' during the Cold War and the pursuit of a wide-ranging menu of intergovernmental Nordic cooperation. With Finnish and Swedish EU membership the distinction between the two frameworks has lessened, but the development of a Nordic bloc has not materialised.

Finally, it would be true to say that arising out of this Nordic affinity, concern with the Baltic states has become another key special relationship. Danish policy makers have been stalwart advocates of bringing the Baltic states within the complex of European cooperation and integration. They have also embarked upon a series of bilateral and multilateral initiatives to support and sustain the transformation and secure the independence of these states.

In terms of issue areas the most obvious and immediate is, of course, security and defence policy. Danish policy makers maintain the opt-out on defence issues won at the 1992 Edinburgh Summit. A second set of issues which excite particular interest are those of human rights and development cooperation. Danish policy makers do not describe these as *domaines reservees* in the same way as they might security policy. However, they do attach particular importance to these sectors of their foreign policy profile since they generate significant domestic interest.

Neither Nordic cooperation, support for the Baltic states, human rights nor development cooperation are necessarily seen to be adversely compromised by EU membership. Indeed in most respects policy makers present the EU as strengthening their hand in achieving nationally defined goals. Only the security relationship with the United States and thus NATO is set deliberately and forcibly apart from the EU framework.

For Ireland the obvious foreign policy priority that lies both within and beyond the remit of EU membership is the search for peace in Northern Ireland and Ireland's broader relationship with the United Kingdom. Northern Ireland – in different respects – has always been close to the heart of Irish foreign policy concerns. It is not, however, correct to characterise this as having been 'ring-fenced'. Indeed, from the very first membership application, European integration was seen as a means by which divisions on the island of Ireland might be reconciled and Ireland's relationship with its neighbouring island might be balanced more equitably.

Ireland's relationship with the United States might also be placed in a special category. The ethnic and demographic links that draw Ireland and the United States together have also been seen to be a powerful attraction to senior US politicians. For Irish policy makers this is a resource that – while currently employed to assist the resolution of conflict in Northern Ireland – may at soon be a resource in Ireland's relationship with its EU partners.

Security and defence policy is perhaps the key issue area that might be deemed to be 'ring-fenced' within Irish foreign policy. This is certainly an area which Irish policy makers have sought to keep separate from the broader canvass of EU foreign and security cooperation. Irish policy makers have nonetheless pursued the vindication of some of the values that underpin neutrality through the EU. They have, for example, pursued initiatives on arms control and nuclear disarmament through EU channels.

In summary, both Danish and Irish foreign policy treats particular relationships and particular issues as 'special' – as deserving of a priority which goes beyond the normal cut and thrust of foreign policy. That does not necessarily translate into a divorce from the EU policy framework. Indeed, in most circumstances the EU context has at least something to offer in the pursuit of these prioritised relationships or issues. In both states, however, security policy is an exception. For both states any cooperation in this area is seen to be difficult, dangerous, or at least of doubtful utility. Both states therefore continue to hold this area of policy apart from the European context.

Conclusion

From all of the foregoing it is evident that EU membership is part of the external environment which impacts upon Danish and Irish foreign policy but it has also been significant as part of the internal environment from which such policy emerges. Elements of 'Europeanisation' have also been clearly noted which do not call into question the existence of national concerns, priorities and even declared interests but which have transformed the way in which such priorities etc. are constructed, seen and pursued by policy makers. The crucial issue is the extent to which these two national foreign policies have internalised the expectations arising from collective European policy making. The fact that 'European policy' in both Denmark and Ireland appears to have been domesticated within national ministries and the evident tensions between foreign ministers and prime ministers, illustrates the extent to which the boundaries between the 'foreign' and the 'domestic' have also been blurred in these two states.

In no sense, again, should this Europeanisation be seen as a zero-sum game *vis-à-vis* national foreign policy goals. The range of 'special' relationships and issues in Danish and Irish foreign policy is clearly broad. In many ways, these define the thresholds at which the internalised norms and expectations of collective policy making are challenged. The crucial point is not that such thresholds exist (it would be truly remarkable if they did not) but whether or not such thresholds are rising over time. It is clear that for most of these *domaines reservees* collective policy-making is at least seen as potentially advantageous. Only in the framework of security policy do both states clearly draw back and seek to 'ring-fence' their policy from the European framework.

To get an understanding of all of these issues it is indeed necessary to move beyond the rather sterile template of traditional (US-centric) FPA with its state-centric focus upon complex bureaucracies and allegedly rational, utility-maximising actors. Certainly, in the examples of Danish and Irish foreign policy it is evident that a model of FPA needs to be able to account for identity, beliefs, norms and expectations arising from a unique endeavour of political integration. Such a model cannot assume any trajectory or direction in these 'non-rational' variables, but it must – at least – promise to come to terms with them.

Notes

1 H. Branner, 'Danish European policy since 1945' in M. Kelstrup (ed.), *European Integration and Denmark's Participation* (Copenhagen, University of Copenhagen, 1992).

2 M. Hederman O'Brien, *The Road to Europe: Irish Attitudes 1948–1961* (Dublin, IPA, 1978); D. H. Maher, *The Tortuous Path: The Course of Ireland's Entry to the EEC 1948–1973* (Dublin, IPA, 1986).

3 Cited in and translated by H. Larsen, *Domestic Constraints in British and Danish European Policy in the 1990s with Special Reference to the Intergovernmental Conferences* (Denmark, Institut for Statskundskab, 1997), p. 10.

4 P. Keatinge, 'Ireland's foreign relations in 1991', *Irish Studies in International Affairs*, 3:4 (1992), p. 89.

5 Larsen, *Domestic Constraints*, p. 14.

6 C. Archer, mimeo, *Security Options for Denmark*, Institutt for Forvarsstudier, No. 2, 1991.

7 H. H. Holm, 'Denmark's active internationalism: advocating international norms with domestic constraints' in B. Heurlin and H. Mouritzen (eds), *Danish Foreign Policy Yearbook 1997*, (Copenhagen, DUPI, 1997) p. 52.

8   B. Heurlin, 'Denmark: a new activism in foreign and security policy' in C. Hill (ed.), *The Actors in Europe's Foreign Policy* (London, Routledge, 1996) p. 166. For the Danish security policy during the Cold War see C. Holbraad, *Danish Neutrality: A Study in the Foreign Policy of a Small State* (Oxford, Clarendon, 1991).

9   P. Keatinge, *European Security: Ireland's Choices* (Dublin, IEA, 1996).

10 All direct quotations of Danish and Irish policy makers are taken from anonymised transcripts of interviews conducted in 1992, 1993 or 1998.

11 F. Mendel, 'The role of parliament in foreign affairs in Denmark' in A. Cassese (ed.), *Parliamentary Control over Foreign Policy* (Sijtoff and Noordhoff, 1980).

12 P. Svensson, 'Parliament and foreign policy decision making in Denmark', *Irish Studies in International Affairs*, 2:4 (1988), pp. 19–39.

13 I. Faurby, 'Decision structures and domestic sources of Nordic foreign policies' in B. Sundelius (ed.), *Foreign Policies of Northern Europe* (Boulder, Colorado, Westview, 1982), p. 43.

14 J. Fitzmaurice, *Politics in Denmark* (London, Hurst, 1981) p. 138.

15 H. Nehring, 'Parliamentary control of the executive' in L. Lyck (ed.), *Denmark and EC Membership Evaluated* (London, Pinter, 1992).

16 P. Keatinge, 'Annual review', *Irish Studies in International Affairs*, 5 (1994).

17 K. E. Jørgensen, 'Denmark' in Brian Hocking and David Spence (eds), *EU Member State Foreign Ministries: Change and Adaptation* (draft manuscript, DG1A European Commission, 1998).

18 B. Tonra, 'Ireland' in Brian Hocking and David Spence (eds), *EU Member State Foreign Ministries: Change and Adaptation* (draft manuscript, DG1A European Commission, 1998).

19 Jørgensen, *Denmark*.

20 Jørgensen, *Denmark*.

21 Tonra, *Ireland*.

22 Martin Heiser, 'Denmark's quest for security: constraints and opportunities within the alliance' in Gregory Flynn (ed.), *NATO's Northern Allies: the National Security Policies of Belgium, Denmark, The Netherlands and Norway* (Rowman and Allenheld, 1985).

13

Conclusion

Ian Manners and Richard Whitman

This study argues that it is time to adopt a distinctive approach to the foreign policies of European Union (EU) Member States. It now seems more appropriate to suggest that the Member States conduct all but the most limited foreign policies objectives inside an EU context. The study finds that traditional explanations for foreign policy need significant modification in order to more appropriately engage in a Foreign Policy Analysis (FPA) of EU Member States. We now suggest that the foreign policy of the EU does not actually represent the European rescue of traditional foreign policy, given the transformation of these foreign policies by the globalised, post-Cold War, post-EU 'European condition'. We argue that these patterns of change do necessitate a significant reconsideration of FPA and its application to the Member States of the EU, but we also maintain that the many tensions we found present in our analysis render the whole notion of 'foreign policy' somewhat problematic.

In this study we have sought to construct and apply a comparative framework which is appropriate and original for the analysis of the foreign policies of EU Member States. Our framework had to be flexible enough to encompass such European diversity as found between 'nuclear states' such as Britain and France, and (post-)neutral states such as Austria and Sweden. In addition the framework would have to be rigorous enough to facilitate comparative analysis in a meaningful way. The framework we devised was able to account for the broad context in which foreign policies were being made through suggesting two elements of change – macro adaptation and micro socialisation. The framework was also able to account for the dynamics of policy making by looking at two elements of this process – domestic environment and bureaucratic mechanisms. Finally, the framework was able to account for the actions of implementing foreign policy through the consideration of policies realised within or without the EU competencies. Thus the framework proved itself more than adequate, and certainly original, in the way in which it encompassed the sometimes juxtaposed factors in the broad context, dynamic process and implementation phase of Member States' foreign policies. As Tonra suggests in his chapter, capturing the features of a 'complex, collective policy-making system' such as is necessary in this study is no easy task if we are looking for meaningful insights.

The value of the framework and its comparative application is only one part of our argument for a distinctive FPA being suggested here. The other argument being put forward is that the study can be characterised by a number of tensions which are highly contextual to the foreign policies of EU Member States. These tensions could not be conceivably arrived at by applying generalisations, or 'questions that travel', from the study of foreign policies of states outside of Europe. In this respect it is useful to briefly present these tensions and the way in which they can be argued to be conditioning features of a distinctive FPA for EU Member States.

Tensions in the foreign policies of EU member states

The foreign policy analysis of EU Member States is subject to a number of tensions. First, there is tension between the need to adapt to the changes brought by EU membership and the post-Cold War environment. The tension here is between the benefits which adaptation may provide for an EU Member State and the desire to maintain the status quo of Cold War international relations that tends to be found amongst those states who believe this would negatively impact on their status as international 'powers'. This tension increases with interaction between Member States and the world outside Europe's door. Secondly, there are tensions between the constitutional/bureaucratic arrangements of foreign policy making within a Member State, public opinion of the citizens of that state, and the activities of socialised civil servants/political elite. These tensions tend to surface more when there is a period of rapid foreign policy change, when legislative approval is sought, or when public awareness is heightened. This tension will continue to increase as European solutions become more common.

Thirdly there is a tension between what may be considered 'foreign policy' and what may be considered 'external policy'. This tension focuses on the political diplomatic functions of a Member State government and its political economy functions. This will grow as the former continues to be retained as a symbol of statehood, whilst the increasingly important substance of the latter is Europeanised at an EU level. Fourthly, the tensions between competing centres of influence continue to seek to render notions of traditional foreign policy somewhat problematic. The abilities of non-state actors, sub-national actors and supranational actors to claim (or reclaim) the landscape of relations between peoples continues to increase through the processes of globalisation/localisation.

Finally there is a tension between foreign policy actions within or without the EU. Increasingly this is a false dichotomy as the realities of attempting to hold separate issues of a political-diplomatic nature from those of a political-economic nature, as well as trying to maintain a clear separation between issues of foreign policy 'special interest' from those of domestic policy 'general interest', tend to illustrate. As is often the case, an attempt to maintain a *domain privé* can be expensive in terms of political capital – as the case studies have illustrated, the costs of special relationships are often to be found hidden in the antagonisms which these can bring to the rest of the EU relationship.

Adaptation through membership

The study sought to consider the degree to which it was possible to recognise the adaptation through membership of the Member States' foreign policies. Following Kenneth Hanf and Ben Soetendorp, the study used as its starting point the definition of adaptation taken from Ernst Haas as 'the ability of a political actor to change its behaviour so as to meet challenges in the form of new demands by altering the means of action'.[1] The study took care to differ from this implied focus in the us~ of the term 'political actor' and the potentially loaded response if this actor is assumed to be 'the state'. The authors were all asked to consider the impact of 'the changing external environment' including membership, treaty changes and the end of the Cold War. However, although the focus was clearly on the adaptation of foreign policy, the interpretation of the actor involved was left open. As the chapters demonstrate, this open interpretation still, inevitably, leads to a primary focus on the Member State as the political actor, but it is interesting to note that all the chapters avoided the pitfalls of attributing anything like a unitary-state rationality to the adaptation processes.

It is valuable to note the way in which many of the authors equated adaptation as meaning 'Europeanisation', despite the fact that the term was not used in this specific context by the editors. Drawing on Robert Ladrech, Sonia Mazey and Jeremy Richardson, Kenneth Hanf and Ben Soetendorp, this study characterises Europeanisation as an incremental process reorienting Member States' politics and policies towards the EU.[2] In his contribution to this study Ben Tonra in Chapter 12 went even further and defined Europeanisation of foreign policy as:

'a transformation in the way in which national foreign policies are constructed, in the ways in which professional roles are defined and pursued and in the consequent internalisation of norms and expectations arising from a complex system of collective European policy making'.

Although not explicitly presented to all the authors in this formulation,

Tonra's definition does provide a valuable contribution to the argument put forward here that the 'complex system of collective European policy making' necessitates a distinctive analytical approach encompassing the transformational context, process and actions of the national foreign policies of EU Member States.

EU adaptation appears to play an important role in the 'modernisation' of Member States' foreign policies as they attempt to come to terms with the challenges of the 21st century. It provides the framework and the opportunity for Member States to adapt to the realities of post-Cold War global foreign policies. Those states that resist adaptation and the processes of Europeanisation are invariably doing so because they are also trying to resist the wider forces at work – to maintain notions of 'national' and symbols of their past. Indications of this were found in particular in the French and British cases, although it might be argued that this was also to be found in the Greek and Danish cases. In the French case, Europe provides the 'optimum multiplier of national power', but 'France must never surrender its independent role, and the status as one of the great historic powers and permanent member of the Security Council'. In the British case, on a 'core sovereignty issue [such] as foreign policy' successive governments have 'tried to use European level policy coordination as a means to strengthen national policy'. In the Greek case there is also evidence of the desire to maintain a veto over its 'national policies', although this is somewhat contradicted by its keenness for more EU foreign policy action (especially in the defence sector). The Danish position during the early 1990s had also been resistant to adaptation in the foreign policy sphere, largely because of its 'traditional ambivalence towards a Euro-centric model'. However, it now appears that since 1998 'Danish foreign policy has been liberated from its worst fear' by the patterns of evolution of the EU and North Atlantic Treaty Organisation (NATO).

In contrast to these questions of resistance to adaptation, those states that embrace adaptation and the processes of Europeanisation appear to be doing so because they are using the EU as a means of overcoming their past – be it a fascist or authoritarian past, be it a colonial past, or be it a past marked by problems of economic development or of achieving economic growth, be it a neutral or non-aligned past. The chapters presented here illustrate the degree to which all four of these pasts can be addressed (or forgotten) through EU membership.

Historical experiences

Historical experiences of fascism or communism are surmounted, as in the cases of Germany, Spain, and Italy, through EU membership. As the German case illustrated, the move to a Berliner Republik suggests that the 'historical other' in this case may be fading out of memory. Although a 'sense of guilt and shame about its Nazi past' and 'historical fears of German hegemony' may still be present, the current debate on normalisation indicates that EU membership provides an opportunity for Germany to become a 'normal civilian power'. Similarly, membership has provided a means for Spain to recover an international confidence in the post-Franco era. As was noted in the chapter, 'a quarter of a century after the death of General Franco, Spain can consider itself as an established middle-ranking power which enjoys considerable international prestige'. In the case of Italy, it seems to 'need' the EU more than most as a means of providing a 'barrier' between itself and its previous or other self. In this case adaptation to membership has provided 'a set of behavioural rules' which are part of 'Italy's path towards ... modernisation'. This is particularly interesting in the military sector where the 'legacy of fascism' has led to low 'prestige of the military'.

Colonial experiences

EU membership can help colonial experiences to be overcome, as in the cases of France, Britain, Portugal, and Belgium, although for larger Member States this is more problematic. For France the EU 'with its pacific reputation and freedom from the taint of imperialism, is a particularly useful vehicle'. For Britain, its Commonwealth relations are 'becoming increasingly less important as an arena' in favour of EU, or bilateral Franco-British, policy in areas such as the Lomé Convention and Africa, although the status of Gibraltar remains problematic. The EU has provided a crucial mechanism for Portugal to help overcome the tragic legacy of its colonial empire. As has been previously stated, it may be possible to argue that Portuguese foreign policy has been shaped by 'the lessons learned ... in solving the colonial problem'. In the case of Belgium the EU provides a means of increasing 'the effectiveness of its own foreign policy' or 'the possibility of "dumping" the intricate and intractable situation in Central Africa'.

Interestingly EU membership has also helped Ireland in its post-colonial rehabilitation to the degree that it has now achieved 'Celtic tiger status'. For Ireland EU membership has provided an opportunity to change an 'overwhelming bilateral relationship' with Britain to one 'balanced more equitably'.

Economic development

The problems of economic development are addressed by EU membership, as in the cases of Italy, Ireland, Greece, Spain and Portugal. As the most economically-backward founding member, Italy has been able to enjoy the 'benefits of membership – markets, modernisation, status' while improving 'the country's overall economic and trade performance'. For Ireland membership of the EU has provided 'significant material benefits' in the form of 'financial transfers from the Community budget' and reduced its 'asymmetrical economic dependence' on Britain. In Greece the questions of economic development are still being addressed, but in terms of avoiding the 'economic suicide' of other Balkan states, EU membership has provided it with 'a European orientation' which is now leading to prosperity. In the cases of Spain and Portugal membership proved itself to be a moderating influence on foreign policy, allowing tough changes to be made, and domestic opposition to be overcome. It also appears to have led to a degree of cross-party consensus over most major areas of foreign policy. In Spain this was most noticeable in the position of the Socialist Party's equation of the two terms Europeanisation and modernisation, as 'the utilisation of European integration as the key element in the all-embracing policy/*leimotif* of modernisation'. In Portugal this was seen in the collapse of the backward-looking authoritarian regime and reorientation towards a 'liberal west European' democratic future within the EC.

Post-neutrality

Finally, neutral or non-aligned positions are adjusted, as in the cases of Ireland, Austria, Finland and Sweden. Although all four seek to retain their international positions on the question of neutrality, it does appear as if membership of the EU has provided a means of redefining the exact nature of these positions in a post-Cold War world. In all four countries, their participation in a post-Cold War EU with a common foreign and security policy raises the question of whether they should now be realistically considered post-neutrals. For Ireland, the last twenty-eight years of membership have not raised any serious questions about its non-participation in European defence arrangements. However, it is now an open question of whether its 'initiatives on arms control and nuclear disarmament' are the only security issues in which Ireland is an active participant in the early 2000s. In this latter period the changed security premise in Europe has led Austria, Finland and Sweden to question their own 'neutral' status. In these three countries it now seems more appropriate to adopt the term 'non-aligned' to describe the way in which their foreign policies have adapted to membership. In Finland and Sweden this adaptation has gone as far as using the term 'non-participation in military alliances'. The Austrians appear to have gone further towards 'reconsidering the value of neutrality', although in all three cases this is done with great caution and with regard to public sentiment.

What is interesting is the degree to which the adaptation to EU membership changes foreign policy orientations and mechanisms. But it is also worth noting that adaptation is more a function of attitude than time, as the contrasts between the changes in the EU's youngest members over the past five years and the oldest members over the past forty years help illustrate. In the cases of all but two Member States adaptation has proved a means of achieving innovation within domestic politics and external orientation. As has been discussed above, this adaptation may be a means of dealing with four types of issues described as 'historical experiences', 'colonial experiences', 'economic development', and 'post-neutrality'. Only in the cases of France and Britain has adaptation been seen as a mixed blessing in foreign policy terms. In both France and Britain the tensions between 'trying to use EU membership to manage and adapt to changes in the international system' whilst trying to 'fight to retain national freedom of action and historic political assets at all costs' ultimately means that adaptation through membership has proved elusive in these two cases.

Socialisation of foreign policy makers

The question of the socialisation of foreign policy makers was considered in this study as a means of understanding the way in which membership can shape ways of thinking amongst policy making elites. However, analysing the socialisation of political actors can be notoriously difficult to do, particularly when using traditional (or 'rational-actor') methodologies. Fortunately, the authors involved in this study were able to blend traditional with more critical methodologies (based on interview and discourse approaches) in order to gain greater insight within their analyses. It is valuable to consider the discourses used within the chapters to refer to processes of socialisation as a form of analysis. While some talked of consultation 'reflexes' or 'habits' in policy making (see, for example, Chapters 2 and 3 on Britain and France), others interrogated notions of 'collective identification' and the 'identity' of policy makers (see, for example, Chapters 4 and 12 on Denmark, Ireland and Germany). The challenge here is to contrast the differing ways of talking about the policy-making processes in order to gauge the extent to which varying degrees of socialisation have, and are, impacting on foreign policy.

Reflexes

In three cases the language of 'reflex' was used to describe the socialisation of foreign policy makers into differing patterns of thinking and behaviour. In Germany its 'reflexive' tradition in foreign policy making has been important in 'enmeshing' it in European norms and common policies. In both the British and Danish cases attention was drawn to a 'first reflex' which had historically involved the non-EU partners of Nordic countries (in the Danish case), and the United States (in the British case). However, in both cases attention is drawn to the gradual break-down of these reflexes as Anglo-American coordination in economic and foreign policy weakens, and the Nordic cooperation changes with the admission of Sweden and Finland to the EU.

Habits

It is worth noting that in six of the states 'habit' forming practices were identified by the authors as being important. In France these habits of working together were seen as being crucial in maintaining the Franco-German relationship by 'fostering mutual respect and a shared understanding' which 'retained some continuity across administrations and presidencies'. In the Netherlands and Belgium the long timescale (over the past thirty years) involved in cooperating within the EU foreign policy processes ensured that the 'fully internalised habits of working together' led to the definition of policy positions for these two states. The role of the EU's foreign policy-making mechanism was also identified as being important in 'creating habits of thinking' in the case of Irish and Danish diplomats. Even for later joining states, 'the habits of working together have gradually altered' behaviour and interests for Greek foreign policy makers.

Norms

A more difficult issue concerns the degree to which foreign policy makers are socialised into 'norms' of behaviour and thinking. In six of the states the authors commented on the way in which European and international norms were becoming integral to the foreign policy-making procedures under examination. In the cases of Britain, Denmark and the Netherlands, explicit reference to the importance of international norms in shaping foreign policy was made. In Britain the 'growing importance of international rules, norms and procedures' is seen as being a significant factor in this respect. Similarly, in Denmark the principal foreign policy norms are those of 'collective security, the rule of law and self-determination'. In the Netherlands the element of foreign policy given highest priority is 'the implementation of human rights norms' which, it is observed, often brings it into conflict rather than harmony with its European partners. In addition to these international norms, in the cases of Germany, Spain, Denmark and Ireland there were references to European norms. The distinctive nature of these norms was spelt out most explicitly in the German case as being 'transparency, consultation and compromise' which maintain 'stability and predictable relations in foreign policy'. In Spain the achievement of 'European norms' was seen to be a means of returning to European and international normality and responsibility in the post-Franco period. For Danish and Irish foreign policy makers participation in the EU system involved 'a consequent internalisation of norms' which are implicitly European in their conception.

Identities

Finally, the language of identity construction was used in the analysis of seven Member States, signifying the role of self-definition (and redefinition) in the socialisation of foreign policy makers. In the cases of Denmark and Ireland is was noted that 'a degree of collective identification' appears to exist which 'internalise[s] the aims of collective foreign policy making'. For German, Swedish and Finnish foreign policy makers 'a European identity ... is formulated in a language characterised by ... notions of a shared European destiny' and the incorporation of this 'European identity and priorities' into the discourses of the governing elite is an indication of shared practices being incorporated into shared identities. There is also evidence of the European orientation and practices in Greek foreign policy making transforming the 'traditional identity' of policy makers through altering the attitudes, self images and interests of those involved. However, in the British case the long timescale of often intense interaction and collaboration 'does not appear to have led to a new and wholly differ-ent European identity' for its policy makers.

In the cases of four of the Member States the question of perception of EU membership was raised by the authors. It was argued in each case that the EU acted as an opportunity or multiplier of foreign policy activ-ity. For France 'Europe is about adding, not subtracting', whilst for Britain membership 'is not a zero-sum game' but offers 'a multiplier effect' in the foreign policy sphere. However, in the Danish and Irish case it is noted that the 'participants do not see this process as a zero-sum game', but as a means by which national and EU interests 'are defined together'.

The EU membership does not simply involve legal and political commit-ments to a union, it provides a community, a textured environment, a part in a process, a social sphere for continued and intensifying interaction. But this socialisation is also part of a broader process of globalisation where links with others, often outside of a geographical context, are intensified. Notions of who is 'local' (in terms of close contacts) and whom one identifies with (in terms of social meaning) are increasingly shaped by the European nature of those involved in the integration process. But we should not be surprised if the opposite is also true – those not directly involved in this process feel disaffection as they seek meaning and community outside of this European context and inside a 'traditional' context of a 'nation-state'. As has been demonstrated in the chapters on the larger Member States, the socialisation processes are less pronounced in the foreign policy processes of France, Britain and Germany. In contrast the chapters on most smaller Member States all draw attention to the importance of socialisation in foreign policy making in Portugal, the Netherlands, Belgium, Finland, Sweden, Denmark and Ireland. It would therefore appear that the impact of socialisation is more noticeable in smaller, rather than larger Member States, although this is by no means the only determining factor. In contrast, this also appears to indicate that length of membership is not as an important factor in socialisation as one might think, with French and German membership being ten times longer than that of Finland and Sweden.

Like adaptation, socialisation forms part of a broader pattern that is shaping both foreign policy and the relationship between Member States and the rest of the world. Those engaged in foreign policy activities have their understanding shaped by the social interaction in which they engage. This in turn shapes the way in which they think about foreign policy and notions of what actually constitutes the 'foreign'. But this process is part of the larger processes of interdependence, shaped by the (freer) movement of people, their experiences and the way in which they interact through travel, personal contact, communication, and shared cultural meanings.

Domestic factors in the policy process

The role of domestic factors can be examined by considering the five elements considered most important by the authors in shaping the foreign policy process – the constitutional design, the role of sub-national governments, the relationships between governments and parties, the role of special interest groups, and the breakdown of the domestic–foreign distinction. Although each of these factors is considered separately here, it is worth remembering that the interplay between them is significant in each national context, particularly if there are active cross-cutting coalitions of interest at work.

Constitutional designs

The first element determining the influence of domestic factors on the foreign policy process identified in this study is the constitutional design of the Member State under consideration. The constitutional design plays a significant role in determining the nature of government, who the lead actor in foreign policy is, what role the political parties play, and the role of parliamentary oversight. All but one of the EU's Member States have governmental systems based on a combination of proportional representation electoral systems and coalition governments which tends to lead to these systems being termed 'consensual' in nature. In Germany, France, Italy, the Netherlands, Belgium, Austria, Denmark and Finland the governments consist of coalitions of between two and five parties in power sharing arrangements. However, it should be noted that France has a two-round majority voting system, while Germany and Italy have mixed voting systems. Elsewhere EU governments are in power with slender majorities or are in power with a minority government which relies on the help of other parties. With one or two exceptions the constitutional design of EU Member States tends to produce patterns of consensual democracy, which relies on consultation and bargaining amongst political groups to achieve policy. The main exception to this pattern is Britain with its 'first past the post' electoral and governmental systems which is not based on consensus politics, although Greece also has a tradition of single-party majority government.

Constitutional designs are also responsible for defining who the lead actor in foreign policy is, and in particular the differences between parliamentary systems and presidential systems. In the European context there is a distinction to be made here between the semi-presidential systems of France and Finland, and the parliamentary systems of the rest of the EU. In the French case, the role of the President is crucial in shaping foreign policy, even when there is a cohabitation of Socialist Prime Minister and Gaullist President, as is the situation from 1997 to 2002. In Finland joining the EU led to an interesting debate where the role of the President in foreign policy was reduced in the area of EU relations in order to adapt to membership (made easier because both were from the Social Democratic Party). In March 2000 the consolidation of the Finnish Constitution ensured that its foreign policy is headed by the President in conjunction with the Council of Ministers, in effect leading to a more parliamentary system involving the President, the Prime Minister and the Foreign Minister in frequent consultations. Although not strictly a semi-presidential system, the Portuguese case showed that the turbulent relationship from 1986 to 1995 between the Prime Minister and the President did not significantly impact on foreign policy making because of the 'consensualism and continuity at the elite level' and the fact that both the Socialists and Social Democrats provided 'consensual political support for foreign policy within European integration parameters'. Since Jorge Sampaio's election in 1996 the Portuguese President has played a less pro-active role (as the President's constitutionally-defined role might suggest).

In contrast, the parliamentary systems have a clearer line of decision making between the Prime Minister and Foreign Minister, although in the case of six of these states the posts of Prime Minister and Foreign Minister are held by people from different parties. This coalition relationship is most obvious in the case of the German Chancellor Gerhard Schröder (Social Democratic Party) and the German Foreign Minister Joschka Fischer (Green Party), although Austria, Belgium, Denmark, Italy and the Netherlands also have power-sharing relations. Only the states of Britain, Greece, Ireland, Spain, and Sweden are currently parliamentary systems with prime ministers and foreign ministers of the same party, although this also happens to be currently true in France and Portugal. In terms of actual foreign policy making these relationships are not as conflictual as might be supposed, as the mostly consensual nature of European politics, combined with years of coalition experience, helps provide for smooth governmental relations. However, it is worth bearing in mind that none of these constitutional arrangements for foreign policy making bears any resemblance to that found in the United States.

The role of parliamentary oversight is also an important factor in shaping foreign policy, particularly in those political systems which cherish open and participatory government. These more open democracies are mostly found within the Nordic tradition of government which in the EU is seen in Sweden, Denmark and Finland. In the Swedish Riksdag, parliamentary oversight is provided by the Advisory Committee on EU Affairs, in the Danish Folketing it is provided by the Foreign Affairs Committee and Committee on Europe, whilst in the Finnish Eduskunta it is provided by the Foreign Affairs Committee. This contrasts strongly with the position in France, Britain and Italy where foreign policy is said to be largely 'unaccountable' (in the French case) with parliamentary scrutiny and oversight considered 'rather ineffective' (in the British case).

Sub-national governments

The second element determining the role of domestic factors is the degree to which Member States may be considered a centralised or decentralised state. Although this is also a function of constitutional design, it is usually shaped by historical factors and questions of diversity within a Member State. Again the EU Member States represent very different positions on a wide spectrum of degrees of centralisation, which is a significant contributing feature of the role of domestic factors in shaping foreign policy. At one end of the centralisation–decentralisation spectrum lies Belgium with its 'federated entities' of regions and communities which are represented within the Union by six different delegations: Federal Government; Flemish Government; Walloon Government; Government of the German-speaking Community; Government of the French-speaking Community; and the Brussels Capital Regional Government. Although the Prime Minister and the Federal Ministry of Foreign Affairs retain competence in foreign policy, given the difficulties in differentiating between domestic policy, European policies and foreign policy encountered in this study, the lack of legal hierarchy leaves 'a rather small foundation for Belgian foreign policy'. Next on this spectrum come the federal states of Austria and Germany with the principles of 'subsidiarity and power-sharing' providing the constitutional means for the provinces and Länder to influence foreign policy. In practice both these states leave the definition of most foreign policy (as distinct from European policy) to the federal government, although it was noted in the German case that the Länder have developed 'extensive competency as sub-national actors in foreign economic policy'. After these federal states we find Spain and Italy next in terms of decentralisation, although the Spanish autonomous communities have far greater influence than the Italian regional administrations. In the Spanish case the external activity of the autonomous communities (in particular Catalonia), and the dependence of the government on the support of the Catalan Nationalist Party since 1993, has enhanced their role in foreign policy making. To a lesser degree a similar pattern developed in Italy during the immediate post-Christian Democratic Party period of 1990–95 with the behaviour of the regional administrations of north-eastern Italy during the collapse of Yugoslavia and the rise of Umberto Bossi's Northern League. Although in contrast this has not led to the same degree of influence over foreign policy as the autonomous communities in the case of Spain.

The only other state worth considering in terms of the impact of decentralisation on foreign policy making is Britain. Since the creation of devolved regional assemblies in Scotland, Wales and Northern Ireland during 1999, the question of the external role of these parliaments and their influence on British foreign policy has been raised (particularly in terms of relations with other EU states).[3] However in Britain, as with the cases of the eight other Member States not mentioned above, the impact of sub-national, regional, or devolved parliaments is currently limited in national foreign policy making. There are several reasons for sub-national governments' external relations or 'paradiplomacy'[4] not having as much of an impact on Member States' foreign policies outside the five cases already discussed, but the absence of significant sub-national identities which have a political or constitutional form remains the main explanation.

Political parties

The third domestic element which has a significant impact on foreign policy making is the role of party politics and their relationship to the government in power. The party political orientation of the government in power in shaping foreign policy appears to be of decreasing relevance in the cases studied here. Most of the cases spoke of party political consensus over the issue of EU membership and foreign policy objectives. What is interesting here is the speed with which, in general, this picture has changed in the last twenty years. There are smaller parties and groups on the far left and far right of most domestic EU political spectra (for example the Communist Party in Portugal and Freedom Party in Austria) which hold more extreme views on foreign policy and EU issues. However, a combination of three factors has led parties across the EU to hold far more similar views on foreign policy issues (despite what they might say in public pronouncements). First, the increasing acceptance of the neo-liberal or free market philosophy in the post-1970s period has tended to minimise the political-philosophical differences between parties. Secondly, the collapse of the Communist bloc and the political alternative it represented has led to a crisis of socialism across Europe. Thirdly, as this study has examined, participation in the EU's dual-decision-making procedures (in the areas of external relations and CFSP) appears to have changed the views and expectations of many of the European political parties on foreign policy issues.

Interest groups

The fourth domestic element is the role of special interest groups in the foreign policy making process. Given the secretive nature of political lobbying and the difficulties of gauging the success of media campaigns, the degree to which these groups are able to influence and shape foreign policy is difficult to judge. However, the role of interest groups was identified across the cases studied here and can be divided into the economic sector and the non-economic sectors, although clearly these are not always so easily delineated. Special interest groups active in the economic sector consist of employers and industrial groups on one hand, and trade unions on the other. Employers groups and federations of industries were seen to be active in Spain, Denmark and Sweden, in addition to the role of the Bank of Italy. The French case gave some interesting insights into commercial interest group lobbying in the arms trade, heavy industrial and high tech industries. In particular, the example of where interest groups are found to be lobbying against one another on the question of French foreign policy towards China, Taiwan and Korea helps illustrate activity which is more commonplace across the EU than was studied here. In contrast, the role of trade unions attempting to shape foreign policy was identified in the Spanish, Danish and Swedish cases, although their influence pervades the policies of left-leaning political parties across Europe.

Special interest groups active in the non-economic sector consist of religious organisations, diaspora groups, global issue groups, and anti-EU groups. The role of religious organisations found in the cases included the powerful influence of the Catholic Church in Italy and the Orthodox Church in Greece. Also found to be influential in the cases were the diaspora groups resident in EU Member States, the two most powerful of which were the Algerians in France and the Cypriots in Greece, although many EU capitals have such groups seeking to shape their hosts' foreign policies (the Kurds for example). Global issue groups included peace and disarmament groups (such as PANA, CND and Saferworld), environmental groups (such as Greenpeace and Friends of the Earth), and human rights groups (such as Amnesty International). The influence which such groups can exert through lobbying and public campaigns was recently demonstrated in the 1995 case of the relations between the former Nigerian government, the Shell Oil company, and the execution of Ken Saro-Wiwa. The final type of interest group in the non-economic sector are those anti-EU groups common in Member States and which seek to reduce participation in EU activities, including foreign policy cooperation. Examples of these types of group were found in Denmark in the form of the June Movement and the People's Movement Against the EU, although there are similar examples to be found in the other Nordic states, in Britain (the UK Independence Party) and in Austria (the Freedom Party).

Domestic–foreign distinction

The final element determining the relationship between domestic politics and foreign policy is the breakdown of the distinction between domestic and foreign issues. The problems which this breakdown presents to the analysis of foreign policy making has recently been identified by authors such as Michael Smith, Roger Tooze and Jens Mortensen who point out that this distinction is fast being eroded because 'trade policy has ... grown into one of the most important foreign policy instruments in the 1990s'.[5] Clearly this change presents significant problems for the study of foreign policy in EU Member States as trade policy is largely a function of external relations, which is regulated by the Commission, rather than the foreign ministries. In the study a number of authors referred explicitly to this breakdown which leads us to 'the overwhelming conclusion that it is no longer possible to make a clear distinction between European foreign and domestic policy', as is the case in Britain.

Thus, for EU Member States the domestic–foreign frontier blurs into obscurity as most areas of economic, and increasingly political, activity are Europeanised. This Europeanisation of domestic issues is not simply about the infraction of the EU into the formerly 'national' sphere. It involves the complicated realities of the management of multifaceted interactions amongst the advanced industrial societies of Europe. In this environment of multi-interaction (economic, political and social), issues that might have formerly been dealt with in the capitals of Europe are increasingly referred to the capital of the EU – Brussels. So the boundary around fifteen domestic spheres is both broadened and permeated by the impact of EU membership. But this raises the 'paradox' of relations between EU states – are they still to be considered 'international' and the activity to be one of 'foreign' policy. Perhaps it is now more appropriate to consider them as 'intranational' and the activity of 'European' policy. In many ways the foreign policies of EU Member States are still coming to terms with this paradox of inclusion–exclusion or self–other.

As with the two previous factors of adaptation and socialisation, the problems associated with the domestic–foreign frontier are not solely a function of EU membership – they are increasingly a reality for all states as the interconnectedness between their societies leads to many questions regarding the policing of the frontier of the state, and the role of foreign policy making in regulating relations between states. In some respects this has led to the observation that foreign policy cooperation/integration within the EU actually presents an opportunity in the face of these challenges to reformulate the domestic–foreign frontier at a European level – and thus might represent the 'rescue' of European foreign policy (see below for a fuller exposition of this rescue).

Bureaucratic politics in the policy process

The question of the role of bureaucratic politics in the policy process is as problematic as that concerning the socialisation processes and takes us into the world of institutional structure and inter-ministry conflict. There are three major issues which need to be addressed here regarding the questions of autonomy and command, the relationship between the foreign ministry and other ministries, and the question of who is responsible for coordinating foreign policy, particularly in a European context.

Autonomy and command

The first issue to be addressed is the question of autonomy and command in the bureaucratic structures under analysis. Implicitly this question is tied up with those issues raised in the previous section concerning the roles of a president, prime minister, coalition partners and parliamentary oversight. However, the determining factors here are broadly about the degree to which any foreign policy making bureaucracy is characterised by centralisation or autonomy in decision making and implementation, as well as how efficiently the lines of command function. To illustrate just how different these factors can be we only have to compare the 'permanent symbiosis between the Élysée and the Quai d'Orsay' in the foreign policy making of the French Fifth Republic with the binding '*einheitliche Stellungnahme*' (a common position agreed by the Austrian provinces) which the federal foreign minister may be trying to use as a basis for foreign policy making.

At the top of this bureaucratic structure lies the presidential and/or ministerial staff and their cabinets which, as discussed previously, can be working in harmony or conflict, depending on constitutional, coalition and domestic pressures. The crucial relationships here are those with the ministries and staff below this top level of decision making. It is helpful to consider three contrasting types of relationship here to illustrate the different ways these lines of command and communication can work. In the French case the President at the Élysée, with diplomatic counsellors, will work closely with the Prime Minister's office, the Foreign Minister and Ministry, as well as other significant ministries as necessary (such as the Defence and Finance Ministries), all in 'uninterrupted contact' and 'informed of the same events'. Compare this dynamic image with that in the German case where the *Bundeskanzler* is responsible for 'the overall coordination and guidelines of . . . foreign policy' which, following extensive consultation and adjustment with the coalition partners and ministries may be implemented by the Foreign Minister. Finally, compare the images of French dynamism and German 'reflexive' consultation, with those of the British 'tightly organised and highly centralised policy making process' but which provides 'little flexibility once a British position is established'. These three examples help to illustrate that the relations between the top decision making level with the ministers and ministries responsible for implementation can be crucial in determining the efficiency and flexibility on foreign policy issues.

Below this level lie the ministries, secretariats, and committees dealing with both foreign policy and European policy. One of the crucial elements raised in the case studies is the quality of the staff in both administrative and diplomatic posts. Another comparison that is useful here is that between the Greek and British case, although in terms of size of foreign ministries this is a little unfair. In the Greek case the 'problem of clientelism in the recruitment process' leads to a bureaucracy which is 'characterised by weak administration'. In contrast, the high level of 'cohesion across the political elite concerning British foreign policy objectives' means that 'few quibble with the efficiency of British foreign policy making'.

It is important to note that there is no one model for the bureaucratic arrangement of foreign and European ministries across the Member States, but there are varying degrees of autonomy for the ministries and the permanent representation. The departments with the greatest autonomy are to be found in the Netherlands, Denmark, Ireland, Spain, Portugal, Greece and Germany. In the Netherlands traditional departmental autonomy has been an important feature of its foreign policy mechanisms. The Danish and Irish foreign ministries are able to benefit from bureaucracies characterised by 'flexibility and adaptability' rather than 'structure and hierarchy'. Although the Spanish Ministry of Foreign Affairs has limited autonomy, the permanent representation for which it is ultimately, via the Secretariat of State for Foreign Policy and the EU, responsible does 'enjoy a fairly high degree of autonomy'. In Portugal the post-1994 reforms of the Ministry of Foreign Affairs laid the emphasis on 'decentralisation but better coordination'. The Greek Ministry of Foreign Affairs also has a high degree of autonomy, but as the case illustrated, it often finds itself having to deal with internal disputes (as with the case of EU relations with Turkey) and inter-ministry disputes with the Ministry of National Economy (renamed from the Ministry of Coordination after EU membership). The very nature of the German federal arrangements and the patterns of coalition governments have tended to lead to relatively high autonomy for the German Foreign Ministry as well. The departments with the least amount of autonomy are to be found within the 'hierarchical form of authority' and 'highly centralised system' of 'tightly focussed ... horizontal coordination' which characterise the French and British foreign policy mechanisms respectively. In the French case this coordination within the EU is provided by the SGCI[6] answerable to the Prime Minister, whilst in the British case EU coordination is provided by the European Secretariat in the Cabinet office, also answerable to the Prime Minister.

Coordinating foreign policy

The cases demonstrated two interesting dynamics at work shaping the role of the Foreign Ministries and the task of coordinating policy within the EU. On the one hand, most of the Member States were in the process of consolidating their EU-policy coordinating mechanisms in the office of the Prime Minister, mimicking the success of the French and British systems. In Germany this has led to the Chancellor's Office playing a more important role in coordinating policy. Similarly in Italy the Prime Minister's office (at the Palazzo Chigi) 'has significantly increased its competencies and supervisory role'. In Spain there is also 'continued centralisation of the policy process around the Prime Minister, who remains the key figure in the field of foreign affairs'. Whilst in both Sweden and Finland the Prime Ministers have assumed responsibility for formulating and coordinating EU policy, providing a 'effective counter-weight' to their often 'cumbersome consensual approaches to policy making'.

On the other hand, most Member States are now witnessing the expansion of the external relations of 'domestic ministries' as they increasingly 'conduct their own foreign policies' with other Member States' 'domestic ministries' through the EU's technical councils, the Commission and the ECB. The increasing activism of other ministries such as finance and trade, was directly acknowledged in six cases (Britain, Belgium, Denmark, Ireland, Sweden and Finland) where their 'autonomous diplomacy' was bringing into question the role of the Foreign Ministry. In the case of Britain it was even remarked that it was 'established practice' for 'individual departments [to] contact the Commission and UKREP bypassing the Cabinet Office and FCO'. The dynamic at work here is that as the activity and autonomy of these other ministries increases so 'the influence of the Ministry of Foreign Affairs decreases in proportion'.

The explanation for these two dynamics lie in the explosion of EU-oriented managerial tasks for the foreign ministries and the loss of non-Europeanised foreign policy tasks, both of which attest to the degree to which the Europeanisation of domestic and foreign policy has made inroads towards the office of the prime minister. As Tonra has said, it serves as 'the best illustration of the fact that foreign policy is no longer quite so "foreign".' What the cases seem to be saying is that the future tasks of foreign ministries will lie in the areas of coordinating the external relations of other ministries and providing monitoring, communication and representatives services – what might be termed 'coordination services'.

Bureaucratic conservatism

The question of the influence of bureaucratic process is one of the most interesting aspects of the impact of EU membership in shaping the foreign policies of its Member States. It is the bureaucratic design which shapes the way in which a state, its government, its civil servants and its citizens are able to interact with other similar hierarchical arrangements in other Member States and in non-Member States. The bureaucratic structure has both a formal and an informal component to it. The informal politics of the 'multi-interactional' world of foreign policy making can often be as important as, if not more than, the formal politics of 'international relations'. Once again these ideas of 'informal circles of consultation' or the impact of 'habits of cooperation' have long been identified as being crucial in the process of *engrenage, Verflechtung,* or the 'locking in' of foreign policy elites in informal patterns of policy making.[7]

What is interesting here is the remarkable conservatism which most EU Member State bureaucracies have demonstrated in coming terms with foreign policy in the post-Cold War world. We should not be surprised at this, however. As early as 1978 Christopher Hill identified the way in which conservatism in foreign policy administrations inhibited change, a situation which appears to have changed little in the intervening twenty-two years contrary to claims that foreign ministries have 'responded to the demands of managing access rather than focussing on ... gatekeeping'.[8] Without exception the traditional structures of a foreign ministry with a foreign minister in charge of foreign policy have been maintained, if not strengthened.

Foreign ministers have adapted to the demands of EU membership by taking on board the task of coordinating external relations in response to the needs and demands of these new conditions. But as the cases studied here demonstrate, other ministries have developed external relations in response to the needs and demands of EU membership and broader international demands. In every case the task of coordinating these cross-cutting responses fall to a European minister who is always subordinate to the foreign minister. It has been observed by many that these arrangements look increasingly anachronistic in a regionalised/globalised world. Many would argue that the foreign ministers and their ministries have been usurped by the finance and economic ministers as the EU's, and its Member States' real ability to influence foreign relations lie in their economic weight. As Paul Kennedy comments in Chapter 6 on Spain, a more accurate measure of foreign policy strength has become the ability to 'punch over [a state's] *economic* weight'.

Within the EU: constriction or opportunity?

The question of whether the EU represents a constriction or an opportunity for the foreign policies of its Member States is central to this study. It is not as simple a question to answer as might be thought, as the four factors outlined above, adaptation, socialisation, domestic factors and bureaucratic factors, will all shape the response in the Member States under consideration. The degree to which the EU is seen to represent a constriction or opportunity is thus dependent on to whom, in what context, and when the question is asked. As has been discussed previously, membership can be seen as an opportunity to use integration to modernise a country, particularly in terms of its foreign policy outlook. Examples of this can be found in the chapters on Italy, Ireland, Greece, Spain and Portugal, all of which refer to modernisation. More recently we have seen modernisers on the left in Britain (New Labour) and Germany (SPD) attempt to use membership as a means to propagate/popularise the policies of the 'third way' and the *neue Mitte*. As has also been seen, the institutionalisation provided by EU membership can help to imbed norms and international obligations as a means to overcome a poor history in this respect, as was seen in the post-fascist/post-colonial cases.

In terms of more explicit advancement of national foreign policy goals, especially in comparison to other Member States, the EU can provide opportunities to take a leadership role. An example of this was seen in the case of Spanish leadership in the Euro-Med initiatives taken from Italy and France. The EU was also seen to provide opportunities for leadership in traditional diplomatic parlance by 'punching above its weight' (as in the case of Britain) or, perhaps more importantly, 'punching over its economic weight' (as in the case of Spain). Examples in these two cases were found in the important role given to British and Spanish diplomats such as Javier Solana (Secretary-General of NATO and High Representative for the CFSP), Carlos Westendorp (chair of the 'reflection group'), Felipe Gonzalez (EU special representative for Yugoslavia), Miguel Moratinos (EU special representative for the Great Lakes region), Peter Carrington and David Owen (EU special envoys to Yugoslavia), Lieutenant-General Mike Jackson (KFOR Commander), and George Robertson (Secretary-General of NATO).

'Extensive' foreign relations

A more important factor in explaining whether EU membership can be viewed as a constriction or an opportunity for foreign policy action is the pre-existing orientation of external relations which Member States may have. Although it would be wrong to see these orientations as overly deterministic, it is possible to talk about three patterns of external relations which may shape the way in which membership impacts on foreign policy actions. The first discernible pattern is that seen in Member States which have an extensive network of external relations outside the EU, which affect its foreign policy behaviour and the way in which it interacts with the EU and other Member States. Clearly the two premier examples of this pattern are to be found in the British and French cases, although it is far too simplistic to argue that this represents the only, or most determining, factor in explaining their foreign policies. In this pattern of external relations, the EU is more often perceived as a constriction, or simply as a means to amplify national foreign policy.

'European' foreign relations

A second pattern may be seen in Member States which have a less extensive network of foreign policy relations than Britain and France, and which tend to work through the EU. In this pattern the Member State involved often seeks to work with the EU or defers most foreign policy prerogatives to the Union. It might also be argued that the EU presents an opportunity within which to hide difficult decisions, or the absence of any preconceived policy. Within this pattern of external relations are two types of Member State – smaller states without the capacity or desire to engage in extensive external relations, and states which for historical reasons wish to enmesh themselves in a European rather than national system of foreign policy making. Examples of the smaller state might be found in Portugal or Ireland, as was argued in the Irish case when it was stated that policy makers 'are quicker to welcome restrictions on the ambitions of larger Member States than they are to bemoan the same limitations being placed on themselves' because of the question of size. Examples of the 'European' state include Italy and Belgium, both of which find EU solutions to difficult historical and domestic problems. An important additional point here is whether the EU can provide a balance between 'Europeanist' or 'Atlanticist' foreign policy trends which satisfy internal tensions. As has been seen in the cases of Spain, Italy, Greece, and to a certain degree Denmark, this second pattern of foreign policy can be viewed as a solution to the tensions between pro-European (read 'EU' or 'anti-US') and pro-American (read 'NATO' or 'anti-EU') forces within these countries. Clearly in this pattern of external relations, the EU is more often perceived as an opportunity for foreign policy action (or perhaps as an excuse for national foreign policy inaction).

'International' foreign relations

A third pattern can be observed in those states which may not have an extensive network of foreign policy relations, but tend to work through other international organisations such as the UN, NATO, or the Organisation for Security and Cooperation in Europe (OSCE). Within this pattern a Member State may seek to act independently of the EU or in concert with the EU in order to assist their foreign policies. Thus not all Member States feel constrained to participate solely in EU foreign policy activity, and may well seek to avoid doing so because of the implications for further integration. This pattern of international rather than European foreign policy relations may also be related to the Cold War experience of a country, in particular its status as neutral or non-aligned. Additionally, this pattern of activity might be directly related to a multilateral foreign policy orientation within a Member State. Examples of the 'international' pattern may be found in the cases of Austria, Finland and Sweden, all of which are active in the OSCE and UN. Examples of the 'multilateral' pattern may be found in the case of Germany which, through its *Sowohl-als-auch* approach pursues its foreign policy through the EU, NATO, OSCE and UN. In this type of pattern EU membership represents not so much an opportunity or a constriction, but merely another forum for its foreign policy (as traditionally conceived).

For the EU Member States participation in the Union represents a mixed blessing for their foreign policy activities. On the one hand it forces them to confront the rigidity or flexibility in their foreign policy making within a European framework, while on the other hand it tends to underline the paramount role which non-traditional foreign policy (external or economic relations) has come to be assume in the twenty-first century.

What is clear is that EU membership involves asking some difficult questions of foreign policy practices, or the absence of them. The challenges and responses this presents can be considered through looking at notions of the 're'-formulation of foreign policy in terms of 'retreat', 'remove', 'rescue', and 'renationalise'. There has, since the crisis of confidence in European states during the 1970s, been much debate about the degree to which the state can be described as being 'hollowed out' and its ability to conduct meaningful foreign policy as being in 'retreat'.[9] Although the strongest assertions of this approach are denied by most, it is now widely accepted that the European state is 'learning new strategies of governing, including collective action at the EU level'.[10] Hubert Vedrine's argument presented earlier illustrates this point, that even for a larger Member State like France 'sovereignty is already formal or illusory, and the exercise of common sovereignty permits the recovery of a little of what has been lost'. These new strategies of response to the 'retreat', or at least 'reformulation' of EU Member States can be conceptualised in foreign policy terms in three ways.

Remove to Brussels

The first response is the attempt by Member States to 'remove' many of the activities of foreign policy making from state capitals to Brussels. It is important to note that this 'Brusselisation' of foreign policy does not mean the wholesale communitarisation of foreign policy making and implementation within the European Community. As David Allen has argued, the Brusselisation of foreign policy making is facilitated by the 'steady enhancement of Brussels-based decision making bodies' such as the Political Committee of the Council of Ministers,[11] although some might wish to include decision making within the NATO Headquarters or the Western European Union (WEU) Headquarters, both located in

Brussels. David Spence goes further when he points out that as the Political Committee is, in theory, subordinate to the COREPER, this 'has implied a shift of focus from national capitals to Brussels'.[12]

EU rescue

The second response goes further than simple 'removal' by attempting to 'rescue' the foreign policies of Member States by using membership of the EU as 'the means by which Member States made their positions less rather than more vulnerable'.[13] In broad terms this second strategy goes far beyond the strategy of simple removal by Europeanising a Member State's foreign policy in an attempt to improve or strengthen its relations. From this perspective, the EU is often presented as an intergovernmental mechanism for rescuing and strengthening the state and its foreign policy.[14] But once again, as David Spence has made clear, the extent to which Europeanisation can 'rescue' foreign policy from the pressures of the supra-national, the sub-national, and the transnational needs to be questioned:

> ... the Europeanisation of domestic policy in EU Member States has tended, in all Member States, to require more rather than less of foreign ministries, given the supranationality of the EU process, the consequent blurring of the distinction between foreign and domestic policy and the continuance of the foreign ministry's gatekeeping role on the margin of the domestic–foreign policy divide.[15]

Renationalisation of foreign policy

The final response to any perceived 'retreat' of Member States' foreign policies is more recent, and for some reflects the crisis of post-Maastricht CFSP, particularly in light of the embarrassing failures (shared with the most powerful state in the world) in the Balkans. This response would appear to be the 'renationalisation' of foreign policy as a means of dealing with the 'failure to progress' through the reassertion of 'traditional national foreign policies' identified by Christopher Hill, William Wallace, David Allen, Michael Smith and Esther Barbé. It is important to note, as they do, that even though 'renationalisation' is 'freely discussed' and a 'drift apart' has been noticed by some, 'vested interest' in the still early stages of the CFSP makes this argument questionable.[16]

As was noted under 'adaptation' in the first section above, the contrasting benefits of 'removal', 'rescue' or 'renationalise' in response to a perceived 'retreat' depend on the viewpoints of those engaged in the foreign policy processes under discussion. For post-colonial states such as France, Britain, the Netherlands, Belgium, Spain and Portugal the use of development policy and external relations provides a convenient conduit for a 'rescue' of these relationships in the guise of a less historically 'loaded' EU policy. For smaller Member States such as Denmark, Ireland

and Greece the EU can represent a rescue of their non-security policies, but the pressure to 'remove' security interests to Brussels is fiercely resisted. For the (post-)neutral states of Austria, Finland and Sweden, the removal of aspects of their Cold War security stance to Brussels provides a means for overcoming domestic resistance, as well as seeing the human rights and development policies of the EU as a means for rescuing, or at least advancing, these issues on a larger stage. But these strategies are not without problems – as was mentioned under 'bureaucracies' in the previous section, vested interest in maintaining the status quo tends to view these developments with suspicion and may seek to find a pretext for the 'renationalisation' of elements of foreign policy, particularly in the larger foreign policy infrastructures of France and Britain.

Without the EU: special relationships and special interests

The final factor considered in this study was the question of the role of the foreign policies which Member States attempt to keep separate or private from the EU context. In the absence of any federal-EU authority with responsibility for foreign relations, Member States would obviously like to pick and choose which aspects of their foreign policy they share, and which they retain. Throughout this study we see that each case under consideration has a range of relationships and interests they see as 'special' and beyond the realm of European consultation. As Magnus Ekengren and Bengt Sundelius have highlighted elsewhere in the case of one of the EU's newest members (Sweden): 'tacit understandings exist among the Member States as regards "special interests". These base lines are recognised by other members as areas where the country in question has priority, and where it is difficult to pursue an assertive policy line'.[17]

Domain privé

Not all these 'special interests' are as strictly ring-fenced as a *domain privé*. There appears to be a dynamic, or a form of hierarchy, to these special issues which we may describe as four 'rings of specialness'. At the core of these rings of specialness is the *domain privé* which encompasses issues deemed 'national security' as they are central to the sovereign discourses of certain Member States. The three clearest-cut policies of this *domain privé* are to be found in the sovereign discourses surrounding security issues and policies. The first security issue is that of the nuclear-armed states of the UN Security Council – France and Britain. The second security issue concerns the 'national issues' of defence found in the EU's only Balkan state – Greece. The third security issue is the security policies of the EU's neutral, non-aligned, and NATO-only states of Sweden, Finland, Austria, Ireland and Denmark. In all three areas, and for all eight states, these questions of security are acknowledged by all Member States as being beyond discussion – laying in a private field.

Bilateral relations

Outside of this inner ring of specialness lies the second ring of bilateral relations which are considered, by the participants, to be of special significance and therefore outside of 'normal' EU foreign policy discussions. These bilateral relations come in two varieties: those of 'special relations' (a form of strong bilateralism) and those of 'semi-independence' (a form of weak bilateralism). In terms of special relations it is fairly common to focus on those traditionally between Britain and the United States (primarily in the defence field), decreasingly between France and Germany (mainly in the integration field), and increasingly Germany's relations with Israel, Poland and the United States. In terms of semi-independence, we can look at the Benelux cooperation, the Nordic relations (particularly in terms of Nordic roles in the UN), the relations of energy-dependent Member States with suppliers (such as Italy with the Maghreb), and several Member States on immigration issues (including both sending states, such as Italy and Ireland, as well as receiving states such as France and Britain). Whilst this ring of specialness based on bilateral relations is more dynamic than the previous inner ring, it still involves Member States exempting from discussion those relations which are acknowledged outside of foreign policy actions.

European multilateralism

The third ring of specialness, lying outside of bilateral relations, can be characterised as European multilateralism, and is becoming more important in the post-Cold War period. European multilateralism consists of a mixture of issues which are regional, normative, or post-colonial in nature and which may be found to be a 'special issue' in the language of one or more Member State. The regional issues are those foreign policy relations which have been significant for historical or proximity reasons, such as those that France, Spain and Italy have with the other (non-EU) Mediterranean states, as well as relations between France/Britain and the Middle Eastern states. The normative issues are those foreign policy issues of significance for reasons of justice and equality, such as the issue of human rights for the Netherlands and Austria, and the question of developing countries for the Netherlands, Sweden and Denmark. Covering similar relations, although not necessarily for similar reasons, are the post-colonial issues which are held to be special for Britain and France (especially in Africa), Belgium and the Netherlands, Spain and Portugal. In all three of these areas of European multilateralism, attempts are made, by differing Member States, to attach special meaning or importance to the issues under consideration. As might be expected, this ring of specialness is far more dynamic that the two inner rings and it is in this area that we might to see the most interesting debates over foreign policy competence, as all three issues seem destined to become more 'Europeanised' in the near future.

Transitional relations

The outer ring of specialness is by far the most dynamic of the four, consisting of special relations and issues which are in a transitional phase and are usually in the process of being communitarised in one form or another. If we think of those foreign policy issues which are the most difficult to place clearly within any one particular policy-making sphere then they are often to be found in this ring. These policies are considered special by perhaps one or some Member States, but are increasingly being drawn into the European sphere. Thus, relations between Member States and neighbouring applicant states would be found here, as well as relations which have a significant economic content to them, and relations which were formerly inter-national in nature, but are now more inter-regional in reality. This ring of special relations is really one full of questions rather than clear-cut answers – how might we best think of German–Polish relations after enlargement? Where do Anglo-South African relations stand in a dispute over free trade? And should Spanish–Argentinean relations be thought of as more special than EU–Mercosur relations?

The chapters present evidence that most Member States have relationships and interests they consider 'special' and worthy of bilateral, rather than multilateral or EU foreign policies. However, not only can these special interests problematise their entire membership, they can also require large amounts of political capital at the bargaining table in order to maintain. Interestingly the case studies here indicate that even some of the traditional special interests of the EU's Member States are in flux. As we have seen, Britain's special relationship with the USA is only really maintained in the security field, and indeed is shared with Germany. Two chapters both seemed to be demonstrating that the Franco-German special relationship is not what it once was, particularly with the absence of François Mitterrand and Helmut Kohl. Similarly, two of the authors were both able to show how the Netherlands and Austria have been able to lift their special issues of human rights onto the EU table in the post-Cold War era. Finally, we saw how the formerly special Nordic relationship has been subsumed within Baltic and EU relationships. Thus, notions of specialness and how they are Europeanised or maintained in a *domain privé* are more fluid concepts than was initially thought, which tells us as much about the distinctly post-Second World War context of many of these issues as it does about the impact of EU membership.

Conclusion: distinctive foreign policy analysis

This study attempted to formulate and utilise an approach to the foreign policies of EU Member States which was both distinctive and appropriate. The study formulated a framework that would allow the contributors to explore the foreign policies of individual Member States, while at the same time facilitating comparison in a search for broader insight. The study utilised the first new framework since William Wallace and William Paterson last aired these questions in 1978. The framework captured elements of context, process and implementation in a way which provided insights which are significantly distinctive and appropriate to the twenty-first century 'European condition'.

It is recognised here that appropriate analysis needs sensitivity and insight into the unique processes that constitute the EU, its Member States' domestic conditions, and the foreign policy-making processes within these Member States. As Helen Wallace has recently argued, theoretical and methodological space must be left for explanations which are intrinsically irrational, based on a combination of middle range theories which may not be metatheoretically consistent in their approach, but which can help to broaden our understanding: 'space needs to be made for irrationality, for confusion and for mistaken judgements'.[18] Or, as Brian White is arguing for in the foreign policy analysis of the EU, 'European FPA can tentatively be characterised as more eclectic epistemologically, focused on more limited theoretical advances . . . and contextual 'middle range' theories'.[19] Our approach attempts to adopt a more appropriate methodology which is suitable for the European context, takes into account processes of integration and socialisation, and is applicable to post-Cold War EU Member States. This approach was summed up very neatly by Ben Tonra in Chapter 12 of this book:

> To get an understanding of all of these issues it is indeed necessary to move beyond the rather sterile template of traditional (US-centric) FPA with its state-centric focus upon complex bureaucracies and allegedly rational, utility-maximising actor . . . it is evident that a model of FPA needs to be able to account for identity, beliefs, norms and expectations arising from a unique endeavour of political integration. Such a model cannot assume any trajectory or direction in these 'non-rational' variables, but it must – at least – promise to come to terms with them.

The second distinctive element of the study is the number of insights which the comparative approach adopted has revealed and which will be briefly restated here.

Separable, not separate

The study consistently finds that the analysis of Member States' foreign policies is separable, but not separate from the EU context. It is not possible to convincingly study one of the foreign policies considered here without accounting for the impact of, and adaptation to, the EU. The comparative framework provides insights into a number of adaptation strategies found in the Member States, but it also demonstrates the degree to which resistance to change is present. The extent to which states like France and Britain attempt to maintain the status quo of foreign policy coordination through intergovernmental means is interesting. Also valuable is the way in which states like Austria, Finland and Sweden use EU membership as a means of adapting from neutrality to post-neutrality.

Context, not abstract

The analysis of Member States' foreign policies is situated within a distinct social context involving high levels of interaction between a relatively small number of policy making personnel, rather than an abstract condition of autonomous decision making located in some form of 'international system'. The study finds that this leads to a degree of socialisation for many of those involved in foreign policy making, although crucially this was not a consistent pattern across all the cases. It is noticeable that policy makers in larger Member States (such as Britain, France and Germany) as well as in more geographically remote states (such as Greece) are less socialised than others. It is also suggested that there is sometimes a tension between this socialised elite and public opinion on foreign policy issues.

European, not domestic

The study supports the view that increasingly the boundary between domestic and foreign policy is permeated as the Member States become part of a 'multilevel political system', in Carole Webb's words. The problems of distinguishing between domestic policies, European policies and foreign policies is heightened, not resolved in this study. As the Secretary-General of NATO has argued, 'European politics are now domestic politics with a vengeance'.[20] If this is true then it may now be more appropriate to talk of Member States' residual foreign policies as being those that have not been Europeanised, and are maintained for their security role (such as defence) or their symbolic role (such as diplomatic missions).

Coordination, not policy

The study finds that foreign ministry bureaucracies are fast having to adapt to the new demands of policy making, coordination and representation. But while this adaptation involves an expansion of scope for most ministries, it is also leading to a change in role from foreign policy to foreign coordination of the policies of other ministries. In the case of certain states, such as Belgium, the foreign ministry might be heading towards a role as an 'escort service' for other ministries. Although this may be a little unfair, the study finds that foreign ministries are playing a broader role in terms of coordinating relations between other departments and the EU, but are having greater difficulty in the making and conduct of traditionally conceived foreign policy. As Michael Smith has argued, one crucial reason for this is that the importance of foreign policy has been displaced by the rise of foreign economic policy, which is increasingly made by a partnership of trade ministries and the Commission.[21] It may be more accurate, therefore, to talk of foreign ministries playing the role of coordination services rather than policy makers.

With or without EU

Lastly, the study finds that the combination of the four insights spelt out above make it difficult to talk of one clear-cut boundary between those policies which are 'Europeanised' or conducted through the EU, and those policies which are retained or excluded from the EU as a *domain privé* because of their 'special' status. Instead the cases analysed here provide evidence of 'rings of specialness' which allow a dynamic interpretation of a range of policies from a central core of a *domain privé* on security issues, through bilateral issues and European multilateral issues, to a number of transitional issues in the process of being Europeanised. Thus, the study confirms its initial assertion that it now seems more appropriate to suggest that the EU Member States conduct all but the most limited foreign policies objectives inside an EU context. And, as we argued at the beginning of this chapter, if such a transformation has taken place then a distinctive approach must be adopted which is able to go beyond de-contextualised explanations and some way towards a more appropriate understanding.

Notes

1 E. Haas, *When Knowledge is Power* (Berkeley, University of California Press, 1990) in K. Hanf and B. Soetendorp (eds), *Adapting to European Integration* (London, Longman, 1998), p. 7.

2 R. Ladrech, 'Europeanisation of domestic policies and institutions: the case of France, *Journal of Common Market Studies*, 32:1 (1994), p. 69; S. Mazey and J. Richardson, 'EU policy-making: a garbage can or an anticipatory and consensual policy style?' in Y. Mény, P. Muller and J-L. Quermonne (eds), *Adjusting to Europe: the Impact of the European Union on National Institutions and Policies* (London, Routledge, 1996), pp. 44–45; K. Hanf and B. Soetendorp, 'Small states and the Europeanization of public policy' in Hanf and Soetendorp (eds), *Adapting*, pp. 1–9.

3 K. Robbins, 'Britain and Europe: devolution and foreign policy', *International Affairs*, 74: 1 (1998), pp. 105–118; B. Hocking, 'Foreign policy and devolution', paper presented to the British International Studies Association, Annual Conference 1999.

4   E. Philippart, 'Le comité des régions confronté à la 'paradiplomatie' des régions de l'union européenne' in J. Bourrinet (ed.), *Le Comité des Régions de l'Union Européenne* (Editions Economica, Paris, 1997), pp. 147–180; F. Aldecoa and M. Keating (eds), 'Paradiplomacy in action: the foreign relations of subnational governments', *Regional and Federal Studies*, 9:1 (1999).

5   J. Mortensen, 'The institutional challenges and paradoxes of EU governance in external trade: coping with the post-hegemonic trading system and the global economy', in A. Cafruny and P. Peters (eds), *The Union and the World: the Political Economy of a Common European Foreign Policy* (Dortrecht, Kluwer Law International, 1998), p. 212.

6   Secrétariat général du comité interministériel pour les questions de coopération économique européenne.

7   H. Wallace, 'The institutions of the EU: experience and experiments' in H. Wallace and W. Wallace (eds), *Policy-Making in the European Union* 3rd edn. (Oxford, Oxford University Press, 1996), p. 51; W. Wallace 'Government without statehood: the unstable equilibrium' in H. Wallace and W. Wallace (eds), *Policy-Making in the European Union* 3rd edn (Oxford, Oxford University Press, 1996), p. 449; C. Hill and W. Wallace, 'Introduction: actors and actions' in C. Hill (ed.), *The Actors in Europe's Foreign Policy* (London, Routledge, 1996), p. 12.

8   C. Hill, 'A theoretical introduction' in W. Wallace and W. Paterson (eds), *Foreign Policy Making in Western Europe* (Farnborough, Saxon House, 1978), pp. 17–18; B. Hocking, 'Foreign ministries: redefining the gatekeeping role' in *'Foreign Ministries: Change and Adaptation* (Houndmills, Macmillan, 1999), p. 14.

9   For the beginnings of this debate in Europe see, R. Cooper, 'Economic interdependence and foreign policy in the seventies', *World Politics*, 25 (February 1972), pp. 159–181; P. Odell, 'The world of oil power in 1975', *The World Today*, 31 (July 1975), pp. 273–282; C. Makins, 'Interdependence: the European example', *Foreign Policy*, 23 (Fall 1976), pp. 139–144. For the counter arguments see, P. Hirst and G. Thompson, 'The problem of globalisation', *Economy and Society*, 21:4 (1992), pp. 357–396; M. Mann, 'Nation-states in Europe and other continents: diversifying, developing, not dying', *Daedalus*, 3 (Summer 1993), pp. 115–140; W. Muller and V. Wright, 'Reshaping the state in western Europe: the limits of retreat', *West European Politics*, 17:3 (1994), pp. 1–11.

10 B. Laffan, R. O'Donnell and M. Smith, *Europe's Experimental Union: Rethinking Integration* (London, Routledge, 2000), p. 71.

11 D. Allen, 'Who speaks for Europe?' The search for an effective and coherent external policy' in J. Peterson and H. Sjursen (eds), *A Common Foreign Policy for Europe? Competing visions of the CFSP* (London, Routledge, 1998), pp. 56–58.

12 D. Spence, 'Foreign ministries in national and European context' in B. Hocking (ed.), *Foreign Ministries: Change and Adaptation* (Houndmills, Macmillan, 1999), p. 257.

13 D. Allen, 'Conclusions: the European rescue of national foreign policy?' in Hill (ed.), *The Actors,* p. 290.

14 Laffan, O'Donnell and Smith, *Europe's Experimental Union*, p. 15.

15 Spence, 'Foreign Ministries', p. 249.
16 C. Hill and W. Wallace, 'Introduction': actors and actions' in Hill (ed.), *The Actors*, p. 14; D. Allen and M. Smith, 'The European Union's security presence: barrier, facilitator, or manager?' in C. Rhodes (ed.), *The European Union in the World Community* (London, Lynne Rienner, 1998), p. 52; C. Hill, 'Convergence, divergence and dialectics: national foreign policies and the CFSP' in J. Zielonka (ed.), *Paradoxes of European Foreign Policy* (The Hague, Kluwer Law International, 1998), p. 36; E. Barbé, 'Balancing Europe's eastern and southern dimensions' in J. Zielonka (ed.), *Paradoxes of European Foreign Policy* (The Hague, Kluwer Law International, 1998), p. 118.
17 M. Ekengren and B. Sundelius, 'Sweden: the state joins the European Union' in Hanf and Soetendorp (eds), *Adapting*, p. 144.
18 H. Wallace, 'Review section: the choice for Europe – piecing the integration jigsaw together', *Journal of European Public Policy*, 6:1 (1999), p. 158.
19 B. White, 'The European challenge to foreign policy analysis', *European Journal of International Relations*, 5:1, p. 59.
20 G. Robertson, 'Britain in the new Europe', *International Affairs*, 66:4 (1990), p. 699.
21 M. Smith, 'The European Community: testing the boundary of foreign economic policy' in R. Stubbs and G. Underhill (eds), *Political Economy and the Changing World Order* (London, Macmillan, 1994). B. Hocking and M. Smith, 'Beyond foreign economic policy' in *Beyond Foreign Economic Policy: the United States, the Single European Market and the Changing World Economy* (London, Pinter, 1997), pp. 5–25. M. Smith, 'Does the flag follow trade? 'politicisation' and the emergence of a European foreign policy' in Peterson and Sjursen (eds), *Common Foreign Policy*, pp. 77–94.

Index